SAMIR KHALAF is Professor of Sociology a... and Director of ... ... behavior
Research, American University of Beirut. He has held academic positions at Harvard University, Princeton University, MIT and New York University. His other books include *Cultural Resistance*, *Heart of Beirut*, *Sexuality in the Arab World* (co-edited with John H. Gagnon), *Arab Society and Culture* and *Arab Youth* (both co-edited with Roseanne Saad Khalaf), all by Saqi Books.

'A timely and provocative reading of Lebanon's postwar malaise. Samir Khalaf, once again, offers an empirically rich and theoretically broad survey of Lebanese society, capturing the excesses and dislocations of violence, consumerism and religious communalism. *Lebanon Adrift* proffers not merely a critique of an indulgent and indifferent traumatized populace, but extends a call to a new civility and convivial future.'

Craig Larkin, University of Exeter

'Samir Khalaf pays due attention to the political culture in Lebanon rather than simply revisiting the shortcomings and failures of our political system. He looks into sentiments of hostility, in times of uncertainty, and how communal politics breed intentions of hostility. Both archaic and modern, tribal and consumerist, Lebanon is not only the battleground for proxy conflicts, it is a society homogenized by commodification and amnesia while torn apart by the exaggeration of minor differences and reinvented memories. In writing about the risks of living in the worst of two worlds and searching for promising signs of resistance and an emerging citizen consciousness, he is subtle and genuine, elegant and sober.'

Tarek Mitri, American University of Beirut

'This is a skilled sociological reading of contemporary Lebanon by a master of the discipline. Against a background of protracted conflict, unreconciled narratives of struggle and suffering, and rival, even self-contradictory identities, Khalaf offers a penetrating critique of Lebanon's society, including its rampant consumerism, kitsch and its appetite for nostalgia seasoned with forgetfulness. He finds scope for optimism in a renewal, fittingly, of Lebanon's youth who have demonstrated—not least through social media—an impatience with divisive boundaries, a penchant for altruism, a quest for civil society, and a revived appreciation of civility in society that retains Lebanon's vitality and its marvelous complexity.'

Augustus Richard Norton,
Boston University and University of Oxford

SAMIR KHALAF

Lebanon Adrift

From Battleground
to Playground

SAQI

ISBN 978-0-86356-434-5

First published 2012 by Saqi Books

© 2012 Samir Khalaf
Preface © 2012 Ghassan Hage

A full CIP record for this book is available from the
British Library.

A full CIP record for this book is available from the
Library of Congress.

Manufactured in Lebanon

SAQI
26 Westbourne Grove, London W2 5RH
www.saqibooks.com

Contents

Preface by Ghassan Hage   7
Prologue   13

1.   On Protracted and Displaced Collective Violence   31
2.   The Spaces of War and Postwar:
      Reflections on Collective Memory, Identity and Nostalgia   75
3.   Consumerism in a Traumatized Society   115
4.   Touting Luxury, Sensuality and Image   161
5.   The Allure of the Spectacle and Kitsch   210
6.   Prospects for Transforming Consumers Into Citizens   240

Epilogue   267
Bibliography   275
Acknowledgments   287
Index   289

Preface

by GHASSAN HAGE

'Eefneh

While visiting Lebanon to conduct what was largely emigration-related research, I gradually became interested in the phenomenal growth of *arghileh* (water pipe) smoking. When I left Lebanon in the mid-seventies, smoking *arghileh* was something largely associated, by middle-class youth like me at least, with older, male, working-class urban cafe culture. That was what such men did as they sat, drank coffee or tea, and played backgammon. Perhaps it was also perceived as something that old or traditional village people did, if I remember well. But what is certain is that youth in my circle would never have fantasized themselves smoking *arghileh* at that time.

I am not sure if the above perception reflected the actual demographic of *arghileh* smoking before the civil war, but there is no doubt that something during or after the war triggered a serious transformation in the social and geographic spread of the practice: everyone now seemed to be smoking *arghileh*, and everyone, particularly young people, seemed to think that it was a really hip thing to do. It is not an exaggeration to say that on any night in the restored city centre, turned into a pedestrian zone and lined with cafes and restaurants, something like thirty or forty percent of the patrons would be smoking an *arghileh* – that's *arghilehs* in their hundreds, and on a weekend night that's perhaps *arghilehs* in their thousands.

Similarly, further down by the sea and heading westward, on the Corniche, the long wide footpath by the sea that is the closest Beirut has to a public space, one can see working- or under-class men and women park their cars, bring out a couple of plastic chairs, and, sure enough, a couple of *arghilehs*. They light up and sit there by the sea, smoking and contemplating the water and the sunset, feeling visibly at peace with themselves ... drifting. Drifting bodies in a Lebanon adrift. I think that there is a lot about this *arghileh* smoking that demonstrates the themes of adriftness that are mobilized in Samir Khalaf's book.

If there is something that characterizes popular forms of Lebanese sociality in postwar Lebanon, it is the remarkable way that they have immunized themselves from the endless political conflict and upheavals that continue to characterize Lebanese politics. On one level, it was like a decision that was made, such as, 'if we are going to wait for the political situation to become normal in order to have fun, we're never going to have fun.' On another level however, it was more than that. It was, 'we're going to have fun precisely so that we don't have to think about the political situation.' This then evolved into: 'we're going to have fun in order not to think about anything too upsetting', 'we're not going to think about the hopeless provision of basic social services such as rubbish removal, water and electricity supply', 'we're not going to think about the state of the roads and traffic congestion', and 'we're not going to think about the very manifest forms of ecological degradation around us.' So, except for the activists and the usual cross-section of socially aware and concerned citizens, the withdrawal of the rest of the population from the social and the political and into a life of 'fun', 'consumerism' and 'shallowness', when they can afford it, is sometimes quite extreme. Samir Khalaf's book is a recording and an analysis of the social and political origins and manifestations of this culture of escapism.

Arghileh smoking is metonymic of this form of escapism and a kind of narcissistic folding of oneself onto oneself to seek a sense of immunity from the traumatizing environment. As a Lebanese person said to me recently: 'if you are sensitive and aware, one walk down the streets is enough to diminish you as a human being here.' So, there is something stoic and heroic about this escapism. One has in mind the image that circulated widely on the net following savage Israeli bombing of Lebanon in 2006: two men sitting in the middle of the rubble of a building flattened by an Israeli bomb, both smoking an *arghileh*. And one cannot help but understand the Lebanese desire to withdraw from Lebanese politics given its injurious, belligerent and yet futile nature that Khalaf describes so well. But at the same time, and again, as Khalaf stresses regarding the various social pathologies he examines, there is also a reneging of one's responsibility towards the political, social and environmental degradation that one is in fact reproducing through this very act of withdrawal from the social. It is as if every *arghileh* smoker, like every mindless consumer, is holding a little sign that says *'eefneh*, a quintessentially Lebanese colloquial exclamation, which means, 'let me be and don't bother me.' Being psychoanalytically inclined like I am, I have always seen this kind of 'let me be' sentiment as having a regressive, infantile nature.

To speak of regressive, infantile sentiments here is to say that within the desire for withdrawal and immunisation from the social is really a desire to regress back to where one has come from: the womb. That is, in every desire to retreat from social life, there is also a desire to retreat from life as such. There are many works, some serious and some less so, that connect smoking with sucking, and imaginatively, with the breast of the mother, which, in psychoanalytic terms, is itself symbolic of a desire to return to the womb. This certainly can apply to *arghileh* smoking, though I know of no studies that make such a connection. Beyond the act of sucking, *arghileh* smoking also provides a visual enhancement of the regressive imagination, given that one sucks on a pipe that suspiciously looks like an umbilical cord. This is further enhanced in the domain of sound by a very womb-like gurgling of water. Add to this the soft buzz that the special aromatic *arghileh* tobacco provides, and there should be no doubt that there is probably no other device capable of producing a 'womb effect' the way the *arghileh* does.

I guess that the extent to which one finds all this productive to think about is correlative to how seriously one takes psychoanalysis. But what is certainly beyond doubt is that recognizing that emotions that are generated by the Lebanese desire for regression and withdrawal, and which are present metonymically in *arghileh* smoking, are a form of infantile regression, can help us understand the paradoxical nature of many forms of irrational violence that often go hand in hand with this type of regression and which are also referred to in Khalaf's book.

When one desires and attempts to regress, one feels good, as long as nothing is disturbing one's peace. Unfortunately, in such situations, many things are perceived to disturb one's peace. For, to act as if one is back in the womb and to demand a womb-like peace, when one is not and is in fact constantly interacting with people, is ambivalent to the extreme. Anything is bound to be found a disturbance. This kind of emotional situation is exemplified by the irrationality of what is called 'road rage': the astonishing amount of anger and violence that can be generated from minor conflictual interaction between car drivers.

What often induces 'road rage' is precisely the ambivalent emotional experience that driving a car can produce: it is both a form of cocooning away from the social and yet an interactive exercise with other occupants of the roads. 'Road ragers' are often those who experience the cocooning effect of the car as a regressive womb-like situation, which heightens a form of infantile aggression that is directed at any other road occupant perceived to have disturbed one's peace. Many interactions in Lebanon, on and off the road, often take the form of road rage; any small occurrence can induce tempers to flare in an irrational way when one is floating about adrift.

I conceived these ethno-psychoanalytic thoughts about the *arghileh* quite a while ago. It is interesting to me that in reading Samir Khalaf's book I feel I have a better understanding of the social processes in which these psychoanalytic experiences are grounded and that the way the two domains interlink. But this would not be the first time that Samir Khalaf lightens up the sociological path for me.

Samir Khalaf was already an assistant instructor at the American University of Beirut and then a university fellow at Princeton in 1957, the year I was born. When I began studying Middle East politics at university, an article of his was the very first piece of Middle Eastern political sociology I read as a student. By that time, he had already engaged in many research projects, which ended in various waves of publications: on prostitution in Beirut (the subject of his very first publication), on Lebanese industrial relations, on Arab intellectuals, on family firms, on Lebanese migration, on the historical sociology of nineteenth-century Lebanon, on Beirut's urban politics, and more generally, on Lebanon's political system. And when I was writing my PhD on the Lebanese Civil War, his work had achieved a classical status that made it obligatory for any scholar of Lebanese politics to engage with it. So, as the reader can imagine, I am unbelievably delighted to be writing this preface. It is not every day that one gets the opportunity to preface a book by someone whose work has had such a defining impact on oneself and on so many others.

But I am also particularly delighted to be writing this as Samir Khalaf's friend and colleague. This is to stress something important. From what I mentioned above, it could be easy for someone to mistakenly assume that this prefacing is a ritual of commemoration of an intellectual from the past by an intellectual from the present. Nothing is further from the truth. This is why: to highlight that Samir Khalaf is my friend and colleague is to highlight the fact that his intellect is still at the very least as productive, innovative, sharp, and alive as mine, with the added bonus of historically acquired wisdom and an impeccable sense of measure in making analytical and political judgments.

Samir Khalaf is nearing his eighties – he will have to forgive me for revealing his age – but he remains one the most dynamic sociological intellectuals in Lebanon today, always willing to write and publish on new topics, always on top of new theoretical literature and always excitedly making it speak to the particularities of the Lebanese situation. And it is precisely this that makes this book, like any other work of his before it, an important book to read. For regardless of whether one fully agrees or not with its various analytical observations and conclusions, one is invariably forced to recognize and respect the analytical craftsmanship that brings them about and make them so engaging.

Finally, I want to conclude by stressing another important quality of Samir Khalaf's writing that manifests itself throughout this book. Lebanese politics is a mean colonizing machine. It devours everything and politicizes anything it touches, even that which desires to remain outside the political. To write as a sociologist in Lebanon and not let oneself be devoured by the political, and to disallow one's view to become partisan and enslaved to this or that political position, is a difficult task to achieve. But Samir Khalaf does it and he achieves this by maintaining a certain intellectual cosmopolitanism that is paradoxically both uniquely Lebanese in its sensibility and concerns, and yet at the same time untimely and out of place. One of the greatest pleasures of this book is that it embodies the survival of this Lebanese, cosmopolitan, intellectual ethos in the face of the many social and political forces that are trying to efface it.

Prologue

On Being Adrift

Lebanon today is at a fateful crossroad in its eventful socio-cultural and political history. At the risk of some oversimplification, it remains adrift because it is imperiled by a set of overwhelming predicaments and unsettling transformations. At least three such disorienting circumstances stand out by virtue of their ominous implications for exacerbating the ambivalences and uncertainties of being adrift. More grievous, they are also bound to undermine prospects for forging a viable political culture of tolerance and genuine citizenship.

First, Lebanon is in the throes of postwar reconstruction and rehabilitation. Postwar interludes, even under normal circumstances, are usually cumbersome. In Lebanon, they are bound to be more problematic because of the distinctive residues of collective terror and strife the country was besieged with for nearly two decades of *protracted, displaced and futile* violence. Despite the intensity and magnitude of damage and injury, the fighting went on. More menacing, as the hostility degenerated into communal and in-group turf wars, combatants were killing not those they wanted to kill but those they could kill. The displaced character of hostility was also manifest in the surrogate victimization of random groups not directly involved in the conflict and of innocent bystanders. Finally, the war was futile since the resort to violence neither redressed the internal imbalances nor ushered the country into a more civil and peaceful form of pluralism or guarded coexistence. One concrete implication of those three aberrant features of collective strife is painfully apparent: though the outward manifestations of fighting and belligerency have ceased, hostility, fear and suspicion still prevail. This is visible in the occasional outbursts of violent clashes between fractious groups. These only serve to compound the fragmented and unanchored character of society and, hence, all the anguishing uncertainties of being adrift.

Second, Lebanon is also trapped in a turbulent region suffused with residues of unresolved rivalries. There is hardly an internal problem – not only crises of political succession, electoral reforms, the naturalization of Palestinian refugees, Hizbullah's arms but also the drain on precious youthful resources, erosion of natural habitat, violation of human rights and civil liberties, freedom of speech – which is unrelated to persisting regional and global rivalries. Hence, it is understandable why a small and defenseless country like Lebanon, embroiled in such a turbulent region, should be concerned about how to ward off or protect itself against such external hazards. Indeed, this is its most compelling predicament.

Finally, and as of late, the country is also embroiled, willingly or otherwise, in all the unsettling forces of postmodernity and globalism: a magnified importance of mass media, popular arts and entertainment in the framing of everyday life; an intensification of consumerism, commodification and the allure of kitsch; the demise of political participation and collective consciousness for public issues and their replacement by local and parochial concerns for heritage and nostalgia. As we shall see, the global surge in mass consumerism has reawakened interest recently in the colonizing and alienating nature of modern consumption. Naturally, such conditions are of particular relevance to a postwar setting already suffused with excessive material desires and wasteful indulgence in extravagant and spectacular display of conspicuous leisure and consumption.

The disheartening consequences of such broad structural transformation are grievous. Three socio-cultural realities are particularly poignant and relevant, and are bound to exacerbate the state of drifting which continues to affect the country and sharpen feelings of enmity and paranoia between and among fractious communities. First, the salient symptoms of *retribalization* are apparent in reawakened communal identities and the urge to seek shelter in cloistered spatial communities. Second, there is a pervasive mood of lethargy, indifference, weariness which borders at times on *collective amnesia*. These two seemingly dissonant realities coexist today in Lebanon. The longing to obliterate, mystify and distance oneself from the fearsome recollections of an ugly and unfinished war, or efforts to preserve or commemorate them are, after all, an expression of two opposed forms of self-preservation: the need to remember and the need to forget. The former is increasingly sought in efforts to anchor oneself in one's community or in reviving and reinventing its communal solidarities and threatened heritage. The latter is more likely to assume escapist and nostalgic predispositions to return to a past imbued with questionable authenticity. Third, another unusual reaction has lately become ascendant, one which could threaten to undermine some of the cherished cultural values of authenticity, conviviality and simplicity. In times of local and regional political instability, mounting economic risks and sharper socio-cultural divisions, one would expect groups to display a modicum of control in their desires for material goods and other lavish and extravagant expectations and whims.

Normally, postwar interludes generate moods of restraint and sobriety. People are more inclined to curb their conventional impulses and become more self-controlled and introspective in the interest of reappraising and redirecting their future options. Rather than freeing them from the prewar excesses, the war in Lebanon has paradoxically induced the opposite reaction. It has unleashed appetites and inflamed people's insatiable desires for acquisitiveness, conspicuous leisure and consumption and guilt-free lawlessness.

In such a setting, public and private events – even the most intimate and personal celebrations – are transformed (or deformed) into objects of curiosity and display appealing or intended to appeal to traumatized and duped consumers. The intention is to dazzle and trap the masses into a simulated mass culture. Today, Lebanon is a living and vivid example of Guy Debord's *The Society of the Spectacle* (1995), where the obsession with appearance and image-making become forms of false consciousness and public distraction. Embittered and rootless masses, impelled by the urge to make up for lost time, are readily seduced by burlesque-like spectacles, trite clichés and cheap sentimentality. Objects, scenes, events, even the cherished icons of Lebanon's archeological, artistic and culinary legacies, are all banalized by the public gaze and the whims of the masses. They become no more than a sensational marvel or curiosity.

Some of these excesses are so egregious that they assume at times all the barbarous symptoms of not-so-moral substitutes for war. Boisterous and disorderly conduct are routinized and hardly invite any moral reprehension or censure: from reckless driving, noise pollution, littering, heedless smoking to the more rapacious offenses such as ravaging the country's natural habitat, violating zoning and building ordinances, embezzlement, fraud, corruption, deficient civic and public consciousness – are all deeply embedded in the cultural ethos of laissez-faire, excessive economic liberalism and political clientelism.

Mercantilism and its concomitant bourgeois values were always given a free rein in Lebanon. As will be seen it has been treated by a score of historians as a 'Merchant Republic'. The outcome of such excessive commercialization was already painfully obvious in the prewar years. With staggering increases in land values, commercial traffic in real estate became one of the most lucrative sources of private wealth. Hence, the ruthless plundering of the country's scenic natural habitat and the dehumanization of its living space became starkly visible. With the absence of government authority, such excesses became more rampant. What was not ravaged by war was eaten up by greedy developers and impetuous consumers. Hardly anything is being spared today. The once pristine coastline is littered with tawdry tourist attractions, kitsch resorts and sleazy private marinas, as much as by the proliferation of slums and other unlawful makeshift shoddy tenements.

Rampant commercialism, greed and enfeebled state authority could not, on their own, have produced as much damage. They are exacerbated by the ravenous postwar mentality. Victims, having suffered human atrocities for so long, become insensitive to these seemingly benign and inconsequential concerns or transgressions. The moral and aesthetic restraints which normally control the growth of cities have become dispensable virtues, as they seem much too remote when pitted against the postwar profligate mood overwhelming large portions of society. Victims of collective suffering normally have other rudimentary things on their mind. They rage with bitterness and long to make up for lost time and opportunity. The environment becomes an accessible target on which to vent their wrath. In a culture infused with a residue of unappeased hostility and mercantilism, violating the habitat is also very lucrative. Both greed and hostility find an expedient proxy victim.

In such a free-for-all, any concern for the aesthetic, human or cultural dimensions of living space is bound to be dismissed as superfluous or guileless. As a result, it is of little concern whether cities are ugly, whether they debase their inhabitants, whether they are aesthetically, spiritually or physically tolerable, or whether they provide people with opportunities for authentic individuality, privacy and edifying human encounters. What counts is that access to land must satisfy two overriding claims: the insatiable appetite for profit among the bourgeoisie and the vengeful feeling of entitlement to unearned privileges among the disenfranchised. By the time authorities step in to restrain or recover such violations, as was to happen repeatedly in the prewar years, the efforts are always too little, too late. By then, officials could only confirm the infringements and incorporate them into the legitimate zoning ordinances.

How can ordinary citizens burdened with the pervasive fears of an ugly and unfinished war, persisting regional rivalries, mounting economic deprivation and diminishing socio-psychological prospects for well-being and the good life, find meaning and coherence (let alone inspiration) in a society which has not only lost its moorings and direction but is also out of control? This is precisely what adrift means and this is how the term, as a metaphor or 'ideal type', is being employed in this work.

If one reviews how the term is formally defined in a handful of unabridged dictionaries, the usage converges on at least three defining features or attributes. First it involves the notion that a society, like a ship floating at random and without any motive power, has lost its anchorage and moorings (Merriam-Webster). Hence, one feels disconnected from the abiding values and primordial loyalties which once served as sources of meaning, stability, order and integration. Second, without any anchorage, one is carried aimlessly, bereft of any firm purpose or direction (Collins). At best, one simply drifts with the flow. At worst, one becomes confused, uncertain but also estranged, abandoned and alienated (Macmillan). Without any solid ties, guidance, or security, people become morally adrift (Merriam-Webster). Altogether, one is overwhelmed by the feeling that one's life has no purpose any more.

Finally, and most definitive for our purposes, when one loses the usual support, one is also inclined to lose restraints and controls (Merriam-Webster). It is in this fundamental sense that I have characterized Lebanon as being adrift. The country has not only lost its anchorage and sense of direction. Most disheartening, it has been displaying lately all the startling symptoms of being uncontained. The exuberance and expectations of the Lebanese are so excessive that they are beyond control or restraint. Hence, they are doomed to a life of constant seeking without fulfillment. More concretely and existentially, as the average Lebanese becomes disconnected from his past moorings, he is also anxious and uncertain about the future directions of his society and his place in it. The Lebanese today are trapped in a disparaging threefold predicament: alienation from the past, anxiety and unease about the present and uncertainty about the future.

Symptoms of being adrift are more compelling in Lebanon because ordinary citizens feel estranged from and abandoned by an inept political culture which remains indifferent to their vital everyday needs. The political system has been for some time now obsessively focused (often ad nauseam) on issues exclusively concerned with peace accords, conflict resolution, electoral and constitutional reforms, political succession, the formation of so-called 'national unity' governments and, as of late, political confessionalism. Hence, the seemingly more elusive but vital problems associated with qualities of the good life, and how to safeguard ties of civility, trust, decency and the enrichment of the aesthetic and cultural legacy of society, are either trivialized or overlooked.

Being adrift is exacerbated further by the modes of collective adaptation the Lebanese have been employing to cope with all its derivative anomalies. The society appears today, perhaps more than any other earlier interlude, engrossed in two seemingly inconsistent, often irresistible, forms of false consciousness. First, a growing segment of the population is seeking shelter in religiosity, communalism or in cloistered groups and self-enclosed defensive spatial identities. Second, even larger portions are finding refuge and temporary relief in the hyped and seductive appeals of mass consumerism, image-making and self-representation.

In the former, as seen in the greater participation in religious rituals, festivals and mass commemoration, confessional and sectarian loyalties are politicized and reduced to symbolic statements. In this sense religiosity is no longer a spiritual longing to find redemption in a deity or divine savior. Instead, it assumes revivalist and assertive bigotry and intolerance of the other. In the latter, consumerism as an enabling venue to fulfill basic human needs is debased and degenerated into a compulsion. As a result virtually no entity today – from the sacred to the profane – can escape being commodified. To allay the fears of remaining adrift, the sacred, as will be seen, is often profaned and the profane is sacralized by worshiping consumer fads, celebrities, brands and logos.

In more mundane and prosaic terms, Lebanon seems to be caught in a pernicious 'catch 22'. At many levels, the very enabling forces which are supposed to offer the ordinary Lebanese social support, coherence and autonomy are also the forces which disable him, undermining his civility and sense of well-being. The formation and deformation of Lebanon are rooted, as it were, in the same forces. At the micro level, one's salvation and victimization are by-products of the same realities. It is in this sense that religiosity and consumerism become forms of false consciousness. They give individuals shelter but mute their sensibilities and dampen their feelings of outrage. Hence, the two most pervasive and defining features of contemporary Lebanon – profaned religiosity and sacralized consumerism – are more likely to exacerbate and reproduce the state of being adrift rather than allay it.

Finally, one cannot overlook the role of the new media and information technologies in accentuating the unsettling symptoms of these disparities. This is most visible today in Lebanon in the way the media is stylizing and romanticizing the products being merchandized. Prior to the advent of the mega-conglomerates, when production of news, culture, sports and entertainment was moderate and reasonable, the average consumer had limited chances to desire material objects beyond his reach. Today, he is taken hostage, or at least at the mercy of the relentless disparity between stimulated and hyped desires and his inability to reach them.

Naturally, Emile Durkheim, and the succession of scholars who reformulated his classical treatment of anomie, reminds us that it is a socio-cultural and not a psychological predisposition. In other words, it is society, through its aggressive and scintillating marketing campaigns, which whets people's appetites but fails to provide the necessary restraints on exuberant commodification. As will be shown, nothing is spared. Once intimate, modest and understated family and communal celebrations fall victim to such spectacles of excessive display. In the process some of the inviting features of genuine authenticity, conviviality and simplicity inherent in such gatherings – always sources of well-being equity and solidarity – are now banalized and kitsched-up.

Is Lebanon irrevocably doomed because it has been unable, at repeated interludes in its checkered history, to contain or reverse some of the disquieting symptoms of being adrift? Being adrift, it should be borne in mind, is essentially a transitory condition, a state of limbo or liminality. Though it conjures up images of being aimless, drifting without any purposive or willed direction or destination, it is nonetheless a state of travel. It is not unlike the intuitive aphorism of Robert Louis Stevenson when he tells us that 'to travel hopefully is better than to arrive'. The condition of liminality also evokes the tenuous experience of being between traveling and settling. Hence, it is also characterized by ambiguity, indeterminacy but also openness to new encounters. As such, normal limits to thought and self-understanding are suspended and relaxed. Mass events – ceremonies, collective celebrations, even sport events, cultural artistic festivals – are said to create such liminal experiences. They could become transcending sources of collective inspiration and mobilization and hence serve to redirect creative energies into more optimal directions.

Two other perspectives come to mind when we consider some of the redemptive features of being adrift: K.W. Wolf's metaphor of 'Surrender and

Catch' (1995) and Edward Said's 'Potentate and the Traveler' (2000). In the former Wolf implies that only when we are released from ordinary and customary routines and fixed constraints do we become able to catch new possibilities. Likewise, to Said, the image of the traveler, unlike the potentate who must guard only one place and defend its frontiers, is more mobile and playful.

> The image of traveler depends not on power but on motion, on a willingness to go into different worlds, use different idioms, and understand a variety of disguises, masks, and rhetoric. Travelers must suspend the claim of customary routine in order to live in new rhythms and rituals. Most of all, and most unlike the potentate who must guard only one place and defend its frontiers, the traveler *crosses over*, traverses territory, and abandons fixed positions, all the time. (Said, 2000: 404)

ON METAPHORS AND 'IDEAL TYPES'

All metaphors and 'ideal types', like any other figures of speech, involve some inevitable distortions of reality. They rarely tell the whole truth. Though I am labeling Lebanon as being 'adrift', other elusive expressions – a 'playground', a society of 'spectacle', 'Janus-like' – are still relevant and informative to this undertaking. Certainly more so, in my view, than the hackneyed labels that have been attached to Lebanon over the years: both the redeeming and the pejorative. The former make it seem like a privileged creation, a 'success story' suffused with unmatched resilience, and natural endowments or the 'Switzerland' or 'Paris' of the Middle East. The latter admonish it with all the epitaph-like slurs which suggest that Lebanon is no more than a congenitally flawed or artificial entity bent on self-destruction. Since it is beyond understanding or cure, some have gone further to propose that, like any pathological organism, the most one can do is to 'quarantine' or contain it lest it contaminate others.

Such denigrating labels are quick to resurface whenever Lebanon lapses into another round of factional fighting or serial political assassinations. Indeed, 'Lebanization' has by now been reduced to an ugly metaphor indiscriminately employed by sensational journalistic accounts and media soundbites. At times it is no more than an allegoric figure of speech, a trite cliché, a mere byword to conjure up images of the grotesque and unspoken.

These, and other hidden abominations, are pardonable. The most injurious, however, is when the label is reduced to a fiendish prop without emotion, a mere foil to evoke the anguish of others. When cataloguing the horrors of Lebanon at a time when it was still newsworthy on American TV (i.e. 1985–92), I kept a ledger of the times this indignant label popped up compulsively in a set of random but dreaded circumstances: a fireman fighting a blaze in Philadelphia, the anguish of an AIDS victim, a jogger facing the fearful prospects of Manhattan's Central Park, survivors of a train crash, dejected Vietnamese 'boat people', evacuees from China, the frenzy of delirious masses mourning Khomeini's death, looting and the chaos in the wake of the Los Angeles earthquake, a shooting rampage of a crazed spree-killer, even the anguish and perplexing bewilderment on the face and demeanor of a psychopath was described by a noted American psychiatrist as if his subject was deranged by the cruelties of war in Lebanon.

At times the pejorative codeword spilled over to include natural catastrophes: fires, earthquakes, hurricanes and the like, and the damage they inflict on vulnerable and defenseless people. Even wanton acts of bestiality, the hapless victims of anomie, entropy and other symptoms of collective terror and fear are also epitomized as analogs to life in Lebanon (see Khalaf, 2002: 10).

Tabloids and sensational image-makers may be forgiven these epithets. Scholars, sadly, continue to appropriate the label. Indeed, considering the growing amount of scholarly writing which readily invokes 'Lebanization' or 'Lebanonization', it has now entered part of the regular lexicon of social science terminology. *Larousse*, the prominent French dictionary, might have well been the first when, in 1991, it introduced 'Libanisation' formally into the French language to mean 'procès de fragmentation d'un État, résultant de l'affrontement entre diverses communautés' (process of fragmentation of a state, as a result of confrontation between diverse communities). *Larousse* goes further to suggest that the term might be considered as an alternate to 'balkanization', to capture more graphically the collapse and dismemberment of the 'Eastern Bloc' in the wake of the Cold War.

James Gillian, in his wide-ranging work on violence, singles out Lebanon (Beirut in particular) – along with the atrocities committed by Hitler, Stalin, Idi Amin, Saddam Hussein, Kamikaze pilots, the Baader-Meinhof Gang, the Red Brigades and the victimization of innocents in Belfast, Bosnia and Bogata – as illustrative 'of the most horrendously destructive of human life around the world in this century' (Gillian, 1996: 95). Rupesinghe does not remain at this broad narrative level. He goes further, to accord 'Lebanization' the attribute of a concept to refer to 'situations where the state has lost control of law and order and where many armed groups are contending to power' (Rupesinghe, 1992: 26).

Even serious scholars could not resist the allure of the metaphor. The most revealing, perhaps, is the way William Harris has chosen to use the label in his book on sectarian conflict and globalization in Lebanon (Harris, 1997). In fact, the distinction he makes between the 'Lebanization' of the 1980s and that of the 1990s informs the guiding thesis of his work. The former referred to 'sectarian strife and temporary cantonization at a time of global transition'. Lebanon then attracted attention as an 'extreme case of regime multiplied across Eurasia' (Harris, 1997: 6). Lebanonization of the 1990 ushers in a new threat. Extreme and militant Shi'ites, by becoming the most potent political force, 'represented the principal extension of the Iranian revolution in the Arab world'. Hizbullah quickly acquires its international bogeyman image and 'Lebanonization' begins to signify 'a black hole of destruction and terror' (Harris, 1997: 7).

These and other such characterizations – particularly those which either exaggerate the innate character of Lebanon's internal divisions and dislocations or those which view it as a victim of external sources of instability – are naturally too generic and misleading. They do not capture or elucidate the rich diversity and complexities of the country's encounters with collective unrest and postwar anxieties. Nor do they do justice to some of the peculiar pathologies and circumstances associated with Lebanon's entrapment in that ravaging spiral of protracted and unappeased hostility and the uncertainties of global consumerism.

The metaphors and 'ideal types' I am proposing to use have nothing in common with this derisive name-calling. In his seminal work on 'liquidity' in contemporary society, Zygmunt Bauman (2000) makes intuitive use of Max Weber's 'ideal types' to elucidate the meaning of liquidity and its implications for understanding an endless inventory of human phenomena, ranging from modernity, love, fear and risk to waste and consumerism. He maintains, much like Weber and others who make use of such constructs, that 'ideal types' are not descriptions of social reality; nor are they snapshots or facsimiles of the real world. Rather, they are attempts to construct models of its essential elements which can help in rendering the otherwise scattered and chaotic evidence of experience more intelligible. Hence, ideal types are not merely descriptions of social reality but the tools for its analysis and, hopefully, its comprehension. In this manner they help us in making more sense of the world out there. To achieve that purpose, Bauman maintains that they 'deliberately postulate more homogeneity, consistency and logic in the empirical social world than daily experience makes visible and allows us to grasp' (Bauman, 2007: 23).

Bauman is keen to remind us that most, if not all, concepts conventionally used in the social sciences – like 'capitalism', 'feudalism', 'democracy', even 'society', 'community' or 'family' – have the status of an ideal type. In line with Weber, if properly constructed, they are not only useful, but also indispensable, cognitive tools for throwing light on certain aspects of social reality (for further details, see Weber, 1947: 110). They are indispensable because they 'leave in the shade some other aspects considered to be of lesser or only of random relevance to the essential, necessary traits of a particular form of life' (Bauman, 2007: 27). Bauman uses Weber's analytical tools to construct his own ideal types of a 'society of consumers', 'consumerism' and 'consumer culture'.

Beyond Bauman's use of ideal types as tools to 'see with' and to be 'thought' within his analysis of liquidity and consumerism, other classical conceptions can also help in grasping the notion of being adrift. Georg Simmel's (2004) 'stranger' in a dense, impersonal and pecuniary metropolis assumes a 'blasé' attitude. To survive, in other words, the city-dweller needs to 'blunt his discrimination'. Hence, one merely 'floats in a constantly moving stream of money'. To Simmel the 'blasé' person is also riddled with symptoms of 'melancholy'. This, as will be elaborated, becomes the generic affliction of the consumer. In Simmel's analysis it stands for the built-in transitoriness and, hence, objects become contrived and simply drift over. This is also close to how we are employing Debord's metaphor of the 'spectacle', which above all stands for not being attached to anything specific or concrete. Interestingly, Rolland Munro in his work on 'Melancholy and the Follies of Modernization' reconciles the insights of Simmel, Debord and Bauman. He argues that, because of the infinity of connections in modern society, the 'melancholic is hooked up to nothing. In short, it refers to a *form* without *substance*' (Munro, 2005: 282).

Altogether then, metaphors like *spectacle, playground*, as analytical constructs serve us well since they give us a measuring rod to ascertain similarities as well as deviations in the concrete cases associated with being *adrift*. Also ideal types in no way imply that they subscribe to moral ideals. In fact, they are fairly neutral and consider both the enabling and disabling features of the problems being investigated.

OVERVIEW OF THE BOOK

Chapter 1, largely theoretical in character, revisits some of the salient perspectives on civil unrest and collective violence. The intention is to extract and account for some of the defining attributes of proxy wars and surrogate victimization. Under what circumstances and why, it will be asked, are ordinary forms of socio-economic and political protests deflected into more belligerent violence? How and why, in other words, was Lebanon transformed into a killing field for other people's wars? More graphically, why do the Lebanese throughout their encounters with collective violence end up killing not those they wanted to kill but those they could kill? Equally distressing, why has the resort to violence had no effect on redressing the imbalances in society or transforming the country's confessional and communal loyalties into more civic entities germane to a nation-state?

In answering these queries, I single out seven rather unusual but distinct features which account for the protracted and displaced character of civil unrest. Inferences are also advanced to suggest how they are likely to affect the state of adrift. First, and perhaps most striking, circumstances which *initiate* or impel oppressed or marginalized groups to resort to political violence are not necessarily those which *sustain* their mobilization or inform the direction, character and outcome of conflict. For example, all three peasant uprisings in Mount Lebanon in the nineteenth century were initially incited by a sense of collective consciousness and concern for justice and public welfare. Yet, at one point or another, they were all deflected into confessional hostilities. As this happens the struggles acquire a life of their own, unrelated to the original conditions which might have propelled them.

Second, another curious anomaly associated with the first, the circumstances in a country's socio-economic and cultural history heighten and radicalize communal identities. This is emblematic of another 'catch-22' in that the communal identities which conventionally serve as vital sources of support and venues of welfare, benefits and privileging networks are transformed (or deformed) into belligerent vectors for radicalization. Once again, in other words, the enabling and disabling features are rooted in the same socio-cultural realities. As will be amplified, it is understandable why traumatized and threatened groups should seek shelter in communal solidarities. But as they do so, fear, paranoia and distance from the other are heightened and, thereby, compound the intensity of enmity and hostility.

Third, the interplay between internal dislocations and external pressures has also not been an auspicious or neutral phenomenon. Western incursions, willfully or otherwise, have always contributed to socio-economic dislocations and political instability. This was most visible in the diplomatic role foreign powers played in the formulation of successive settlement schemes. In virtually all episodes of collective strife – communal hostilities and peasant uprisings in Mount Lebanon, the civil war of 1958 and the extended civil unrest of 1975–92 – foreign intervention almost always touched off renewed outbreaks of civil unrest and political violence. Dipping into the rich sources of diplomatic history and international studies (e.g. Gerges, 1997; Korbani, 1991; Arkali, 1993; Hanf, 1993), persuasive evidence is marshaled in support of this thesis. For example, Henry Kissinger's disengagement diplomacy as the war broke out in Lebanon and his subsequent step-by-step approach actually increased the prospects of proxy wars. More recently, the unsettling by-products of unresolved regional and global rivalries – Arab–Israeli conflict, nascent Islamophobia and Islamic militancy in the aftermath of 9/11, global struggle between the US and Iran, etc. – have all had a definitive impact on the pattern and intensity of conflict.

Fourth, employing the distinction James Rule (1988) makes between *consumatory* and *instrumental* violence, one is able to throw further light on how violence became domesticated and routinized. In one respect there is much to substantiate the 'consumatory' or expressive type of collective strife, the kind impelled and sustained by group solidarity, in which the sharing of emancipatory excitement and the frenzy of agitated gatherings are pronounced. In other words, the sheer ardor and devotion to collective struggle becomes the glue which cements people together. In other respects, one also encounters evidence to support what Rule labels 'instrumental' violence. Here the insurgents are not only incited by the impulse to correct injustices and seek some respite from abuse and marginalization. They are also driven by a utilitarian desire to secure basic amenities and material rewards.

Fifth, Lebanon remains adrift largely because – as the explicit title of the chapter suggests – it is gripped by two aberrant features of hostility: it is displaced and protracted. The two aspects feed on each other and, thereby, exacerbate the pathological consequences of each. This is understandable. I take my hint from the seminal work of Rene Girard (1977), who tells us that when grievances and feelings of anger are not pacified, agitated groups are prone to release their unappeased hostility on any accessible and vulnerable target. Episodes of protracted strife in Lebanon are replete with such instances of displaced violence. In the language of Girard, innocent victims just happened to be there: 'vulnerable and close at hand'. Concrete evidence will be provided from all interludes of civil unrest to substantiate this proxy and surrogate character of victimization. For example, Syrian forces in the early stages of the war (1975–7) were in combat with Christian militias or Palestinian fighters. Neither though were their ostensible enemies. In this regard, they should have been fighting either the Israeli or Iraqi forces. Yet neither of those regional powers was vulnerable or close at hand.

Sixth, the prosaic distinction between 'horizontal' and 'vertical' divisions will be introduced here to shed further light on the circumstances that radicalize communal identities. 'Horizontal' socio-economic disputes, though aroused by embittered feelings of injustice, loss of status, material advantage and privilege, are likely to remain less militant unless deflected into confessional or communal hostility. 'Vertical' divisions, on the other hand, particularly when engendered by communal and sectarian loyalties, are threatened by more compelling and existential issues such as the loss of freedom, identity, autonomy and heritage. In the language of Theodor Hanf (1995) it is then that the conflict shifts from a struggle over *divisible goods* to *indivisible principles*. As this happens, the intensity of violence is bound to become more savage and, hence, the prospects for resolving the conflict peacefully all the more remote. Expressed more concretely, struggles over the former (that is, *divisible goods*) normally involve contests of distributive justice as to who gets what and how much. Such struggles, as I have argued elsewhere (Khalaf, 2002), are bound to be contained and 'civil' in character. It is when they spill over, as they often do, into primordial and confessional rivalries (that is, *indivisible principles*), those based in the ingrained kinship sentiments of kinship, community, faith and creed, that they are bound to become bloodier.

Finally, Lebanon remains adrift because in its prolonged and recurrent encounters with collective violence, and despite the ferocity of the wars, none ever ended, or was permitted to end, with a clear victor or vanquished. Indeed, and with the intercession of foreign emissaries, hostilities were redressed by short-lived cease-fires or abortive political settlements (Khalaf, 2010). Comparative evidence, as will be shown, is not very encouraging in this regard. In at least six other instances of civil unrest (Colombia, Zimbabwe, Greece, Yemen, Sudan, Nigeria and the American Civil War), when conflict is primarily communal or ethnic in character, the likelihood of a negotiated peaceful settlement becomes very slim. There must be, in other words, a victor or a vanquished before combatants begin to consider negotiation.

Chapter 2 shifts the analysis to issues of collective memory, contested space and attempts to forge new cultural identities. Vital as these issues are, they have not been given the focused and critical attention they deserve. How much and what of the past needs to be retained or restored? By whom and for whom? In Lebanon these are particularly pertinent questions on which, as we shall see, there is no consensus. Some are inclined to argue that any sense of amnesia is a dreaded condition to be resisted. Others, in view of the atrocious recollections of the war, are more likely to maintain that, without an opportunity to forget, the prospects for accord and coexistence are slim. Within this context the chapter explores a few dimensions which have some implications for the liminal and elusive state of being adrift.

First, some of the most striking spatial transformations will be highlighted to better understand the interplay between space, memory and how territorial identities are being redefined by the spatial logic of war. Second, given what I term the 'geography of fear', an effort is made to identify how various communities are reacting to some of the global forces presumed to undermine their local identities. Given the re-emergence of the Bourj as a vibrant and cosmopolitan public sphere, I will review its eventful transformations to elucidate further how it managed to reconcile local, regional and global incursions to reinforce its predisposition to experiment with divergent lifestyles. Finally, under the rubric of the 'mediating agencies of social forgetting', I consider some of the poignant dilemmas the Lebanese are facing today in their efforts to recall all the atrocities of the war without sanitizing or lessening their horrors.

In Chapter 3 we begin to focus on what is singled out as one of the defining, often aberrant, features of contemporary Lebanon: the unprecedented surge in mass consumerism, particularly its stylized, sensational and hedonistic features. Normally, postwar interludes are expected to invite moods of moderation, introspection and restraint. By stark contrast, they have unleashed the opposite conditions in Lebanon. The passions for consumption, acquisitiveness and display have become so irresistible that they stand out today as some of the most compelling and coveted cultural features. Indeed, and not unlike the experience of Euro-American societies, consumerism has been transformed into commodification, where marketable goods and services are substituted for personal relationships, cultural, artistic expressions and other sources of well-being and identity. In short, and hence one of the leitmotifs of this chapter, 'it is in acquiring, using and exchanging things that individuals come to have social lives'.

With this in mind, the chapter is in two parts. An attempt is made first, briefly and eclectically, to identify a few promising theoretical perspectives from the rich and growing volume of literature on consumerism (from Veblen, Durkheim, Simmel to Goffman, Bourdieu, Bauman and Giddens) to account for some of the striking manifestations of the changing character of consumerism. To substantiate the link between cosmopolitanism and commodification, the bulk of the chapter focuses on three interludes in Beirut's epochal history: its swift urbanization by the end of the nineteenth century as an *entrepôt* and epicenter of banking and trade, the concomitant emergence of the early symptoms of merchandizing, and the gadgetry of modern consumerism and marketing. It is then, for example, that department stores like Orosdi-Back became precursors of global franchises for upscale and elite consumerism.

By the early decades of the twentieth century emancipated youth started to discover the novelty and marvels of the cinema as an accessible form of public entertainment. Unlike other cities in the Levant, cinemas in Beirut were not contested forms of leisure. Indeed, by the 1940s the proliferation of movie theaters was so striking that they overwhelmed the cityscape of Beirut. More important, as will be seen, as a popular pastime movie attendance had significant proletarian and gender implications. It was the one public form of entertainment which drew together diverse status groups. It also prodded women to defy customary inhibitions which restricted their appearance in public venues. Finally, with the proliferation of other venues for self-expression, in the two decades preceding Lebanon's descent into civil unrest (also the country's golden/gilded age), different groups of all persuasions and backgrounds started to experiment with new ideas and lifestyles. The nascent patterns of consumerism remained largely restrained, participative and convivial in character.

During the past few years, Beirut has become unrivaled in being the marketing, media and graphic design capital of the Arab world. The proliferation of new media – with the latest state-of-the-art technologies – has had a profound effect, accentuating both the seductive appeal and pitfalls of consumerism. Chapter 4 considers first some of the relevant conceptual perspectives to elucidate the impact of marketing on mass consumerism. As will be demonstrated, nothing is spared commodification: from the secular features of Lebanon's political culture, resistance movements, popular entertainment to the deepest and most intimate character of communal and family life. This is most evident in the thriving of the sex industry, the prevalence of sensuality and the commercialization of religion and spirituality.

The chapter then, and in more concrete details, substantiates textually and graphically the merchandizing strategies Lebanese entrepreneurs are employing in transforming consumers into commodities. The marketing of six basic amenities and public needs are exposed: buying a home, cosmetics, fashions, entertainment, nightlife and religious tourism. The basic premise of the chapter is that the more exuberant the marketing strategies in the promises they make, the more delusional they are. Hence, they are destined to embody an inevitable dissonance between their extravagant claims and what they objectively deliver. The ordinary Lebanese consumer is, as a consequence, doomed to a condition of constant seeking without fulfillment.

In Chapter 5 we consider two extreme by-products of excessive commodification and global consumerism: the spectacle and kitsch. As in earlier chapters, the basic premise here is that some of the very sources which accounted for Lebanon's openness, malleability and cosmopolitan character and which rendered it more receptive in fostering cultural experimentation, also brought with them some of the disheartening symptoms of the spectacle and kitsch. These manifestations are becoming increasingly visible in an obsessive concern with image-making, virtual and artificial commodification and debasement of cultural products. More important, it is argued that their special appeals as forms of false consciousness are inherent in their ability to shelter traumatized groups from the realities of being adrift. The chapter dwells on some recent riveting public events to demonstrate how they are kitsched-up and deformed into spectacles.

Chapter 6 is devoted to a consideration of some of the likely alternatives to a commodified consumer society and the prospects for transforming the consumer into a citizen. The chapter first recaptures some of the basic arguments of the book with special emphasis on the circumstances associated with the paradigm shift in consumerism as seen in the preponderance of commodification, mindless hedonism and the longing for glamour, luxury, sensuality and image-making. Rather than seeking answers in the incursion of petro-dollars and the so-called irresistible and homogenizing forces of globalization, we focus instead on manifestations of hybridity, eclecticism and *glocalization*, where global consumer items are rearranged to render them more amenable to local needs.

I then employ the metaphor of a playground which, in my view, is a realistic and judicious label to capture some of Lebanon's distinctive but anomalous features. It is certainly more meaningful than the hackneyed and binary clichés which either celebrate the country as a dazzling and inviting place or malign it as a flawed and foreboding entity; that is, a perennial battleground for other people's wars or a lascivious place of sexual abandon and ephemeral pleasures. The chapter identifies five features of a playground which epitomize Lebanon's seemingly lopsided and Janus-like character. In all those features – such as the country's laissez-faire ethos, the spirit of gamesmanship, conviviality and the spectacle – we find many of the enabling and disabling attributes of a *playground* as a metaphor. It helps us to elucidate Lebanon's 'success story' and those which render it more vulnerable to all the internal and external contradictions.

In other words, though some of the symptoms of commodification – particularly visible in excessive commercialization mass and popular culture and conspicuous leisure – are becoming more salient in Lebanon, they are not the colonizing, pathological and sinister demons they are often made out to be. The concluding chapter also dwells on some recent promising examples, mostly the venues of advocacy and civic-consciousness groups and NGOs (e.g. Green Party, Consumer's Lebanon, Transparency International, the Youth Association for Social Awareness and non-corporate architecture), which provide alternatives to commodification and shelter ordinary citizens from being deformed or denatured into duped consumers.

Finally, the parting thoughts of our epilogue leave us with a few promising and enabling inferences. Foremost, it questions the prevailing and essentialist perspective which posits a binary relation between the assumed seductive and manipulative merchandizing forces and the so-called docile and gullible consumer. Neither are the forces of commodification that irresistible, nor are the Lebanese consumers that pliant and undiscerning. It is also in this sense that the state of being adrift which currently besets Lebanon need not be treated as a perpetual or irredeemable condition of aimless wandering. Nor are all its symptoms aberrant and dismaying. When its impulsive and excessive features are contained, this liminal state of surrender and wandering may well prove to be rejuvenating. At least it carries the prospect, remote as it may seem, of averting some of the bleak destinations ahead.

Chapter 1

On Protracted and Displaced Collective Violence

When unappeased, violence seeks and always finds a surrogate victim. The creature that excited its fury is abruptly replaced by another, chosen only because it is vulnerable and close at hand.

(René Girard, *Violence and the Sacred,* 1977)

The animus was always the same: Whether nation, province, or city, whether religion, class or culture – the more one loved one's own, the more one was entitled to hate the other ... Through the centuries politicians had exploited this human trait. In the knowledge that hatred can be cultivated with a purpose, they constructed enemies in order to bolster domestic concord.

(Peter Gay, *The Cultivation of Hatred,* 1993)

In cases where conflict is primarily of an ethnic, communal character in contrast to those provoked by economic and/or political issues, the likelihood of a negotiated non-belligerent resolution becomes very slim. Indeed, all communal wars end in blood. There must be a victor and a vanquished before combatants begin to consider negotiation.

(Jay Kaplan, 'Victors and Vanquished', 1980)

Lebanon's perilous and extended encounters with collective violence continue to invite a relentless output of speculative writing, both scholarly and journalistic. Despite its diversity, and much like the broader and conventional literature on civil unrest, the output converges on a set of recurrent themes. In fact, one can identify five general perspectives, which have gained currency during the past two decades or so, in accounting for the sources and patterns of political violence.

First, some scholars focus on the fragmented character of political culture in new states in transition. The voluminous output of scholars like Huntington (1993), Eisenstadt (1966), Pye (1966), Apter (1965), Geertz (1968), Deutsch (1961), Black (1966), Shils (1965), Lerner (1958) etc, particularly during the 1960s, consisted mostly of efforts to elucidate the dialectical relationship between fragmentation and political instability. Fragmentation is, on the whole, treated here as a by-product of both traditional divisive and segmental loyalties or the asymmetrical growth and cultural differentiation generated by processes of development and modernization. Hence, vertical and horizontal divisions, particularly in plural societies like Lebanon, are prone to pull the society apart and threaten the delicate balance of forces. In short, fragmentation generates political unrest which, in turn, accentuates the cleavages in society.

Second, there are those who, armed with dependency theory and conspiracy models, advance some version of 'inside–outside' polemics. Internal disparities, the argument goes, prompt threatened and dispossessed groups to seek external patronage. External forces, through direct forms of foreign intervention, growing dependence on world markets or patronage of local client groups, produce pronounced shifts in the relative socio-economic and political positions of the various religious communities. These dislocations almost always touch off renewed outbreaks of civil unrest and political violence.

Virtually all peasant uprisings and communal hostilities in Mount Lebanon during the second half of the nineteenth century, much like the civil war of 1958, were replete with the escalating disruptive consequences of such 'inside–outside' dialectics. This polemic became sharper and more devastating during the extended hostilities of 1975–92. More recently the adverse by-products of unresolved regional and global rivalries – such as nascent Islamophobia and Islamic militancy in the wake of 9/11, the global struggle between the US and Iran and its implications in precipitating and compounding the intensity of hostility between pro and anti Syrian and Iranian factions and the inveterate belligerent Israel and Palestinian resistance factions – have all had a decisive impact on the pattern and intensity of collective violence.

Third, drawing upon theories of cognitive dissonance and relative deprivation – as expounded by Festinger (1957), Gurr (1980), Feierabend and Feierabend (1966) and others – this group of scholars tends to focus instead on the socio-psychological strains generated by the growing gaps and disparities between aspirations and opportunities. One of the most celebrated versions of this perspective is, of course, that of relative deprivation, treated here in terms of the group's perception of a discrepancy between what they believe they are legitimately entitled to get, and their estimation of what they are actually able to receive under existing conditions. According to this analysis, feelings of relative deprivation will produce anger and frustration, which in turn will trigger violent action. This is inevitably compounded by the inherent dissonance between subjective perception and objective conditions.

Fourth, and by contrast, theories of so-called 'collective action' are more inclined to argue that what matters is not so much that people have grievances and unmet needs, but rather that they possess the political resources which will enable them to translate their discontent into action. Noted examples here are Tilly (1978), Hirschman (1970) and Moore (1966), who in much of their research concentrate on the conditions conducive to the mobilization of groups and their predisposition to participate in collective action.

Finally, a growing number of scholars in recent years have shifted their concern to the analysis of the impact of rapid urbanization on domestic political violence. Particular emphasis here is placed on the revolutionary potential of the urban poor and 'urban marginals', and the impact of communal networks on the pattern and intensity of civil strife. Theoretical reformulations by Tilly (1978), Bienen (1984) and Wilson (1992), among others, reinforced by empirical surveys in regions undergoing rapid urbanization, are beginning to reveal some telling but inconsistent trends. For example, while the survival of communal networks in Latin American and African cities has been generally associated with the reduction in the incidence of political violence, preliminary results from a selected number of Middle Eastern cities provide evidence to the contrary (Karpat on Turkey, Kazemi on Iran, Ibrahim on Egypt and Khalaf and Denoeux on Lebanon).

Instructive as such analyses have been, they are predominantly concerned with the inception and etiology of civil unrest. Consequently, they have had little to say about (1) why violence has been sustained, (2) the forms and intensity it has assumed or (3) how people cope with chronic unrest and unsettled times. At least in the case of Lebanon, the exercise has become rather futile; at best a laborious and painful elaboration of the obvious. For example, it is quite common for a pluralistic society like Lebanon to display a high propensity for violence. The lack of political integration in new states has, after all, been cited over and over again as a major cause, indeed a prerequisite for violence. One could, likewise, write volumes about the destabilizing impact of the presence of Syrians, Palestinians and Israelis, or the unresolved regional and superpower rivalries, without adding much to what we know already.

What is, however, unusual is the *persistence, growing intensity* and *shifting targets of hostility*. By the early 1990s, in fact, the conflict was fractured even further as inter-communal rivalries degenerated into intraconfessional hostilities. The ecology of violence, reinforced by all the psychological barriers of restructured enmities, began to assume more intensive forms as street and quarter in-fighting displaced and/or compounded the earlier communal violence. Hence, much of the former characterization of the initial stages of civil unrest – 'Christian versus Muslim', 'right versus left' – generally became outmoded. It clearly does not help in accounting for the upsurge in the level of hostility between Sunnis and Shi'ites, Druze and Shi'ites, Kurds and Shi'ites, Palestinians and Shi'ites, Maronites and Armenians ... or between Maronites and Maronites. Indeed, by the early 1990s victims and casualties of intraconfessional violence had started to outnumber those generated by intersectarian or inter-religious hostility.

Doubtless, the most menacing was the displaced and surrogate character of violence and victimization. As the hostility degenerated into internecine fighting between fractious groups, combatants were often trapped in localized turf wars where they ended up taking vengeance on almost anyone, including their own kinsmen. This is, clearly, the most perfidious feature of the incivility of violence. Fighters were *killing not those they wanted to kill but those they could kill.* In repeated episodes of such in-group hostility, wanton killing was the bloodiest in terms of its victimization of innocent bystanders.

Considerations of this sort, along with all the other ruinous manifestations of civil unrest, clearly suggest that violence has become counterproductive and self-defeating. Contrary to what is often suggested, it has had little to do with the rebirth or recovery of justice and virtue, which are unlikely to rescue Lebanon from its deepening crisis and transform it into a secular and more civic social order. I take my cue here from Hannah Arendt (1958) who has suggested that the practice of violence, like all action, changes the world, but the most probable change is to a more violent world.

Expressed in more explicit political terms, the resort to violence has had little effect so far on (1) redressing the gaps and imbalances in society, or (2) transforming Lebanon's communal and confessional loyalties and institutions into more civic entities typical of a nation-state.

Yet, renewed cycles of violence went on unabated. Though Lebanon is often dubbed as an instance of 'low-intensity conflict', violence began to assume all the aberrant manifestations of endemic and autistic hostility. Unlike other encounters with civil unrest, which are often swift, decisive and localized, and where a sizeable part of the population could remain sheltered from its traumatizing impact, the Lebanese experience has been much more protracted and diffuse. The savagery of violence was also compounded by its randomness. In this sense, there is hardly a Lebanese today who is exempt from these atrocities either directly or vicariously. Violence and terror touched virtually everyone. It was everywhere and nowhere. It was everywhere because it could no longer be confined to one specific area or a few combatants. It was nowhere because it could not be identified or linked to one concrete cause. Recurring cycles or episodes of violence erupted, faded and resurfaced for no recognized or coherent reason.

The warring communities also locked themselves into a dependent relationship with violence and chronic conflict became both protracted and insoluble. Personal memories and recollections of the war, which for a while became an appealing genre of literary writing, reveal how perceiving and coping with the ugly everyday episodes of the war were domesticated and routinized. It is then that violence became both protracted and insoluble. It was also then that it was sustained by a pervasive feeling of helplessness, demoralization and obsessive dependency on external patrons and foreign brokers.

Within such a context, it became more instructive to shift the analysis from the partial and almost exclusive concern with the etiology of violence and extend it to incorporate those features that sustain and escalate the belligerency. Only by so doing can we begin to understand fully some of the socio-psychological and cultural attributes of protracted violence and, more importantly, suggest possible courses of action or strategies to constrain its aberrant consequences.

More specifically, this shift in concern from the *initiating* to the *sustaining* factors accompanying protracted conflict can help us better in elucidating at least two distinctive features of civil unrest in Lebanon: (1) the tendency for both pluralism and violence to become more pathological, and (2) the existence of ideologies of enmity through which warring

communities reinvent strategies for mutual debasement and demonization to rationalize acts of aggression, particularly when the victims of that
aggression might well be their own co-religionists or groups they coexisted
with previously.

When we extend our concerns to those features which sustain and escalate
the intensity of hostility, then we must part company with some of the
conventional perspectives and consider other sources and paradigms more
appropriate for the analysis of such overlooked features of protracted conflict.
Fortunately I discovered, as seen in the rich and diverse sources I consulted,
a rather substantial volume of writing which could be more imaginatively
applied to the instances of communal conflict under study.

Since I am assuming a dialectical interplay between the reassertion of
communal identities and heightened magnitude of collective strife, it is
necessary that the three persisting features underlying this interplay be
explored. Indeed, these features stand out, perhaps, as the defining elements in Lebanon's checkered political history: (1) the reawakening of primordial identities, (2) foreign intervention, and (3) the escalation of protracted violence. I have elsewhere (Khalaf, 2002) identified and accounted
for how the unresolved regional and global rivalries have contributed to
the protraction and escalation of conflict and the reassertion of communal
solidarities. The aim here is to document a few of the persisting features
underlying the survival of communal loyalties, particularly those aspects
of Lebanon's 'retribalization' exacerbated by the inside–outside dialectics.
How and under what circumstances, to be more concrete, are communal
loyalties radicalized?

By focusing on different episodes – ranging from peasant uprisings, factional feuds, 'class' and ideological struggles to other intermittent incidents
of civil strife – it is possible to elucidate how, regardless of their origins and
overt manifestations, they are all transformed (or deformed) into sectarian
hostility. It is also then, as will be seen, that the conflict becomes bloodier,
uncivil and more mired into the tangled world of foreign intervention.

For purposes of analysis, three different layers or magnitudes of violence
are identified. There is first *social strife*, the product largely of socio-economic
disparities, asymmetrical development, ideological rivalries, relative
deprivation and feelings of neglect and dispossession. These, normally, are
non-militant in character and express themselves in contentious but non-
belligerent forms of social protest and political mobilization. Second,
if the socio-economic disparities persist and the resulting hostilities are

unappeased, particularly if accompanied by feelings of threatened communal legacy and confessional loyalties, conflict and discord are inclined to become more militant and bellicose. It is here that social discord is transformed into communal violence; or in the words of Bouyer-Bell (1987) that the *civil strife* passes the point of no return into *civil war*. Finally, civil violence is not, or does not always remain, 'civil'. When inflamed by atavism or reawakened communalism, enmity and deep-seated suspicion of the 'other', internecine feuds and unresolved regional and global conflicts, collective violence could readily degenerate further into the incivility of proxy war and surrogate victimization. It is here that violence acquires its own inherent self-destructive logic and spirals into an atrocious cycle of unrelenting cruelties.

Within this context, it is meaningful to identify and account for some of the circumstances associated with the tenacity of communalism and its various manifestations. An effort is also made to consider how social strife is deflected into communal violence and ultimately descends into further barbarism and incivility. Queries of this sort are not only of historic significance. There has been recently renewed theoretical interest in the nature, manifestations and consequences of renewed 'tribalism' and reassertion of local and communal identities, particularly as they relate to the forces of globalization and postmodernity.[1]

Despite the varied circumstances associated with the repeated episodes or armed conflict Lebanon has been beset with for so long, they do evince features which have become distinctive elements in its checkered political culture. The purpose of this chapter is to highlight, albeit briefly, a few of those defining features.

DISSONANCE BETWEEN INITIATING AND SUSTAINING SOURCES OF VIOLENCE

Perhaps one of the most striking anomalies of the character and pattern of violence is the disparity between the factors which initiated it and those which sustained and accounted for its growing intensity and magnitude. Clearly, the circumstances which impelled groups to resort to political

---

1 There has been a profusion of writing recently exploring various dimensions of the globalization of ethnic and communal violence. Interested readers may wish to consult the following: Barber, 1996; Brezezinski, 1993; Esman and Rabinovich, 1988; Geyer, 1985; Hanf, 1995; Ignatieff, 1994; Kakar, 1996; Kelly, 1994; Moynihan, 1993; Wirston, 1992.

violence were not necessarily those which sustained their mobilization and informed the direction and outcome of conflict. What this in essence means is that as hostility is released it is likely to acquire its own momentum, almost a life of its own unrelated to the original sources which might have sparked it. It is then that embattled groups become trapped, as it were, in an escalating spiral of vengeance and retribution.

For example, all the peasant uprisings were initially sparked off by a sense of collective consciousness and a concern for public welfare. Yet all were deflected, at one point or another, into confessional hostility. Likewise, episodes of communal conflict, originally provoked by socio-economic disparities and legitimate grievances, were transformed into factional rivalry. The enthusiasm for 'class' struggle and collective mobilization among Christian peasants in the north found little appeal among their counterparts in the Druze districts. By arousing latent confessional enmity, traditional Druze leaders could easily manipulate such sentiments to ward off or caution against such involvement. The lapse of nearly forty years, in 1820–60, had done little in transforming the loyalties and attachments of peasants. Expressed more concretely, confessional, local and feudal allegiances continued to supersede other public and collective interests. A Druze remained a Druze first, a Jublatti second, a Choufi third, and then a fellah or part of the 'ammah or commoners.

This need not be dismissed lightly. In some significant respects had these 'class' rivalries been more successful in undermining the hegemony of feudal and communal leaders, the tribal and neo-feudal loyalties might not have retained their primacy in shaping the country's political culture. As a result, the resilience of primordial ties and subnational loyalties were still in evidence a century later during the civil disturbances of 1958. Here, as well, the resort to collective violence was initially rooted in legitimate socio-economic and political grievances. The issues underlying the conflict were non-sectarian. So were the composition and motives of the main adversaries. Both insurgents and loyalists were broad and loose coalitions of religiously mixed groups. Yet fighting in urban and rural areas assumed a sectarian character. Indeed leaders, on both sides, incited such sentiments to reawaken communal solidarities and extend the basis of their mobilization. The same patterns of reawakened confessional and sectarian hostilities were, of course, very salient during the protracted interlude of civil strife of 1975–92.

What I am trying to infer is that the recurrent episodes of social unrest during the nineteenth century, in 1958 and the latest so-called 'civil war' and its unresolved latent hostilities all share a common anomalous feature: as violence unfolded, it acquired its own self-generative cycle of enmity and violence. Leaders themselves often helplessly admitted that, once incited, violent episodes were escalating out of control and that there was little they could do to quell the fury of aroused passions. This, too, supports another basic premise of this chapter; namely that the origin of violence is not necessarily located in enduring structural and attitudinal conditions but in the flux of events associated with outbreak of hostility. Here as well one is able to account for another seeming paradox inherent in collective violence: leaders were initially reluctant to entertain belligerency but, once it erupted, they were inclined to romanticize its redemptive and regenerative attributes.

One need only review the political rhetoric and acrimonious attributions of protagonists to realize the depth of dissonance between the outward assertions, of tolerance and peaceful coexistence, and the belligerent realities on the ground. Such disjunctions have become more acute recently. This also accounts, as will be demonstrated later, for why virtually all attempts to establish permanent cease-fires or resolution of conflict were always short-lived.

Drawing on the mundane distinction between 'horizontal' and 'vertical' divisions, one may better understand or at least elucidate the difference between 'civil' and 'uncivil' violence. As long as disputes remain predominantly horizontal in character (that is, grievances over distributive justice, feelings of relative status and material well-being, deprivation, even political succession), the conflict is likely to remain fairly mild and contained. Deprived, neglected, underprivileged groups feel that their socio-economic standing is being undermined. They resort to various forms of collective mobilization (street protest, demonstrations, boycott, public outcries of dissent) to dramatize their dispossession or political marginalization. These, however, remain 'civil' in at least three senses: civilians are the ones generally involved in initiating and mobilizing discontent; the conflict is likely to be less belligerent; and, finally, as long as it remains a genuine socio-economic rivalry it is less predisposed to turn into a proxy and surrogate venue for other sources of conflict.

RETRIBALIZATION: EMBLEM OR ARMOR?

For some time mainstream theoretical paradigms – that is, those associated with modernization, Marxism and their offshoots – were quite tenacious in upholding their views regarding the erosion of primordial ties and loyalties. Despite the striking ideological differences underlying the two meta-theories, they shared the conviction that ties of fealty, religion and community – which cemented societies together and accounted for social and political distinctions – were beginning to lose their grip and would, ultimately, become irrelevant. Indeed, to proponents of modernization theory, notions like familialism, tribalism and confessionalism were not only pejoratively dismissed and trivialized, they were seen as obstacles to modernity. So-called 'traditional' societies, in other words, were expected to break away and disengage themselves from such relics of pre-modern times if they were to enjoy the presumed fruits of modernity or to become fully fledged nation-states. Given the resilience of traditional loyalties, some proponents made allowances for interim periods where 'transitional' societies might linger for a while. Eventually, however, all such precarious hybrids will have to pass. They cannot, and will not, it was argued by a generation of social scientists in the 1960s and 1970s, be able to resist the overpowering forces of industrialization, urbanization and secularization.

Likewise to Marxists, communist and socialist regimes these, allegedly irresistible, transformations were perceived as 'giant brooms' expected to sweep away pre-existing loyalties. If non-class attachments and interests survive or resurface, they are treated as forms of 'false consciousness' to mask or veil fundamental economic and social contradictions. Theodor Hanf (1995) has alerted us that such ethnic and primordial loyalties were often treated as transitory phenomena by modernization theorists and as epiphenomena by Marxists. Both agreed, however, that primordialism was destined to disappear. Both, of course, have been wrong. It is a blatant misreading, if not distortion, of history in both advanced and developing societies. It is a marvel in fact that such misrepresentations could have persisted given persuasive evidence to the contrary.[2]

Ernest Gellner (1987: 6–28) provides such evidence while exploring the nature of nationalism and cohesion in complex societies. He finds it conceptually fitting to re-examine the role of shared amnesia, collective forgetfulness and anonymity in the emergence of nation-states. Among other things, he argues that the presumed erosion of primordial allegiances

---

2 For a representative cross-section of the literature see Almond and Coleman, 1960; Almond and Powell, 1966; Apter, 1965; Eisenstadt, 1966; Lerner, 1958; Pye, 1966; Shils, 1965.

is not a prerequisite to the formation of cohesive nation-states. Likewise, the formation of strong ruthless centralizing regimes is not the monopoly of any particular state or culture. Seemingly cohesive and integrated old states are not as culturally unified and homogeneous

Of course here Ottoman Turkey became the prototype of the 'mosaic' where ethnic and religious groups not only retained much of their so-called primordial and archaic identities, but they were positively instructed – through edicts, centralization, fiat, etc. – never to forget. As such, the Ottomans were tolerant of other religions but they were strictly segregated from the Muslims. The various *millets*, in other words, mixed but never truly combined in a homogeneous and unified society. Today such a dread of collective amnesia is amply visible in the dramatic events surrounding the collapse of the USSR and the unfolding disintegration of Eastern Europe.

Nor are the nascent new nations today bereft of the loyalties and institutions often attributed exclusively to civil and secular nation-states. Perhaps conditions of anonymity are true in time of swift or revolutionary social change and turmoil. But after the upheavals, when the deluge subsides, when social order is restored, internal cleavages and continuities resurface. New memories are invented when the old ones are destroyed. Indeed, 'most societies', Gellner reiterates, 'seem allergic to internal anonymity, homogeneity and amnesia' (1987: 9).

Lebanon's political history, in both good and bad times, reinforces this self-evident but often overlooked or misconstrued reality. Throughout its epochal transformations – the emergence of the 'principality' in the seventeenth and eighteenth centuries, the upheavals of the mid-nineteenth century and the consequent creation of the Mutesarrifate of Mount Lebanon (1860–1920), down to the creation of Greater Lebanon in 1920, the National Pact of 1943, the restoration of unity and stability after the civil war of 1958, and the aftermath of almost two decades of protracted violence – some salient realities about the ubiquity of recurring retribalization are reconfirmed. One might argue that Lebanon has not been detribalized sufficiently to be experiencing *retribalization*. The term, nonetheless, is being employed here rather loosely as a catch-all phrase to refer to the resurgence of communal loyalties, particularly the convergence of confessional and territorial identities. As has been demonstrated by a score of socio-economic and political historians, the sweeping changes Lebanon has been subjected to – from internal insurrections to centralized and direct rule by foreign powers or the more gradual and spontaneous changes associated with rapid urbanization, spread of market economy and the exposure of a growing portion of the population to secular, liberal and radical ideologies, etc – did little to weaken or erode the intensity of confessional or sectarian loyalties. Indeed, in times of social unrest and political turmoil such loyalties became sharper and often superseded other ties and allegiances.[3]

Confessional loyalties have not only survived and retained their primacy, they continue to serve as viable sources of communal solidarity. They inspire local and personal initiative, and account for much of the resourcefulness and cultural diversity and vitality of the Lebanese. But they also undermine civic consciousness and commitment to Lebanon as a nation-state. Expressed more poignantly, the forces which motivate and sustain harmony, balance and prosperity are also the very forces which on occasion pull the society apart and contribute to conflict, tension and civil disorder. The ties that bind, in other words, also unbind (Khalaf and Denoeux, 1988; Khalaf, 1991).

As the cruelties of protracted violence became more menacing, it is understandable why traumatized and threatened groups should seek shelter in their communal solidarities and cloistered spaces. Confessional sentiments and their supportive loyalties, even in times of relative peace and stability, have always been effective sources of social support and political mobilization. But these are not, as Lebanon's fractious history amply demonstrates, unmixed blessings. While they cushion individuals and groups against the anomie and alienation of public life, they also heighten the density of communal hostility and enmity. Such processes have been particularly acute largely because class, ideological and other secular forms of group affiliation have been comparatively more distant and abstract and, consequently, of less relevance to the psychic and social needs of the uprooted and traumatized. Hence, more and more Lebanese are today brandishing their confessionalism, if we may invoke a dual metaphor, as both *emblem* and *armor*. It is an *emblem*, because confessional identity has become the most viable medium for asserting presence and securing vital needs and benefits. It is only when an individual is placed within a confessional context that his ideas and assertions are rendered meaningful or worthwhile. Confessionalism is also used as *armor*, because it has become a shield against real or imagined threats. *The more vulnerable the emblem, the thicker the armor. Conversely, the thicker*

---

3   Substantive and persuasive evidence can be extracted from a score of studies in support of such views. See, among others, Chevallier, 1971; Harik, 1968; Khalaf, 1979; Picard, 1996; Salibi, 1965.

the armor, the more vulnerable and paranoid other communities become. It is precisely this dialectic between threatened communities and the urge to seek shelter in cloistered worlds which has plagued Lebanon for so long.

Massive population shifts, particularly since they are accompanied by the reintegration of displaced groups into more homogeneous, self-contained and exclusive communities, have also reinforced communal solidarity. Consequently, territorial and confessional identities, more so perhaps than at any other time in Lebanon's history, are beginning to converge. It is in this sense that *retribalization* is becoming sharper and more assertive. Some of its subtle, implicit and nuanced earlier manifestations have become much more explicit. Political leaders, spokesmen of various communities, opinion-makers and ordinary citizens are not as reticent in recognizing and incorporating such features in their daily behavior or in bargaining for rights and privileges and validating their identities. Even normally less self-conscious and more open communities such as Greek Orthodox, Catholics and Sunni Muslims, are beginning to experiment with measures for enhancing and reinventing their special heritage and particular identity.

Recently such symptoms of retribalization have become more pronounced. Ironically, during the prewar and pre-Taif periods when confessionalism was recognized, its manifestations and outward expression were often subtle and attenuated. Groups seemed shy, as it were, to be identified by such labels. This was especially so during the decades of the 1950s and 1960s when nationalism and often secular and so-called progressive and ideological venues for group affiliation had special appeal (Melikian and Diab, 1974).

Today, as the sectarian or confessional logic is consecrated by Taif and, to the same extent, by public opinion, the overt expression of communal and sectarian identities has become much more assertive. Political leaders and spokesmen of various communities, of all persuasions, are not at all reticent or shy in invoking such parochial claims. Indeed, dormant and quiescent communal identities are being reawakened, often reinvented, to validate claims for special privileges.

Universities, colleges, research foundations, voluntary associations, special advocacy groups, radio and TV stations are all being established with explicit and well-defined communal identities. So are cultural and popular recreational events and awards to recognize excellence and encourage creative and intellectual output. Even competitive sports, normally the most transcending and neutral human encounter, have been factionalized by sectarian rivalries.

These and other such efforts can no longer be wished away or mystified. They must be recognized for what they are: strategies for the empowerment of threatened groups and their incorporation into the torrent of public life. The coalition of confessional and territorial entities, since it draws upon a potentially much larger base of support, is doubtless a more viable vector for political mobilization than kinship, fealty or sectarian loyalties. Hence, it was not uncommon that protest movements and other forms of collective mobilization of social unrest, sparked by genuine grievances and unresolved public issues, were either aborted or deflected into confessional or communal rivalries.

The dismaying outcome of the 'Cedars Revolution' of 2005 is one vivid and fateful example of such derailing. All the public outcries and massive mobilization sparked by the 'Revolution', doubtlessly one of the most momentous and spontaneous collective demonstrations in Lebanon's recent history, have since dwindled away. Even the brutal serial assassination of a string of the country's political and public leaders – the most grotesque of Lebanon's bloody history – has done little to bring the political factions closer together.

In other words, over close to 200 years – from the aborted outcome of the peasant uprising of 1820 to the 'Cedars Revolution' – primordial and communal loyalties remained resilient. As I write (early September 2011), the two major political factions – March 14 and March 8 – are split further apart in the wake of the release from custody of the four security and military officers arraigned after the assassination of Prime Minister Hariri. The divisive political rhetoric and acrimonious attributions have resurfaced again with sharper bellicosity. Indeed, there is hardly an issue – those of the 'higher order', which involve controversy over the UN Special Lebanese Tribunal (SLT), Hizbollah's arms, electoral laws, constitutional reforms, ties with the Syrian regime, or those of the 'lower order' involving violations of zoning ordinances, illegal construction or how to rehabilitate the country's deficient power resources, even child abuse and family violence – which does not arouse factional rivalry. Such inveterate dissonance between civic and primordial loyalties continues to account for Lebanon's deficient civility. More perhaps that any feature, it tells why communal, sectarian and personal loyalties always prevail over the broader concerns of national and state allegiances.

THE INTERNATIONALIZATION OF COMMUNAL CONFLICT

To assert that Lebanon's entrapment in protracted strife is largely a by-product of the interplay between internal dislocations and external pressures is, in many respects, an affirmation of the obvious. Yet it is an affirmation worth belaboring, given some of its persisting complexities and disruptive consequences. The catalog of the recent horrors of nearly two decades of bloody strife makes it abundantly clear that, unless we consider alternative strategies for neutralizing external sources of instability and pacifying internal conflict, Lebanon's precarious polity will always be made more vulnerable to such pressures.

There is nothing novel about this kind of polemic. Throughout Lebanon's eventful political history, this inside–outside dialectic has clearly not been an auspicious or neutral phenomenon. Western incursions and exposure to the mobilizing impact of advanced technology and liberal thought associated with such contacts have not always been sources of regeneration. Willfully or otherwise, they have also contributed to asymmetry, socio-economic dislocations, political instability and discord between communities. Ironically, this was most visible in the diplomatic role foreign powers played and their efforts to formulate successive settlement schemes, peace accords and political covenants.

In the nineteenth century, during the relatively short span of forty years, Mount Lebanon experienced successive outbreaks of collective strife. Typical of small, highly factionalized societies, many of these episodes often assumed a befuddling medley of factional feuds, peasant insurrections and sectarian rivalries. On at least three occasions – 1820, 1840 and 1857 – peasants and commoners were incited to rebel against some of the repressive abuses of feudal society.

Initially, virtually all the uprisings employed non-confrontational strategies of collective protest. Rallies, gatherings, petitions, mass agitation were very common. In some instances, particularly in 1858 when peasants felt strong enough to resist impositions of their feudal lords, they ceased payments of rent they owed their Khazin sheikhs. When this failed, rebels had no aversion to experimenting with other more contentious strategies.

Indeed, in all three uprisings, conflict spiraled into violent scuffles, armed hostilities and frontal clashes between masses of armed peasants and state-sponsored armies. In some instances, particularly in 1840, peasants employed the conventional logistics of guerrilla warfare, such as ambushing and attacking Egyptian convoys transporting ammunition and supplies (Smilianskaya, 1972: 81; al-Shidiaq, 1954: 2. 226). On the whole, however, the instruments of violence involved little more than the ordinary rifles and hatchets common at the time in factional combat and local rivalries. It was when regional and European powers were drawn into the conflict that violence, in most instances, escalated into actual warfare with regular armies, reinforced by the technologies of mass destruction, for example massive troop movements, naval blockades, bombardment, heavy artillery and the like. It was also then that the damage to life and property became more devastating.

It should also be noted that insurgents, peasants, rebels rarely acted alone. In all episodes of peasant uprisings, for example, organizational and ideological leadership was assumed by Maronite clerics. It was they who first articulated the peasants' revolutionary attitude toward the feudal system. They organized them into village communes and appointed *wakils* as spokesmen for the *'ammiyyah*.

In addition to ecclesiastical intervention, the peasants almost always received either the direct or moral support of Ottoman authorities and foreign consuls who manipulated the uprisings for purposes unrelated to the grievances or interests of the *'ammiyyah* as a genuine protest movement. The Ottomans were always eager to undermine the privileged status of Mount Lebanon and the local authority of feudal chiefs. Indeed, pitting one group against another, through alternating strategies of ingratiation and manipulation, became a popular shorthand for Ottoman barbarity and repression.

Foreign powers, eager to gain inroads into the Middle East and win protégés, also resorted to the same divisive strategies. This was poignantly apparent in 1840. While European powers – France, Britain, Russia, Austria and Prussia – were acting in concert to rescue Syria from its Egyptian occupiers, each had their own diplomatic agenda. Sometimes, discord within a country (e.g. the conflict in France between Prime Minister Thiers and King Louis-Philippe) left its reverberations on the course and outcome of the rebellion. Consequently, a genuine local uprising was, literally, appropriated and deflected into a global crisis. Indignant peasants, already violated by the adverse effects of European economic transformations, were victimized further. Kisrwan, in the process, was assailed into a proxy killing field for other people's wars.

In all earlier episodes of collective strife, though foreign powers and regional brokers had a role in inciting and escalating hostilities, they also stepped in to contain the conflict when it began to undermine their strategic interests. Both, for example, in 1860 and 1958, conflict ended largely because the interests of the super-powers were better served by stabilizing Lebanon. It took thirty-two weeks and about fifty meetings of intensive diplomatic negotiations between the concerned foreign actors at the time (i.e. France, Great Britain, Austria, Russia, Prussia and Turkey) to arrive at the Réglement Organique which reconstituted Lebanon as an Ottoman province under the guarantee of the six signatory powers. Through French initiative, the international commission was set up to fix responsibility, determine guilt, estimate indemnity and suggest reforms for the reorganization of Mount Lebanon.

Likewise, in 1958 the strategic stature and significance of Lebanon was at its height. The region was seething with political ferment and ideological disputes. The Cold War had transformed the region into a proxy battlefield for super-power rivalry. The Baghdad Pact of 1955, the Suez Crisis of 1956, unrest in Jordan in 1957, the formation of the United Arab Republic (the abortive union between Egypt and Syria), the military coup in Iraq in 1958, all had unsettling implications. Since Lebanon at the time was identified with the Western camp, by virtue of its support of the Eisenhower Doctrine, the events had, naturally, direct bearings on the political standing of Lebanon. Indeed, the peace accord which ended the war was brokered by the US and Egypt.

It should be noted, however, that before the Iraqi coup Eisenhower was reluctant to intervene directly despite the repeated requests made at the time by President Chamoun and foreign minister Charles Malik. Even when the US finally decided to commit its marines, as Secretary of State Foster Dulles put it, 'Lebanon was not very important in itself' (for this and other details, see Gerges, 1997: 88–9). Hence, the intervention should not be taken as evidence of Western commitment to the security of Lebanon as such. Rather, Lebanon served as a proxy for other broader regional interests. The ultimate concern of the Eisenhower administration at the time was, of course, to curtail the spread of communism and radical Arab nationalism which were perceived as threats to America's vital interests in the region, mainly oil supplies.

The deployment of American troops was intended to demonstrate America's military clout and its determination to protect its regional and global interests. The US was also beginning to realize that with Nasser's charisma and growing influence in the region, Egypt was fast becoming the epicenter of Arab politics. This must account for its inclination to abandon Chamoun and work jointly with Cairo to arrive at a resolution of the crisis in Lebanon. This, as in earlier and subsequent crises, served to reconfirm what was to become a recurrent modality in the resolution of conflict in Lebanon: the state is so enfeebled and divided that foreign and regional brokers take on this responsibility. Lebanon's impotence, or at least the failure of the state to protect itself against regional destabilizing forces, was of course translated into the ironical political doctrine, namely that the 'country's strength lies in its weakness'. In effect this meant that the state was to surrender or relinquish its national security responsibility to other regional and global actors.

Lebanon in the early and mid-1970s was not even in that mildly privileged diplomatic or bargaining position. The détente between Russia and the US defused much of the Cold War tension. Egypt under Sadat shifted towards the US. American inroads into the Arab Gulf and Iran became more substantive. Hence the major powers, in the wake of the first round of the war of 1975–6, had no immediate or vital interests at stake to encourage them to interfere in the conflict. France was in no position to mobilize international initiative on behalf of Lebanon as it did in 1860. Unlike 1958, the US also found little justification (at least initially) to dispatch their marines or to engage in sustained diplomatic effort in settling the conflict.

Little wonder that when the war broke out in 1975, neither Washington nor Moscow felt the need to be involved in any direct diplomatic engagement as long as the conflict did not affect their vital interests. Henry Kissinger's disengagement diplomacy toward Lebanon, as Fawaz Gerges has persuasively argued, was 'informed not only by his perception of the inherent precariousness of the country but also by the strategic need for a safety valve where Arab–Israeli tensions could be released without the threat of a major Arab–Israeli confrontation' (Gerges, 1997: 78). Theodor Hanf (1993) was even more explicit in arguing how, by abandoning the search for a comprehensive peace settlement in the Middle East, Kissinger's step-by-step diplomacy had actually increased the risk of proxy war in Lebanon. Indeed, Lebanon's suffering seemed of little or no concern as long as the internal hemorrhaging did not spill over to contaminate or destabilize other vital spots in the region.

The 'quick-fix' diplomacy the Reagan administration resorted to was ill-perceived, ill-timed and mismanaged. There was, of course, more than just a civil war raging in Lebanon at the time. The country was already a proxy battlefield for other people's wars and a succession of unresolved regional/global rivalries. Reagan's rash adventure (or misadventure) undermined completely the balance of power equation between the regional and super-powers and placed the US in an illusory superior standing.

Agnes Korbani (1991), in her evaluative study of the two American interventions in Lebanon (i.e. 1958 and 1982), concludes that, while Eisenhower's 'move was effective, it brought peace without the use of force. As a result, the marines withdrew peacefully and proudly and were welcomed back home as heroes. Reagan's move however was defective. It left Lebanon in shambles. And the victim marines were carried away to their last rest' (Korbani, 1991: 124). More devastating, Lebanon's victimization from then on was compounded.

It must also be kept in mind that in both 1860 and 1958 the fighting was summarily ended with a political settlement, backed by major powers and reinforced by internal public opinion. The settlements also brought auspicious times. During the second half of the nineteenth century, Mount Lebanon was wallowing in an enviable 'silver lining' (Hitti, 1957) and enjoyed a blissful interlude of 'long peace' (Arkali, 1993). In the wake of the 1958 crisis the country was also privileged to enjoy another felicitous interlude of political stability, state-building and cultural enlightenment.

Although Lebanon was released from the specter of global rivalry, it was caught instead in the more foreboding web of regional conflict. As long as the Arab–Israeli conflict was unresolved, Lebanon was once again an expedient and surrogate killing field. Indeed, all the fierce battles which inaugurated the prolonged hostilities in 1975 (PLO–Lebanese war, the PLO–Syrian war and the PLO–Israeli war) had little to do with internal dislocations and political tensions.

More perhaps than other political observers, Ghassan Tueni has been propounding this persuasive thesis (i.e. Lebanon as a proxy killing field for other people's wars) with relentless tenacity, first as head of Lebanon's UN delegation and subsequently in many of his trenchant weekly columns in *an-Nahar* (Tueni, 1985). Charles Issawi, another astute observer of Lebanon's unsettled history, was equally poignant in contemplating Lebanon's victimization in the wake of 1958 crisis. He had this to say about the moral indifference of the regional and international community:

> Lebanon is too conspicuous and successful an example of political democracy and economic liberalism to be tolerated in a region that has turned its back on both systems ... It may be answered that such fears are unfounded, that the conscience of the world would not allow any harm to befall such a harmless country as Lebanon, that the neighboring world

would not want to have a recalcitrant minority on their hands, and that it is their interests to preserve Lebanon as 'a window on the West.' But to anyone who has followed the
course of national and international politics in the last fifty years, such arguments are sheer
nonsense. Minorities have been very effectively liquidated, windows have been violently
slammed and hardly a ripple has stirred in the conscience of the world. (Issawi, 1966: 80–1)

CONSUMATORY AND INSTRUMENTAL VIOLENCE

Another pertinent conceptual element can be inferred from the changing
forms and consequences of the three major interludes of collective strife;
namely the peasant uprisings and communal conflict in the nineteenth
century, the civil war of 1958 and the prolonged strife of 1975–92 and its
unresolved disruptive repercussions. All three interludes provide vivid evidence in support of two broad perspectives on the dynamics of civil strife
elucidated by James Rule (1988). On the one hand, one encounters much to
substantiate the 'consumatory' or expressive character of collective strife, the
kind which is incited and sustained by group solidarity, the sharing of revolutionary excitement engendered by the insurrections. Here, the flux of events
themselves, the unfolding episodes associated with the outbreak of hostilities, served to draw insurgents together. Mass rallies, animated gatherings,
collective agitation, the resourcefulness of *wakils,* the camaraderie of *shuyukh
al-shabab* (youth leaders) and the exhilaration of combat all contributed to
this. It is also here that one sees manifestations of emotional contagion, the
frenzy of aroused peasants incited by anger, rage, vengeance, and hence their
predisposition to vent their wrath through unrestrained looting and plunder.
In short, the appeals to express solidarity with one's group, assail one's enemy
and destroy hated symbols provided the catalyst for collective violence.

On the other hand, one also sees perhaps more evidence of the 'instrumental' character of collective strife, the type which bears closer affinity to
the rational calculation of costs and benefits inherent in protest movements.
Here rebels were not only driven by an impulse to correct injustices and
seek some reprieve from feudal abuse but also by a desire to secure material
benefits and basic necessities. For example, acts of looting and confiscating
Khazin property and crops were more part of organized operations designed
to place expropriated property at the disposal of the rebellion. Hence, they
were not symptoms of unrestrained acts of marauding and pillaging or a
compulsion to wreak vengeance for its own sake. Indeed, particularly in 1858,
the expulsion of the Khazins lasted long enough to be accompanied by their

de facto expropriation and, hence, a substantial redistribution of property in favor of commoners (Baer, 1982: 300–1).

In 1958 these expressive and consumatory elements became more visible. As an 'uprising', 'sedition', 'insurrection', 'revolt', or 'civil war' – to mention a few of its many labels – it must not be judged by the structural transformations it unleashed. By standards of the day, the ensuing violence and destruction were massive. It took a toll of some 3,000 lives, had dire economic consequences, deepened communal enmity and rendered Lebanon more vulnerable to regional and international rivalries. Yet the insurrection did not result in any fundamental restructuring of society or its political system. Indeed, since the call for armed struggle was largely made by a disgruntled political elite, demanding little more than the resignation of President Chamoun, the 'revolt' ended by the restoration of the status quo.

If measured against the protracted cruelties of 1975–92, it pales by comparison. It seems more of a benign and sporadic excursion into violent politics. Yet it produced an immense jolt throughout the country. It drew together, albeit on a limited scale, diverse elements that had not before been commonly engaged in collective protest. In that sense it offered political tutelage and initiated a wide spectrum of individuals and political parties into the fray of political mobilization and violent politics. Leaders of the insurrection had little in common, other than their hostility to the regime and its pro-Western policies and, to a lesser extent, a transient ideological infatuation they shared with Nasserism. They were drawn from different regions, articulated varying justifications for their participation in an armed struggle and displayed distinct political styles. It is rather odd that a coalition of tribal feudal chiefs, landlords, urban gentry, clerics, revolutionary pamphleteers, intellectual dilettantes, militant commoners, etc should find common cause in rebellion. They did. They also drew around them a coterie of young political upstarts and activists: mostly intellectuals, journalists, artists, professors sparked by the novelty and idealism of collective struggle and the prospects of launching a career in public life. In addition to the organized commands, councils and other revolutionary committees that leaders in the various war zones established, they also relied on an informal network – a medley of close relatives, friends and hangers-on – of personal assistants and advisers. These often served as self-appointed think-tanks; they gave interviews, issued press releases, drafted speeches, suggested strategies.

Mass support was also a broad and loose coalition of peasants, blue-collar workers, lower-middle-class elements, progressive students and other marginal recruits and volunteers. Armed men received nominal wages, family allowances and a daily ration of cigarettes, beverages and snacks in return for their services. Palestinian refugees, already in Lebanon for nearly a decade, many of whom had strong pro-Nasserist sympathies, took active part in the fighting. At the time, Palestinians in diaspora were not as yet politically organized. Their involvement, nonetheless, sent a warning signal and provoked the fear of the Christian community.

To many of the participants at all three levels (that of leadership, hard-core supporters and the mass of rank and file activists and fighters) the events of 1958 served as a venue for their initiation into militancy, the clamor of street fighting and communal strife. Since many of the actors were still around in 1975, their experience came in handy. Indeed, an activist like Ibrahim Qulailat, an impressionable adolescent of eighteen at the time, had hardly completed his high school education in 1958. Like other lower-middle-class Sunni Muslims from West Beirut, he was a Nasser enthusiast, maintained close ties with Fatah and radical and populist elements of the 'street' and was involved in successive acts of violence. Shortly after 1958, he established *al-Murabitun* as an independent Nasserist movement which was to play a prominent role in the civil war of 1975.

Altogether, the nature and consequences of the events of 1958 reinforce certain attributes which have become embedded in Lebanon's rather unusual legacy with civil strife. One sees relics of the earlier forms of communal and factional hostility, those aroused and sustained by deep-seated animosities, atavistic fears of local groups coexisting in close and dense socio-political settings. But one also sees features which prefigure much of what was to come; namely, the violence of deprived and dislocated groups, Lebanese or otherwise, inspired by nationalist and secular ideologies, transcending endemic sources of conflict and with nebulous allegiances to Lebanon or concern for its sovereignty. Obviously the involvement of groups like the PPS, Ba'ath, Palestinians, Communists, the coalitions they formed, and the character of their militancy were bound to be different from those of the more endogenous factions. Much of the violence in this latter instance became more proxy in character and more devastating in its cruelties. It was also then that Lebanon became, because of its political vulnerabilities, a battlefield, so to speak, for the wars of others.

Given these anomalous features, the civil war of 1958 seemed more of a 'structural' and 'negotiated' phenomenon rather than one primarily driven by an irresistible urge to inflict reckless injury and damage on others. There was, clearly, a discrepancy between the outward, often dramatic and stirring rhetoric of war and the rather cautious and non-deadly form of combat actually assumed on the ground. The war, in short, was much too voluble in words but short on casualties.

Indeed, the unfolding pattern of violence seemed surreal at times; more of an incredulous spectacle, and 'opera bouffe' than a real insurrection: an army that would not fight; opposition leaders officially declared as 'rebels' with warrants for their arrest, yet free enough to circulate, hold press conferences and appear on public television; pitched battles would suddenly stop to permit army trucks to supply rebel forces with amenities and rescue casualties (Qubain, 1961: 71; Hottinger, 1961: 132). Emile Bustani, who kept contacts with both factions and bore close witness to the actual course of fighting, observed that the 'uprising was both launched and contained with a certain old-fashioned courtesy more in keeping with a private duel between members of the nobility than a political revolt' (Bustani, 1961: 86).

Accounts of fighting are replete with episodes displaying similar disarming courtesy and concern for the niceties of conduct. Fighters, for example, were known to apply for curfew passes before they staged their raids. Others took out licenses for carrying arms. Fighting in Beirut usually took place in the afternoon and at night, often over weekends, as if not to disrupt too drastically the orderly regularities of daily routines. Truces were mutually arranged to relieve the pressure of combat. After a particularly fierce bout of fighting in the Chouf, a cease-fire permitted Christian villagers to be provisioned from Beirut. In return, wounded Druze were brought to Beirut for medical treatment (Hottinger, 1961: 32). Deliberate efforts were made, by both sides, to avoid random and unnecessary victims. Explosives were placed at times when it was reasonably certain that premises would be vacant. Desmond Stewart, who claimed acquaintance with a bomb-thrower named Adnan, noted that he 'has undoubtedly taken scrupulous care only to make noises, symbols. When he bombed Dory Chamoun's shop, he made sure there was no one in the house upstairs at the time' (Stewart, 1959: 61).

The role of the army is perhaps most intriguing in this regard. It maintained its neutrality, refusing, despite its superiority, to crush the insurrection. It acted as an arbiter between the embattled factions. Often it went further to shelter one group from onslaught of the other. For example, it repelled advances of the rebels upon regions inhabited by partisans of the government. It also gave protection to the rebels by prohibiting the PPS from starting fighting in Beirut. During the marines' landing, it acted as a buffer between American troops and the insurgents (Hottinger, 1961: 134).

These and other symptoms of the domestication and routinization of violence became much more pervasive in 1975–92. It is, nonetheless, instructive to encounter such manifestations in 1958, whereby some of the grotesque features of the war were already becoming a form of discourse or political language stripped of any belligerent undertones. This was also happening in a political culture where light arms are accessible and widely used on festive occasions.

In retrospect, the brush with civil unrest in 1958 was instructive precisely because it marked the threshold at which the character of political contests dramatically changed from a subject of 'leisurely mental and oral strife into an issue of life and death'. Or, in the language of Theodor Hanf invoked earlier, it is then that the conflict degenerates from a struggle over 'divisible goods' to a struggle over 'indivisible principles'. The moment, in other words, socio-economic rivalry is transmuted into confessional or communal enmity, with all its attendant fears of marginalization, erasure, threats to identity and collective consciousness, that hostility descends into the incivility of atavistic violence.

Episodic feuds, personal slurs, grievances and minor provocations normally dismissed as tolerable manifestations of a fractious political culture were transformed into sources of bitter hostility and polarization. Any move by either side became suspect and was always imputed with the worse possible interpretation. Parliamentary debates, electoral campaigns, political pronouncements became forums for exchanging insults and invective. Being barred from entering parliament was, suddenly, a legitimate justification for armed insurrection. Attribution and demonization of the 'other' evolved into common strategies for rationalizing belligerency. Insurgents became 'outlaws', 'infiltrators', 'terrorists' and 'unanchored masses', wreaking havoc in society and undermining its sovereignty and autonomy. Loyalists became a malicious 'clique', a den of 'criminals', 'traitors', 'western stooges' and 'infidels'. Every atrocious misdeed from political corruption, bigotry to prostitution, drugs and thievery was attributed to Chamoun and his maligned 'gang' (Jumblat, 1959: 32).

Enmity, in such a charged political milieu, can become highly combustible. It is then that politics becomes, to borrow Henry Adam's axiom, 'the systematic organization of hatred' (Wills, 1990: 3). When provoked, it could easily spark off hostility and heighten the predisposition for belligerency. This is, in fact, what was transpiring at the time. Grievances, demonstrations and other forms of collective protest were being transformed into riots, clashes and violent confrontations. Charting the networks of such enmity, that is, who hates whom, where and why, provides, at times, a better understanding of the shifting character of political alliances than ideological disputes and public issues.

Such episodes of expressive and consumatory manifestations of violence were legion throughout the protracted civil war of 1975–92. They account for much what seemed bizarre, often grotesque and unpredictable (for further substantiation, see Khalaf, 2002). A few more recent instances are worth noting, particularly in the wake of the unsettling events surrounding Rafik Hariri's assassination in February 2005.

By coincidence, two momentous events coincided in Lebanon on 14 February 2008. While the parliamentary majority was commemorating the third anniversary of former Prime Minister Rafik Hariri's assassination, Hizbullah laid to rest Imad Mughniyeh, the party's chief of operations assassinated in Damascus a day before. Because the media covered the events simultaneously, viewers could witness their unfolding on the same screen. At no moment in Lebanon's history had rival political factions ever seemed so dissonant.

The March 14 commemoration was an exultant spectacle. Throngs of people braved foul weather to converge on Martyrs' Square in numbers far exceeding expectations. They filled open spaces and blocked all major arteries leading to the once-vibrant city center. The gathering was a spontaneous blend of broad constituencies drawn from all of Lebanon's communities, representing a wide cross-section of socio-economic sectors. Women in headscarves and turbaned religious figures mixed amiably with more stylish compatriots. The rippling flags, banners, placards, umbrellas and protective caps transformed the rally into an animated work of art, one akin to a Jackson Pollock canvas. Incidentally, since then the 'March 14 Alliance' has evolved into a Sunni-Druze-Christian coalition that takes its name from the date of the Cedar Revolution in 2005, when Lebanese took to the streets in mass protest to demand the end of Syria's 29 year occupation. The overwhelming mass protest in the Center of Beirut, was triggered by the assassination of Prime Minister Rafik Hariri on February 14, 2005. The Alliance has succeeded in mobilizing the popular Cedar Revolution into a political movement.

Just a few kilometers away, in Beirut's southern suburbs, the funeral ceremony for Mughniyeh was the antithesis of the March 14 gathering. It had all the appearance of being based on a prearranged set of totalitarian precepts. The women, in black chadors, huddled together, looking like a motionless polka-dotted tapestry. The bearded men, wearing party headgear, occupied an adjoining space. Hizbullah secretary general Sayyed Hassan Nasrallah's vituperative speech was met by an orchestrated, rhythmic response, as the men present punched the air with their fists. Nasrallah highlighted his eulogy by saying that Hizbullah had declared 'open war' against Israel, a state destined to be wiped off the map.

Underlying those differences was an ideological rift. To March 14, the paramount aim is retributive justice for Hariri's killing and countless others since. Only when justice is fulfilled, the majority believes, will Lebanon regain its independence. The opposition, in turn, boasts of its occupation of central Beirut. Rather than remembering the number of days since Hariri's assassination, they list the number of days since opposition parties began the wasteful sit-in in the downtown area. Bizarre as these two dissonant approaches are, their interplay has come to mold the destiny of Lebanon's traumatized society.

Despite the striking differences between March 8 and March 14, they share an aberrant feature which largely accounts for Lebanon's political deadlock. For over three years, the two sides have been trapped in an escalating war of mutual rhetorical vilification, depicting the 'other' as a repository of all the pathologies that more often characterize enemies. Since this sense of enmity is directed internally, it involves effectively dehumanizing a brother to better justify the rancor against him.

The current political impasse has a puzzling edge to it. As the two recalcitrant groups disavow any resort to violence, they adamantly maintain their belligerent rhetoric. One group is seething with anger and bitterness; the other with fear and resilience. All efforts at reconciliation have thus far been in vain.

Just as fractious political leaders have violated all the basic ingredients of participatory democracy, they have also made a mockery of the civic virtues of public protest. In democracies, controversy, disputes and tolerable conflict are healthy signs. The public interest is well served by spirited public debate. But when disagreements are distorted by extremist rhetoric, the public debate degenerates into futile meta-politics, or worse mere exchanges of invective; democratic discourse becomes a spectator sport, a destructive pastime.

The primary victim of all this is the democratic citizen. He or she is denigrated, deceived and demeaned. Witness the waste of resources as the media, day and night, insult our intelligence and debase our aesthetic sensibilities by hosting talk shows that remind us of cockfights in a tribal culture. The level of demonization has never been so vulgar or abusive.

While one might point the finger at the unwavering strategies of March 14, it is the escalating demands of March 8 and the Aounists that have crippled all possible venues for consensus. The opposition failed at the time to realize any of its objectives: the resignation of the Siniora government, electing a president with Syrian approval, compelling the army's leadership to abandon the government, persuading the Arab League and foreign powers to make a deal with Syria and, perhaps most important, derailing formation of the Hariri tribunal.

Yet despite its failure, perhaps because of it, the opposition escalated its rhetoric, its single-minded, dogmatic inclinations, and its righteous insistence on the supremacy of its views while denigrating all others. In their public appearances, opposition groups have embodied two of Nietzsche's concepts: *schadenfreude*, taking pleasure in the suffering of others, and *ressentiment*, blaming others for one's own frustrations.

To the opposition, obstruction has become a cherished agenda. Hizbullah unilaterally provoked the summer 2006 war which had ruinous consequences for Lebanon's economy and infrastructure, not to mention the far more painful toll in lives and personal property. The destruction was even more acute because the war erupted at a time when the country was displaying signs of recovery and solidarity. Oddly, Hizbullah continues to celebrate that war as a 'divine victory'.

By far the most spiteful expression of *schadenfreude* was the occupation of Beirut's old city center. Just as the downtown area was emerging as an open, cosmopolitan public sphere, perhaps because of its notoriety in hosting the Cedar Revolution of 2005, it became a target of desecration. Its ruin was accomplished with indifference, as though the epicenter of the capital was enemy territory. This malice could well have been a reflection of unresolved sectarian tensions. Otherwise, it would not have been characterized by vengeful disregard for the well-being of others. Indeed, the opposition dismissed the damage it wreaked on the area as no more than curtailing the business prospects of a parking lot belonging to the Hariri family.

We are at a fateful crossroads in Lebanon's political history. When conflict sparked by communal and sectarian rivalries is transformed from a dispute over *divisible problems* (electing a consensus president, power-sharing, the prerogative of the cabinet, a new electoral law and the like) to one over *indivisible issues* (such as the future, defining character, and existence of Lebanon as a plural, open and independent state), then the character of the conflict is bound to become more belligerent.

It should be remembered that social strata become embittered by loss of status, material advantage and privilege. Lebanon's communal formations feel threatened by the loss of freedom, identity, heritage, even their own national existence. This is precisely what has been at stake in the country. And this is why March 8 and March 14 seem so inflexible. Once again, the political future of the country is shrouded in uncertainty. The usual interplay between internal divisions and external rivalries is exasperating the crisis. In the absence of an unforeseen cataclysmic event, the country is destined to remain adrift.

The latest protracted government crisis is, once again, nothing but a tired replay of this same inside–outside dialectic which has beleaguered Lebanon for so long. Five months after the national elections of May 2009, Saad Hariri finally succeeded in forming the so-called 'national unity' government. Internally, the basic issue is Hizbullah's arms and its militant posturing and, hence, how to integrate the Shi'ite community (presumably the most populous community in the country) into the state's political institutions. Externally, the crisis is also a reflection of the persisting struggle between the so-called 'axis of evil' in the Middle East spearheaded by Iran, and the 'moderate' camp led by Saudi Arabia and Egypt. The elections in Lebanon were thus perceived as a test case, in which Iran's ability to advance its ambitious aspirations, through the surrogate mediation of the Syrian regime, in the Arab world is put to the test.

Within such a contested and precarious setting, the new cabinet, much like its precursors, is destined to be based upon a balance of fear; particularly between Hizbullah and Prime Minister Hariri and the Sunni community he heads. This is bound to imply that the vulnerability of the Lebanese–Israeli border will remain precarious and volatile.

DISPLACED HOSTILITY AND SURROGATE VICTIMIZATION

The destabilizing consequences of the interplay between internal divisions and external dislocations, as we have seen, is not of recent vintage. Virtually all episodes of collective strife, even petty factional feuds and sectarian rivalries, were all predisposed to being manipulated by the quicksands of shifting regional and global interests. To this day, observers continue to differ in their assessment as to where the faultlines lie. There are those who exaggerate the fractious innate character of the country's internal divisions, deficient civic consciousness and national loyalties. Others are more inclined to view it as a victim of external sources of instability. Naturally both views are too generic and misleading. They do not capture or elucidate the rich diversity and complexities of the country's encounters with collective unrest. Nor do they do justice to some of the peculiar pathologies and circumstances associated with Lebanon's entrapment in a ravaging spiral of protracted and unappeased hostility.

These two features – *displaced* and *protracted* hostility – remain the most defining elements in the country's encounters with collective strife. They also feed on each other and compound the pathological consequences of each. This is understandable when grievances or feelings of anger are not allayed or pacified. Agitated groups are prone to release their unappeased hostility, as Girard (1977) reminds us, on any accessible and vulnerable target. Episodes of protracted strife in Lebanon, as I have demonstrated elsewhere, are replete with such instances of displaced enmity (Khalaf, 2002).

The character of communal strife and peasant uprising, in the early and middle decades of the nineteenth century, displayed many of these symptoms. Aroused peasants, aggrieved by the oppressive exactions of distant pashas or *amirs*, turned against the relatively weaker and more accessible feudal lords. Likewise, an *amir* or *hakim*, unable to resist the demands of an Ottoman sultan or *wali*, would vent his outrage on his defenseless feudal lords, often by playing one faction against another. Feuding cousins, sometimes brothers, vying to win the patronage of a *wali*, end up in a fractious and bloody tribal rivalry. More decisive, in all these and related instances, the original character of the conflict was transformed in the process. A genuine social protest was deflected into confessional rivalry; a sedition of oppressed peasants was muted and derailed into factional belligerency.

Foreign intervention in the 1958 crisis, by regional and global powers, also generated its odd coalitions and proxy and divisive turf wars. Here again an internal crisis over political succession and the intractable issues of socio-economic disparities, grievances of neglected groups and regions and Lebanon's contested national identity and foreign policy orientation, degenerated into sectarian and communal strife. It was then that the largely non-belligerent forms of collective protest started to slip into vengeful cycles of reprisals with atavistic and free-floating violence. It was also then that innocent citizens became proxy victims of unprovoked hostility. They just happened to be there, 'vulnerable and close at hand' (Girard, 1977). With the absence of public order, unanchored masses were released from the conventional restraints. Acts of hooliganism, banditry, pillage, looting and disdain for law and order became rampant.

The grievous consequences of displaced hostility were naturally far more barbarous during the protracted strife of the past two decades. Indeed, when one re-examines some of the most ominous episodes, particularly those which were fateful in redirecting the pattern of collective violence and escalating its intensity, they were all by-products of such surrogate victimization. For example, when Syrian forces were alternating their targets of hostility – by shelling Christian militias' strongholds or, conversely, when warding off the logistical gains of Palestinian fighters – they would rather have been attacking their more ostensible enemies, namely, Israeli or Iraqi forces. Yet neither of these regional super-powers were defenseless or at hand. Displaying their military power over lesser and more compliant groups also allowed them to extend or reinforce their patronage over alternate client groups. This accounted for much of the protraction of hostility and miscarried cruelties.

Transforming South Lebanon into a relentless battlefield is a glaring instance of such proxy violence. It has had little to do with the internal disparities or contradictions within Lebanon. The war began when the ousted Palestinians from Jordan relocated their bases and resumed their guerrilla operations from South Lebanon. From then on the South became an embattled war zone with grievous repercussions in escalating the levels of hostility elsewhere in the country. The war in the South, by unleasing throngs of uprooted Shi'ites, ultimately congested and radicalized the destitute suburbs encircling Beirut and in other urban fringes. From such slums of squalor and dereliction Hizbullah emerged during the Israeli invasion of 1982. Ironically, when Israel expelled the PLO from Beirut it had in effect created a more ferocious and recalcitrant enemy. Hizbullah, like the PLO before it, is now embroiled in the same interlocking web of regional and global rivalries. Hence much of its activities are profoundly shaped by its two principal backers, namely Iran and Syria. Iran is, after all, the fount of Hizbullah's brand of Shi'ite fundamentalism and a source of an estimated $2 billion in support since the early 1980s. Syria remains the sole vector through which the arms supplied by Iran continue to flow.

The slightest shift in the balance of such exogenous forces, or the conduct of the intermittent Arab–Israeli peace talks, is bound to reactivate the cycle of belligerency. It is not only the defenseless and innocent villagers in the South who have to suffer the outcome of such assaults. Israeli reprisals for Hizbullah's Katyusha rocket attacks on their settlements are rarely directed against those ultimately responsible for them, namely Syria, Iran or the military bases of the Shi'ite resistance forces. The reprisals are massive and disproportionate when compared to the limited damage generated by Hizbullah's rocket lobs or forays into the nine-mile 'security zone' Israel has occupied in South Lebanon since 1985. Such attacks always devastate civilian installations, power plants, villages, towns and families very far removed from Shi'ite guerrilla bases. In the latest bouts of Israeli belligerency (June 1999 and early February 2000) three power stations were destroyed, thereby leaving 80 percent of the country in utter darkness.

In fact, it does not really matter who provokes Israel's wrath. Nor does it need to fabricate alibis to justify its reprisals. Over the years its government has not been able to refrain from taking out its wrath and pent-up hostility on Lebanon. In a recent editorial, aptly titled 'when in doubt, just bomb Lebanon', Charles Glass expressed no surprise, in this context, if Israeli war planes were to be dispatched over Lebanon because 'the Orthodox vigilantes in Jerusalem's Mea Shearim throw rocks at people driving on the Sabbath'. Such an affront may be farfetched. Still, thirty years of relentless war in South Lebanon is one of the saddest tales of modern times, precisely because it is the one prime proxy war that does not seem to go away. The recent round of bellicosity attests to this. If anything, Hizbullah's stepped-up military offensives against Israel were most certainly encouraged by Syria by way of wresting concessions that Israel has refused to agree upon in the suspended talks.

Much of the internecine in-fighting, because it often involved spilling the blood of one's own kinsman, has been clearly more perfidious. Unlike the analog in biblical mythology, Cain and his many facsimiles were not banished by avenging God for killing Abel. Rather than wondering fearfully, they were instead trapped in a relentless carnage of renewed blood baths. In such heightened emotional contagion, belligerent groups find themselves avenging almost anyone. *Instead of killing those they wanted to kill, they end up victimizing those they could.*

Instances of such proxy victimization are legion. A notorious few are worth highlighting. For example, on the infamous day Kata'ib Party leader Pierre Gemayel made a reconciliatory visit to Damascus (6 December 1976), the bodies of four slain Kata'ib activists were found on a hillside east of Beirut. Without waiting even for Gemayel's return from Damascus, Kata'ib militiamen went on a rampage and rounded up and summarily killed more than seventy Muslims picked at random on the basis of their ID notification of their religious affiliation. This 'Black Saturday' became a grim threshold for ushering in other such mindless vendettas.

When in the fall of 1976 the Kata'ib and other Christian militias launched their 'cleaning' up operations culminating in the siege and 'liberation' of Tel al-Zaatar and other suburbs (such as Dbayyeh, Maslakh, Qarantina, Jisr al-Basha, Nabaa and other mixed neighborhoods in areas under their control) the LNM and their Palestinian allies retaliated by besieging the Maronite town of Damour on the coast south of Beirut. More than 500 people, it is assumed, lost their lives in Damour, almost identical to the numbers of those victimized in Qarantina.

When Kamal Jumblat was assassinated, along with two of his close associates, on 16 March 1977, on his way home in Mukhtara, his outraged Druze kinsmen sought revenge among their most likely surrogate enemies. Though the assassination was attributed to Syrian agents, his frenzied followers went on the rampage and slaughtered more than 170 Christians in adjacent villages. In a vengeful act of impassioned *quid pro quo*, the proverbial Christian–Druze coexistence in the Shuf was dealt a grievous and irretrievable blow.

Avenging the death of Bashir Gemayel was much more gruesome in substance and implications. When the youthful president-elect was killed in the massive explosions which ripped through the Phalangist headquarters in East Beirut (14 September 1982), it did not take long for his bereaved followers to retaliate. The incident released a flush of contemptuous outrage. As in other such episodes, the fury was not, of course, directed against those who might have had a hand in the tragedy. Instead, it was discharged on the most vulnerable and accessible proxy targets: Palestinian refugees in Sabra and Shatila camps. Given the outrage and the protection the perpetrators of the massacre had received, the victimization was bound to be gruesome. It turned out to be more barbarous than all expectations. Though the area was monitored at the time by the Israeli Defence Forces (IDF), Gemayel's own militia, reinforced by members of Major Haddad's South Lebanese Army (SLA), managed to get through and indulged in two days of utter bestiality. Indeed, they were deliberately let in by the Israelis. Close to 2,000, mostly children, women and elderly, were butchered. The IDF clearly did nothing to stop or contain the pogrom.

Even state-sponsored invasions have not been averse to such tit-for-tat strategies. When no legitimate grounds for retaliatory measures were available, alibis or 'provocations' were willfully fabricated. The Israeli invasion of

1982 was one fully documented instance of such strategies. Begin, as Israeli Prime Minister, had promised President Reagan that Israel would not launch an attack on South Lebanon without a clear provocation from Palestinian or Syrian forces. For over a year the Lebanese Southern borders were fairly quiet. The 'Sinai Observers Agreement' between Egypt and Israel was signed. Saudi Arabia issued their bold declaration, the first to be made by an Arab regime, regarding Israel's right to exist. The US, Egypt and Israel were engaged in negotiations towards some kind of self-rule for the Palestinians in the West Bank and Gaza. Yet, despite all these reassuring signals, Israel sought to officially annex the Golan Heights captured from Syria in 1967. Shortly before the invasion (9 May 1982), Israel shot down two Syrian MIGs during a routine reconnaissance over Lebanon. But the real pretext, the immediate 'provocation' for the invasion, came when the Israeli Ambassador to Britain was shot and seriously wounded in London.

The incivility and futility of strife became more visible precisely because such atavistic forms of self-administered retributive justice were bereft of any redemptive or restorative value. The more merciless the scope and intensity of vengeful violence, the more remote the likelihood of reconciliation. It was also then that the vertical divisions started to assume a more fractious character. Communities became more cloistered and hence less inclined to entertain schemes for coexistence and cooperation.

Much of the internecine and intra-communal rivalries between the major combatants took the form of such 'turf battles'. These conflagrations had, naturally, more in common with tribal and factional feuds than with conventional warfare, revolutionary struggles or class and ideological conflicts. They are also much bloody than the label 'low-intensity conflict' suggests. Indeed, they are all the more baffling and painful because the bloodletting is endogenous; as abhorrent as the muted cruelties of 'domestic violence' or the futile deaths by 'friendly fire'. All the malevolent and self-destructive inner logic of violence are manifest here: that is, the corrosive proclivity of groups embroiled in conflict to eliminate potential competitors within their own groups to enhance and consolidate their belligerency against their enemies without.

Here again the sources which might have provoked the initial hostilities become irrelevant. Caught up in the frenzy of bloodletting, combatants began to kill those they could, not those they wanted. Little wonder that such internecine violence turns out to be the most atrocious. Its ultimate pathos is not only the heavy toll of innocent victims it generates. More perfidious, it is often inflicted upon, and by, groups with known identities and histories. People were literally killing their neighbors and friends of yesterday. This is why in the early rounds of fighting, militias and fighters in close combat often resorted to wearing masks to conceal their identities.

Virtually all the militias have had their hands stained by the blood of their own brothers. Initially, this was most apparent in the in-fighting between and among Palestinian factions. Early in 1977, mainline Palestinians of the PLO were already engaged in pitched battles with those of the PFLP-General Command and the Arab Rejection and Liberation Fronts. At other times, the Syrian-sponsored Sa'iqa were fighting others, particularly those with leanings toward Iraq or Libya. Often rival factions within single camps (such as those between Arafat and Abu Musa loyalists within Fateh) fought in fierce clashes.

Among Shi'ites, the in-fighting between Syrian-supported Amal and Iranian-supported Hizbullah was equally ferocious. This was exacerbated by their shifting global and regional sponsors. For example, when Iran became suspicious of Syria's rapprochement with Washington, after 1988, it gave Hizbullah a freer hand in undermining Syria's proxy powers within the Shi'ite community. More perplexing, sometimes Hizbullah would be at war with a Syrian-supported militia in the Beqaa while fighting on the side of another Syrian-supported militia in South Lebanon.

The most ruthless, however, were the turf wars among the Maronite militias and their contentious warlords. Coalitions and alliances readily broke up into factions, each vying to extend and consolidate its powers. Bashir Gemayel's swift political ascendancy was largely a by-product of the ruthlessness he displayed in eliminating potential rivals (e.g. Tony Franjieh and Dany Chamoun, both presidential hopefuls) in his quest to claim the leadership of the Maronite community and, ultimately, Lebanon. In May 1978 he encountered little resistance when his Phalangist militias attacked the coveted and strategic region of Safra and destroyed the military infrastructure of Chamoun's Tigers, the militia of the National Liberal Party (NLP). The elimination of Tony Franjieh was far more gruesome. Masterminded and led by Elie Hobeika, Phalangist forces raided Ihden (13 June 1978) and massacred Franjieh, his wife and child and twenty-five of his followers.

The rivalry and intermittent clashes between Samir Ja'ja and Elie Hobeika for the leadership of the Lebanese Forces, and the final showdown in September of 1986, were costlier and much more divisive. Hobeika's militia reinforced by Syrian-backed Muslims from West Beirut crossed over to confront the Ja'ja–Gemayel coalition. Though Hobeika's incursion into the Christian enclave was repelled, it was the first such fateful cross-over. It left grievous repercussions other than the heavy toll of casualties and destruction.

By far the most destructive of the intra-Maronite turf wars was the final confrontation between Ja'ja and General Aoun. This was more than just a turf war since it pitted two Maronite diehards who entertained two distinct visions for safeguarding and bolstering Christian sovereignty. Ja'ja was calling for a 'Federal Lebanon' to be partitioned among its various sectarian communities. Aoun, on the other hand, favored a broader, more Lebanonist vision, hankering to 'Greater Lebanon' of the past, than the constricted Maronite nationalist view envisioned by Ja'ja and the Lebanese Forces. Much like the cryptic biblical story of Abel and Cain, the sibling rivalry between Ja'ja and Aoun evoked hidden meanings. This morbid legacy was clearly alive in Lebanon and equally brutal. Given the urban density of the Christian enclave and the technologies of destruction available to both (thanks to Iraq's Saddam Hussein), the campaign was bound to be devastating in its terror and ferocity. Patriarch Nusrallah Sfeir, like other outraged Maronite leaders, bemoaned this round of bloodletting as 'collective suicide'. After six weeks of reckless fighting and abortive cease-fires, over 1,000 lives were lost. This was more, incidentally, than the toll of devastations brought by six months of artillery bombardment by the Syrians in 1989 (Winslow, 1996: 276–7).

CONFLICT OVER DIVISIBLE GOODS OR INDIVISIBLE ISSUES

One can extract another disconcerting inference from Lebanon's successive but unresolved encounters with collective strife, one with prophetic implications for the course and magnitude that violence has come to assume in the country's checkered political history. As long as the conflict remained a 'class' rivalry, exacerbated by fiscal pressures, socio-economic disparities, political coercion and the like, it was more likely to remain comparatively mild and less belligerent. Once it was transformed or deflected into a confessional or communal hostility, the magnitude and intensity of violence became much more menacing.

This, as René Girard reminds us, has even more ominous implications. 'Religion shelters us from violence just as violence seeks shelter in religion.' As this happens, communities are trapped in a vicious circle of vengeance and reprisal. 'The mimetic character of violence is so intense it cannot burn itself out ... Only violence can put an end to violence and that is why violence is self-propagating' (Girard, 1977: 24–6).

Theodor Hanf (1995) coins the term *ethnergy* to highlight such conscious invention and politicization of ethnic identity. Circumstances associated with the emergence and mobilization of such identities are instrumental in accounting for the pattern and intensity of intra- and interstate conflict. Since all societies are, to varying degrees, horizontally stratified with vertical cultural cleavages, conflict is bound to reflect both horizontal socio-economic disparities and deep cultural divisions. By themselves, however, the strata and cleavages will not become sources of political mobilization unless groups are also made conscious of their distinctive identities. Differences in themselves, horizontal or vertical, become politicized only when those who share common distinctive attributes also share awareness of their distinctiveness. Analogically Hanf translates Marx's 'class-by-itself' and 'class-for-itself' into ethnic group loyalties. Hence, only an ethnic group 'for itself' can become a source of political mobilization.

Within this context it becomes meaningful to identify circumstances in Lebanon's socio-political and cultural history which have heightened and mobilized the political and radical consciousness of communal and confessional identities. Of course, technically speaking, communal and confessional attachments are not 'ethnic' in character, if by that is meant that the assignment of special or distinct status within a culture or social system is arrived at on the basis of purely racial or physical characteristics. But if 'ethnicity' is broadened to incorporate variable traits associated with religion, communal, ancestral affiliations, dialect and other behavioral and subcultural distinctions, then confessional and sectarian identities may well assume some ethnic attributes (Horowitz, 1985). It is also then that these identities become sharper and more militant. They acquire a density of their own and coalesce around sentiments of solidarity and collective self-consciousness.

Popular accounts then were keen on depicting, often with noted amazement, the eagerness with which impressionable teenagers flocked to the barricades, just as their older brothers only a few years back had taken to frivolous pastimes, such as nightclubbing, fast cars, pinball machines and sleazy entertainment (Randal, 1984: 112–13). This is all the more remarkable since we are dealing with a fairly quiescent political culture, one without much background or tradition in military service, conscription or prior experience in paramilitary organizations.

In short, what these and other manifestations imply is that religion is not resorted to as a spiritual or ecclesiastical force. It is not a matter of communing with the divine as a redemptive longing to restore one's sense of well-being. Rather, it is sought largely as a form of ideological and communal mobilization. Indeed, it is often people's only means of asserting their threatened identities. Without it, groups are literally rootless, nameless and voiceless. Results of a survey conducted in 1982, in the wake of the Israeli invasion, revealed that as the intensity of religiosity (as measured by concrete behavioral conduct such as incidence of observation of religious duties and obligations) was declining, and confessional loyalties, distance from and intolerance of other religious groups, were becoming sharper (Khalaf, 1991). In other words, as religiosity was declining bigotry was becoming more salient.

Such realities, incidentally, are certainly not unique to Lebanon. In an insightful and thoroughly documented study of Hindu–Muslim rioting and violence in India, Sudhir Kakar reaches essentially the same conclusion (Kakar, 1996). The author also draws on other historical encounters – such as the anti-Semitic pogroms in Spain in the fourteenth century, or sixteenth-century Catholic–Protestant violence in France, and anti-Catholic riots in eighteenth-century London – to validate the inference that all such instances of collective mobilization were more a by-product of cultural identities and communalism than a reflection of religiosity or revitalization of religious zeal as such.

To Kakar, communalism is a state of mind elicited by the individual's assertion of being part of a religious community, preceded by the awareness of belonging to such a community. He goes further to maintain that only when what he terms the 'We-ness of the community' is transformed into the 'We are of communalism' can we better understand the circumstances which translate or deflect the potential or predispositions for intolerance, enmity and hostility and how these are ultimately released into outward violence (Kakar, 1996: 192). Enmity after all can remain at a latent level. As has been demonstrated, hostility between the various communities in Lebanon has not always erupted in bloody confrontations. Rather, it managed, and for comparatively long stretches, to express itself in a wide gamut of non-violent outlets and arrangements ranging from mild contempt, indifference, guarded contacts and distancing to consociational political strategies and territorial bonding in exclusive spaces.

This is why it is instructive to identify those interludes in Lebanon's checkered history – the critical watersheds so to speak – during which feelings of communal identity are undermined and when the vague, undefined threats and fears become sharper and more focused. It was during such moments that communities sought efforts to reconnect and revive communal solidarity and mobilization. Identifying with and glorifying the threatened virtues of one's own group is heightened and rendered more righteous – as the psychology of in-group/out-group conflict reveals – if it is reinforced by enmity towards the out-group (Kelman, 1987). If uncontained, especially when amplified by rumors and stoked by religious demagogues, the hostility could easily erupt into open violence. By then only the slightest of sparks is needed for a violent explosion.

A drop of blood here and there, in moments of aroused communal passions, always begets carnage. If I were to express this prosaically or more crudely, there is a relationship after all between hot-headedness and cold-blooded violence. The more impassioned and impetuous groups are, the more likely they are to be merciless and guilt-free in their brutality. Hot-headedness should not here be mistaken for mindlessness. Hard-core fighters, by virtue of both their youthfulness and effective resocialization, are normally impelled by an ardent, often sacrificial, commitment to the cause and strategies of combat. Hostility is thus made more legitimate by dehumanizing, depersonalizing and reducing the enemy into a mere category: a target to be acted upon or eliminated. The 'other' becomes no more than an object whose body is worthy of being dispensed with (see Volkan, 1979, 1985; Keen, 1986; Zur, 1987). Assailants can commit their cruelties with abandon and without shame or guilt. It is also then that collective violence degenerates into barbarism and incivility.

By drawing on the rather prosaic distinctions we employed earlier between 'horizontal' and 'vertical' divisions, we can begin to isolate the circumstances which radicalize communal loyalties. At least we can better gauge and ascertain the magnitude and direction conflict is likely to assume as ordinary social strife is deflected into communal and fractious violence and how this may escalate or degenerate into barbarism and incivility.

Horizontal socio-economic disputes, at least as far as the experience of Lebanon is concerned, are more likely to remain comparatively mild and less belligerent. Affected strata are prone to experience various degrees of deprivation and neglect. Their social standing is undermined. They become less privileged. Like other impoverished, aggrieved and dispossessed groups, they resort to collective protest to dramatize and, hopefully, correct the injustice and inequities. Such mobilization, however, unless it is deflected into confessional and communal hostility, rarely escalates into violent confrontations.

Communal and sectarian rivalries are of a different magnitude. While social strata are embittered by loss of status, material advantage and privilege, 'ethnic' groups (in this context, confessional and communal formations) are threatened by the loss of freedom, identity, heritage and even their very national existence. As Hanf aptly puts it, 'politicizing ethnic distinctions shifts the struggle from divisible goods to indivisible principles' (Hanf, 1995: 45).

At precisely such junctures, as socio-economic and political rivalries in Lebanon are transformed into confessional or sectarian conflict, the issues underlying the hostilities become 'indivisible'. The intensity of violence is bound to become more savage and merciless. It is also then that prospects for resolving the conflict non-belligerently become all the more unlikely.

In his probing analysis of civil strife in Ireland, Bouyer-Bell (1987) expresses this poignant dilemma in terms which are applicable to Lebanon, particularly with regard to that fateful threshold when civil strife crosses over the 'point of no return into civil war'.

A prolonged civil war is the most overt indication of an attenuated societal schism. In the preliminary civil discord – no matter how divisive and mutually contradictory the elements involved are, no matter how long-standing the opposing values or how deep-seated the distrust – a society, however strained or artificial, continues to exist. Once civil strife has passed the point of no return into civil war, however, the prewar society has, for better or worse, committed suicide. There can be no restoration of the uncomfortable but familiar past, for civil war can lead only to the ultimate triumph and imposition of a new society, cherished by the victors, inconceivable to the vanquished (Bouyer-Bell, 1987).

NO VICTOR, NO VANQUISHED

Alas, this is a lesson the Lebanese are yet to learn despite their repeated encounters with both civil strife and civil wars. It is in this explicit sense that prolonged or recurrent wars are the most overt indication that something is not changing. The *belligerent equality* so to speak has never transformed itself into the *peaceful inequality* that entails the designation of one as victor and the other as vanquished. Despite the intensity, massiveness and depth of damage and injury, the wars went on. They imperiled and tainted everyday life. There was perpetual hurt and grief with no hope for deliverance or a temporary reprieve. Like a malignant cancer, it grows but refuses to deliver its victim from the anguish of his pain. The enfeebled patient lives on, doomed as it were to be rejuvenated by the very sources of his affliction.

This is why Lebanon's experience in this regard, both past and more recent, is not very encouraging. In fact, it is quite dismal. Throughout the hostilities of 1975–92, cycles of violence were interspersed with efforts of foreign emissaries interceding on behalf of their shifting client groups to broker a short-lived cease-fire or an abortive political settlement. Lebanon's political landscape is strewn with the wreckage of such failed efforts. Cease-fires, in fact, became the butt of political humor and popular derision. As soon as one was declared, it was summarily violated. These were more ploys to win respite from the cruelties of war and recoup losses than genuine efforts to arrest the fighting and consider less belligerent strategies for resolving conflict.

Incidentally, comparative evidence on the relationship between civil violence and conflict resolution is very instructive. Unfortunately, much of this evidence tends to reinforce Lebanon's bleak prospects. A recent analysis of how six other instances of civil unrest have ended – Colombia, Zimbabwe, Greece, Yemen, Sudan, Nigeria and the American Civil War – suggests that in cases where conflict is primarily of an ethnic, communal character, in contrast to those provoked by economic and/or political issues, the likelihood of a negotiated non-belligerent resolution becomes very slim (Rutgers, 1990). Indeed, all communal wars end in blood so to speak. There must be a victor and a vanquished before combatants begin to consider negotiation (Kaplan, 1980).

Fred Ikle arrives at the same conclusion, particularly when he distinguishes civil conflict from international wars. 'Outcomes intermediate between victory and defeat are difficult to construct. If partition is not a feasible outcome because belligerents are not geographically separable, one side has to get all, or nearly so, since there cannot be two governments ... and since the passions aroused and the political cleavages opened render a sharing of power unworkable' (Ikle, 1971: 95). More interestingly, even if a major adversary is defeated, other participants may not admit or recognize such realities. This, too, has plagued Lebanon for so long. Defeat is a state of mind; everyone decides for themselves when they are defeated (Carroll, 1980: 56).

Being trapped in such a setting of unresolved and protracted hostility is inflammable. The most trivial slight or petty personal feud can become, as has happened time and time again, an occasion for the shedding of blood. Also, as Peter Gay reminds us, groups caught up in the frenzy of vengeful blood-letting do not normally resort to violence to avenge a slight. Rather, they are more prone to seek, or invent, a slight in order to release their impulse for aggression (Gay, 1993: 31). Hypersensitivity to being insulted or violated, nurtured by muted enmity, almost always provokes a tendency to retaliate out of proportion to the initial offense. This was clearly the case in the massacres of 1860, not as much in 1958, but much more pronounced in 1975–90.

Quickly during the early rounds of the war in 1975–6, the conflict started to display many of the features of confessional struggle. The two major combatants – the Christian Phalange and their allies and the Palestinians and the Muslim-Left Coalition – behaved as if their very existence was at stake. Little wonder that the fighting quickly descended into the abyss of a zero-sum deadly rivalry, where the perceived victory of one group can only be realized by annihilating the other. Spurred by the fear of being marginalized or swept by and subjugated in an Arab-Muslim mass, the Kata'ib reacted with phobic fanaticism to what seemed to them at the time an ominous threat. They felt that they were fighting not only for the violated authority of state sovereignty but for their way of life, unique heritage and national existence. Often the threat was willfully dramatized to incite and awaken communal solidarity and, thereby, mobilize reticent Christians to the cause of militancy.

Moderation is hard to sustain in the midst of distrust and fear. Progressively the Kata'ib, more so perhaps than other Christian communities, departed from their earlier support of pluralist social arrangements and their preference for a democratic dialogue for progressive reform. They reverted, instead, to a more fanatic anti-Islamic rhetoric. Such awakened parochialism associated with sectarian hostility was given added stimulus by the cultivation of reflexive hatred.

Palestinians were likewise threatened by the fear of being liquidated. Lebanon, by the mid-1970s, was their last abode so to speak. It had become their most strategic stronghold. After the loss of its Jordan base, the PLO was more entrenched in Lebanon. It also jealously guarded the political and strategic gains it had managed to carve out there. The 1969 Cairo Accord, by putting Palestinian refugee camps under PLO control and, virtually, inaccessible to Lebanese authorities, was tantamount to an act of national liberation. The logistical and ideological support they were receiving from Arab radical and rejectionist regimes, particularly after the Egyptian–Israeli peace accord, made their presence in Lebanon all the more vital for their survival. Hence, they were protecting not merely the privileges and freedoms they had acquired in recent years, but also the political setting which had nurtured and safeguarded their very existence.

So both major combatants were locked into that deadly zero-sum duel. As the magnitude of sectarian fighting became bloodier, so with each renewed cycle of violence did the intensity of vengeance and enmity. Sometime ago Anthony Storr warned that 'it is more difficult to quell an impulse toward violence than to arouse it' (Storr, 1968). Once aroused it acquires a logic of its own. It feeds on itself and becomes self-propagating. Again and again, the omnipresent binary categories of diabolic 'them' and virtuous 'us' resurfaces with sharper and more deadly intensity. The enemy is demonized further and the conflict is seen as a war between light and darkness, between the virtuous and the damned. As ordinary, quiescent citizens are drawn into the vortex of such bellicose hostility, they too become more amenable to being engulfed in this pervasive and ferocious enmity. Almost overnight they are transformed into passive, helpless pawns caught up in an inexorable process. Aroused communities buzz with pejorative anecdotes. Adversaries compete in assigning blame and trading invectives. Attribution and name-calling escalate to new heights. Especially in the early rounds of fighting, it is elevated to a high art of rancorous political discourse. The repressed residues of the past resurface. Adversaries, once perceived as rigid, become hopelessly intransigent. 'Isolationists' degenerate into bigots and traitors. Disenfranchised and unanchored masses become aliens with 'green faces'. 'Borrowed ideologies' become repressive, chaotic and obfuscating. In short, the bad become worse; the unsavory and undesirable degenerate into the repulsive and the demonic.

One only has to read a sample of war diaries and accounts by combatants, and even by dispassionate observers or neutral bystanders, to highlight the war-like implications of such predispositions. This seething enmity and fanaticism were naturally more visible in the polemical platforms of warring factions, militias and their affiliated political pressure groups and parties. It also permeated the rest of the society. Pamphleteering, local historiographies, position papers and public pronouncements became legion and more rancid and divisive in tone and substance. So were church sermons and Friday mosque *khoutbas*. Colorful wall graffiti, expressive sheet displays, propaganda campaigns, elaborate obituaries of fallen fighters also evolved their own popular images and art forms.

Though largely symbolic, in that such manifestations may not inflict direct and immediate damage, they are nonetheless responsible for preparing the psychological and moral justifications for outward aggression. Violence is thus rendered socially acceptable and tolerable. Even wanton and gratuitous violence becomes, in the words of Robin Williams, 'virtuous action in the name of applauded values' (Williams, 1981: 26–7).

Like other such 'ideologies of enmity', as John Mack (1979, 1988) calls them, they all converge on three overriding but related objectives. First, there is the glorification of one's community and the ominous threats to it. Communalism in this regard becomes a rapacious scavenger. It feeds upon the awakened sense of a privileged but threatened territorial identity. Second, there is the propagation of mutual vilification campaigns whereby each group depicts the 'other' as the repository of all the ills and pathologies of society. Ironically, the 'other', as John Keane aptly puts it, is treated 'simultaneously as everything and nothing' (Keane, 1996: 125). The enemy is dreaded and feared, but is also arrogantly dismissed as inferior and worthless. Finally, these inevitably lead to the legitimization of violence against the defiled other (Mack, 1988; Pinderhughes, 1979).

The moral and psychological implications of such strategies, though self-evident, should not be overlooked. By evoking such imagery the 'other' is transformed into a public menace, a threat to security and national sovereignty. Hence it becomes easier to inflict violence against him. At least the moral inhibitions, associated with such acts of aggression, are suspended or removed. Indeed, aggression against the 'other' assumes a purgative value. It becomes an act of liberation, the only way to preserve or restore national dignity and integrity. More palliating, it obviates much of the guilt of having blood on one's hands. And this is not necessarily the blood of strangers and distant enemies. Remorse in these instances is not as poignant. But as the ferocity of combat descends into the callused atrocities of internecine, intra-communal and turf warfare (as it did when Christian militias were eliminating their Christian rivals, in the in-fighting between Palestinian factions or between Amal and Hizbullah), the blood is quite often the blood of brothers and kinsmen.

Alas, as the recent history of other episodes of 'ethnic cleansing' tells us, the alleviation of guilt in the frenzy of battle is only momentary. When wars are nurtured by religious passions and the visceral hatreds that go with them, they acquire a self-destructive momentum of their own and they spiral, inexorably, out of control. They become harder to forget and even much more difficult to resolve. Trapped in such an unyielding and atrocious cycle of vengeance and reprisal, fighting in Lebanon started to display many of the pathologies of barbarism inherent in uncivil violence.

I still vividly recall the lineup of politicians sharing the rostrum at the funeral of Pierre Gemayel (21 November 2006), another victim of such visceral barbarism. Almost every one of them was related to someone who had suffered a similar fate. They now live in fear of being the next generation of targeted victims. That fear is justified.

Beirut's streets and those of its suburbs are decked with billboards of the dead or those who miraculously survived assassination attempts. Had we brought to justice but one of those guilty for these crimes, the cycle of killing would not be so easy to perpetuate. In any other civil society Rafik Hariri, Basil Fuleihan, Marwan Hamadeh, Samir Kassir, George Hawi, May Chidiac, Gebran Tueni, Pierre Gemayel, Walid Ido, Wissam Eid, Antoine Ghanem and Francois El Hajj would be celebrated as rare mavericks. They would not be intimidated and slaughtered without a hint of remorse.

The billboards entreat us not to forget. But the problem is not forgetting, but stopping the carnage. Lebanon is much too enfeebled and harassed to consider reconciliatory strategies on any of the issues dividing its leaders. The prospects for resuming a national dialogue are grim. How, after all, can a motley crew of rancorous politicians vilify each other in public and then convene in good faith to arrive at a unified vision of their country's future? This impasse is rendered more intractable by the fact that one group insists on keeping its arms on the haughty pretext of redeeming the damaged dignity of the *umma*. The enmity, spurred by growing inter-sectarian hostility, could well escalate into open conflict. This is symptomatic of how corrosive the faultlines in Lebanon have become.

What can be done to remove Lebanon from this vicious cycle? The Hariri tribunal is an auspicious step in that direction. But much more is needed. It is not just about identifying those who have embroiled Lebanon in collective dread. The very existence of Lebanon as an open, plural and cosmopolitan entity is now in jeopardy. In addition to all the chronic uncertainties that are beleaguering the country, a new fear looms on the political horizon. With the ascendance of Iran as a regional power, Lebanon must now confront the foreboding prospect of falling under the sway of a local version of *wilayat al-faqih*, the system of clerical-political leadership adopted by the mullahs in Tehran.

Chapter 2

The Spaces of War and Postwar: Reflections on Collective Memory, Identity and Nostalgia

Fear is at its most fearsome when it is diffuse, scattered, unclear, unattached, unanchored, free floating, with no clear address or cause; when it haunts us with no visible rhyme or reason, when the menace we should be afraid of can be glimpsed everywhere but is nowhere to be seen. 'Fear' is the name we give to our *uncertainty*: to our *ignorance* of the threat and of what is to be *done* – what can and what can't be – to stop it in its tracks – or to fight it back if stopping it is beyond our power.

(Zygmunt Bauman, *Liquid Fear*, 2006)

For nearly a decade I have been privileged to live in Saifi Village, a gentrified urban neighborhood, on the eastern fringe of Beirut's Central Business District. Every day I alter my half-hour brisk stroll to the American University of Beirut (AUB), to observe the massive reconstruction underway. Much like the recollections of the traditional commuters of old, I note their *sens pratique*; the sun is behind me in the morning and behind me on my return at dusk. The city-scape is sharper and crisper to behold. The daily commute becomes a bewitching, often beguiling experience, both existentially and conceptually. At such a close and intimate range, not only one is struck by the massive physical and material transformations underway but one also gains insight into how new socio-cultural spaces and territorial entities are invested with new meanings. One becomes aware of how disembedded groups and communities are recreating and reinventing their familiar and daily rhythms.

Beirut today is akin to an ongoing living laboratory where one is in a sustained state of being captivated by the new discoveries unfolding, as it were, before one's eyes. It is a marvel to live in such an urban milieu where one, literally, never encounters the same familiar and unchanging street or neighborhood. One is liberated, in an existential sense, from the deadening effects of habit and the sterility of familiar places. A daily stroll always carries with it the visceral sensation of surprise and the prospects of levitating, as it were, into another world. It always heightens one's visual and aesthetic sensibilities. To borrow the metaphors of Ghassan Hage, one is in a sustained state of being pushed, pulled, propelled upward and whirled downward. The elation of stupendous and instant change is dampened by irrevocable feelings of a city adrift and pulled apart by forces beyond its control. One is engulfed by symptoms of promise and hope but also by ambiguity and fear.

More compelling, Beirut is at another critical threshold in its checkered history. A restless and buoyant city is in the throes once again of redefining itself. I say once again because it has been in this predicament many times before. It has reinvented itself on numerous earlier occasions. This is, however, the first time that the process has incited such a contested public debate regarding the rehabilitation scheme itself and its impact on the envisioned or projected public image of Beirut. Indeed in the popular imagination a plurality of images is invoked: a future Hong Kong or Monaco; a Mediterranean town or Levantine sea port; a leisure resort, a playground or touristic site.

To better understand the nature and character of this ongoing interplay between collective memory and obsession with 'heritage', the reassertion of space, and the forging of new cultural identities, I intend to address five related dimensions. First, I will highlight briefly a few of the most striking spatial transformations associated with the war, particularly those that have some bearing on the dialectics between space, memory and collective identity. All three are in flux and are being contested today. This is not a prosaic concern. How this is resolved will prefigure much of the emerging contours and future image of Beirut. Second, by elucidating what I term the 'geography of fear', an attempt will be made to identify and account for how various communities in Beirut are resisting or accommodating themselves to some of the global forces presumed to undermine their local heritage and identities. Third, considering the postwar period, I focus on the historic transformation of Beirut's most commanding central square (the Bourj) to account for its survival as a fairly open, pluralistic and cosmopolitan public sphere. I then move to consider, extracted from the historic and recent experience of the Bourj as a central space, the interplay between local, regional and global encounters and the contested issue of collective memory and amnesia as they relate to the ongoing process of constructing meaningful collective identities. These also help us to elucidate and account for some of the striking manifestations of the liminal and elusive state of being adrift which have beleaguered Lebanon for so long.

Let me first, and very briefly, situate the discussion within a pertinent and ongoing conceptual debate or discourse. Lebanon today is at a fateful crossroads in its political and socio-cultural history. At the risk of some oversimplification, the country continues to be imperiled by a set of overwhelming predicaments and unsettling transformations. At least three stand out by virtue of the ominous implications they have for the massive reconstruction underway and the prospects for forging a viable political culture of tolerance and peaceful coexistence.

First, Lebanon is in the throes of postwar reconstruction and rehabilitation. Given the magnitude and scale of devastation, the country will most certainly continue to require massive efforts in virtually all dimensions of society to spearhead its swift recovery and sustained development. Processes of postwar reconstruction, even under normal circumstances, are usually cumbersome. In Lebanon, they are bound to be more problematic because of the distinctive character of some of the residues of collective terror and strife the country was besieged with for almost two decades and which set it apart from other instances of postwar reconstruction. The horrors spawned by the war are particularly galling because, as we have seen, they were not anchored in any recognizable or coherent set of causes. Nor did the violence, ugly as it was, resolve the issues which sparked the initial hostilities.

In this poignant sense the war which destroyed Beirut was wasteful, futile and unfinished. This is why the task of representing or incorporating such inglorious events into Beirut's and the country's collective identity becomes, understandably, much more problematic. But it needs to be done. Otherwise, the memory of the war, like the harrowing events themselves, may well be trivialized and forgotten, and hence it will be more likely to be repeated. Some of the disheartening consequences of unfinished wars are legion. Two are particularly poignant and of relevance to the concerns of this chapter. First, the symptoms of *retribalization* are apparent in reawakened communal identities and the urge to seek shelter in cloistered spatial communities. Second, there is a pervasive mood of lethargy, indifference, weariness which borders, at times, on *collective amnesia*. Both are understandable reactions which enable traumatized groups to survive the cruelties of protracted strife. Both, however, could be disabling as the Lebanese now consider less belligerent strategies for peaceful coexistence.

Second, Lebanon is not only grappling with all the short-term imperatives of reconstruction and long-term need for sustainable development and security, but it has to do so in a turbulent region suffused with a multitude of unresolved conflicts. Impotent as the country may seem at the moment to neutralize or ward off such external pressures, there are measures and programs, which have already proved effective elsewhere, which can be experimented with to fortify Lebanon's immunity against the disruptive consequences of such destabilizing forces. Such efforts can do much to reduce the country's chronic vulnerability to these pressures. As will be argued, urban planning and design, architecture, landscaping, among other overlooked forms of public intervention, can offer effective strategies for healing symptoms of fear and paranoia and transcending parochialism.

Finally, Lebanon is also embroiled, willingly or otherwise, in all the unsettling forces of postmodernity and globalism: a magnified importance of the mass media, popular arts and infotainment in the framing of everyday life; an intensification of consumerism; the demise of political participation and collective consciousness on public issues and their replacement by local and parochial concerns for nostalgia and heritage. Some of the aberrant manifestations of such features, particularly mass consumerism and kitsch, will be elucidated in the next chapter.

Within this context, issues of collective memory, contested space and efforts to forge new cultural identities begin to assume critical dimensions. How much and what of the past needs to be retained or restored? By whom and for whom? Common as these questions may seem, they have invited little agreement among scholars. Indeed, the views and perspectives of those who have recently addressed them vary markedly. Some, as we shall see, argue that collective forgetfulness or shared amnesia are conditions to be resisted at any cost. Others maintain, particularly when the atrocious memories of the war are still alive, that without an opportunity to forget there can never be a chance for harmony and genuine coexistence.

Both manifestations – the longing to obliterate, mystify and distance oneself from the fearsome recollections of an ugly and unfinished war and efforts to preserve or commemorate them – coexist today in Lebanon. Retribalization and the reassertion of communal and territorial identities, as perhaps the most prevalent and defining elements in postwar Lebanon, incorporate in fact both these features. The convergence of spatial and communal identities serves, in other words, both the need to search for roots and the desire to rediscover or invent a state of bliss that has been lost. They also serve as expedient means of escape from the trials and tribulations of war.

Expressed more concretely, this reflex or impulse for seeking refuge in cloistered spatial communities is sustained by two seemingly opposed forms of self-preservation: to *remember* and to *forget*. The former is increasingly sought in efforts to anchor oneself in one's community or in reviving and reinventing its communal solidarities and threatened heritage. The latter is more likely to assume escapist and nostalgic predispositions to return to a past imbued with questionable authenticity.

If there are then visible symptoms of a 'culture of disappearance' evident in the growing encroachment of global capital and state authority into the private realm and reconstruction schemes which are destroying or defacing the country's distinctive architectural landscape and urban heritage, there is a burgeoning 'culture of resistance' which is contesting and repelling such encroachment and dreaded annihilation or the fear of being engulfed by the overwhelming forces of globalization (for further details, see Khalaf, 2001).

One unintended but compelling consequence of all this is that through this restorative venture, and perhaps for the first time in recent history, a growing segment of the Lebanese are becoming publically aware of their spatial surroundings. Their spatial sensibilities and public concern for safeguarding the well-being of their living habitat have been enhanced in appreciable ways. By doing so, consciously or otherwise, they are transforming their tenuous, distant and instrumental attachments to 'space' into the more personal and committed identities engendered by deep and supportive loyalties to one's 'place'. These loyalties after all are receptive to the needs of urbanity and civility. Hence, rather than berating and maligning one's *roots* and primordial attachments (religious, sectarian, kinship, communal and otherwise) as sources of retrograde or infantile nostalgia, they could, if judiciously mobilized, become *routes* for forging new cosmopolitan identities and transcending loyalties and commitments.

THE SPACES OF WAR

For almost two decades, Lebanon was besieged and beleaguered by every possible form of brutality and collective terror known to human history: from the cruelties of factional and religious bigotry to the massive devastations wrought by private militias and state-sponsored armies. This generated an endless carnage of innocent victims and an immeasurable toll of human suffering. Even by the most moderate of estimates, the magnitude of such damage to human life and property is staggering. About 170,000 have perished, twice as many were wounded or disabled; close to two-thirds of the population experienced some form of dislocation or uprootedness from their homes and communities. By the fall of 1982, UN experts estimated that the country had sustained $12–15 billion in damages, i.e. $2 billion/year. Today more than one-third of the population is considered to be below the poverty line as a result of war and displacement.

The latest string of serial assassinations, beginning with Prime Minister Rafik Hariri on 14 February 2005 and close to twenty prominent politicians and public figures, the 'summer war' of 2006 between Israel and Hizbullah and the military incursion of Hizbullah forces into West Beirut and the mountain in May 2007 (the former predominantly Sunni Muslim and the latter Druze), have all compounded sectarian tensions and heightened public fear.

For a small, dense and closely knit society of about 3.5 million and less than 4000 square miles, such devastations are, understandably, very menacing. More damaging, perhaps, are some of the socio-psychological and moral concomitants of protracted hostility. The scars and scares of war have left a heavy psychic toll, in terms of pervasive symptoms of post-traumatic stress and nagging feelings of despair and hopelessness. In a culture generally averse to psychoanalytic counseling and therapy, these and other psychic disorders and fears are more debilitating. They remain masked and unrecognized and, hence, unattended to.

The spiritual consequences of the war are also visible in symptoms of pervasive trauma, vulgarization and impoverishment of public life and erosion of civility. The routinization of violence, chaos and fear only compounded the frayed fabric of the social order. It drew groups into the vortex of conflict and sowed a legacy of hate and bitterness. It is in this fundamental sense that Lebanon's pluralism, radicalization of its communities and consequent collective violence have become pathological and uncivil. Rather than being a source of enrichment, variety and cultural diversity, the modicum of pluralism the country once enjoyed is now generating large residues of paranoia, hostility and differential bonding.

REDEFINING TERRITORIAL IDENTITIES

The first striking and, perhaps, unsettling feature is the way the Lebanese have been, since the outbreak of the war in 1975, caught up in an unrelenting process of redefining their territorial identities. Indeed, as the fighting blanketed virtually all regions in the country, few have been spared the anguish of uprootedness from their spatial moorings. The magnitude of such displacement is greater than commonly recognized. Recent estimates suggest that more than half, possibly two-thirds, of the population have been subjected to some transient or permanent form of uprootedness from their homes and communities.

Throughout the war, in other words, the majority of the Lebanese were trapped in a curious predicament: the painful task of *negotiating, constructing and reconfirming* a fluid and unsettled pattern of spatial identities. No sooner had they suffered the travails of dislocation by taking refuge in one community than they were again uprooted and compelled to negotiate yet another spatial identity or face the added humiliation of re-entry into their profoundly transformed communities. They became homeless, so to speak, in their own homes or furtive fugitives and outcasts in their communities.

The socio-psychological consequences of being dislodged from one's familiar and reliable landmarks, those of home and neighborhood, can be quite shattering. Like other displaced groups, they become disoriented and distressed because the terrain has changed and because there is no longer a neighborhood for them to live in and rely upon. 'When the landscape goes,' says Erikson (1976) 'it destroys the past for those who are left: People have no sense of belonging anywhere.' They lose the sense of control over their lives, their freedom and independence, their moorings to place and locality and, more damaging, a sense of who they are. The dismaying implications of such relentless dislocation and the trepidations of being adrift are self-evident.

Bereft of place, groups become homeless in at least three existential senses. First, they suffer the angst of being dislodged from their most enduring attachments and familiar places. Second, they also suffer banishment and the stigma of being a *muhajjar*; outcasts in their neighborhoods and homes.

Finally, much like the truly exiled, they are impelled by an urge to reassemble a damaged identity and broken history. Imagining the old places, with all its nostalgic longings, serves as their only reprieve from the uncertainties and anxieties of the present.

DESTRUCTION OF COMMON AND POROUS SPACES

Equally devastating has been the gradual destruction of Beirut's and, to a large extent, the country's common spaces. The first to go was Beirut's central business district which had served historically as the undisputed focal meeting place. Beirut without its Bourj, as the city center is popularly labeled, was unimaginable. Virtually all the vital public functions were centralized there: the Parliament, municipal headquarters, financial and banking institutions, religious edifices, transportation terminals, traditional souks, shopping malls, entertainment activities, etc, kept the prewar Bourj in a sustained state of animation, day and night. There, people of every walk of life and social standing came together.

With decentralization, other urban districts and regions in the country served as supplementary meeting grounds for common activities. They, too, drew together, albeit on seasonal and interim bases, groups from a wide cross-section of society, thereby nurturing outlets germane for coexistence and plural lifestyles. There were very few exclusive spaces beyond the reach of others. The social tissue, like all seemingly localized spaces, became fluid and permeable.

The disappearance of such common, porous and malleable places – one of the pronounced features of postwar Lebanon – is bound to have adverse implications on prospects for tenable coexistence, let alone civility and national consciousness.

THE CREATION OF EXCLUSIVE AND INSULAR SPACES

Alas, the war destroyed virtually all such common and porous spaces, just as it dismantled many of the intermediary and peripheral heterogeneous neighborhoods which had mushroomed with increasing urbanization in cities like Tripoli, Sidon and Zahleh. It not only destroyed common spaces, but also encouraged the formation of separate, exclusive and self-sufficient spaces. Hence, the Christians of East Beirut need not now frequent West Beirut for cultural and popular entertainment. Likewise, one can understand the reluctance of Muslims and other residents of West Beirut to visit resorts and similar alluring spots in the Christian suburbs. With internecine conflict, quarters within urban districts, just like towns and villages, were often splintered into smaller and more compact enclosures. Spaces within which people circulated and interacted shrank still further. The socio-psychological predispositions underlying this urge to huddle in insulated spaces is not too difficult to trace or account for.

Massive population shifts, particularly since they are accompanied by the reintegration of displaced groups into more homogeneous, self-contained and exclusive spaces, have also reinforced communal solidarity. Consequently, territorial and confessional identities, more so perhaps than at any other time, are beginning to converge. For example, 44 percent of all villages and towns before the outbreaks of hostilities included inhabitants of more than one sect. The sharp sectarian redistribution, as Salim Nasr (1993) has shown, has reshuffled this mixed composition. While the proportion of Christians living in the southern regions of Mount Lebanon (i.e. Shuf, Aley, Upper Matn) was 55 percent in 1975, it had shrunk to about 5 percent by the late 1980s. The same is true of West Beirut and its suburbs. Likewise, the proportion of Muslims living in the eastern suburbs of Beirut has also been reduced from 40 percent to about 5 percent over the same period (see Nasr, 1993, for more details).

The war has also transformed the perception and use of space in a more compelling sense. When a 'playground' (as pre-war Lebanon was legitimately labeled) turns into a 'battleground' inevitably this is accompanied by a dramatic turnover in land use. Hashim Sarkis (1993) has demonstrated how space during episodes of civil strife develops its own logic and propels its own inhabitation. He tells that 'it precedes, resists, yields to, and survives those who assume it to be a neutral site for their control.' He also advances the view that 'inhabitants are more elusive in their relationships with places they inhabit. They move across given boundaries ... negotiate and renegotiate their spatial identities.' Here again the meaningful and reinforcing intimacy of coherent *places*, as primary sources of well-being and authenticity, is transformed or deformed as they become amorphous, impersonal and commodified *spaces* to enhance their speculative and commercial real estate prospects.

THE SPATIAL LOGIC OF WAR

Most graphic, of course, is the way spaces of war asserted their ferocious logic on virtually every nook and cranny of public and private space. Equally telling is the ingenuity of its besieged hostages in accommodating this menacing turnover in their spatial surroundings.

Public thoroughfares, crossroads, bridges, hilltops and other strategic intersections which served as links between communities were the first to be converted. They became 'Green Lines', treacherous barriers denying any crossover. Incidentally, the infamous 'Green Line' acquired its notorious label when shrubs and bushes sprouted from its tarmac after years of neglect. It is ironic that the great divide which rips the city in two was none other than the major thruway (i.e. the old Damascus Road) connecting Beirut to its hinterland and beyond. Likewise, major squares, traffic terminals and pedestrian shopping arcades, once the hub of gregarious activity and dense interaction, became desolate 'no man's lands', *al-Mahawir al-taqlidiya* (traditional lines of confrontation) or *khutut al-tamas* (lines of confrontation).

While prominent public spaces lost their identity, other rather ordinary crossings, junctures, hilltops, even shops, became dreaded landmarks. The war produced its own lexicon and iconography of places (see Makdisi, 1990). By virtue of their contingent location these and other inconsequential places and spaces became fearsome points of reference and demarcating lines, part of the deadly logistics of contested space.

Private space was not spared these tempestuous turnovers in land use. Indeed, the distinctions between private and public space were blurred and lost much of their conventional usages. Just as basements, rooftops and strategic openings in private homes became part of the logistics of combat, roadways were also 'domesticated' as family possessions, discarded furniture and bulky items spilled into the public domain to improvise barricades. Balconies, verandas, walk-ups, doorways and all the other open, airy and buoyant places the Lebanese craved and exploited with such ingenuity, became dreaded spaces to be bolted and shielded. Conversely, dingy basements, tightly sealed corridors, attics and other normally neglected spaces became coveted simply because they were out of the trajectory of snipers and shellfire. They became places of refuge.

Even the intimacy and security of private space were not spared the anguish of being adrift. The symbolic meanings and uses of a 'house', 'home' or 'dwelling' space, as Maha Yahya (1993) has demonstrated, were also overhauled.

The most compelling, of course, is the way the family unit and its private space has been broadened to accommodate other functions, as disengaged and unemployed household members relocated their business premises to their homes. The thriving informal war economy reinforced such efforts and rendered them more effective.

Perhaps most unsettling is the way the tempo of war has imposed its own perilous time frames, dictating traffic flows, spaces to be used or avoided. Time, space, movement and interaction all became enveloped with contingency and uncertainty. Nothing was taken for granted anymore. People lived, so to speak, situationally. Short-term expediency replaced long-term planning. Everything had to be negotiated on the spur of the moment. The day-to-day routines which once structured the use of space and time were lost. Deficient communication and irregular and congested traffic rendered all forms of social interaction fortuitous and unpredictable. One was expected to accomplish much of one's daily activities at unexpected hours depending on the merciless whims of fighters or the capricious cycles of violence. Beirutis became, as a result, astonishingly adept at making instant adaptations to such jarring modulations and precipitous shifts in the use of time and space.

THE GEOGRAPHY OF FEAR AND ITS BY-PRODUCTS

All wars, civil or otherwise, are atrocious. Lebanon's encounters with civil strife are particularly galling because its horrors were not anchored in any recognizable or coherent set of causes, nor did they resolve the issues which had sparked the initial hostilities. It is in this poignant sense that the war was altogether a wasteful and futile encounter with collective violence.

The muted anguish and unresolved hostilities of the war are now being compounded by all the ambivalences and uncertainties of postwar reconstruction and the encroachment of conglomerate global capital as it contests the efforts of indigenous and local groups in reclaiming and reinventing their threatened spatial identities. What we are witnessing in fact is a multi-layered negotiation or competition for the representation and ultimate control of Beirut's spatial and collective identity. Much of Beirut's future image will largely be an outcome of such discrepant claims and representations. The contesting groups (i.e. funding and state agencies, planners, property and shareholders, advocacy groups and voluntary associations, concerned public), by virtue of their distinct composition and objectives, vary markedly in their proposed visions and strategies.

The ongoing competition and the public debate it has incited have also served to accentuate the fears of the public, particularly since the struggle is now intimately aligned with the intrusions of global capital, mass culture and consumerism. Hence the fears of disappearance, erasure, marginalization and displacement are assuming acute manifestations. The overriding reactions have much in common, in fact, with the three neurophysiological responses to fear and anxiety, namely: *freeze, flight* and *fight*. While the first two normally involve efforts to disengage and distance oneself from the sources of fear, the third is more combative since it involves a measure of direct involvement, negotiation and/or resisting the threats of erasure (Nan, 1997). All three, in varying proportions, are visible today in Lebanon.

1. The first, and perhaps the most common, is a relic of the war. To survive all its cruelties, the Lebanese became deadened and numbed. Like other victims of collective suffering, they became desensitized and overwhelmed by muted anguish and pain. During the war, such callousness (often masquerading as resilience) served them well. It allowed them not just to survive but also to inflict and rationalize cruelties on the 'other'. By distancing themselves, or cutting themselves off, from the 'other', the brutality of embattled communities was routinized. Violence became morally indifferent. People could engage in guilt-free violence and kill with impunity precisely because they had restricted contacts with their defiled victims. To a large extent, it is 'the group boundaries', as Randall Collins tells us, 'that determine the extent of human sympathy; within these boundaries, humanity prevails; outside them, torture is inflicted without qualm' (Collins, 1974: 417).

    There is a painful irony in this mode of response. That which enabled embattled groups and communities to survive the atrocities of strife is clearly disabling them now as they are considering options for rearranging and sharing common spaces and forging unified national identities. Here again, Collins is quick to remind us that 'the point is not to learn to live with the demons, but to take away their powers' (Collins, 1974: 416). The issue, here as well, converges on who is to mobilize or speak on behalf of those who have been rendered 'frozen'; namely, disengaged, inactive and bereft of speech.

There is after all something in the character of intense pain, Elaine Scarry tells us, which is 'language destroying'. 'As the content of one's world disintegrates, so the content of one's language disintegrates ... world, self, and voice are lost, or nearly lost, through the intense pain' (Scarry, 1985: 35). This is also a reflection of the fact that people in pain are ordinarily bereft of the resources of speech. It is not surprising that the language for pain should in such instances often be evoked by those who are not themselves in pain but by those who speak on behalf of them. Richard Rorty expresses the same thought. He, too, tells us that victims of cruelty, people who are suffering, do not have much in the way of language. That is why there is no such thing as the 'voice of the oppressed' or the 'language of the victims'. The language the victims once used is not working anymore, and they are suffering too much to put new words together. So the job of putting their situation into language is going to have to be done for them by somebody else. (Rorty, 1989)

This is where civil society groups, and Lebanon has a comparatively vibrant civil society, can begin to create a critical mass movement to establish priorities and formulate effective and permanent pressure groups of professional activism to address such overlooked problems.

2. A second more interesting and complex response is not purely one of *flight* but an effort to distance oneself from the atrocious residues of protracted strife and the disenchanting barbarism of the postwar period. This nostalgic retreat is a search for 're-enchantment', evident in the revival of heritage or the imagined nirvana of an idyllic past. Three manifestations of such escapist venues are becoming increasingly visible in various dimensions of daily life and popular culture: (1) the reassertion of communal solidarities, (2) nostalgic longings and (3) the proliferation of kitsch. I will elaborate here on the first two and defer my remarks on kitsch to the next chapter.

As mentioned earlier, it is understandable why traumatized and threatened groups should seek shelter in their communal solidarities and cloistered spaces. Confessional sentiments and their supportive loyalties, even in times of relative peace and stability, have always been effective sources of social support and political mobilization. But these are not, as Lebanon's fractious history amply demonstrates, unmixed blessings. While they cushion individuals and groups against the anomie and alienation of public life, they also heighten the density of communal hostility and enmity.

There is a curious irony here. Despite the many differences which divide the Lebanese, they are in a sense homogenized by fear, grief and bafflement. Fear, as it were, is the tie that binds and holds them together. But it is also fear which keeps them apart. This 'geography of fear' is not sustained by walls or artificial barriers as one observes in other comparable instances of ghettoization of minorities and ethnic groups. Rather, it is sustained by the psychology of dread, hostile bonding and ideologies of enmity. Also, as Zygmunt Bauman reminds us, and certainly more perilous, is when fear is everywhere and nowhere to be seen.

Fear is at its most fearsome when it is diffuse, scattered, unclear, unattached, unanchored, free floating with no clear address or cause; when it haunts us with no visible rhyme or reason, when the menace we should be afraid of can be glimpsed everywhere but is nowhere to be seen. 'Fear' is the name we give to our uncertainty: to our *ignorance* of the threat and of what is to be *done* – what can and what can't be – to stop it in its tracks – or to fight it back if stopping it is beyond our power. (Bauman, 2006: 2)

The challenges for urbanists and architects are immense and daunting. At the least one should recognize and understand the implications of such pervasive forms of hostile bonding in cloistered spaces as legitimate reactions to fear. Indeed, this is doubtlessly the most pressing problem which confronts urbanists: how to transform this geography of fear, as seen in the symptoms of mistrust, paranoia and exclusion, into a geography of genuine tolerance and coexistence. Expressed more broadly this will demand the transformation of such dreaded necessities into civil, cosmopolitan and convivial encounters.

3. By far the most promising are the strategies to which various communities have been recently resorting in resisting threats to their local heritage and identity. Here responses to fear and uncertainty – whether generated by internal displacement, global capital or mass culture and consumerism – have reawakened and mobilized local groups to reclaim their contested spaces and eroded cultural identities. The emergent spaces reveal more than just residues or pockets of resistance. There are encouraging signs of so-called 'third spaces' or in-between cultures of hybridity, mixture and tolerance.

This is, after all, what Bennett implied by 'cultures of resistance', that is, how a 'local spatial system retains many of its traditional institutions and utilized these to manipulate and control the extreme forces' (as cited in Milnar, 1996: 80). Hence, many of the public spaces, more the work of spontaneity than design, are in fact spaces of bargaining and negotiation for national memory and indigenous re-emergence. More so than in other such instances of 'globalization', what we are witnessing in Lebanon today are manifestations of local groups becoming increasingly globalized and, conversely, global incursions being increasingly localized. In other words we see symptoms of 'inward shifts' where loyalties are redirected towards renewed localism and subnational groups and institutions. We also see 'outward shifts', where loyalties and interests are being extended toward transnational entities (DiMuccio and Rosenau, 1992: 62).

This is, incidentally, a far cry from the portraits one can extract from recent writings on the spatial and cultural implications of this global/ local dialectics. For example, in his polemical but engaging work on the interplay between 'Jihad' and 'McWorld', Benjamin Barber (1996) pits McWorld, as the universe of manufactured needs, mass consumption and mass infotainment against Jihad, shorthand for the belligerent politics of religious, tribal and other forms of bigotry. The former is driven by the cash nexus of greedy capital and the bland preferences of mass consumers. The latter is propelled by fierce tribal loyalties, rooted in exclusionary and parochial hatreds. McWorld, with all its promises of a world homogenized by global consumerism, is rapidly dissolving local cultural identities. Jihad, by recreating parochial loyalties, is fragmenting the world into tighter and smaller enclosures. Both are a threat to civil liberties, tolerance and genuine coexistence. 'Jihad pursues a bloody politics of identity, McWorld a bloodless economics of profit. Belonging by default to McWorld, every-one is a consumer; seeking a repository for identity, everyone belongs to some tribe. But no one is a citizen' (Barber, 1996: 8).

We see little of such sharp dichotomies and diametrical representations in postwar Lebanon. While many of the emergent spatial enclaves are cog-nizant and jealous of their indigenous identities, they are not averse to experimenting with more global and ephemeral encounters and cultural products. Likewise, global expectations are being reshaped and rearranged to accommodate local needs and preferences. Expressed in the language of globalization and postmodernity, the so-called 'world without borders', the 'collapse of spatial boundaries' is not a prerequisite for global encoun-ters. At least this is not what has been transpiring in Lebanon. Indeed, as Martin Albrow argues, one of the key effects of globalization on locality is that people 'can reside in one place and have their meaningful social relations almost entirely outside it and across the globe'. This, Albrow goes on to say, 'means that people use the locality as site and resource for social activities in widely different ways according to the extension of their sociosphere' (Albrow, 1996: 53).

Recent case studies of three distinct sites in Beirut (Ain al-Mryseh, Gemmayze and the 'Elisar' project in Beirut's southern suburb) provide instructive and vivid evidence for how local groups and communities have been able to resist, avert and rearrange the powers of global agendas. Indeed, in all three instances, globalization has contributed to the strengthening and consolidation of local ties, thereby reinforcing the claims of Persky and Weiwel when they speak of the 'growing localness of the global city' and the 'globalization' of urban structures. (For further details see Khalaf 1998: 140–64.)

This strip or corridor (roughly not more than five hectares or about 50,000m²), which is often dubbed by archeologists the 'nursery of Homo Sapiens', has served as an abode for man almost since his appearance on the surface of the earth. Indeed, some of the implements which continue to be unearthed on the site have been traced back to the lower Paleolithic, that is, about two or three million years ago. From its eventful past, much like its most recent history, three distinct but related elements stand out: first, its predisposition to incorporate and reconcile pluralistic and multicultural features; second, its inventiveness in reconstituting and rearranging its collective identity and public image. Finally, by virtue of its role in hosting and disseminating popular culture, consumerism, and mass entertainment, and as a setting for political and public protest, the Bourj becomes a paragon, almost a textbook case of a public sphere destined to remain a focal mode or national image in Beirut's future.

THE BOURJ AS A COSMOPOLITAN PUBLIC SPHERE

Despite its checkered history, the Bourj, more than its adjoining quarters and eventual outlying suburban districts, has always served as a vibrant and cosmopolitan 'melting pot' of diverse groups and socio-cultural transformations. While other neighborhoods and districts of the expanding city have attracted distinct sectarian, ethnic, class and ideological groups and communities – and eventually evolved into segregated and bounded urban enclosures – the Bourj always managed to remain a fairly open and homogenizing space.

It is this openness and receptivity to new encounters, particularly foreign cultures, competing educational missions, European trade and an incessant inflow of goods, itinerant groups and borrowed ideologies, which account for both its resonant pluralism and assimilating character. These two forces, *pluralism* and *tolerance* to others, became the defining elements of Beirut's center. This was very evident during the first half of the nineteenth century. Partly because of its compact size and predominantly commercial character, the intermingling and collaboration between the various communities was both inevitable and vital for their coexistence and survival. Typical of a so-called 'merchant republic', traders and entrepreneurs of various communities were partners in private business ventures. They assisted each other in times of austerity and financial need. More important, they perceived themselves as members of an urban merchant elite, resisting the hostile elements that threatened their common economic interests.

This symbiotic coexistence between traditional outlets and the more specialized, commercial and corporate-like organizations continued throughout the post-independence period and beyond. Indeed, this proclivity to accommodation was a distinctive attribute of the Bourj. The growth of secular and impersonal associations throughout the 1960s, and until the outbreak of civil hostilities in the mid-1970s, did not displace the conventional shopkeeper, artisans and neighborhood stores. They merely enriched the plurality and diversity of outlets. Hence, seemingly disparate groups felt equally at home: the villager and regular neighborhood customer who was seeking familiarity and personal contacts and the itinerant visitor and tourist after novelty and adventure. In other words, neither the foot-loose *flâneur* nor the rooted conformist felt any dissonance in the spaces they were sharing.

Throughout its eventful history and largely because of the multicultural and pluralistic layers of ancient civilizations it sheltered, the Bourj had to reinvent itself repeatedly, to accommodate the relentless succession of imperial occupations. The most intractable public label has, of course, been the Bourj, referring to the imposing tower guarding its sea-front ramparts. Consistent with its ubiquitous and evolving national character, the popular labels and nomenclatures attributed to it have always been in flux and contested. It is rather telling that the first urban form the Bourj assumed was 'Al Maydān', which prefigured some subsequent striking developments, particularly its role as a collective common ground (public sphere) for itinerant and unanchored social groups. The *Maydān* should not be dismissed as merely a fortuitous and insignificant passing interlude. As it evolved, it incorporated elements which account for the dual role it came to play and, hopefully, will continue to do so in yet another reinvented form: an open space – *Sāha* – that is not a wilderness; a common ground that is not home.

From its inception as an open, amorphous *Maydān* (and this is how it was first labeled), the Bourj never served as a distinct enclosure or sanctuary. Rather, it acted as an open ground that exacted a measure of collective attachment. This is, after all, what the notion of *Maydān*, in its Persian origins, conjures up. It came to be identified with images of plains, meadows, grounds or fields. In its Persian context it was primarily associated with pilgrims, traders, militias. As it found expression in other contexts like Cairo, Bombay, Ahmedabad, Calcutta etc), it embraced many other elements and uses. Throughout, however, the idea of *Maydān* emerged as a result of human intervention directed not toward the addition of identity, events or character but rather towards keeping land free and indeterminate, and hence negotiable. Therefore the *Maydān* should not be confused with enclosed courtyards or cultivated parks. Nor is it a desolate wilderness, a dreary, parched stretch of land. Rather, as M. Mathur (1999) suggested, it is somewhere in between; it is both nomadic and collective. It is in fact close to what Ivan Illich calls 'commons', or

> that part of the environment that lay beyond a person's own threshold and outside his own possession, but to which, however, that person had a recognized claim of usage – not to produce commodities but to provide for the subsistence of kin. Neither wilderness nor home is commons, but that part of the environment for which customary law exacts specific forms of community respect. (Illich, 1980: 18)

A striking feature of the *Maydān*, which is of particular relevance to the Bourj's emergence and metamorphosis, is its predisposition to embrace a diversity of cultures while containing neutrality, anonymity and transcending attributes. As Mathur puts it:

> In cities of increasingly circumscribed social, racial, or economic enclaves, the *maidan* has come to both symbolize and provide neutral territory, a ground where people can gather on a common plane. It is a place that offers freedom without obligation. This ability to accommodate a diverse range of social and political structures makes the *maidan* an extremely significant space in the city. It is a place where people can touch the spirit of commonness. (Mathur, 1999: 215)

Given the scarcity and inevitable intensification and competition for the use of precious urban space, a realistic reappropriation of a *Maydān* in its original concept or form is naturally a remote likelihood in central Beirut. Its underlying spirit and sentiment is however still realizeable. Indeed, because of the disappearance of many historical *Maydān*, efforts are being made today to appropriate landscapes that lend themselves to both settled and nomadic or ephemeral elements. Hence, open spaces and *Sāhas* made once again available for urban redevelopment are rare and challenging interludes for urban designers. Leveled and open spaces can offer rare opportunities to reclaim a measure of freedom and spontaneity within the enclosure of the city. All adjoining areas radiating from Beirut's center are increasingly commodified, deliberately monitored and exploited in ways that are bound to discourage any spontaneous appropriation or unplanned development. Within such seemingly impervious constraints, when urbanists and landscape architects are seeking to promote qualities of indeterminacy and open-mindedness, the Bourj offers such a rare and coveted opportunity.

Naturally as a reality, the *Maydān* life-span was short-lived. No sooner had itinerant groups started settling within and adjoining the remains of the fortified medieval embankments, than the Bourj became literally, *Sāhat-al-sūr*. The imperial Russian fleet in 1773 installed five massive pieces of artillery on its elevated fortifications. Hence the appellation of Place des Canons. By 1860, it was the imperial canons of the French fleet which this time reinforced that label. Prior to that and for a brief interlude (after 1850) when Beirut's center was largely desolate, other than the few nomadic bedouins from the interior who occupied one of its remaining fortified towers, it bore the designation of *Sāhat Bourj el Kāshif.*

Shortly after, by 1863, the Beirut–Damascus road (originally planned in 1851) was completed, thereby strengthening the link with Damascus and territory beyond Mount Lebanon and the coast; the centrality of the Bourj was reinforced further. A tolled caravan route extended from Bourj square in a valley between the Ashrafiyeh area and the western regions of Moussaytbeh and Mazr'a. Under Dāwūd Pasha (1861–8) the streets of Beirut were widened and macadamized to accommodate carriages of the French Damascus Road Company. Greek Orthodox merchants benefited financially from the improving regional economic role of Beirut.

During the Mutasarrifiyya, the Municipal Council of Beirut in 1879 launched a series of magisterial and eye-catching projects. It is interesting to note in this regard that, unlike other Ottoman provinces, private initiative and foreign capital contributed heavily to changing the urban landscape, particularly in the wake of the economic boom during the last decade or so of the nineteenth century. Initiated at that time, this form of private intervention or concern for the regulation of public space became, off and on, a recurrent feature. For example, as early as 1879, when Fakhrī Bek launched his landscaping project of the public garden in the Bourj, about thirty families contributed to the effort. Incidentally, the uniqueness and novelty of a public garden prompted municipal authorities to enforce restrictive measures to safeguard it from envisaged public abuse by neglectful and disorderly urban masses. An elaborate fence made the garden inaccessible to the public. For a fairly long time it remained a well-tended and jealously guarded public space.

This *Muntazah*, as it was initially labeled, became the edifying centerpiece of the Bourj. Perhaps because of its novelty and the patrons it drew from a cross-section of the social fabric, the Bourj started to attract other outdoors cultural outlets for public entertainment. A music kiosk was built. From then on, the Bourj began to evolve into an urban hub or loop which drew in and around it a variety of activities ranging from official state and municipal bureaucracies, travel termini, hotels, locandas, side-walk cafes, to business and retail stores, popular souks, other more seamy outlets such as brothels, bars, gambling joints and houses of assignation.

During the Ottoman period (1889–1918), the Bourj underwent successive changes in its popular identity. First, it acquired the label of *Sāhat al Ittihād* or *al Hamīdiyyah* in reference to its Ottoman legacy; the former as an expression of the desired national unity under Ottoman sovereignty and the latter in commemoration of Sultan Abdul Hamīd. By the time Prince Faysal Ibn al-Husayn made his triumphant visit in May 1919, *Sāhat al Hamīdiyyah* became *Hadīqat al Hurriya*; that is, freedom or liberation from Turkish oppression.

Freedom and liberation from Ottoman oppression did not, of course, occur without exacting a heavy toll on a select group of recalcitrant nationalists. Beginning 21 August 1915, Jamal Pasha used the open square of the Bourj to execute, by public hanging, the first group of eleven martyrs. This was followed in 1916 by three other executions (5 April, 6 May and 5 June). Journalistic accounts of the day reveal widespread feelings of collective anguish, trepidation and pride (see Tueni and Sassine, 2000). In 1937, 6 May was declared a national memorial day. The memoralization of martyrs, given the repeated victimization of innocent civilians the country has been beleaguered with, is naturally a solemn and fitting commemoration.

Interestingly, the most lasting labels and collective identities of Beirut's center have always oscillated between three common nomenclatures: a bourj, *Sāha* or Martyrs' Square. The first makes reference to the one remaining relic of its medieval walled ramparts. The second marks the *sahat*, open *muntazah*, or *maydān*, which it was during the second half of the nineteenth and early twentieth centuries. Finally, martyrdom is also a befitting and felicitous national commemoration.

Just as one can understand and account for the resurgence of religious identities in postwar Beirut, one can likewise appreciate the seductive appeal of the Bourj as a *playground*, an open setting conducive for both personal, intimate and familiar ties, along with more fluid, protean and changeable encounters. Indeed, as we have seen, throughout its checkered history the Bourj has been quite adept at accommodating both the 'sacred' and the 'profane', the communal and associational, the universal and particular, the global and local. These, and other such seemingly polarized dichotomies, have been malleable and porous entities. Being dialectical in character, they reinforce and enrich each other.

It is this malleability and liminality which rendered the Bourj more receptive for fostering mass and popular culture, mass politics, popular entertainment and, as of late, global consumerism with all its disheartening manifestations of commodification, kitsch and the debasement of the threatened residues of high culture, fine and performing arts. I will amplify these features in Chapter 5. What needs to be emphasized here is that the proliferation of popular meeting spaces, most visible around the Bourj and adjoining areas, has been very conducive for fostering mass and popular culture. During the Ottoman and Mandate interludes, the Bourj – by virtue of its Petit Serail and public square – was fully used for ceremonial functions, official and magisterial declarations and receptions for dignitaries. But it was also a *muntazah*.

The Mandate period saw the emergence of distinctly bourgeois spaces and lifestyles, but also introduced a new mass culture. What was restricted to the elite in the late Ottoman period started to spread to middle and lower strata. By the mid-1920s, a new phase of capitalist penetration swept in a multitude of imported consumer goods and practices. By then, Thompson (2000: 181) indicates that little girls in the mountains of Lebanon were already importing French dresses. By the early 1940s a set of household inventories showed that average families in Lebanon already were enjoying the use of many imported or Western-style products: electric irons, imported dress shirts, toothbrushes, aspirin, electric lamps, telephones, packaged cookies, canned meat, tuna and sardines, chairs made of iron and wood, and even some gramophone records.

Electricity not only made family soirées and charity balls more glamorous. It also expanded the horizons of the urban public with extended tramlines, radios and telephones. Electricity was introduced to Beirut before World War I. In less than a decade Beirut had already close to a 1,000 subscribers. Telephones, long confined to military networks, spread gradually during the 1930s to homes, offices and public spaces. By 1935, there were already phone booths at most busy intersections in Beirut (for these and other details, see Thompson, 2000: 180–2).

This same intensity in social mobilization and mass communication – and more so since they were exacerbated by rapid and unrelenting urbanization – was sustained throughout the 1950s and 1960s. It was also then that Beirut's image as a cosmopolitan, sophisticated polyglot meeting place of world cultures was being embellished.

All the indicators, crude and refined, attest to this overriding reality. From the sharp increases in the flow of domestic and foreign mail, in the number of telephones, and in that of passenger vehicles to the more stupendous growth in the volume and diversity of media exposure (particularly TV, radio and movie attendance), all bespeak appreciable increases in physical and psychic mobility and high levels of consumption throughout society. On these and other related indices, Lebanon enjoyed disproportionately higher rates than those observed in adjoining Arab states. Shortly after independence, for example, Lebanon could already boast over 8,000 passenger vehicles, or about 7 per 1,000 people – considerably more than what Syria, Jordan, Iraq and Egypt had in 1960. By then Lebanon had leapt to 73,000 or close to 40 cars per 1,000, compared to an average of 4 to 6 among those neighboring Arab states (UNESCO statistical yearbook, 1985; Khalaf, 1992). By the early 1920s, Beirut had already three or four cinemas. Unlike in other cities in the Levant, cinemas were not socially and politically contested forms of public entertainment. Cinemas made their first appearance in traditional quarters, sharing makeshift tents with itinerant shadow-puppet shows (karakoz). Others were temporary, located in the upper floors of cafes, merchant hostels (khans) or locandas. As in the case of other novel outlets of popular culture (cafes, bars, billiard lounges, brothels etc), it was the Bourj which became the first permanent space for movie houses. Incidentally, because of their commodious premises and capacity to accommodate large audiences, cinemas were often used as lecture halls, auditoria for French-sponsored charity events and other cultural venues.

Early in the 1950s, if measured by the number of movie seats per capita, Beirut was already living up to its reputation as the movie capital of the world. By then, per capita movie attendance was five per year. In another decade, it increased by fivefold, a close second to Hong Kong (UNESCO, 1965). During the same period, the number of movie theaters leapt from 48 to 170, an increment of twelve new premises per year. The accessibility of such theaters, rendered more appealing by the variety of films, plush surroundings and low prices, only served to whet the appetite of the Lebanese of all classes for this form of public entertainment. Indeed, by then, before the advent of TV and home videos, anticipating, attending and talking about movies was already the undisputed most popular and most absorbing national pastime.

If Lebanon boasted of being the movie capital of the world, on a more enabling and vital dimension it was also a 'nation of journalists'. Their accomplishments in this field were both pace-setting and of long standing. Since the appearance of their first paper in 1858, the Lebanese have long displayed a distinct predilection and talent for establishing papers and periodicals sustained by an irresistible compulsion for reading them. As in other dimensions of public life, the striking penchant the Lebanese evinced for journalism was nurtured and cultivated within a network of family tradition. This intimate association between families and careers in journalism is of long standing. Families, in fact, more than ideological parties, advocacy groups or political platforms have provided the settings within which some of the most gifted journalists received their tutelage and commitments to journalistic careers. Illustrious families such as Aql, Khazin, Taqla, Tueni, Zaidan, Sarruf, Jumayyil, Tibi, Mukarzil, Awad, Taha, Nusuli and Mashnuq, among others, have all produced successive generations of journalists. Fathers served as mentors and role models and, often, had direct impact in initiating scions into the venerable family tradition and in honing their skills and cultivating contacts (for further biographical details see Tueni, 1995).

By 1975, the eve of the civil war, Lebanon had over 400 valid publication licenses. For a country of about 3 million, this is an incredible density of newsprint, perhaps the highest in the world. The majority were politically independent, though a small number might be associated with political groups. Indeed, so independent the press had become that it evolved into an autonomous institution, a 'Fourth Estate', along with the executive, legislative and judicial authorities.

Economic and social historians are keen on attributing Beirut's cosmopolitanism and tolerance to foreign cultures to its mercantile predisposition. Commerce, trade and the exchange of goods and services rest, after all, on the willingness to mix and interact, in a productive mode, with others. Throughout its history, Beirut has lived up to its image as being part of a 'Merchant Republic'. The Bourj, in particular, acted as an irresistible magnet for banks, credit houses and exchange outlets. Look how Charles Issawi depicts the profile of this emblematic prototype:

> Fabulous, yet perfectly authentic, stories are told of the transfer of gold from Mexico to India and China, of the shipment of copper from Franco's Spain to Stalin's Russia and of the sale of a huge consignment of toothbrushes from an Italian firm to a neighboring one – and all directed from and financed by some mangy-looking business house in Beirut. In 1951, when Lebanon's gold trade was at its peak, it was estimated that 30 percent of world gold traffic passed through the country. (Issawi, 1966: 243)

As in virtually all other commercial and industrial enterprises, many of the early resourceful banking and financial houses were strictly family establishments bearing the family's pedigree (Haddad, Chiha, Safar, Sabbagh, Audi, etc). Kinship and family sentiments were not sources of lethargy and wasteful nepotistic favoritism. Rather, they acted as a spur for inventiveness and fierce competition. Banks were so overwhelming in the life of the Central Business District (CBD) that ultimately one of the most important avenues took their name. Recently some of the successful banks have begun to patronize the arts and other outreach cultural programs to rehabilitate traditional artifacts and artisans.

Beirut's ebullient cosmopolitanism was not only reinforced by its Levantine mercantilism and tolerance for foreign incursions. By virtue of its location, composition and historic role as a hybrid place of refuge for dissidents or a gateway for itinerant groups, Beirut has always been a fairly open and free space. Exit from and entry into society has been relatively easy. Indeed, Lebanon and particularly the Bourj at times became much too open, too hospitable and, hence, much too vulnerable to all the vicissitudes of internal and regional disturbances.

The spectacular events sparked by the 'Independence uprising' in the wake of Rafik Hariri's assassination on 14 February 2005 were so riveting in their manifestations and consequences that they drew the attention of the world and drove global powers to take remedial action. Spontaneous and self-propelled, the uprising – largely because it could exploit the commanding setting of Beirut's historic center – displayed so much daring and inventiveness that it evolved into a formidable public sphere. Sustained demonstrations and expressions of collective grievances allowed the protesters to articulate a coherent set of demands and to mobilize normally passive and quiescent groups to participate in popular grass-roots movements in support of the uprising. The by-products were vast in their immediate consequences and promise to be more consequential in their anticipated future reverberations. The massive sustained uprising forced the resignation of the government and precipitated a sharply contested political crisis. It expedited the formulation of two decisive UN resolutions: 1559, calling for the immediate withdrawal of Syrian troops and security agencies from Lebanon, and 1595 to set up an international commission of inquiry into the assassination of Hariri. Perhaps more compelling, in view of its future consequences, the uprising initiated the country's youth into a hands-on and direct education in civic virtues and emancipatory political struggle.

LOCAL, REGIONAL AND GLOBAL ENCOUNTERS

As we have seen, Lebanon has always been caught in the persistent interplay between local, regional and global sources of conflict. The unresolved rivalries at all three levels have compounded the intensity and magnitude of hostility. Since the country, despite contested efforts, is yet to work out a national covenant or pact which can protect it against the disruptive consequences of such destabilization, it continues to be vulnerable to this chronic state of being adrift.

Clearly this is not then the first time that the country – Beirut in particular – faces such predicaments. During earlier confrontations with both Ottoman and French attempts at the production of social space, local builders, architects and other indigenous groups displayed considerable awareness, knowledge and skills relevant to processes of construction and reconstruction underway at the time (Khalaf, 2006).

Since Beirut as capital and imposing port city was subjected to successive planning schemes and the construction of monumental edifices, thoroughfares and public squares, it is instructive to re-examine how such attempts were perceived and implemented. Were local groups, in other words, merely passive recipients in such instances of struggle for power and control over lived space? Or were they active participants who often succeeded in resisting and changing the imperial and colonial impositions? The experience of Beirut, particularly its central square and contiguous urban spaces, is instructive in conceptual and comparative terms. In this respect, Beirut offers another grounded and living instance of the production of social space which departs from common experiences and patterns observed in other settings (see e.g. King 2003; Nasr and Volait, 2003). Beirut's experience was not and is not merely a process of transfer, transplantation or imposition of external visions and schemes on a willing, compliant and non-participating public. More vital perhaps, by disclosing the interplay between the inevitable plurality of forces – local, regional and transnational – involved in the construction of the collective identity of a particular settlement, one is also probing the elements which make up the 'imagined community' of the Bourj, Beirut and Lebanon as a nation-state.

Regardless of what perspective or paradigm one adopts for contextualizing the nature of spatial identities – that is, the perspective of world systems, globalization, postcolonial or postmodern – in the final analysis this requires an understanding of both the broader macro and structural transformations and the nature, scale and the particular manner in which local considerations continue to make their presence felt in redefining and reconstituting social space. Indeed, in some instances, so-called 'postmodern' attributes – i.e. fragmentation, fluid and multiple identities, the mixing of different histories, pastiche, irony, the destruction of the vernacular and provincial – were present in Beirut long before they had appeared elsewhere, including Europe and the US.

No matter, for example, how we define globalization, it involves, as Roland Robertson (1992) reminds us, 'an increasing consciousness of the world as a whole'. He goes on to suggest that:

> [T]he contemporary concern with civilizational, societal (as well as ethnic) uniqueness – as expressed via such motifs as identity, tradition and indigenization – largely rests on globally diffused ideas. In an increasingly globalized world … there is an exacerbation of civilizational, societal and ethnic self-consciousness. Identity, tradition and indigenization only make sense contextually. (Robertson, 1992: 130)

While Anthony King is in agreement that identities are established and validated contextually, he does not maintain that they are usually the outcome of the broad and distant forces of 'globalization'. Instead, he argues that they are usually 'constructed in relation to much more specific, smaller, historical, social and spatial contexts'. He goes on to say that people do 'express their resistance to the global political and economic situations that engulf them, and at the same time may also immerse themselves within these situations' (King, 2003: 10). Such consciousness and proclivity to engage with cosmopolitan encounters were also present in Beirut before the advent of globalism and postmodernity. The identity of some urban Beirutis – if one were to infer this from the architectural styles of their residences, their mannerisms, fashions and other cultural manifestations of everyday life – was also a hybrid of seemingly dissonant and inconsistent features. Expressed more concretely, the Lebanese are certainly becoming more interconnected at all three levels: globally, regionally and locally. They cross over with greater ease. At least they seem less guarded when they do so. They visit areas they never dared to visit before. These and other such symptoms of interconnectedness should not, however, be taken to mean that they are becoming more alike or that they are becoming more homogenized by the irresistible forces of globalization and postmodernity.

On the contrary, and in many instances, attachments to place are becoming more important, not less. Geography, location, territorial and spatial identities have become sharper and more meaningful at the psychic and socio-cultural levels. Such manifestations should not be dismissed as nostalgic or transient interludes destined to 'pass' into 'secular', tenuous and more impersonal or virtual encounters. Indeed, one of the central premises of this book is that we can better understand the emergent socio-cultural identities – even the political and economic transformations – by seeing their manifestations in this ongoing dialectic between *place* and *space*. How, in other words, are *spaces* being transformed into *places* and how, in turn, places degenerate into mere spaces to be occupied and exploited for commercial and mercenary pursuits. Yes, of course, notions like space and place are ordinary, mundane, common-sense everyday terms. Yet they are suffused with meaning and symbolism. Hence they are vital to individual and group identity. It behoves us to explore how they are being played out in Beirut's postwar setting.

If the geography of fear is largely a by-product of the perpetual state of being adrift – unanchored and without direction – where and how does one allay such fears? Manifestations of such fluidity have become more salient recently. A cursory stroll round the rehabilitated districts of central Beirut, and of those under reconstruction, quickly reveals symptoms of such dissonance. First, and doubtless the most striking, is the pronounced dominance of religious edifices, mosques, cathedrals, churches and shrines. In the process of rehabilitation some have appropriated added property and, through the stylistic use of modes of architectural illumination and electronic digital amplification, they have been rendered physically and audibly more overwhelming. While mosques are restrained from extending the use of their premises to non-sacred activities, churches and monasteries have made efforts to host musical recitals, poetry readings and other secular performances and events. Incidentally, Greek Orthodox churches are also restrained from using their premises for other than Gregorian chants and religious choral recitals.

The gargantuan Al-Amin Mosque, inaugurated in 2010, occupies a massive space of about 4000m². It literally dwarfs everything around it. It was funded by three benevolent foundations: Walid Ibn Talal, Rafik Hariri and Al-Amin Mosque Association. Because of its colossal proportions there have been contested negotiations to scale down its height and the number of its protruding minarets so that it will not overshadow the adjoining St George Maronite Cathedral.

If the *sacred* features have become more conspicuous and redoubtable, then so are the *profane*, to invoke Durkheim's classic dichotomy. Any land-use mapping of the district is bound to reveal the dominance of mass consumerism, retail shops, boutiques, restaurants, coffee shops, side-walk cafes, nightclubs and bars. But here as well the global and postmodern (i.e. shopping arcades, internet cafes, chat rooms, fast-food franchises and elegant fashionable boutiques) coexist with provincial outlets. Quite often global franchises (McDonalds, KFC, Pizza Hut, Dunkin Donuts, etc) 'go native' by appropriating local elements such as valet parking and other semiotic images of the vernacular to enhance the appeal of their products and services. Likewise, traditional outlets often copy the scintillating features of their global counterparts to validate their own public images and marketing ploys. Within such a context, it is no longer meaningful to talk about local/global, provincialism/cosmopolitanism, vernacular/universal, space/place, being/becoming, village-in-the-city/global-village etc as though they are distinct, irreconcilable dichotomies. Such polarization and ideal typologies, much like the earlier misplaced dichotomies between the sacred/secular, traditional/

modern, mechanical/organic, are not a reflection of what is in fact grounded in the real world (see Short, 2001: 7–20, for further elaboration).

Such realities must be borne in mind as we explore or anticipate the future national image or collective identity Beirut's Central Square is likely to assume at this juncture in its checkered history. We are, after all, dealing with the convergence or interplay of three problematic and tenuous realities or considerations: postwar Beirut, regional uncertainties and global incursions. Hence the emergent identities in Beirut are blurred and are in perpetual states of being reconstituted and redefined. The views of a growing circle of recent scholars – Ulf Hannerz (1996), H. Bhabha (1994), A. Appadurai (1996), John Short (2001), among others – support such expressions of cultural diversity and hybridity.

COLLECTIVE MEMORY VS. COLLECTIVE AMNESIA

Beirut is not only grappling with the three demons which have ensnared it for so long: the trials and tribulations of a postwar setting, local fragmentation and the unsettling manifestations of unresolved regional and global rivalries. These three demons are not new to Beirut. More recent, however, are some of the compelling consequences of postmodernity and globalism which compound feelings of uncertainty, the vulnerabilities of being adrift and, hence, pervasive fear.

Within this context, issues of collective memory, contested space and efforts to forge new cultural identities begin to assume critical dimensions. How much and what of the past needs to be retained or restored? By whom and for whom? Common as these questions might seem, they have invited little agreement among scholars. Indeed, the views and perspectives of those who have recently addressed them vary markedly. To Ernest Gellner (1987), collective forgetfulness, anonymity and shared amnesia are dreaded conditions to be resisted in all social orders. Perhaps conditions of anonymity, he argues, are inevitable in times of turmoil and upheaval. But once the unrest subsides, internal cleavages and segmental loyalties resurface. MacCannell (1989) goes further to assert that the ultimate triumph of modernity over other socio-cultural arrangements is epitomized not by the disappearance of pre-modern elements but by their reconstruction and artificial preservation in modern society. Similarly, Jedlowski (1990) also maintains that a sense of personal identity can only be achieved on the basis of personal memory.

Paul Connerton (1989) argues that it is collective memory – that is, commonly shared images of the past – which legitimate a present social order. To the extent that people's memories of a society's past diverge, then its members will be bereft of common experiences, perspectives and visions. These memory claims figure significantly in our self-perceptions. Our past history, imagined or otherwise, is an important source in our conception of selfhood. In the final analysis, our self-knowledge, our conception of our own character and potentialities, is, to a large extent, shaped by the way in which we view our own past action (Connerton, 1989: 22). Likewise, Halbwachs argued persuasively that it is primarily through mediating groups such as religion, national ideological or class membership that people are able to acquire and then recall their memories (Halbwachs, 1991). These become the venues for creating and sustaining shared memories. We often forget that for man, as for no other creature, to lose his past is to lose his memory. To lose himself is to lose his identity. History, in this case, is more than just a record of how man becomes what he is. It is the largest element in his self-conception.

Persuasive as such pleas on behalf of collective memory are, particularly with regard to their impact on reconstituting the frayed symptoms of social solidarity and national allegiance, a slew of other scholars make equally persuasive claims on behalf of collective amnesia and social forgetfulness. Benjamin Barber, for example, argues that successful civic nations always entail a certain amount of 'studied historical absentmindedness.' 'Injuries too well remembered', he tells us, 'cannot heal' (Barber, 1996: 167). What Barber is, of course, implying here is that, if the memories of the war and its atrocities are kept alive, they will continue to reawaken fear and paranoia, particularly among those embittered by it. Without an opportunity to forget there can never be a chance for harmony and genuine coexistence. David Lowenthal, in his preface to an edited volume on *The Art of Forgetting* (2001), goes further to underscore the close etymological connection of 'amnesia' with 'amnesty'. He invokes one of the basic premises of Hobbes who, he reminds us, treated forgetting as the basis of a just state and amnesia as the 'cornerstone of the social conduct'. What he termed 'remedial oblivion' was a common strategy of seventeenth-century statecraft (Lowenthal, 2001: p. xi). Lowenthal advances, in this regard, another compelling inference: that much forgetting turns out to be beneficial and enabling rather than a bereavement, a 'mercy' rather than a 'malady': 'To forget is as essential as to keep things in mind, for no individual or collectivity can afford to remember everything. Total recall would leave us unable to discriminate or generalize' (ibid., p. xi).

To reinforce his plea in favor of forgetting as a merciful as well as a mandatory art, Lowenthal makes a distinction between individual and collective forgetting. While the former is largely involuntary, collective oblivion, on the other hand, is mainly:

> Deliberate, purposeful and regulated. Therein lies the art of forgetting – art as opposed to ailment, choice rather than compulsion or obligation. The art is a high and delicate enterprise, demanding astute judgment about what to keep and what to let go, to salvage or to shred or shelve, to memorialize or to anathematize. (Ibid.)

Adrian Forty (2001), in supporting the view that forgetting is an intentional, deliberate and desirable human response, invokes the classic tradition, particularly the perspectives of Durkhiem, Freud, Ernest Renan, Martin Heidegger and a sampling of a few contemporary cultural theorists and philosophers like Michel de Certeau, Walter Benjamin and Paul Connerton. By fulfilling this universal need to forget, which to Forty is essential for sustaining normal and healthy life, groups normally resort to or take shelter in two rather familiar and well-tried strategies. They either construct an artifact, by building monuments, war memorials and the like, that is, a material proxy or substitute for the delicate and fragile nature of human memory. The trauma, senseless destruction and sacrifices are in this case redeemed. Or, and more likely, society resorts to iconoclastic predispositions, by effacing and destroying relics and material heritage from the past.

Both these traditions have been quite salient in Beirut. Indeed, they have provoked an ongoing, often heated, polemic over the architectural heritage of the city and how to memorialize the country's pathological history of protracted civil strife. Critics of Solidere's massive rehabilitation scheme of downtown Beirut continue to decry and berate how much of the city's distinctive archeological heritage was needlessly destroyed in the process of reconstruction. If the recurrent cycles of random violence had devastated much of the city's center and adjoining urban neighborhoods, the reconstruction schemes, the critics often charge, compounded the ruthless destruction by acting more like a merciless bulldozer. When the more divisive issues associated with the war's collective memory – i.e. how, where and in what form can they be recalled – are invoked, manifestations of discord and ambivalence become equally contentious. They always generate and reawaken sharp and heated debate and, thereby, bring out layers of hidden hostility and unresolved fear.

These, clearly, are not merely rhetorical or benign concerns. Nor are Beirut's experiences in this regard unique or unusual. They are embroiled with the tricky issues of collective memory, space and national identity. More explicitly they inform the entangled discourse regarding the connection between objects, memory and forgetting. Adrian Forty in fact (2001) takes us back to the Aristotelian tradition to show us how it was inverted by Freud, by Ernest Renan and, more recently, by Michel de Certeau.

To Forty, the Western tradition of memory since the Renaissance has been founded on the Aristotelian premise that material objects, whether natural or artificial, can act as the analogs or correlates of human memory. As a result such objects may be interpreted as the means by which members of a society may get rid of what they no longer wish to remember. This was predicated on the assumption that memory loss is inevitable through the attrition of time.

Freud's theory of mental process is the antithesis of such an Aristotelian conception of memory. He questioned the presumed relationship between objects and memory. Since to Freud memory is no more than a mental process, he advanced the thesis that in 'mental life nothing that has once been formed can perish – that everything is somehow preserved and in suitable circumstances ... can once more be brought to light' (Freud, 1969: 6). In other words, rather than memory loss taking place over time, as Aristotle had assumed, Freud considered that memory, and thus forgetting, is an active, intentional and desired force, not passive, natural and involuntary. The French philosopher Michel de Certeau views this connection between memory and objects from an interesting and telling perspective. He writes, intuitively, that 'memory is a sort of anti-museum: it is not localizable.' For him, the defining element of memory is that 'it comes from somewhere else, it is outside of itself, it moves things about' (de Certeau, 1984: 108). This is taken to imply that if and when it ceases to display such alteration, when it becomes fixed to particular objects or local artifacts, then it is destined to decay and may well suffer oblivion. Seen in such a light, objects become the enemy of memory. Confining memory will most certainly produce forgetfulness.

Within this context, the reaction of the Lebanese to all the unbearable atrocities and traumas with which they were beset, that they should try to forget, or at least distance themselves from and sanitize, as they appear to be doing, the scars and scares of almost two decades of cruel and senseless violence, is understandable. As the country was preparing itself to commemorate the thirtieth anniversary of its misbegotten civil war on 14 April 1995 a score of voluntary associations were declaring their birth and pronouncing their envisaged programs and strategies for healing, reconciliation and enhancing national consciousness through voluntary and cross-communal work-camps and social welfare projects which cut across and transcend sectarian and local attachments. Interestingly the leaders and spokespersons of these associations are on the whole too young to have witnessed at first-hand the treacherous events of the war. They are also perceptive in launching their programs on the dreaded 'green line' adjoining the National Museum, a site which conjures up images of demarcation, distance and the bounded territoriality of warring factions.

It is the ambivalence and uncertainty with which we behold the past, along with the fear of disappearing, which account for what Lowenthal aptly calls the 'heritage crusade'. In postwar Lebanon this crusade has become so pervasive that it is beginning to assume all the trappings and hype of a national pastime and a thriving industry. Escape into a re-enchanted past has obviously a nostalgic tinge to it. This, however, need not be seen as a pathological retreat into a delusionary past. It could well serve, Bryan Turner has argued, as a redemptive form of heightened sensitivity, sympathetic awareness of human problems and, hence, it could be 'ethically uplifting' (Turner, 1987: 149). As will be argued in the next chapter, it is less of a 'flight' and more of a catharsis for human suffering.

MEDIATING AGENCIES OF SOCIAL FORGETTING

What are the mediating agencies or artifacts in the Bourj which can evolve into effective vectors for the process of social forgetting, or what Hobbes termed 'remedial oblivion'? There is no shortage of candidates. The envisioned 'Archeological Trail', the 'Garden of Forgiveness' under construction, some of the distinct architectural icons or edifices can easily play such a role since they all embody elements of cultural pluralism, tolerance, hybridity and peaceful coexistence. Likewise, some of the debated proposals have also addressed the issues of how to incorporate the Martyrs' Monument (which commemorates the national heroes executed by the Ottomans in 1915 and 1916), or how to envision a war memorial or a monument to celebrate or memorialize all the victims and sacrifices of the civil war. Such efforts become pertinent not to help us dwell on the pathologies of civil and uncivil violence but they can serve as the socio-cultural venues for cultivating the sorely needed outlets for forgetting. Generations of Lebanese, either directly or vicariously, are still old enough to remember those years. In no way have they or can they forget such dark and misbegotten episodes of their past. Indeed, they often remember it so well that they deeply resent being reminded of it. In this sense, as will be shown in the next chapter, the carefree abandon, exuberance and the proclivity of the Lebanese to embrace novelties, crazes and popular pastimes are largely symptomatic of their eagerness to distance themselves from the dreaded memories of the war.

Here again, the longing of the Lebanese for a respite from the beleaguering elements of their collective memory finds parallels in other comparative instances of internecine hostility. For example, the outbreak of violence in former Yugoslavia may well be seen as the outcome of the refusal to forget past events. Likewise, the Northern Irish protracted conflict is symptomatic of the fact that the protagonists – both parties and religious groups – were reluctant to forget the elements of their belligerent past that other groups might no longer feel the urge to remember. Neil Jarman's (2001: 171–95) account of the Irish in Belfast epitomizes graphically the consequences of a people so trapped in their past, so embroiled in reliving their contentious and bloody history, that they are unable to free themselves from the constraints of that conflict-prone history. Selective retention implies that some of the more redemptive and beneficent elements of that past are not celebrated or commemorated with the same passionate intensity. In short, what we remember and what we forget are socially constructed.

From these instances, it is clear how essential to stable political life – indeed to the well-being of individual life as well – is a certain measure of amnesia or social forgetfulness. By re-examining the checkered history of the Bourj it is our hope to reconstruct from its rich and diverse past a history, to paraphrase Forty, 'not of memorials but of amnesiacs!' (Forty, 2001: 8).

It is in this sense that the experience of the Lebanese, particularly their ambivalence regarding how to cope with, let alone incorporate, the barbaric legacy of the war, is not at all unique. The setting in postwar Europe is very instructive in this regard. Indeed, as some historians argue, the relative stability of Western Europe since 1945 has in part been due to that colossal act of collective, consensual forgetting; for example, the divisions between wartime partisans and collaborators which, whatever may be said in private, have been largely forgotten in public (see Forty, 2001: 7). As indicated earlier the very word 'amnesty' denotes a certain measure of public forgetfulness. As Ernest Renan reminds us, most of the social contract theories of the state, upon which modern democracies are based, assume that their members are prepared to forget the more divisive differences which on occasion pull them apart. Renan was unequivocal when he asserted that the 'essence of a nation is that all individuals share a great many things in common also that they have forgotten some things' (quoted in Wolin, 1989: 37). Jens Hanssen and Daniel Genberg (2002) have coined the term 'hypermnesia' to refer to instances in postwar Lebanon of the abundance of overlapping, conflicting and rivaling memories of the war. In their view, such celebrity conceptions of history, indeed, the frequent public debates about collective forgetting, have served to amplify and reinforce this notion of 'collective hypermnesia'. To them the loss of memory is no more than an 'antonym to amnesia ... the inaccessible, passive *other* memory that is triggered inadvertently, to denote a situation where memory is constantly present, multiple and celebrated' (Hanssen and Genberg, 2002: 233). In this sense, the whole experience of Solidere in the reconstruction of downtown Beirut became a hotly contested public debate precisely because it was emblematic of and embodied the discourse over versions and visions for the past and future of city and country.

The threatening effacement of dilapidated vestiges of the past falling prey to early 'clean slate' ideologies ironically produced a public sphere pregnant with divergent versions and visions for past and future of city and country. At this particular juncture the debate represented an effort and commitment to effect a moratorium on the seemingly inevitable and ever accelerated, globalization-induced forgetting. (Hanssen and Genberg, 2002: 234)

The relentless polemics over the remembrance of the Holocaust, America's experience in Vietnam, the repeated *naqbas* (disasters) and *naqsas* (setbacks) Arabs have had to suffer in their misbegotten confrontations with Israel – from the colossal defeat in the Seven Days War to other equally treacherous failures, including the collapse of the Saddam regime in Iraq – and other such atrocities of modern times, always reinvite the some poignant and anguishing public debates. Of course, forgetting always runs the risk of repetition. In this sense, had the Lebanese recalled and learned from all their earlier encounters with civil strife, perhaps the atrocities would not have been as recurrent. The basic dilemma the Lebanese face today is to know how to remember all the ugly atrocities of the war without lessening their horrors. To put it differently, the problem is how to recall the hideous episodes of the war without sanitizing them by making them more tolerable to remember. To attribute the war to external forces by which the country, and Beirut in particular, became no more than a proxy battlefield for other people's wars, is one such effective strategy or alibi the Lebanese continue to resort to. It obviates their guilt and, hence, their direct responsibility for partaking in the horrors. They become no more than surrogate victims of other warring and belligerent groups.

Solidere launched on 18 June 2004 an international competition – 'International Urban Design Ideas' – for Martyrs' Square and the Grand Axis of Beirut. The competition, under the auspices of the Union of International Architects (UIA), drew some 420 applicants from sixty-five countries. Though the results of the competition were announced on 6 May 2005, – National Martyrs' Day – the venture still remains an unrealized design.

This is, of course, regrettable since virtually all the finalists, in one way or another, addressed the issue of what, how and where in the reconstructed Central Square of the city's capital we can memorialize or celebrate some of the disparate elements in the country's checkered history with civil strife. This, too, is a tricky and probing issue. It was bound to invite heated polemic, given the contested views the Lebanese continue to uphold about the war. Will the commemorization be a sober, subdued *memorial* to recall and dwell upon tragic, lamentable and mournful events? Or will it be a celebratory *monument* to revel and bask in the glories of past heroic events?

We often associate dramatic iconoclastic reactions, the deliberate acts of destruction of national symbols, with efforts to mark or celebrate moments of transition from one political era or regime to another. Such riddance of monuments (e.g. destruction of the Berlin wall, Lenin's statue, the Buddha statues in Afghanistan, and more recently Saddam Hussein's statue in Baghdad), often accompanied by the frenzy of aroused masses, is more than just a vengeful act of sheer retribution. It must be seen as a collective attempt to permanently erase or withdraw representations of the maligned or discredited old system that might serve again as vehicles for popular recollection (Küchler, 2001: 53).

The importance we conventionally assign to memorial or monuments, or any visual imagery, is clearly not an invention of the modern world. In a fascinating work, Frances Yates (1966) persuasively traced this back to the age of scholasticism and medieval memory where *memoria,* the conscious evocation of past experience through visual imagery, served to facilitate the spread of devotional learning to laymen. From medieval times onwards, the destruction of such visual imagery appeared to be tantamount to acts of forgetting (Yates, 1966: 99).

Although we are often inclined to use terms like 'memorials' and 'monuments' interchangeably, James Young insists on clarifying the distinct meanings of each. To him *memorials* 'recall only past death or tragic events and provide places to mourn'. On the other hand, there is an element of triumphalism in *monuments*. 'They remain essentially celebratory markers of triumphs and heroic individuals' (Young, 1993: 3). Bearing this subtle distinction in mind, Arthur Danton, in his assessment of the contested Vietnam Veteran Memorial, situates his observations within the polemics of collective memory or the social art of forgetting. Danton is very explicit in this regard. He tells us that

> we erect monuments so that we shall always remember and build memorials so that we shall never forget. Thus, we have the Washington Monument but the Lincoln Memorial. Monuments commemorate the memorable and embody the myths of beginnings. Memorials ritualize remembrance and mark the reality of ends ... Monuments make heroes and triumphs, victories and conquests, perpetually present and part of life. The memorial is a special precinct, extruded from life, a segregated enclave where we honor the dead. With monuments, we honor ourselves. (Danton, 1986: 152)

It is hoped that these introductory considerations, conceptual and otherwise, will serve as a meaningful context to situate and inform the 'story' I narrated about the Bourj's historical transformation and the role it is envisaged to play at this critical juncture in Lebanon's history. From its eventful past, much like its most recent history, a few distinct but related elements stand out: (1) the predisposition of the Bourj to incorporate and reconcile pluralistic and multicultural features; (2) its inventiveness in reconstituting and refashioning its collective identity and public image; (3) its role in hosting and disseminating popular culture, consumerism, mass entertainment and, often, nefarious touristic attractions.

Most of all, as amplified by the riveting popular and emancipatory expressions unleashed by the murder of Hariri, the Bourj can also nurture and play host to some formidable socio-cultural and political transformations. Yes, and perhaps unavoidably, the uprising has given free vent to some of the festive, light-hearted and frivolous forms of popular entertainment and fun-loving activities. These, however, should not detract from the more weighty and consequential concerns and public issues it has already aroused.

FUTURE PROSPECTS

The present is, doubtlessly, a momentous and critical watershed in Beirut's history. Once again, the city center is in the throes of reinventing itself. No other area or space in Lebanon is more ideally situated to serve as an open and engaging public sphere than the Bourj. The chameleon-like receptivity of the Beirutis to adapt to new settings and to experiment with hybrid and cosmopolitan lifestyles must be restored and safeguarded.

By virtue of its openness and fluidity, the Bourj was not only receptive to a diversity of lifestyles and ideological trends. It was akin to a gadfly. It has seemed at its best when playing host to unconventional activities, or unorthodox events which run against the grain and defy normative expectations. In this sense, it served as a safety value, a cultural broker, a playground or sanctuary to test society's limits of tolerance.

Given all the internal, regional and global uncertainties, it is understandable why the Lebanese today seem inclined to find refuge either in religious and primordial affinities or in the faddish and seductive appeals of mass culture and commodified consumerism. Both spatially and otherwise, such efforts of proxy refuge have become much more pronounced in postwar Beirut. The challenge of urban planning and design is to consider strategies through which the redemptive, healing and enabling features of a common public sphere or playground can be nurtured and reinforced while safeguarding the Bourj from slipping into a 'dystopia' of a fashionable resort or a ritualized sanctuary for competing confessional communities trying to assert their public identities. Beirut's history in this regard, as alluded to earlier, has not been an unmixed blessing.

By virtue of its location, composition and its historical role as a place of refuge for dissidents or a gateway for itinerant groups, the Bourj has always been a fairly open and free space. Exit from and entry into society has been relatively easy. Indeed, some argue that Lebanon became much too open, too hospitable and, hence, too vulnerable to the vicissitudes of internal and regional disturbances. It made itself vulnerable to abuse by the very forces which sought it as a haven from repression or homelessness. A free press, uncensored media, absence of exchange controls, a 'free zone' in Beirut's port, secret bank accounts, liberal migration laws, receptivity to novelties and fads, progressive and permissive lifestyles all reinforced the discordant dualism inherent in its character as a free and open society. Hence its generative and positive attributes were often undermined by subversive elements and deplorable consequences. Beirut became all too often no more than an expedient conduit, a transit point, for the trafficking and recycling of displaced groups, goods, capital and ideas.

Naturally, such trafficking was not always of a desirable and lawful character. Inevitably, Beirut became notorious for smuggling, arms-running, trading in drugs, black-marketing of illicit contraband products and other nefarious activities. Perhaps more damaging was the abandon with which dissident groups exploited this freedom to launch vilifying press campaigns and plots against repressive regimes in the region. This only served to arouse the suspicion and retributive strategies of the targeted states or groups against Lebanon. On both counts, the country, and Beirut in particular, were unjustly victimized.

Throughout its long and checkered history, the Bourj, as we have seen, has always been able to preserve some of the malleable elements of its local traditions without being indifferent to the incessant transformations and novel encounters it has had to accommodate. It is this receptivity to being eclectic and adaptive in its cross-cultural contacts which accounts for its survival as a cosmopolitan public sphere. Incidentally there is consensus among scholars who have recently been revisiting the intellectual roots of cosmopolitanism (as a concept, mental predisposition, way of life or political project) that it is fundamentally shaped by ideals of citizenship and civil virtues which the potential cosmopolitan derives from the supportive networks of his small social groups and how these are transferred to broader forms of solidarity, autonomy and empowerment (Nussbaum, 1997). Here, again in other words, *roots* could well serve as *routes* or venues through which seemingly cloistered communities could retain their local and parochial attachments while being receptive to new cultural encounters.

The politics of civil society, as John Keane (2001) and Iris Young (1990) among others insist on reminding us, is emancipatory in at least two vital senses. First, it enlarges the sphere of autonomy, particularly by providing public spaces based on trust, reciprocity and dialogue. Second, it provides venues for the mobilization of multiple voices and, hence, political empowerment. Incidentally, Young here makes a useful distinction between *autonomy,* which is largely the sphere of the private, where groups can make decisions that affect primarily their own welfare without interference by others, and *political empowerment* which calls for effective participation in all decisions that affect the public welfare (Young, 1990: 250–2).

Both are particularly relevant strategies at this critical watershed in

Lebanon's history caught between the throes of postwar rehabilitation and the disquieting manifestations of global and postmodern transformations. The promise of autonomy is inherent after all in this ability to encourage the active engagement and self-management of the myriad of local voluntary associations which have mushroomed during the past decade. Among other things this calls for dissenting and oppositional politics and the provision of venues for cultural resistance. Political empowerment, on the other hand, implies a shift from the essentially private and parochial concerns of civil society to the sphere of political community. Here politics become a struggle for inclusion, an opportunity for self-actualization and a form of social justice that acknowledges the needs and priorities of different groups.

There is also another sense in which the concern for autonomy and empowerment can be particularly redemptive in Lebanon. Given the regional and global constraints, it is understandable why Lebanon might not be able to safeguard its national sovereignty or contain some of the global forces which undermine its political independence and economic well-being. At the sociocultural and psychic level, however, the opportunities to participate in such voluntary outlets can do much to nurture some of the civil virtues which will reinforce prospects for greater measures of autonomy and empowerment.

Chapter 3

Consumerism in a Traumatized Society

It is in acquiring, using and exchanging things that individuals come to have social lives.

(Celia Lury, *Consumer Culture*. 1996: 12*)*

To consume is to make more sense of a world where all that is solid melts into air.

(Néstor García Canclini, *Consumers and Citizens,* 2001: 42)

Consumer society manages to render non-satisfaction permanent. One way of achieving such an effect is to denigrate and devalue consumer products shortly after they have been hyped into the universe of consumer's desires ... What starts as a need must end as a compulsion or addiction.

(Zygmunt Bauman, *Consuming Life,* 2007: 21)

The most striking and unmistakable impression Lebanon evokes, doubtless a reflection of its Janus-like character, is the arresting beauty of its captivating landscape and the jarring intrusion of the marketing features of its mercantile and consumer culture. Hence, it is understandable why its merchandizing attributes, particularly since they are also associated with the proletarization of society, should arouse mixed reactions.

The penchant for dazzling display among Lebanon's nouveaux riches and their impulse to outdo one another in ostentatious spending have become a national pastime and the most defining elements in their national character. Consumer society, as George Orwell depicted it, is the 'air we breathe'. This irresistible desire, the acquisitive impulse to amass and display material goods, is expected to disappear during dark times of uncertainty, economic risks or political unrest. Postwar interludes are supposed to invite moods of introspection, sobriety and restraint. In Lebanon they have instead unleashed forces of exuberance and an insatiable appetite for novelties, acquisitiveness and frivolities.

Over the years, Lebanon and Beirut in particular have in this regard enjoyed a slew of auspicious and flattering descriptions: a Paris or Switzerland of the Arab world, a fairly open, engaging and spirited cosmopolitan capital. Recently however, representations have been far from inviting or favorable. Beirut's public image, at least the one most salient in the global media and on websites, has degenerated into being a perverse chameleon-like city, catering to any nefarious whim or reprehensible desire. Hence, attributions bordering on the grotesque and obscene are legion: 'Sin City', 'Sex tourist capital', 'Gay and Lesbian capital', 'Nightlife capital', 'Hedonistic Playground', 'Plastic Surgery capital', a 'haven for shoppers' and of course 'Hizbullah Land'.

Such perceptions, sensational as they might be, do not depart much from grounded and lived realities. Lebanon today is virtually blanketed by advertizing billboards displaying the latest state-of-the-art technology. In certain regions, like Metn and Kisrwan, one could easily imagine having been transposed to Las Vegas or any of the suburban sprawls adjoining major Euro-American cities. The barrage of billboards, giant posters and neon-logos which assault the gaze is testimony that Lebanon's advertising sector, with all the setbacks it has suffered since 2005, is still the most creative and dynamic powerhouse in the Arab world.

This is largely a reflection of the country's laissez-faire traditions, a climate of free-market competition, liberal censorship restrictions and, above all, the ingenuity and aspirations of the Lebanese to be one of the most vibrant retail centers in the Middle East. The media and publicity industries have proven credentials, particularly in being able to deliver inventive products employing the latest electronic and digital technologies, and under unstable and adverse conditions. This has enhanced their credibility as export industries. Many of the fairly young and gifted talent in the region, particularly the Gulf, Iraq and Jordan, 'are bred, groomed and nurtured here' (Oxford Business Group, 2006: 149).

Incidentally, although programs in marketing and graphic design have been established during the past decade, universities and colleges train about 6,000 students per year. Lebanon, clearly, cannot absorb all this talent. Hence, as in other sectors of 'the creative industries', they become part of the country's major exports and thereby contribute further to its brain-drain.

The surge in consumerism, as this chapter will argue, particularly its stylized, sensational and hedonistic features, is also an expression of the anxieties and uncertainties of the new petty bourgeoisie and other excluded and marginalized groups. These in Lebanon make up largely the lower echelons of the service class, semi-professionals and small business, along with the unemployed and disenfranchised youth. In a traumatized society, which is also highly commodified, accessible outlets for shopping, popular entertainment and mass culture become expedient venues to allay some of the uncertainties of individuals groping to find meaning and a coherent self-identity. As will be amplified later, in times of public stress, people are more inclined to find comfort and excitement in the ever-changing variety of goods and cultural products. Under the pressure of advertising, it becomes increasingly difficult to avoid such temptations, even if they are delusionary and artificial.

Though the current, almost global, concern with consumerism, particular overconsumption, has an environmental edge to it, some of the recent sociological literature makes an effort to transcend the fairly narrow and partly biophysical perspectives. Instead, it embraces issues of community, work meaning, freedom and the overall quality of life. One such treatment is the edited volume by Princen, Maniates and Conca (2002) in which they make a plausible distinction between *consumerism* and *commoditization*. The former involves the 'crass elevation of material acquisitions to the status of a dominant social paradigm' (Princen et al., 2002: 3). Commoditization, on the other hand, involves the 'substitution of marketable goods and services for personal relationships, self-provisioning, culture, artistic expression and other sources of well-being' (ibid., p. 3).

By recognizing that consumer choices are not isolated acts of rational decision-making, the concern shifts to considering such choices as part of an individual attempt to find meaning, status and identity. Hence, commoditization in this regard becomes the 'tendency of commercial forces to colonize everyday action, converting more and more of life's activities to purchasing decisions' (ibid., p. 15). Anthony Giddens (1991), two decades ago, was keen to remind us, in almost identical terms, that forging a meaningful self-identity becomes transformed into a process of acquiring the desired goods and lifestyles:

> To a greater or lesser degree, the project of the self becomes translated into one of the possession of desired goods and the pursuit of artificially framed styles of life ... The consumption of ever-novel goods becomes in some part a substitute for the genuine development of self; appearance replaces essence as the visible signs of successful consumption come actually to outweigh the use-values of the goods and services in question. (Giddens, 1991: 198)

Giddens also notes that though mass consumption is inevitably associated with standardization, the consumer is far from a duped and passive recipient. He reacts creatively by combining or rearranging the items of mass consumption to accommodate his own preferences.

As in other commercial ventures where the promise of quick returns and the cash nexus prevails, unrestrained liberalism easily spills into uncensored permissiveness. Hence racy lingerie ads and other graphic erotic images not only tower above busy motorways but can be encountered next to schools, religious establishments and other sensitive places. So explicit and suggestive are the campaigns that they have lately provoked a public outcry over their risqué, indecent and outlandish character. Political parties and religious figures have called on the government to apply more stringent controls, but these appeals do not appear to have had any tangible effect in restraining such excesses. Lebanon, as will be shown later, remains the only Arab country to still permit tobacco advertising. Efforts to control some of the detrimental consequences of excessive smoking in public places (and there have been quite a few initiatives) have all been in vain thus far.

Given this rampant commercialization, it is not surprising that the average Lebanese, whether aware of it or not, faces everyday situations where he is being enticed, nudged or compelled to convert himself and the objects he consumes into an attractive and desirable commodity. This self-presentation, particularly in a small and closely knit society, becomes highly marketable. Groups, as a result, try hard, using every possible means at their disposal, to enhance their 'social capital' by catching the attention of the public gaze. In this sense, as will be elaborated in the next chapter, appearance, style and image become the basis for decision-making in everyday life. Put simply, *the question is no longer 'is this a good thing to do?' but 'does it look good?'*

PERCEPTIONS OF CONSUMERISM

If consumerism has become such an important vector through which vital and consequential discourses are being formulated, then it should not be dismissed as merely a superfluous diversion. At this particular socio-cultural interlude in the checkered political history of Lebanon, its manifestations and consequences can no longer be overlooked. Virtually all the vital issues of collective identity, socio-cultural differences, lifestyle inequalities and exclusions (gender, ethnicity, communal and sectarian loyalties, social status) are shaped and reinforced through consumerism. To Alan Warde, the purposes and functions of consumption, despite its underlying complexity, are very clear:

> Consumption comprises a set of practices which permit people to express self identity, to mark attachment to social groups, to accumulate resources, to exhibit social distinction, to ensure participation in social activities, and more things besides. Among issues still subject to debate is the extent to which consumption practices respond to these different social objectives. This provides some potentially rich sources of theoretical disagreement. (Warde, 1996: 304)

Initial reactions to consumerism, at least in its early eighteenth-century phase in most Western societies, acquired traditional Christian moral undertones. Typically, three underlying pathologies were seen as intrinsic in excessive consumerism: greed, gluttony and pursuing false gods (Stearns, 2001: 62). By the early nineteenth century, the attacks started to focus on issues of poverty and how the underclass were being driven into deeper impoverishment by purchasing things they did not actually need. These ethical perceptions prevailed as critics started to associate a growing level of illness with overindulgence – in the words of R. H. Tawney (1920), 'the acquisitiveness of a sick society'.

Two closely related views can be discerned here. In the first place, as reminded by etymologists, consumption itself had two meanings: the buying of goods, but also respiratory diseases associated with tuberculosis. Hence, in the latter sense, one can actually die from consumption. In fact, some critics deliberately employed this double meaning to reinforce their rapacious attacks on consumerism. In the second pathological treatment, reference was normally made to specific diseases of the stomach; namely appetite, where overindulgence could literally have a deleterious effect on the body. This, of

course, spoke of the virtues of plain food, using this as a symbol of moderation and self-restraint.

At the time of rapid urbanization the abuses of consumerism began to be
associated with the alienating and unsettling features of the city life. In the
United States, in particular, around the 1930s, a series of so-called purifica-
tion movements were directed against the twin evils of commercialism and
sexuality. Of particular interest was the campaign of Sylvester Graham, to
shelter Americans from the excesses of market society. His remedies, which
ultimately were widely accepted and globalized, focused on the virtues of
pure food and plain diets to guard against commercial products with excessive fats and other impurities. Vegetarianism was not only associated with
healthy grains (e.g. those contained in the Graham cracker and eventually
Kellogg and other pure products), but also to prevent overstimulation associated with unrestrained sexuality and shopping. These and other crusades
legion at the time continued to sustain this linkage between excessive consumerism and the moral and physical well-being of a society (for further
details, see Horowitz, 1993; Williams, 1985). Obsessive concerns with satisfy-
ing private material desires are often denigrated, perhaps reflecting on the
word's original meaning: 'to devour, waste and spend' (Williams, 1985).

The escalation of consumerism, especially during the late nineteenth
century and into the early twentieth, generated another and more acute
round of disparaging reactions against it. This time, European critical voices
became more ascendant. They also addressed fairly Euro-centered issues,
namely, gender, class distinctions and anti-consumerist elements. Workers
and lower-class groups came under attack because, in their emulation of the
upper and leisure classes, they were impelled to consume items not on the
basis of legitimate needs but for their symbolic status distinction. Women,
incidentally, were not spared. Indeed, adverse reactions became visibly
sharper and derogatory. In France, Emile Zola devoted an entire novel *Au
Bonheur des Dames* (*Shop Girls of Paris*, 1833) to department stores and their
allure for 'flighty and frivolous' women. He was ambivalent as to who was
more at fault: the greedy storeowners for their salacious temptations or the
'empty-head' women for dutifully succumbing to their devious ploys.

In the same year (1833) Balzac came out with another classic which berates
women for their 'romantic fantasies, cajolements and impotent affectations
of the boudoir'. Balzac was also contemptuous of the indolent moneyed
classes, suffused with greed, vanity and hubris, who 'seek pleasure without
ennui':

The irrationality of this world is equaled by its weakness and its licentiousness. It is greedy of time to the point of wasting it. Seek in it for affection as little as for ideas. Its kisses conceal a profound indifference, its urbanity a perpetual contempt. It has no other fashion of love. Flashes of wit without profundity, a wealth of indiscretion, scandal, and above all, commonplace. This hollow life, this perpetual expectation of a pleasure which never comes, this permanent ennui and emptiness of soul, heart, and mind, the lassitude of the upper Parisian world, is reproduced on its features, and stamps its parchment faces, its premature wrinkles, that physiognomy of the wealthy upon which impotence has set its grimace, in which gold is mirrored, and whence intelligence has fled. (Coser, 1963: 248)

Balzac was most disparaging about the 'exorbitant movement of the proletariat and the corrupting influences of the two classes ... who are whipped on by an inexorable goddess – the necessity for money, glory, and amusement'. He went as far as to blame such excesses for the ugliness of the Parisian physiognomy. In his sardonic and biting style, he drew a stark contrast with some of the positive things he said about the humanity in the East:

The excessive pleasure which is sought for incessantly by the great, explain the normal ugliness of the Parisian physiognomy. It is only in the Orient that the human race presents a magnificent figure, but that is an effect of the constant calm affected by those profound philosophers with their long pipes, their short legs, their square contour, who despise and hold activity in horror, whilst in Paris the little and the great and the mediocre run and leap and drive, whipped on by an inexorable goddess, Necessity – the necessity for money, glory, and amusement. Thus, any face which is fresh and graceful and reposeful, any really young face, is in Paris the most extraordinary of exceptions; it is met with rarely. Should you see one there, be sure it belongs either to a young and ardent ecclesiastic or to some good abbé of forty with three chins. (Coser, 1963: 248)

Naturally, consumerism could not avoid being politicized. Changes targeted specific groups. In Europe, for example, a new kind of anti-Semitism developed in the final decades of the nineteenth century. Jews were vulnerable on many issues, but their prominent roles as owners of department stores loomed very high. More so since they were blamed for arousing the appetites of otherwise fairly moderate and ascetic Christians. By the 1920s, Nazism, partly as an extension of earlier anti-Semitic sentiments, harbored a pronounced anti-consumerist bias. Jewish store keepers were resented for being ruthlessly competitive and chauvinistic and, hence, bound to draw business away from other groups. Nazis, it should be recalled, placed primacy on and expected absolute loyalty and deference to the state, race and the Fuehrer. Any diversion, by way of individual consumption, was denounced as a distraction. It seems they were particularly repulsed by new fashions, since they enticed consumers to discard some of the traditional costumes like the flowered skirts and aprons popular in Austria and Southern Germany (see Stearns, 2001: 64). Socialists and left-leaning intellectuals were naturally averse to consumerism, particularly when associated with class inequalities under capitalism. They particularly decried frivolous and unproductive spending and light-hearted leisure.

Such polemic aside, there is already a substantial and growing theoretical tradition from Thorstein Veblen, the Frankfurt School to Pierre Bourdieu, Zygmunt Bauman, Mike Featherstone and, more recently, Celia Lury, Alan Warde, Elizabeth Wilson and John Fiske – to mention a few – that can be judiciously applied to elucidate and account for some of the striking manifestations and consequences (both enabling and disabling) of excessive consumerism in Lebanon. Without taxing the reader with a tedious theoretical exposition, I will briefly extract a few conceptual considerations to shed light on some of the unusual manifestations of consumerism in Lebanon. A good beginning is Veblen's classic, *The Theory of the Leisure Class* (1899). Though written over a hundred years ago and was the product of a particular time and place, what he was describing, often with a detached and bemused eye, we take now for granted. It also allows one to expose some of the unusual anomalies of consumerism in Lebanon.

Veblen grew up on a farm of rural Minnesota and was reared in a Norwegian Protestant family. This was the Midwest of America before the advent of mass consumption; before the mass media and mass advertising; before credit cards and shopping malls. Given his Puritan upbringing, Veblen praised workmanship and other derivative precepts of the work ethic, frugality and accountability for one's time and resources. Such premises must have informed his thinking about conspicuous consumption and leisure. While conspicuous consumption is generally defined as the ostentatious display of wealth, the value Veblen placed on what he termed the 'instinct of workmanship', or productive work, is evident in his perception of conspicuous consumption as the 'unproductive consumption of goods' and leisure as the 'non-productive consumption of time' (Veblen, 1899). Hence, the element of waste is common to both consumption and leisure.

It is pertinent to point out that, in the evolutionary model of Veblen, conspicuous consumption eventually replaces conspicuous leisure as the primary means of displaying one's pecuniary status. The implications of this are self-evident. In any fairly modern society, characterized by a high degree of anonymity and mobility, it is difficult to display free time. It is far easier to be conspicuous on the basis of the goods one has purchased. Strangers passing each other on the street have no other option but to judge reputability or worth by observing the consumer goods each is displaying. *What and how one consumes, in other words, says a lot about who we are.* Increasingly, it is becoming our paramount source of identity and well-being. The most visible way to show that one has wealth is to conspicuously consume goods; to demonstrate that one has enough money to waste it on useless or on overtly expensive goods. Social worth or honor is above all based on wealth. This to Veblen is the 'fundamental canon of conspicuous waste'. In order for expenditure to be reputable, in other words, it must be wasteful. This is also a reflection of the disdain and contempt groups have for manual labor.

In his interpretation of the conspicuous display of wealth Veblen included prestigious items such as clothes, furs, jewels and even wives. One aspect of consumption that Veblen did try to clarify was the propensity for emulation or 'invidious comparison' (Veblen, 1899: 109). This propensity, he suggested, was a pervasive trait of human nature and stemmed from the need to detach and distance oneself from the mundane (Slater, 1998). It is understandable in this regard why distancing oneself from productive labor, that is, not having to work, particularly in demeaning occupations, goes a long way to set the 'leisure classes' apart from the rest (for further elaboration, see Szmigin, 2003: 134–6).

Veblen's theory of consumption has been described as a 'trickle-down' model (Davis, 1992: 110). The leisure class is the point of origin for all reputable consumer goods. And 'each class envies and emulates the class next above it in the social scale' (Veblen, 1899: 103). Veblen claims that when the lower strata adopt a certain consumer product, the leisure class loses interest in it. A consumer product is no longer a luxury nor a signifier of wealth if both the lower classes and the leisure class are consuming it. Thus the leisure class is forced to search out new consumer products, and in a way reproduce itself (Ritzer, 2001: 212).

Many of the recent manifestations of consumerism in postwar Lebanon can still be understood within the context of Veblen's classic depiction of the 'leisure class' as a new social group in society. This new 'class', or social category, is currently seeking to demonstrate its status publicly through the use of consumer goods in leisure practices. Its defining feature, according to Veblen, is 'a conspicuous abstention from all useful employment'. This abstention or disregard for work is made more visible or conspicuous by a spectacular display of consumption or indulgence in idle forms of *dignified repose*. The elevation of one's taste or public image becomes an expression of distance from the world of work. One is more 'refined' or 'cultivated' when one is not soiling or demeaning oneself with cheap manual labor. This is, after all, what defines the so-called nouveaux riches: emerging social groups who seek material goods or idle leisure to disguise their humble origins and assert their social pretensions.

Observers differ as to whether such manifestations are part of a 'trickle-down theory' or the opposite. Does it, in other words, assume a downward or upward direction? Some of the conventional perspectives – particularly when exploring change in fashion, lifestyle and popular culture – speak of the former. They maintain that basically it is a process of emulation of the upper classes once the lower classes appear to have caught up with them. This implies, of course, that conspicuous consumption – whether it is manifested in fashions or as we shall see in the conversion of intimate family gatherings and celebrations into spectacles – is largely a by-product of class competition. Those who support a upward trend speak of a 'chase and flight' process, since in most societies lower status groups are actively chasing after and emulating those above them (McCracken, 1988).

Incidentally, Veblen, though inclined towards a trickle-down paradigm, did not uphold a strictly class perspective. To him the desire for status and prestige, as suggested earlier, is a 'natural' feature of all human societies. It could be observed everywhere, even in relatively egalitarian groupings. 'No class of society, not even the most abjectly poor, forgoes all customary conspicuous consumption' (Veblen, 1899: 85). More pertinent to the situation in Lebanon, Veblen spoke of the pleasures of purchase as a form of exhibitionism. *Wealth in such instances is not a triumph over others but a means of attracting attention, of standing out and being seen* (Finkelstein, 2007: 202–3).

It should be remarked, as noted by Featherstone (1991), Campbell (1987) and Warde (1991), among others, that the impulse to emulate is not only driven by a desire for social status. It is also sparked and sustained by hedonism, escapism, fantasy and, as we shall see, by the allure of kitsch and the spectacle. These, along with the thrills of novelty, become strategies, in the language of Erving Goffman (1963), to bolster a damaged or vulnerable identity.

One of the most aberrant and grotesque manifestations of this compelling impulse is that it comes, in Lebanon as elsewhere, at a high price: the preponderance of piracy and counterfeiting. In meeting the mounting demand, retailers display no restraint in selling pirated products. Nor are consumers likely to entertain any moral qualms in purchasing them. No commodity or product is spared, particularly fashionable brand names, since visible labels readily attract the public gaze. Consequently, fashion outlets are prime victims, with unscrupulous retailers and wholesalers hawking cheap imitations at fractions of the price. This is also true of other commodities linked to global networks such as car parts, pharmaceuticals, entertainment and sportswear. Despite its comparatively small size, the music and video industry stands out in this regard. Beirut can boast of being the Middle East's most vibrant music industry. Perhaps because Virgin's anchor Megastore is located in the exclusive downtown district of Beirut, the entire industry is handicapped by the fact that it is estimated that 70 percent of all music purchases are pirated. Sportswear famous brands, like Adidas and Nike, claim that they could be losing over one-third of their revenue from piracy (for further details, see *Oxford Business Group*, 2005: 130–1).

The open disdain the average Lebanese harbors for manual work is compounded by his indulgence in both leisure and consumption. In other words, contrary to Veblen's basic premise that consumption will displace leisure, what one can readily observe in Lebanon is that both coexist. Unlike other societies Lebanon has not as yet made the transition from conspicuous *leisure* to conspicuous *consumption*. Hence the country suffers the consequences of both. Take a casual stroll through any of the neighborhoods or quarters of Beirut, especially in urban settings dense with coffee houses and side-walk cafes. At any time of the day they are usually full of able-bodied, middle-aged men squandering precious time in idle chatter or in playing backgammon or cards while puffing on their sweet-scented hookahs. Yes, this is perhaps a stereotypical image; a hackneyed cliché. It carries though more than just a hint of truth. One would not decry such behavior as only an occasional reprieve from the toils of work. Given the mounting incidence of disguised unemployment, along with a culture which values dignified repose and not soiling one's hands with demeaning labor, such outlets are bound to become excessive and wasteful.

This is not, it should be noted, a purely urban phenomenon. On a drive through any suburb, town or villages, on a Sunday, the outward manifestations are striking and of fairly recent origins. One is struck by the preponderance of itinerant, mostly Asian and foreign unskilled labor. On Sundays they are more visible because they seem to have overhauled the demographic composition of the host villages and towns. There are estimated to be about 200,000 Asian domestic workers (i.e. about one for every four households) in Lebanon. Since Sunday is their day off, they virtually take over the public squares, side-walks and gathering haunts. With their colorful national garb, distinctive ethnic dialects and habit of bonding in groups, they seem more preponderant. Lately, they have discovered the joys of scooters and motor-bikes. They can be seen swerving back and forth through the town's main streets. They too, in Veblen terms, have earned the privilege to display their conspicuous consumption.

The growing volume of foreign, and mostly itinerant, labor is not just made up of Asian domestics – Filipinos, Sri Lankans or Ethiopians. Virtually all other low-skilled occupations are a monopoly of non-nationals, such as Egyptian gas-station attendants, Palestinian and Syrian construction workers, Asian street-cleaners and garbage collectors. As elsewhere, Russian and East European women are employed in other stigmatized forms of employment: massage parlors, nightclubs, bars, commercialized sexwork and prostitution. A common scene in downtown Beirut, particularly on weekends when it is open to pedestrian traffic, is the large number of Asian domestics who are carrying babies or looking after infants playing in open courtyards and squares. Clearly the entrenched contempt the Lebanese continue to harbor for manual and other demeaning work, along with the availability of foreign labor willing to be engaged in such forms of employment, allows a fairly large portion of the population to pursue seemingly non-productive pastimes.

Conspicuous leisure and conspicuous consumption provoked the moral outrage of Veblen, but it was the compelling tradition of the Frankfurt School which sustained this concern. Even prior to the threats of postmodernity and globalization, scholars like Max Horkheimer, Theodor Adorno, Walter Benjamin and Hebert Marcuse were already aware of the inevitable and dire consequences of popular culture and mass consumerism. Hence in much of their writing, especially during the period between two world wars, they were exposing the pathologies of cultural mediocrity, the tendency to induce passivity, uniformity of mass consumerism, narcissistic and hedonistic personalities, the demise of public participation and environmental damage. Such critics were often associated with some of the more general critique of capitalism, especially the disparaging consequences of excessive commodification.

It was Erich Fromm in *Escape from Freedom* (1941), in the tradition of the Frankfurt School, who alerted us further – by a judicious combination of Marxist and Neo-Freudian perspectives – to some of the unsettling consequences of modern capitalism. As people are released, he tells us, from the primordial ties of kinship, community and religion, they gain freedom and emancipation. They are made more rational and secular but paradoxically more vulnerable and anxiety-prone. In other words, greater opportunities for choice open doors to an increase in anxiety. In the language of Fromm, man gained freedom *from*, but not the positive sense freedom *to* mobilize this liberation in creative and purposive forms of participation in the public sphere. One way out of this anxiety is to seek refuge in any of the new modes of 'false consciousness' – from gurus, religious figures, political extremists to self-help purveyors. Writing in the early 1940s Fromm was naturally trying to account for why totalitarian ideologies and political regimes started to appeal to the uprooted and unanchored masses.

In his classic, *The Hero with a Thousand Faces*, Joseph Campbell (1949) advanced the interesting thesis, paraphrasing the seminal work of Max Weber on charisma, that heroes and their associated myths help us make sense of our lives. They help us in understanding better how ordinary public figures, often with questionable qualifications, are endowed with charisma and supernatural powers and elevated into mythical popular leaders. To Campbell the need for magic, ritual, heroes and celebrities is greatest in a techno-science culture where the concept of God and spirituality are undermined. Lebanon is clearly not such a setting. There it is the pervasive culture of fear, uncertainty and ambivalence which induces people to invest celebrity and stardom with symbolic meaning to bolster their threatened identity. Though not of direct concern here, one could easily account for the emergence of such populist political figures in various segments of Lebanese society. The 'aura' and 'charisma' such leaders enjoy can only be partly due to their exceptional personal endowments or the cogency and relevance of their message or its rational and ideological underpinnings. To a large extent, as Weber reminds us, it is also a reflection of mass psychology and the symbolic meanings uprooted and anxious groups assign to leaders.

Kaelen Wilson-Goldie prefaces her recent essay on 'Guerilla Marketing' (2009) with the following:

Walk through the streets of virtually any neighbourhood in Beirut and you'll find the faces of political leaders – past and present, local and foreign – plastered onto construction walls; building facades and shuttered storefronts. Lebanon's president, Michel Suleiman, has gone so far as to call for an end to the relentless postering, but his pleas have been largely ignored, and the city is still marked by ubiquitous images, large and small of Hassan Nasrallah, Imad Mughniyeh, Nabih Berri, Musa Sadr, Michel Aoun, Rafik Hariri, Saad Hariri, Samir Kassir, Gebran Tueni, Pierre Gemayel, Bashir Gemayel, Elie Hobeika, Egypt's Gamal Abdel Nasser, Syria's Hafez and Bashar Assad and Iran's Ayatollah Ruhollah Khomeini.

Some of the city's posters are tattered and torn while others are freshly pasted, evidence of the ongoing process of marking territory as loyal to one faction or another. Some of the names and faces on the posters have changed over the years, but the poses, slogans, sentiments and styles are recycled again and again, an apt metaphor for the politics of a country that seems cursed to continuously replay the sectarian conflicts of its civil war. (Wilson-Goldie, 2009: 1)

She goes on to maintain that 'what haunts the streets of Beirut is not the scars of wars past – though they are still visible, on buildings pockmarked by bombshells and bullet holes – but the specter of conflicts future, whose scripts are foretold by the posters jostling for prominence in what passes for public space' (ibid., p. 2).

Beyond Weber some psychoanalysts have gone further to argue that the 'discourse of capitalism' does not leave room for love and human tenderness, especially not any space for sublime courtly love. Instead, what we are witnessing today is an increase in narcissistic illusions and a push towards sexuality and permissiveness that hopefully brings some lost *jouissance*. But this is far from being an unmixed blessing. In a society fixated on the idea of choice, matters of sexuality and love may at first seem liberating. For young Lebanese adults how wonderful it might seem to finally feel liberated from parental control and the normal constraints of society. But, as Renata Salecl rightfully cautions us, such 'freedom' does not bring satisfaction. On the contrary, it actually limits it:

In analyzing human desires, psychoanalysis has from the beginning linked desire with prohibition. For the subject to develop a desire for something, there have to be boundaries and objects of desire that are off limits. The solution is not to get rid of the limit in order to finally fuse with the object of desire, but to be able to somehow 'cherish' the very limit and perceive the object of desire as worthy of our striving precisely because it is inaccessible. (Salecl, 2008: 363)

Salecl goes further to expose a special problem of particular relevance to the frustrations of young Lebanese. She argues that 'when the will to *jouissance* dominates the social field, brotherly solidarity is replaced by competitive rivalry. This is where exacerbation of social hate emerges' (ibid., p. 364). In Lebanon this is also a reflection of an unusual demographic reality. As will be amplified later, given the disproportionate brain-drain in manpower, the sex ratio is dramatically skewed. Estimates suggest that the imbalance could be as high as four or five women for every one man. Hence, the eligible young man, because he is scarce, becomes a cherished cultural 'catch'. Women compete, employing a variety of ploys and strategies – from eroticizing their bodies to sexual permissiveness – to exclude other women from the competition. In the process female bonding, sentiments of sisterhood or participation in female social movements to challenge patriarchy take a back seat (Yazbek, 2007).

Furthermore, and this is certainly a reflection of the enduring wisdom of the Frankfurt School, particularly Horkheimer and Adorno, the postmodern marketplace retains the idea that subjectivity is created and naturalized through consuming. Indeed, the commodity form continues to gain stature as the preeminent site through which people experience and express the social world even as the worlds that are channeled through it are orchestrated less by marketers than by consumers.

In a contemporary marketplace, escaping the commodity form becomes increasingly difficult. In fact as of late, resistance, dissent and opposition to some of the abusive consequences of excessive commodification are resurfacing as consumables. A recent popular anti-consumerism manifesto by Naomi Klein has its own, as it were, 'Nologo' logo. In this way an oppositional advertisement required the creation of another advertisement (Schor and Holt, 2000: p. xxi). In Lebanon occasional use has been made of such acts of resistance or campaigns. Recently, eye-catching billboards, with vivid imagery and graphic slogans and aphorisms, have been installed as part of campaigns to prohibit or control smoking, plastic bags, forest fires and corruption or to safeguard shorelines, archeological relics and the country's threatened architectural legacy. Though fairly limited in their impact, they are proof that it is possible to bring a modicum of restraint to a world of such ubiquitous commodification.

It was not, incidentally, until the 1980s and 1990s that some of the basic premises of Veblen started to be questioned; particularly the view that consumer innovation flowed from top to bottom. A growing core of scholars argued instead that commodities were used to construct individual and creative selves. Instead of being a passive form of mass conformity, consuming was seen 'as a resistant, libratory and creative act. They wrote about the pleasure, enjoyment, escape and fantasy of consuming' (Schor and Holt, 2000: p. xvii). Consumption, in effect, had eclipsed production as the driving force in society. It was Colin Campbell (1987) who first contended that just as the Protestant ethic provided the spirit of production, Romanticism – with its cult of the expressive individual – was central in generating the spirit of consumption. If the working classes were instrumental in the development of production, readers of novels and those who dabbled with the creative arts were crucial in the development of consumption. This is true, as we shall see, in post-Mandate Lebanon where much of consumerism at the time assumed genuine expressive, innovative and participatory manifestations.

John Fiske (2000) is frequently cited for offering the most celebrated view of the ways in which structures of social domination can be resisted through consumption. Drawing on the views of Antonio Gramsci and Michel de Certeau, he analyses a variety of consumer activities – shopping, watching television, listening to rock music, etc – to expose what he calls 'tactical raids' on patriarchal capitalism. He finds, for example, that subordinate groups (i.e. women, people of color, the working class) use commodities to pursue their own socio-cultural interests. He cites examples of how what he labels as 'proletarian shopping' is largely an activity of the underclass who frequent shopping malls to engage in window shopping with no intention of buying. In such cases, and they are very prevalent in Beirut and its suburbs, shopping malls become outlets for a variety of activities not available for them elsewhere. In other words, 'young people, cut off from normal consumer power are invading the space of those with consumer power' (Fiske, 2000: 308).

These premises also underline Pierre Bourdieu's monumental work, *Distinction: A Social Critique of the Judgment of Taste* (1984). Making use of extensive French consumer surveys he argued that taste is an important factor in the reproduction of class and status differences. For Veblen, it must be recalled, it was the cost of an item that was the crucial differentiator. Bourdieu instead showed that differentiation extended to areas where cost was hardly a factor, as in styles of art, music, décor and film, and *how*, rather than simply *what*, one consumed. Consumer tastes varied, according to Bourdieu, in predictable ways and depended on 'cultural capital'; namely, family upbringing, formal education, as well as economic resources. At each place in the social hierarchy, individuals were inculcated into specific 'taste' groups. Bourdieu went on to show that the:

> Class patterning of consumption had become far more sophisticated and complex. Those in the higher reaches of the hierarchy used their superior taste to create 'distinction' for themselves, and to distance themselves from those inferior tastes. Thus, the possession of 'good' taste became a mechanism whereby individuals assured their social and economic position; consumption, then, was an integral part of the reproduction of inequality. In Bourdieu's account, one gained the authority to be a manager, or a professional not merely by specific skills but also by one's style of life. Consumption was no longer innocent, trivial, personal, or apolitical, but was directly linked to inequalities in production. Changing how people consume would be a necessary part of any egalitarian social transformation. (Schor and Holt, 2000: p. xvi)

Bourdieu goes further to suggest that what is popularly called 'taste' must be in sociological terms understood as that 'which brings things and people together that go together' (Bourdieu, 1984: 241). In the ironic style of Bourdieu, taste becomes the ultimate 'match-maker':

> Is a match-maker; it marries colours and also people, who make 'well-matched couples', initially in regard to taste ... This spontaneous decoding of one habitus by another is the basis of the immediate affinities which orient social encounters, discouraging socially discordant relationships, encouraging well-matched relationships, without these operations ever having to be formulated other than in the socially innocent language of likes and dislikes. (Bourdieu, 1984: 243)

The symbolic significance of consumption, particularly the value of material processions, cultural knowledge and participation in cultural events as well as preferences, has been increasingly attracting the attention of cultural sociologists. The massive and relentless output is testimony to the sustained interest in probing the changing character of consumption. As part of the so-called 'cultural turn' in the 1970s, attention has increasingly shifted away from the instrumental aspects of consumption, from *use-values*, to the symbolic dimensions of the process, i.e. to *sign-values*. Consumption has come to be seen as a means by which individuals and groups express their identities (see Warde, 2006: 88–90).

Studies on poverty, feelings of deprivation, being dispossessed or excluded from many forms of consumption have shown that the relationships between economic wealth and participation in material culture are highly complex and historically variable (see Lury, 1996: 6–8). There are no direct relationships between an individual's economic standing, and their ownership of goods, perception of which goods count as necessities or luxuries, understandings of needs or wants, their tastes, or the sense of style. As Bauman points out, consumer inequality is felt...

> As an oppression and a stimulus at the same time. It generates the painful experience of deprivation, with...morbid consequences for self-esteem ... It also triggers off zealous efforts to enhance one's consumer capacity – efforts that secure an unabating demand for market offers. (Bauman, 1990: 211)

It is important to bear in mind that the terms of participation in a consumer culture are profoundly unequal. This inequality, incidentally, is not directly tied to economic inequality. Rather, it reflects the culture itself. Contemporary Lebanon, in this regard, does not depart much from the models of Euro-American societies where privilege and self-perception are intimately related to pecuniary emulation and conspicuous consumption. This is, of course, a reflection of the central belief that *to have is to be*; that is, that the emergence of individualism and mass consumer culture is rooted in the predisposition of people to define themselves and others in terms of their material possessions or, and more likely, in terms of their conspicuous emulation of such possessions. In his passionately personal book on *Loneliness as a Way of Life* (2008), Thomas Dumm advances the notion that, in a highly commodified culture, the lonely self seeks to possess something to call its own, and ends up confusing that something with itself. To Dumm, in fact, this is not unusual since the 'great drive of capital is to turn everything into a commodity, including the self' (Dumm, 2008: 52). He goes further, by citing the work of John Wiske (1977), to maintain that the etymology of the word '*behaving*' is grounded in 'being' and 'having', a compound derived from *be-have* – where our 'very *reality* is fundamentally shaped by *realty*' (Dumm, 2008: 53).

All this, of course, implies that the utility of goods, in the conventional tradition of symbolic interactionism, is always constructed and framed by a cultural context. From this perspective, material goods are not only used to do things, but they have a meaning, and act as meaningful meaning-markers of social relations. Indeed, as Lury suggests: 'It is in acquiring, using and exchanging things that individuals come to have social lives' (Lury, 1996: 12). Helga Dittmar is even more explicit in accounting for how identities are shaped by the symbolic meaning we attach to material possessions:

> In Western materialistic societies ... an individual's identity is influenced by the symbolic meanings of his or her own material possessions, and the way in which s/he relates to those possessions. Material possessions also serve as expressions of group membership and as means of locating others in the social-material environment. Moreover, material possessions provide people with information about other people's identities. (Dittmar, 1992: 205)

Bourdieu's notion of *Social Capital* is also of relevance here. In other words, consumer culture is a source of contemporary belief that self-identity is a kind of social resource. More generally, Bourdieu, much like Mike Featherstone, associates this with the emergence of the new bourgeoisie who are normally keen on validating their identities through expressive and liberated lifestyles. This new petty bourgeoisie – which normally make up the lower echelons of the service class – are seen to be developing a lifestyle in which they actively struggle for self-improvement and self-expression. Incidentally, in two successive essays, Mike Featherstone (1990 and 1991) identified three different approaches to the study of consumer culture. First, consumption can be understood in terms of an expanding capitalist commodity production. In this case, consumption is functional to the demands of a prosperous and expanding economy. Second, the concern shifts to the different ways in which people use goods in order to create social bonds or distinctions. Finally, the third approach is concerned with the emotional pleasures of consumption; that is, the dreams, desires, fantasies associated with the world of goods.

Featherstone offers concrete and relevant examples which are also becoming salient in Lebanon. He suggests that the petty bourgeoisie are usually uneasy in their own bodies. Hence, they are constantly self-consciously checking, watching and correcting themselves. This, he suggests, explains the current popularity of body maintenance techniques, sports and forms of exercise such as aerobics and health products – vitamins, ginseng, royal jelly and the like. They are also keen on acquiring the desired taste, style and lifestyle (Featherstone, 1991: 90–1).

Allan Warde (1991) also looked at consumption from three different perspectives. In terms of the functions and meanings attached to consumption, he distinguishes between *use-value* and *exchange-value*. His third approach, reminiscent of Featherstone, is concerned with *identity-value*. In other words, the socio-symbolic value of goods is actualized whenever people engage in consumption with a view to expressing their social identity. In exploring the social theories of Anthony Giddens, Ulrich Beck and Zygmunt Bauman, Warde identifies a common theme all three of them share, despite their disparate views. Interestingly their common themes converge on the role of commodities in self-identity and how they manipulate and manage appearances in creating and sustaining such identities:

> One feature common to the social theories of Ulrich Beck, Anthony Giddens and Zygmunt Bauman is the notion that, today, people define themselves through the messages they transmit to others through the goods and practices that they process and display. They manipulate or manage appearances and thereby create and sustain 'self-identity'. In a world where there is an increasing number of commodities available to act as props in this process, identity becomes more than ever a matter of the personal selection of self image. Increasingly, individuals are forced to choose their identities. (Warde, 1994: 878)

To allay this deep-seated anxiety, the items people consume must have a direct bearing on their social standing. Hence, the affectation of the Lebanese to drive Range Rovers, SUMs and three-digit-license-plated limousines with tinted glass, cannot be explained by the utility of the car as a means of transportation. Likewise one does not wear Armani clothes, Celine handbags, Lacoste or Polo Sportswear, Gucci or Chanel accessories, and pay exorbitant sums for them, in order to be decently clad. Nor does one frequent exclusive restaurants and lounge bars in five-star hotels to fulfill the need for an ordinary meal or to quench one's thirst for an alcoholic beverage. The obsession of the Lebanese with seeking attention has prodded him to extend his ostentatious and ceremonial consumerism to other image-making and branded ventures. Boutique-like clinics, medical centers and five-star hospitals are doing a thriving business. As we shall see, wedding ceremonies, business banquets and symposia are transformed into spectacles of self-indulgent extravaganzas. It is not unusual, for example, for a doting father to spend up to $5–7 million on a wedding ceremony for his daughter or son. The zealous media is always there to memorialize the event. The dozen or so tabloid periodicals are ready, for another handsome fee, to display the event on their glossy pages. No wonder that a new line of expertise – the 'event manager' – is

quickly emerging as a form of entrepreneurship. It is also a new export industry for young talented Lebanese.

Finally, mention must be made of at least three of Bauman's defining
features of consumerism in what he terms the *liquid* modern society where
'society is increasingly viewed and treated as a network rather than a structure' (Bauman, 2007b: 3). In such an ever-changing socio-cultural setting,
Bauman maintains that consumer society 'manages to render non-satisfaction permanent'.[4] One way of achieving such an effect is to denigrate and
devalue consumer products shortly after they have been hyped into the
universe of the consumer's desires: 'What starts as a need must end up as a
compulsion or an addiction' (Bauman, 2005: 80). Second, if this search for
fulfillment is to continue, particularly if the new promises are to be alluring and catching, Bauman then maintains that 'the promises already made
must be *broken* and those hopes of fulfillment frustrated' (ibid., p. 81). This
is why to Bauman consumerism is not about the *satisfaction* of desires but
about *arousing* them:

> Contrary to the declared (and widely believed) promise of the commercials, consumerism
> is not about the *satisfaction* of desires, but about *arousing* desire for ever more desires – and
> preferably the kinds of desires that cannot in principle be quenched. To the consumer,
> a satisfied desire should be just about as pleasurable and exciting as a faded flower or an
> empty plastic bottle; to consumer market, a desire satisfied would also be a portent of
> imminent catastrophe. (Bauman, 2005: 92)

Third, and like kitsch which will be explored later, it becomes part and parcel
of the economics of deception, excess and waste. 'For the expectations to be
kept alive and for new hopes to promptly fill the void left by hopes already
discredited and discarded, the road from shop to garbage bin needs to be
short and the passage swift' (ibid., p. 82).

More recently Joanne Finkelstein (2007) reiterated the same theme
when she maintained that 'the buoyancy of a consumer society requires
every purchase to disappoint ... and the act of purchase must destroy the

---

4   Beginning with *Modernity and Ambivalence* (1991) to *Life in Fragments* (1995), *Liquid
    Modernity* (2000), *Liquid Love* (2003), *Wasted Lives* (2004), *Liquid Life* (2005), *Liquid
    Fear* (2006), *Liquid Times* (2007b), and *Consuming Life* (2007a), Zygmunt Bauman has
    explored, perhaps more than any other living scholar, the impact of liquid modernity on
    transforming individuals into the promoters of commodities and the commodities they
    promote.

very promise that the object offers us' (Finkelstein, 2007: 157–8). Though in a different context, Ghassan Hage, while talking about the distribution of hope in a nationalist capitalist order, made a similar inference by arguing that 'the power of these hopes is such that most will live their lives believing in the possibility of upward social mobility without actually experiencing it' (Hage, 2003: 14).

COSMOPOLITANISM AND COMMODIFICATION

If one were to single out one contemporary defining attribute with pervasive consequences in shaping the underlying incentives and outward conduct of the average Lebanese, it would be the passion for consumption and acquisitive impulse. Because it is so coveted it is also a source of apprehension, anxiety and fear. In the words of Zygumnt Bauman, it is a 'sinister demon' which haunts and torments the social fabric with diffuse, unanchored and ambient fears (Bauman, 2007a: 124). For Bourdieu as well, as we have seen, much of one's worth, status and class in society is gained, lost and reproduced largely through everyday acts of consumer behavior.

The irresistible drive for commodification, retail shopping and conspicuous consumption have been reinforced by the ingenuity of the Lebanese for marketing and advertising of new images and brand names. The two impulses are wedded together and are clearly rooted in the country's history as a 'Merchant Republic' where mercantilism and its concomitant bourgeois values were always given a free rein (for discussion of the economic and political implication of the Merchant Republic, particularly in 1943–52, see Traboulsi, 2007; Gates, 1998). Beirut's reputation as a 'shopper's Paradise' is not an idle or undeserved claim. I recall how during the darkest moments of the civil war, when essential amenities like water and electricity were cut off, and the streets were treacherous, private ingenuity always found a way to prevail. Hence the privileged class of consumers was never denied its whims for foie gras, cigars, caviar or aged whisky. As home to a fairly large international community and with an educated, fairly well-traveled cosmopolitan population, Lebanon's reputation for being a retail and shopping paradise is not, as often assumed by observers, of recent origin. Nor is it the outcome of global consumerism and postmodern commodification.

Travelers in the late 1830s and early 1840s were already describing Beirut as the 'Paris of the East'. As the seat of diplomacy, residence for consul-generals, headquarters for French, American and British missions and growing center of trade and industry, Beirut was 'rapidly increasing in wealth, population and dimensions ... Stupendous new mansions, the property of opulent merchants, were daily being built; beautiful country houses, summer residences of the wealthy; hotels and billiard rooms and cafes, elegantly fitted ... Everywhere utility was blended with magnificence' (Neale, 1852: 209). Travelers, particularly those coming to Beirut after visiting other towns and cities in Syria and Palestine, were struck by the 'European' and 'cosmopolitan' character and amenities of the city.

It is interesting to note that most of the impressions Beirut left on early and subsequent visitors were favorable. What drew their attention was how utility blended with elegance, how parties broke up before midnight so as not to interfere with their mercantile work habits and how new freedoms and liberties were enjoyed but were observed with modesty and restraint. Those same attributes, often associated with Lebanon's 'success story' and its so-called 'miraculous' economy, survived and predated the inflow of Arab oil capital by more than a decade. They were largely an indigenous reaction to some of the favorable circumstances generated by World War II. Unlike the massive privations and suffering inflicted on Lebanon during World War I, the circumstances associated with World War II were clearly more auspicious. For example, the expenditure of Allied Forces, along with expanded employment opportunities, generated appreciable revenues, particularly among the entrepreneurial and working classes. Reserves accumulated during the war exceeded $100 million (Issawi, 1966: 284) and were judiciously invested in building and extending the country's infrastructure, particularly its airport, road network and electricity. By the early 1960s, thirty-seven international airlines were already making daily flights into the airport. In no time Beirut evolved into the main financial center of the Middle East and one of the leading centers in the world.

It was also then that Lebanon began to upgrade its stature as a transit center. In the early 1950s, and clearly much earlier than the impetus it was to receive from the Persian Gulf shaykhdoms, Lebanon was already acting as the main trade intermediary for the neighboring countries. Some 50,000 passengers and 400,000 tons of goods, other than petroleum, passed through Lebanon in that year. Likewise, Beirut was already the headquarters of a growing number of multinational firms (Issawi, 1964: 285). This is another indication that Lebanon's economic growth preceded the oil boom. Nor was it, as often assumed, merely the outgrowth of free enterprise and reckless private initiative. Even the presidency of Bishara Al-Khoury (1943–52), notorious for championing tenets of economic liberalism, did not release the state from its prerogatives and policies of investment in public utilities and services. Camille Chamoun (1952–8) likewise, despite his ardent laissez-faire leanings, did not undermine the role of the state in either enacting legislation to favor such intervention or establishing special institutions to encourage economic development.

Economic and social historians are keen to attribute Beirut's cosmopolitanism and tolerance of foreign cultures to its mercantile predispositions. Commerce, trade, the exchange of goods and services, after all, rest on the willingness to mix and interact in an instrumental resourceful way with others. Throughout its history, Beirut has lived up to this image of being part of a 'Merchant Republic'. In Chapter 2 I quoted Issawi's description in the mid-1960s of trade in the city. Around the same time Micheal Hudson, in his otherwise guarded treatment of Lebanon's political prospects as a 'Precarious Republic', had this to say about symptoms of the 'ultramodern', salient at the time:

> The tales of spectacular profiteering and the Horatio Alger stories of the time are part of the folklore of modern Lebanon. From the Peasant who found a job as chauffeur with the British 7th Army to the *homme d'affaires* who made a fortune selling tank barricades, nearly everybody benefited. The boom has never really ended. Twenty years after the expulsion of the Vichy regime, the inhabitant of Beirut, rich or poor, can hardly avoid the ultramodern world around him. (Hudson, 1968: 71)

Like in virtually all other commercial and industrial enterprises, many of the early resourceful banking and financial houses were strictly family establishments bearing the family's pedigree, such as Haddad, Chiha, Safar, Sabbagh, Audi, etc. Kinship and family sentiments were not sources of lethargy and wasteful, nepotistic favoritism. Rather, they acted as a spur for inventiveness and fierce competition. Banks were so overwhelming in the life of the Central Business District (CBD) that ultimately one of the most compelling avenues was named 'The Banks' Street'. As of late some of the most successful banks are beginning to patronize the arts and other outreach cultural programs to rehabilitate traditional artifacts and artisans.

ANOMIE: THE PREDICAMENT OF SEEKING WITHOUT FULFILLMENT

One of the recurrent themes of this work is the corrupting impact of Lebanon's unusual postwar setting. The country is *adrift*, I have been arguing, because it has not only lost its moorings and direction, but it has also lost control. Postwar interludes, particularly in the wake of prolonged periods of civil disorder, anarchy and random violence, normally generate moods of restraint, disengagement and moderation. War-weary people are inclined to curb their ordinary impulses and become more self-controlled in order to reassess their belligerent past and redefine their future options. Somehow, postwar Lebanon has had the opposite reaction. The Lebanese, rather than being released from their prewar excesses, have discovered insatiable desires for extravagant consumerism, acquisitiveness and longing for immoderate forms of leisure and sterile recreation. Some of the dismaying by-products of this have become quite egregious. Even the ordinary courtesies and decencies, a modicum of attention to the needs and expectations of others, are overlooked, often with callous indifference. The conventional standards of politeness and etiquette which one expects in public amenities and civilities are ruthlessly disregarded. Queuing for one's turn, waiting in line, geniality, showing some deference to those in need of assistance, are all readily neglected.

Social order in any society is predicated on the premise of regularity and recurrence of expected patterns of behavior. More important, it also depends on trust and reciprocity. How and where does one find shelter, security when basic elements – ties of decency, trust and civility – are discarded with impunity? The trauma, fear and apprehension evident in public reflect this uncertainty and ambivalence. Nietzsche's *resentment* and *unappeased hostility* come to mind. This large residue of diffused and unrequited hostility finds release, as René Girard (1977) tells us, in proxy targets. Surrogate victims are almost always subordinate and marginalized groups who are accessible and vulnerable, particularly those who are bereft of the powers to resist or cry foul. In Lebanon, embittered and excluded groups, seething with anger and bitterness, vent their unappeased hostility on a variety of such victims.

One dismaying aspect is how the Lebanese are abusing and debasing the country's scenic beauty, its archeological heritage and living spaces. Regrettably, these have no one to speak on their behalf. Literally nothing is spared, from the sacred to the profane. Hence, ethical and normative precepts, as well as individual conscience and perceptions of right and wrong, are willfully violated. Such transgressions are legion. Reckless driving, strident and boisterous street conduct, deafening car horns, excessive smoking and littering in public spaces and the violations of ordinances regulating public hygiene and civil conduct are much too apparent. They are also committed with much bravado, swaggering display of defiance and vain machismo. Though not openly regarded as aberrant, they contribute to undermining and compromising the country's cultural and aesthetic heritage and authentic lifestyles, along with excessive consumerism, commodification, wasteful leisure, cheap entertainment and mass cultural expressions.

Such symptoms often assume pathological manifestations during holidays. Holiday seasons in Lebanon have always invited moods of compulsive, almost manic, shopping and extravagant spending. Celebrations of the past few years, possibly because of the sharp contrasts and incongruities in public life, have had more grotesque and ludicrous manifestations. Department stores, malls, shops, makeshift stalls and street vendors display a dazzling assortment of goods, and new products. It is hard to prove this empirically, but there seems to have been an increase in the number of shops selling frivolous and dispensable knick-knacks, gadgets, decorative objects, cosmetics, jewelry, clothes and other items which feed on the Lebanese proclivity for vain and indiscriminate buying. Oddly enough, the disheveled streets, congested because of excessive construction and reckless traffic, do not seem to restrain such impulses, nor do anxiety over the political situation or soaring prices. The compulsion to buy has become almost a national pastime, an outlet for traumatized individuals in their futile attempt to restore their damaged self-regard and personal worth.

The inauguration of new restaurants, hotel lounges and bars, which are stunningly frequent, are always occasions which invite a rush of revelers, eager to be among the first and to be seen consorting with the well-heeled and connected. Event managers have now introduced a new ploy dubbed as 'soft opening'. Hence this hyped interlude of curiosity, display and savoir-faire is extended further.

In more conceptual terms, Lebanon at the moment is a textbook example of Durkheim's 'anomie': a social state in which society's norms can no longer impose effective control over people's impulses. In times of rapid social change, people face considerable confusion, uncertainty and conflict in their expectations. Not only do the norms themselves become ambiguous, but people's desires and expectations become extravagant and excessive.

The limits between the possible and the impossible are unknown, as are those between what is just and what is unjust, between what is moderate and immoderate, between legitimate claims and hopes and those which are illegitimate. Consequently, people become victims of a chronic condition of constant seeking without fulfillment. (For an elucidation of Durkheim's classical treatment of anomie see, among others, Clinard, 1964: 1–56.) The deprived and not-so-deprived feel cheated and denied, particularly when rampant commercialism, sustained by the resourceful and aggressive mass media, constantly whets consumer appetites for limitless goods and creates expectations that are beyond the reach of the average Lebanese. It is then that they acquire the belief that they are entitled to such items, by fair means when possible and foul means if necessary. And it is in this precise sense that the corruption of values has become endemic in Lebanon; foul and illegitimate means have become necessary to secure desired goals. Such foul play has become so widespread, it is transformed into a normal and guilt-free predisposition.

The Lebanese today is not only being denied his/her natural claims to live in a decent, orderly, affordable and edifying environment. He is also beginning to realize that he cannot secure even his daily needs for food, shelter, security, safety and public utilities unless he compromises himself and violates society's norms or his own moral principles. He is compelled, for example, to resort to irregular, often devious, means to guarantee his water, electricity, fuel and telecommunication needs. In short, he is a victim of extortion and fraud.

The exorbitant prices one pays cannot be a result of natural inflationary market tendencies; they reflect the extortion and heavy exactions that agents and self-appointed guardians, patrons and middlemen impose. For example, fuel oil, petrol and gas prices have more than tripled during the past few years. Rents, medication, clothing, schooling and some food products have done the same. The yearly rent of a three-bedroom flat, in some urban districts of Beirut, ranges from $20,000–40,000. As will be shown later, Lebanon has been undergoing an unprecedented construction boom of immense proportions. Upscale luxury buildings are sold prior to their completion. Transactions and investment in real estate are largely sparked by speculative considerations. Hence it is not uncommon for a large portion of the built apartments to remain vacant.

Another dramatic example of this nagging disjunction is the failure thus far to impose a modicum of control on the abuses of smoking. The most scintillating ads are for tobacco. Those for liquor, lingerie, cellphones, cars, entertainers and singers compete for their share of advertising space. Public highways and desolate country roads are decked with imposing billboards beckoning one to Marlboro country. Even politicians and public figures (presumably the country's most illustrious role models) cannot part with their cigarettes, even when they make TV appearances.

With smoking such a part of everyday life, all attempts to launch a comprehensive country-wide tobacco control strategy or plan of action to curb some of the adverse derivatives of smoking have been abortive so far. Even the laws passed in 1995 banning smoking in hospitals, infirmaries, pharmacies, theaters, public transportation terminals, health clubs, schools, universities, elevators, etc are ignored and unenforced. A proposal for a law banning all tobacco advertisements on television, radio and print media failed to be endorsed by the Council of Ministers.

A recent public protest seeking to declare Gemayzeh, Beirut's most successful hotspot for party-goers, a smoke-free zone was well received and publicized. But given the deeply embedded mood of popular intransigence, the public is not likely to entertain any restrictions on their addictive dispositions to pollute their surroundings. Even if smoking in public spaces were to be prohibited by decree, the Lebanese would almost certainly brush the injunction aside like all other restrictions on their impulses and extravagant appetites. Lebanon, as a result, is today a haven for smokers.

Since cigarettes are fairly cheap, lack warning labels and are readily accessible to young vulnerable adolescents, influenced by peer pressure and the seductive lifestyles of the cool, they are the most susceptible to addiction and its stressful withdrawal syndromes. Given the intensity of tobacco toxicity, addiction and its hazards to secondary smokers become inescapable. For example, the World Health Organization (WHO) recommends less than 15 micrograms of tobacco pollution per cubic meter. Twenty out of thirty restaurants and pubs tested in Beirut revealed an incidence of about 310 micrograms. This staggering rate, as identified by WHO, places Lebanon way beyond 'emergency conditions'. The most recent estimates released by the Ministry of Public Health and WHO are truly horrendous at all levels. The perils to public health are so menacing that at last the press is talking about the 'killer smoke': more than 3,500 people die every year because of tobacco-related diseases. The state uses about $900 million annually of its roughly $28 billion GDP to treat such afflictions (*Daily Star*, 5 Nov. 2007).

One does not need such empirical findings to realize how pervasive smoking is in public spaces. If one pauses on a street corner, enters a shop or a restaurant, rides a taxi or attends to an errand in a government offices, one is bound to be overwhelmed by the number of smokers. Unlike smokers in countries with stringent anti-smoking attitudes and legislation, the Lebanese smoker is far from furtive, prudent or discreet about his habit. It is flaunted like a badge of honor. The way one reaches for the packet, the way the cigarette is lit and the virtuosity one displays in inhaling, puffing or balancing it as it dangles from the comer of one's mouth – all demonstrate élan and dash. Perhaps even more than the mobile phone, it is an object which has become an extension of one's body and a prop to shore up one's vulnerable being.

When this subject is considered in comparative terms, it becomes more striking. The sources cited earlier also reveal that about 66 percent of the adult male population are smokers, as are 47 percent of women. By contrast, in most developing countries the percentage of women smokers never exceeds single digits. For example, it is not more than 2.3 percent in Egypt and 7.1 percent in Jordan. Lebanon continues to fall behind many countries in the region which have introduced smoking bans, such as Syria, Turkey, Iraq, Qatar, Bahrain, UAE and Israel. Increasingly, the offence of smoking is being posed in human rights terms since the right of human beings to breathe clean air should supersede the rights of those who are polluting it. In this regard it is painful to recognize that Lebanon – presumed to be a more open, liberal and cosmopolitan society – has now fallen behind in liberating its citizens from murderous second-hand smoke in public places.

The incidence of smoking is bad enough. More egregious, however, is the bravado with which smokers flaunt their addictive habits. They do so with total disregard of its public health menaces or the rights of non-smokers for fresh air. And, of course, ads for the ubiquitous cigarette beckon one to a liberal, cool and fashionable life.

The Lebanese today are victims of the prosaic distinction Ghassan Hage makes between *hope* and *joy*. They live in perpetual hope without any intrinsic or genuine joy or inner fulfillment. Being impetuous, with notoriously short attention spans, the average Lebanese is not predisposed to any form of delayed gratification. Hence waiting, another matter of concern to Hage, is not a psychological and existential state which is compatible with the precipitous and headlong inclinations of the Lebanese. They are too narcissistic and so indulgent in their unappeased longing for *jouissance* that they cannot possibly 'wait properly' (Hage, 2009).

SWIFT URBANIZATION AND POPULAR CULTURE

Most accounts of Beirut's surge in the nineteenth century stress the role of external, generally Western incursions, particularly as they relate to colonial and military expeditions. Such perceptions naturally overlook, as several historians have pointed out, local and regional circumstances, especially the interplay between migration and Beirut's urbanization and the role of urban notables and other displaced groups in becoming the vectors of far-reaching economic and socio-cultural transformations (see Salibi, 1965; Issawi, 1977; Owen, 1981; Fawaz, 1983; Bouheiry, 1987; Hourani, 1962; Khalaf, 1979). The first substantial symptoms of change in areas relevant to our concerns in this work – i.e. communication, cultural and intellectual dimensions, the media, consumerism and lifestyle – swiftly became visible.

Towards the end of the nineteenth century, the old town started to show a few of the early symptoms of urbanization. By the 1880s Beirut's population had already reached the 100,000 mark and its compact labyrinthine alleyways and dirt roads were much too dense with human and animal traffic. More importantly, it was also at this time, due to the growing problem of security and law and order, that a growing number of Beirutis started to build their permanent residences outside its walls. On his return visit to Beirut in 1873, William Thomson had this to say:

> Forty years ago, when I came to Beirut, there was scarcely a house outside of the walls fit to live in; now hundreds of convenient dwellings, and not a few large and noble mansions, adorn its beautiful suburbs, and two-thirds of the population reside in the gardens. The massacres of 1860 led many of the inhabitants of Damascus, the Lebanon, and elsewhere, to settle in Beirut, which added largely to its inhabitants, and many of the public buildings that attract the notice of visitors now have been erected since that deplorable event.

> The population is now estimated at eighty thousand, more than one-half of which is made up of the various Christian sects and denominations. No city in Syria, perhaps none in the Turkish Empire, has had so rapid an expansion. And it must continue to grow and prosper, with but one proviso to cast a shade of doubt upon its bright future. Should a railroad ever connect the head of this sea with the Euphrates and the Persian Gulf, that will inevitably dictate where the emporium of Syria is to be. If Beirut can attract that line of trade and travel to its door, it will rank amongst the important cities of the world; if it cannot, then must it wane before some other rival queen of the East. (Thomson, 1886: 49)

It is of interest to note Thomson's prophetic projection of Beirut's future role as 'emporium' of Syria and other regions of the Turkish Empire. In unequivocal terms, Thomson asserted that Beirut had no choice but to nurture its trade and merchandizing prospects. Otherwise it was bound to wane. Before the turn of the century the spatial and land-use character of the old town became less residential and started to attract more commercial and business activities. The old dirt roads and alleyways gave way to rectilinear streets and paved, avenue-like thoroughfares. The first to be converted in the summer of 1894 into a broad street was Souk al-Jamil (literally, 'the Elegant' or 'the Beautiful'). Because it was at the time the only street in the city which could boast paved side-walks, it attracted a large number of craft shops and make-shift hawkers. Somehow, it managed to retain its character as a fashionable venue for the latest European products.

The old Roman road, Decumanus Maximus, a vestige of the old Roman grid, was rendered more visible as it dissected the town from east to west: that is, from Bab Edriss to Bab Es Saraya. For a while it acquired the nickname of 'El-Fashkah' (literally 'a stride' or 'step') to epitomize the diminutive character of the central avenue of the old town. Fouad Debbas recollects a story handed down by a distant uncle of his, claiming that he had arranged a kind of pulley system across the street which saved him the trouble of going back and forth through the mud and dirt to attend to the needs of his clients in both stores (Debbas, 1986: 52). During the Mandate, El-Fashkah was renamed Weygand Street in 1924.

Part of this narrow street, which originally bordered the eastern side of Bab Edriss, survived as Souk el-Frange. With its colorful and vibrant tiny shops, mostly selling perishable local produce, it became a favorite haunt for foreigners and residents of the western neighbourhoods. Another street which witnessed this structural transformation was the picturesque Serail Street, which was formerly entirely residential; it began south of Bab Es Saraya and skirted the former Emir Fakhreddine Palace and was bordered by colorful Japanese lilacs. This evolved first into Souk Soursock, since prosperous Greek Orthodox families such as Sursock and Tueni were the prominent property-holders in the neighbourhood. Ironically, after World War I this same street 'degentrified' into Souk El-Nourieh, the site of the city's bustling open and popular retail market for fresh agricultural produce, knick-knacks, household items and second-hand products.

The fairly swift urbanization of Beirut demanded more than just piecemeal efforts of planning and control. The first attempts to subject the burgeoning

city to some concerted organization along civic lines, particularly with regard
to hygiene, quarantine regulation and policing of law and order, date back to
the Egyptian occupation from 1831 to 1840. But these and subsequent efforts
were imposed by a distant authority not too receptive to local interests. It was
not until the first municipal or town council was officially set up in 1867 that
local citizens, particularly the emancipated and civic-minded intellectual and
business elites, were instrumental in prodding Ottoman administrators to
enact more extensive schemes for modernization of their city. It was then, for
example, that measures were taken to prevent sheep, goats and other domestic animals from passing through the center of the town en route to the
harbor. The maze of congested and narrow dirt roads and alleyways gave way
to the novelty of rectilinear, broad thoroughfares and parallel arterial road
networks. Most prominent were streets like Foch, Allenby and Fakhreddine
whose southern stretch was later called al-Maarad in commemoration of the
first international fair hosted in Beirut's center in 1921.

Of course, this surge of new development meant the disappearance of
some of the distinctive icons and vestiges of the old town. The devastation of World War I and the ravages of epidemics and other treacherous
visitations had left their debilitating imprint on the city. Ottoman authorities were equally unsparing in subjecting the city to further destruction.
In quick succession, from the mid-nineteenth century onwards, a string of
other monumental buildings and imposing infrastructural facilities (particularly port, rail, postal services, *khans, aswaqs, sahas,* the electric tram-
ways, gaslights and the like) did much to embellish the urban setting. A
handful of prodigious and towering structures started to appear on Beirut's
skyline and define its character: the Grand Serail (1853), the Ottoman
Bank (1856), Capucine St Louise (1863), the Petit Serail (1884), Beirut's
train station (1895), the Ottoman clock tower (1898), Orosdi-Back, the
Ottoman department store (1900) and Sanayeh, Arts et Métiers Vocational
school (1907).

One striking example and an unusual milestone in this regard was the
establishment of Orosdi-Back as the first and largest department store of its
kind in Beirut and, perhaps, the largest in the Mediterranean. In retrospect,
it stands out as a precursor of global franchises and the production of spatial
enterprises for upscale and elite consumerism. Three global capitalists –
Leon and Philippe Orosdi and Joseph Back – opened branches of their store
in Paris, Istanbul, Alexandria, Cairo, Tunis and other cities in the Ottoman
Empire. Beirut's branch was inaugurated, with much fanfare, on 1 September

1900 to coincide with the citywide commemoration of Sultan Abdulhamid's silver jubilee (Hanssen, 2005: 251–3). The logistical location of the store – at the intersection of the quay and the port's warehouses and custom offices – proved instrumental in several respects. It was a precursor to the expediting of Beirut's 'free zone' and *entrepôt* mentality. Hence, the store could import luxury items from Europe and then export them regionally.

At the time, Beirut was just emerging as a port city with extensive connections with the hinterland. The Beirut–Damascus road was constructed by a French company in 1858, and a branch of the Ottoman Imperial Bank was established in 1905. The appeals of Beirut were more than just a reflection of its infrastructural and communication facilities. One could already discern the early manifestations of the *nahda* or cultural renaissance. For example, *Hadiqat al-Akhbar*, the first newspaper of the city, was published in 1858 and, within a decade or two, a large number of journals and periodicals surfaced in quick succession. By the turn of the century Beirut was already the uncontested economic, financial, intellectual and communication center in the region (see Hourani, 1962; Owen, 1981; Salibi, 1988; Khalaf, 2002). More compelling for the purposes of this book, this was also the interlude when the concomitant transformations in lifestyle and the 'Occidentalisation' of public manners and fashions were taking place (Fawaz, 1983; Bouheiry, 1987).

Naturally, the foresighted entrepreneurs must have appreciated the pivotal and speculative character of its spatial location. At the hub of this interplay of local, regional and international forces, it was bound to exploit and facilitate propitious windfalls. As an elite store, Orosdi-Back took advantage of the transit and *entrepôt* features of its setting and became an appealing site for local, regional and international customers: more so once the newly constructed railway line (DHP), serving the Syrian interior, became a transit stop for Muslim pilgrims to Mecca as well.

A few of its spatial and architectural elements are worth noting. As a private enterprise, and since local architects were not involved in its design, no effort was made to blend the outward façade of the store with the prevailing architectural style. Other than its monumental and ostentatious character, it had very few Ottoman traces. Nor did it incorporate any features of the local vernacular. Hence, it stood out in sharp contrast to its surroundings. Its building material, the color of the two-story façade and the triple-domed grey rooftops seemed out of sync with the conventional sandstone and red-tiled roofs of adjacent *khans, qaysariyyas* and *wikalas* (Hanssen, 2005: 253). Furthermore, it was also innovative as a *magazine des nouveautés,* which was fashionable at the time as a European marketing gambit. Indeed, in Paris it took the form of an 'Oriental bazaar' which was reproduced in world exhibitions (Girouard, 1985).

Hence, for the first time, the gadgetry of modern consumerism and marketing (elevators, in-house telephones, window displays and layout of merchandise) appeared in Beirut and became a pacesetter for other such features. Finally, and most importantly, by reclaiming the landfill upon which it was built, Orosdi-Back played a significant role in the 'gentrification' of that as yet undeveloped stretch of the cityscape. The Port Company, with a speculative eye on real estate, introduced measures to attract such urban development. A score of notable urban bourgeoisies, such as the Badawis and Tabits, quick to respond to the demand for office space, constructed buildings on the wharf and leased them out as business establishments. This early instance of gentrification predated by over a century developments that were to become pivotal in Beirut's spatial reproduction.

Most visitors and observers at the time were talking about the occidentalization of lifestyles and manners among its privileged urban elite. Christian and Sunni Muslim merchant notables such as Sursock, Boutros, Trad, Daouk and Beyhum were already living in fairly exclusive urban neighborhoods dotted with gated palatial houses – in the words of Kamal Salibi, 'in large Italianate mansions furnished and decorated in European style with a distinctive Beirut Baroque atmosphere and sensibility' (Salibi, 1965: 142). A Daouk, Beyhum or a Jumblat palatial residence would not differ from the mansions of the Sursocks, Boutros or Trads. Most probably they would have all gone to Francophone schools, participated in joint leisure activities, spent their summer months in resort towns like Aley and Soufar, plus of course making occasional trips to Paris and other European capitals, to embellish their aura of taste and savoir-faire.

It was also at this time that Beirut witnessed a marked expansion of banking, money-lending and associated financial ventures. By 1929, Beirut could boast 52 banks, 43 credit and exchange houses, 21 real estate brokers and 518 negotiators (Bouheiry, 1987: 10). After the devastations of World War I, the French administration launched a crash program of relief and reconstruction. Emergency supplies were brought to feed a population shrunk to about one-third by postwar destitution and famine. Health clinics were set up. The number of hospitals tripled within two years of the French arrival. Equally important was the French contribution to the restoration of confidence in the market. With that in mind, a successful international fair was organized in Beirut in 1921, again perhaps a first in the region.

A high priority item for the French was the modernization of Beirut, particularly through urban and spatial planning. This left an indelible mark on the center of the city, particularly the harbor and the three avenues (Foch, Allenby and Weygand) adjoining it. Another elegant quarter, in the familiar *étoile* pattern, was built next to it. This incorporated some of the traditional architecture, with a Parliament House gracing the central Place de l'Etoile. By 1928–9, hardly a decade after the French presence began, the city experienced a widespread real estate boon, with prices doubling or tripling in less than five years (Bouheiry 1987: 9).

Radio-Orient was founded as a modern communication center with powerful transmitters at Khaldeh and supplementary receivers in Ras-Beirut. This was another milestone because it linked the capital with Paris and New York, and places such as Persia. In the early years of the Mandate, the Haut Commissariat was also keen on turning Beirut into a broadcasting center for the whole region. Such infrastructural developments had an instant and demonstrable impact. Between 1923 and 1929, for example, the number of hotels increased from thirty-five to sixty-two. Restaurants and cafes increased from about twenty to more than thirty. Travel agencies and travel goods shops witnessed similar increases. Interestingly, in 1929 there were already seven advertising agencies, where none had existed a decade earlier (see Bouheiry for further details, 1987: 10–11).

THE CINEMA AS PUBLIC ENTERTAINMENT

Most striking perhaps, was the relatively early initiation of the cinema as a popular form of entertainment and a sustained leisure outlet. By 1923, there were already six cinemas and by 1929 there were ten. In the public imagination, and as often noted in personal memoirs of those in their early youth during the 1930s and 1940s, the Bourj as the popular central business district of downtown Beirut was always associated with when they were just discovering the novelty and marvels of the cinema as a form of entertainment. Some speak about it with considerable nostalgia as if it were an irresistible but blissful addiction. Since in some circles protective parents were likely to harbor ethical concerns about its dubious impact, the forbidden fruit became all the more seductive. For nearly half a century the Bourj continued to be the exclusive and uncontested preserve for movie-going. In other words, almost three or four generations of Lebanese youth must have been indelibly marked by the experience. The Bourj and the cinema became contiguous entities.

It should be noted that, unlike in other cities in the Levant, cinemas were not socially and politically contested forms of public entertainment. They made their appearance first in traditional quarters, sharing makeshift tents with itinerant shadow-puppet shows (*karakoz*), picture shows (*Sandouq al Firje*) and, most notably, storytellers (*hakawatis*). For a while, the modern form of mass entertainment did not displace the popularity of the *hakawatis*, who continued to draw their conventional devotees. At dusk, and not unlike the 'happy hour' for today's corporate set, the pressured and overwrought found soothing release on their way home in the conviviality, engaging humor and accomplished virtuosity of the celebrated *hakawati*. After his makeshift stage is assembled (no more than a high table or wooden platform), usually in a familiar cul-de-sac or intimate intersection in the old souks, he ascends the platform with his traditional garb, *tarboush* and proverbial stick, his sole prop which he rhythmically taps to sustain the enthralled attention of his audience. Gradually, the gathering, as coffee and *arghilehs* are served, turns to an amiable, often rambunctious, interactive performance.

The *hakawati* should not be trivialized or dismissed lightly as a passing or nostalgic interlude. It clearly was more than just an entertaining outlet. It epitomized the coveted virtues of conviviality and camaraderie as they were being eroded by the nascent spatial and socio-cultural realities associated with the dislocating forces of urbanization. More relevant to our concerns, the *hakawati* represented a productive and interactive genre of public entertainment. The audience was not a passive and casual group of indifferent consumers. They were devoted and active participants. The *hakawatis* represent some of the features inherent in street theater and modern-day sitcoms: as 'third spaces' they were precursors to formalized stage productions in theaters designed and built for such purposes.

Gradually, movie houses were temporarily located in the upper floors of cafes, restaurants, merchant hostels (*khans*), locandas or congested residential compounds. Zahrat Suriyya was the first projection theater in Beirut, built in 1909. At the time, it was still primitive and elementary and only operated manually. It did not survive for too long. It was destroyed by fire in 1921 and then rebuilt as the Parisienne coffee house. Crystal (1913), Cosmographe (1919) and Chef d'Œuvre (1919) were the first three movie houses specially built for that purpose. The last was converted in 1924 to the Royal. From then on, and in a quickening succession, a string of movie theaters was built, mostly by local Lebanese architects.

Most prominent, perhaps, was Opera (1931), built by Bahjat Abd el-Nour, evidently inspired by features of classical Egyptian antiquity. The Opera stood out as a distinct architectural icon. For a while, it was emblematic of the new massive structures that eventually punctuated the square around the Bourj. It was so photogenic that it served as a majestic and picturesque back-drop for commemorating visits of foreign dignitaries. The triumphal visit of Charles de Gaulle in 1942 was one such spectacle. The Opera, incidentally, was restored and rehabilitated into the Virgin Megastore in 2000.

Given the stupendous popularity of the cinema as a popular pastime, in less than two decades, the Bourj and its outlying streets were virtually decked with movie theaters. Some like the trio, the Roxy, the Dunia and the Empire, literally adjoined each other. The Roxy, designed by Elias Murr in 1932, introduced for the first time elements of Art Deco. This set the pattern to be emulated in the Dunia, the Empire and the Majestique, built approximately around the same time. The proliferation of movie theaters, many with strik-ing and monumental architecture, started to overwhelm the cityscape of the city center by the mid-1940s. Its identity and public image, in fact, became almost synonymous with cinemas. One's orientation and points of reference were almost always related to a particular movie house. By sheer number and the compact area within which they are located, their density is truly staggering. Perhaps it is unmatched elsewhere. By the early 1950s, just before cinemas started to decentralize in pursuit of greener pastures elsewhere, there were about twenty-five such outlets within the Bourj area alone.[5] Many of the cinemas, particularly those built during the French Mandate, were instru-mental in introducing contemporary architectural novelties – Art Nouveau and Art Deco – imported from across the Atlantic. The reproduction of such composite styles was visible in theaters like the Dunia, the Roxy, the Rivoli, among others. These dark theaters reflecting Americanism, with rigorous and refined lines and sometimes in monumental shape and volume, were also landmarks because they were the first instances of concrete being used (Yacoub, 2003: 243). Many were designed by leading architects of the day,

5   Zahrat Suriyya (1909), Crystal (1913), Cosmographe (1919) Chef d'Œuvre (1919), Chautecler (1920), Familia (1920), City Palace (1920), Royal (1924), Empire (1926), Opera (1931), Roxy (1932), Rex (1933), Majestique (1934), Metropole, Dunia (1946), Schehrazade (1952), Gaumont Palace, Hollywood, Capitol (1947), Byblos, Grand Theatre, Rivoli (1946), Radio City.

such as Farid Trad (Dunia), Bahjat Abdel Nour (Opera), Said Hjeil (Rivoli), George Araman and Giorgio Ricci (Capitol). With the exception of Opera all these buildings were demolished in 1993 to make way for the Square's reconstruction. The variety of the premises, in terms of their aesthetic and socio-economic standards (first, second or third degrees), the programs they offered (crime, comedy, western, romance) and language (English, French, Arabic) extended choice by the monetary affordability and the particular genre each of the houses specialized in (Arabi, 1996: 38).

This is why, it should be noted, movie-going had already become one of the most popular pastimes. And it was, incidentally, a truly proletarian experience. All social groups, because of the demarcation of seats into three distinct categories, could find themselves in the same public space. The democratizing implications of such venues should not be overlooked. During World War I German films had predominated in the three-to-four movie houses existing at the time (Arabi, 1996: 38). After 1918, French and American silents started to prevail. Local favorites included Tarzan, police serials, cowboys and the comedies of Charlie Chaplin and the French star Max Linder (Thompson, 2000: 198). It was not, it seems, until the early 1930s that cinemas were equipped with projectors. A measure of the popularity of cinema is that most newspapers introduced regular movie columns.

Movie-going had become so popular for young people that, as early as 1931, students staged a march to Bourj to demand more affordable tickets, just as they had earlier protested for cheaper tramway fares and electricity charges. If anything, this was symptomatic of how pervasive movie attendance had become. About the same time it began to arouse serious concern and public debate in the press. For example, in 1928 the Jesuit newspaper *al-Bashir* called for more stringent censorship, particularly with regard to the presumed detrimental impact on the young.

In a series of editorials, *al-Bashir* addressed issues of censorship and proposed the formation of such boards to prevent the corruption of young morals by movie stars. A Catholic Youth Circle was established and, among other things, urged families not to let their daughters to go to the cinema alone. They proposed instead that the whole family attend only the Circle's own, censored films. In 1933, a group of concerned mothers petitioned the Lebanese president to increase censorship. The French High Commissioner interfered to veto their demand, it seems (Thompson, 2000). By the time movies spread to other segments of society, Muslim leaders likewise demanded increasing measures of control over films perceived to be offensive to public morality. The Mufti, for example, strongly denounced the film *Adam and Eve* which had been seen in Beirut earlier without any objection. He invoked Ottoman law to justify his opposition since, in his view, the film presented a demeaning portrayal of holy personages (ibid.).

So polemical did the issue of cinema and public morality become that Catholic students began publishing a special movie magazine *L'Ecran* which became their platform to vent concerns about how to shelter the young from the corrupting influence of films deemed offensive to public taste. For example, one of their demands was to have heads of households represented on the censorship board. The Maronite Patriarch, Antoine Arida, pronouncing himself guardian of public morality, went on in 1935 to demand the closure of all cinemas and houses of prostitution. He declared that 'it is France that perverts our people and introduces immorality to them'. Muhi al-Din al-Nusuli, editor of *Bayrut* daily, in 1936 denounced cinemas as seedy pockets of vulgarization: 'they are favored places for foreign women to seduce innocent Lebanese men and, thereby, corrupting their national loyalty' (*Bayrut,* 1936).

L'Ecran did not remain passive. As French authorities dragged their heels, the periodical along with L'Equipe (a voluntary association of Catholic students in Beirut) developed their own advocacy strategies. *L'Ecran* started to provide readers with its own assessment and rating of films. L'Equipe resorted to confrontational measures by often disrupting popular films perceived as damaging to public morality. For example, in January 1940, twelve members of this group were detained by police for protesting at nudity in a film at the Rex Theater (*L'Ecran,* 1940).

Women's accessibility to the cinema also became, as one might expect, a contested issue. Initially, women were permitted to attend in segregated movie houses. By the mid-1930s there were women-only screenings three or four times a week (Tarcici, 1941: 145–52). This is an interesting development since women were denied access to street theaters (*hakawatis*) or other performances in makeshift places like cafes and *khans.* Naturally, because regular movies were in enclosed spaces, they were deemed more acceptable than outdoor and live performances. Actors on a screen cannot, after all, see the faces of women in the audience. Reference is made to such episodes to disclose the awareness of the public and the concern of moral entrepreneurs – e.g. clerics, state and Mandate authorities, educators, parents and consumer associations – to impose some control over the permissive impact of the cinema as a popular venue of entertainment.

The inference one may readily extract from this is that the Bourj – as in other aspects of popular culture, socio-economic and political mobilization – was the epicenter where such controversies were initiated and debated. Is this not what a public sphere is all about? Although no reliable surveys exist as yet to ascertain the actual magnitude of women's participation in such forms of popular entertainment, it is clear from the public debate the cinema had aroused at the time that a fairly large portion of the upper and middle classes were already movie-goers and that such opportunities were beginning to trickle down to lower-class groups. The comparative study by Prothro and Diab on changing family patterns in the Arab world, although done considerably later, presented evidence from the sample of respondents to indicate that, indeed, some women had already been exposed to movies by the 1930s and that, by a decade later, all of them had (Prothro and Diab, 1974). It is in this sense, as Elizabeth Thompson correctly argues, that the issue becomes of particular significance. It allows us to consider its implications at three levels: colonial, class and gender (Thompson, 2000: 205).

Mandate authorities, given their 'civilizing mission', were naturally eager to use the glamor of the cinema to disseminate and, hopefully, endear, the diverse communities of Beirut to aspects of French culture and lifestyles. Its class context is also meaningful since this was also the period – to recall the views of Veblen, Bourdieu and Featherstone – when the nascent bourgeoisie was groping to validate its commitment to some of the instrumental, utilitarian and consumer expectations of middle-class values. Finally, the subtle and contested gender implications were also unavoidable, since women in Beirut had already a headstart over their cohorts in other cities in the Arab world in grappling with issues of emancipation, justice, autonomy and equal access to avenues of participation in the public sphere. For example, we are told that by 1930 women in Beirut had already stopped seeking their husband's consent before leaving home. Hence outdoor shopping in stores was no longer the exclusive chore or privilege of men (al-Dabbur, 1943: 8). A score of social historians have also confirmed that Christian Beirutis had generally adopted Parisian styles by 1914 and that, if their Muslim compatriots continued to wear the veil, they were inclined to take it off downtown and put it back on as they returned to their neighborhoods (Daghestani, 1931: 126–31).

This is another revealing symptom of the emancipatory and liberating proclivities of the Bourj as a public sphere. It predisposed women to part with some of the confining elements of their local culture. By doing so, they were in effect, crossing boundaries and negotiating more adaptive and fluid identities and lifestyles.

The Bourj's monopoly as an exclusive movie preserve, it should be noted, started to decline by the late 1950s and early 1960s as movies started to relocate their premises to the new suburban quarters of Hamra, Verdan, Achrafieh, Sodeco and the like. The shift carried with it some distinct changes in both architectural style and scale. During the 1930s and 1940s there were, it must be recalled, less than a handful of architects who designed the twenty-five movie theaters that once graced the Bourj's cityscape and shaped its public image. Lebanon is blessed today with an expansive generation of gifted and resourceful young architects. They are all proficient and skilled in the use of modern and postmodern architectural styles and their associated technologies. In no time the outlying suburbs of Beirut were and continue to be punctuated by a relentless stream of massive structures of shopping malls accommodating often a set of six to eight theaters: Planet Abraj, Sodeco Square, the Concorde, the Dunes, the ABC, the Espace, the Galaxy, Sofil, the St Elie, etc.

For the moment, the Bourj and its adjoining CBD are without any movie houses. As already noted, Opera was the only one of the twenty-five movie houses to escape destruction in the civil war or being bulldozed as the grounds were cleared for reconstruction. It is very unlikely that the square could once again attract the independent single units of old. If they are to resurface, they will most likely be part of the overbearing towers intent on celebrating monu-mentality. Indeed, a few such projects are currently being considered.

Although the Bourj is no longer the focus for movie-going, Beirut and its suburbs have not been timid in this regard. Early in the 1950s, if meas-ured by the number of movie seats per capita, Beirut was already living up to its reputation as the movie capital of the world. Per capita movie attendance was five per year. In another decade, it increased fivefold, a close second to Hong Kong (UNESCO, 1965). During the same period, the number of movie theaters leapt from 48 to 170, averaging twelve new houses per year. The accessibility of such theaters, rendered more appealing as we have seen, by the variety of films, plush surroundings and low prices, only served to whet the proverbial appetite of Lebanese from all classes and age groups for this form of public entertainment. Indeed, before the advent of TV and home videos, anticipating, attending and talking about movies was already the undisputed most popular and most absorbing national pastime. Despite the advent of other forms of public and home entertainment, nothing as yet has replaced the irresistible allure of movie-going for virtually all groups in society.

VENUES FOR SELF-EXPRESSION AND CONVIVIALITY

Beirut's cosmopolitanism was not, naturally, limited to movie-going and other popular forms of entertainment. Throughout the 1950s and 1960s, Beirut was also in the throes of all the transformations associated with social mobilization, mass communications and popular consumerism. This was also the interlude when Beirut, more than other coastal cities and those of the interior, was undergoing its rapid and unrelenting urbanization. It was then that Beirut's image as a cosmopolitan, sophisticated, polyglot meeting place of world cultures was being established. It was also then that opportunities to seek and fulfill conspicuous consumption increased almost exponentially.

All the socio-cultural indicators, crude and refined, attest to this over-riding reality. From the sharp increases in the flow of domestic and foreign mail, number of telephones and passenger vehicles to the more stupendous growth in the volume and diversity of media exposure (particularly TV, radio and movie attendance), all spoke of appreciable increases in degrees of physical and psychic mobility and high levels of consumption throughout society. On these and other related indices, Lebanon enjoyed disproportionately higher rates than those observed in adjoining Arab states.

If one were to look for one defining element which accounts for Beirut's cosmopolitanism and the changing character of popular culture and mass consumerism, then certainly what stand out are some of its playful, convivial and carefree attributes. These residues of its traditional folklore reinforce its receptivity to being immersed in changing patterns of consumerism, fashions and taste as venues of self-expression and validation of one's identity. It is also these attributes that generate greater prospects for aesthetic sensibilities germane to the proliferation of cultural and artistic expressions capable of transcending the rigidities of time and space. This is why, perhaps, as a metaphor, the Bourj as an urban setting approximates some of the redemptive features of a *playground*. As an ideal type a playground after all conjures up images of an open space conducive to both personal, intimate and familiar ties along with more fluid, protean and changeable encounters. Indeed, as we have seen, throughout its checkered history, the Bourj has always been adept at accommodating both the 'sacred' and the 'profane'. But both, as will be elaborated later, are forms of false consciousness. As restless and traumatized groups seek shelter in religion, its spiritual and sacred elements are secularized and ritualized, often degraded and rendered impious to accommodate their mundane and sacrilegious interests. Likewise, profanities, as is abundantly apparent, are often invested with the aura, grace and charisma of sacred idols.

These seemingly dissonant elements are not as mutually exclusive as they appear. Just as one can understand and account for the resurgence of religious and parochial identities in postwar Beirut, one can likewise appreciate the seductive appeals of secular spaces where groups can let down their guard. Indulgence becomes a testing ground for assessing how far they can stray without inviting the censure and reprimand of their society. This is why, as suggested earlier, those seemingly polarized dichotomies – the sacred and profane, cosmopolitan and provincial, universal and particular, global and local – have all been along malleable and porous lines. Being dialectical in character, they reinforce and enrich each other.

Much like the Latin quarter in Paris, Soho in London, or Greenwich Village in Lower Manhattan, the Bourj had many of the features – such as they were at the time – of an avant-garde and counter-culture setting. Hence groups with leanings to experiment with new ideas and lifestyles or to let off steam against some injustice in society were drawn to it. Intellectuals, journalists, poets, political aspirants, activists and ideological groups of all persuasions created their own venues for self-expression, conviviality and camaraderie. In the absence of sanctioned outlets, virtually any space – a private office or shop, a discarded portion of a house, an atelier or workshop, even the coffee house, the restaurant and the hotel lobby – could be readily converted into proxy meeting places.

The proliferation of such surrogate public spheres, which often assumed the form of an *arrière boutique* approximating Goffman's 'back-stage', were legion, particularly during the 1930s and 1940s. Typically, such places would first emerge on a tentative, casual basis involving no more than a small core of devoted friends consumed by a common passion or interest. Quite often a disquieting occurrence, a serendipitous event would gradually extend the appeal and notoriety of the place.

Another definitive milestone which sparked and sustained Beirut's legacy as a cosmopolitan public sphere was its space-setting role in nurturing the genesis and growth of journalism. The earliest Lebanese paper – *Hadiqat al-Akhbar* (the *Garden of News*) was established in 1858 on the narrow and as-yet-unpaved street connecting the Bourj to the port. Just as the Bourj was the pacesetter in launching and accommodating the first movie houses, night-clubs, cabarets, bars, public reading rooms, brothels and public gardens, on a more enabling and vital level it can also boast of ushering in and sustaining Lebanon's credible image as a 'nation of journalists'. Although newspapers had appeared a little earlier in Egypt, Beirut has had the longest and continuous press history in the Arab world (Rugh, 1979: 94).

Because of their country's comparatively higher and earlier rates of literacy and exposure to liberal forms of Western education, the Lebanese have long displayed a distinct predilection and talent for establishing papers and periodicals, sustained by an irresistible compulsion for reading them. Soon after *Hadiqat al-Akhbar* appeared, and in quick succession, the number of daily papers and periodicals increased exponentially. By the turn of the century, there were already about forty such publications (Tarazi, 1914: 4–21). This is certainly a dense volume of newsprint for a population of about 120,000. More important, they were also elitist in content and style, published by intellectuals with a literate and critical reading audience in mind. Since the commercial and service facilities were all at the time still concentrated around the city center, the Bourj and adjacent neighborhoods were home to virtually all the founding papers.

The critical, liberal foundation of Beirut's papers could not have fared well within the despotic and centralized reign of Sultan Abdul Hamid (1876–1909). Many Lebanese journalists were compelled to flee to Egypt to escape the strict and periodic censorship imposed by the Ottomans. They joined there the core of so-called 'Lebanese secularists', such as Yaqub Sarruf, Faris Nimr, Salim and Bishara Taqla, who had already made a start in launching some of the leading Arab journals and periodicals. Others sought refuge in the capitals of Europe from where they sustained their unsparing, often vitriolic, opposition to Ottoman despotism.

Those who stayed behind did not, however, restrain their critical stance. Like their expatriates, they were not just oppositional in their stance. They were instrumental in spearheading the surging sentiments in support of the Arab nationalist movement. They paid dearly for it. Sixteen out of twenty-one martyrs hanged on 6 May 1916 were journalists.[6] Indeed, it is telling that so many journalists were martyred on their own turf as it were; on the very

---

6 The following were the journalists: Said Akl, Ahmad Tabbarah, Aref al-Chehabi, Betro Pouli, Jurji al-Haddad, Abdel Ghani Uraysi, Muhammad Mahmasani, Nayef Tellou, Ali Armanazi, Abdel Karim al Khalil. The identity of the remaining six could not be ascertained.

ground which nurtured their voices of dissent, protest and liberation. Their acts of 'treason' were attributed to nothing other than stirring up public opinion against Ottoman despotism and of demanding freedom and independence. The Martyrs' Square and the National Holiday on 6 May have remained fitting memorials for their legendary and heroic acts of nationalist sacrifice.

During the French Mandate (1920–41), the penchant of the Lebanese for publishing periodicals and newspapers was revived. Some forty papers and more than 300 specialized magazines devoted to literature, education, political satire, women's issues, religion and cinema, appeared during these two eventful decades. The French were liberal in granting licenses but they also imposed their restrictive measures on recalcitrant journalists. These were not sent to the gallows, but the French did, often arbitrarily, suspend a few of the intractable voices who at the time championed their country's territorial integrity and rights of self-determination. For example, during its first six years, from 1933 to 1939, *an-Nahar* was suspended by the government no less than fifteen times because of its criticism of the Mandate powers and its campaigns for constitutional government (Tueni, 1971).

Lebanon's independence was tenuously held together by the *Mithaq al-Watani* (National Covenant) of 1943, which was based on a delicate consociational arrangement which allowed various sectarian communities and interest groups with varied ideological leanings to sustain a modicum of coexistence and power-sharing. Such a pluralist political culture was naturally reflected in a fragmented, often contentious media. Despite its partisan character, the overall quality of the press, the diversity and scope of its coverage, made it particularly appealing to readers outside Lebanon. Indeed, a handful of its papers had a much wider circulation in various Arab capitals. Their critical exposure of the pitfalls of overcentralized regimes became a source of protracted inter-state suspicions and hostility, particularly since political dissidents could use the relatively free and uncensored setting of the Lebanese press to hit back at the sources of their discontent and political dispossession.

Jealous about its freedom and independence, the Lebanese press was tenacious in resisting all measures to curtail or undermine its hard-won freedoms. Naturally some papers could not resist being 'sponsored' or 'subsidized'. Given the stakes, some editors were known to be 'patronized', rented or bought (*Ma'jurah*) in return for more charitable and favorable presentations of the country's public image. Such realities notwithstanding, the leading papers were resolute in defying efforts at muffling or censoring their stories and editorials. Their defiant dispositions were quite costly. *An-Nahar*, in particular, suffered more than its due share of outright intimidation and punitive reprisals. For example, the year Ghassan Tueni took over the editorship of the paper after his father's sudden death in 1948, he was summoned to court. From then on, virtually every year – in 1949, 1950, 1951, and 1952 – he ended up in prison serving terms of three months or more for writing what were deemed 'offensive' articles.

Finally, passing mention must be made that newspapers and magazines in Lebanon, like elsewhere, are prime venues for advertising. Hence, they need to grapple with the delicate balance between selling space to promote new products and maintaining the autonomy, freedom and quality of its coverage of news items worthy of print.

Chapter 4

Touting Luxury, Sensuality and Image

The postmodern world is very much one where culture, broadly understood, plays a major role. Instead of consuming the goods themselves, we consume the meanings of goods as constructed through advertising and display.

(Mike Featherstone, *Consumer Culture and Postmodernism*, 1991)

Logos do not simply signify goods, they serve as a marker to remind us that there are no public spheres, desires, practices, and needs that can escape being commodified. They are central to a politics of identity.

(Henry Giroux, *Disturbing Pleasures*, 1994)

On a short drive or casual stroll through any of the built-up regions, neighborhoods, streets and alleyways in Lebanon, one becomes painfully aware how the entire country is now blanketed by billboards, ads and other offending gimmicks touting a new product. Such merchandizing ventures, and they have become a major industry in Lebanon, do not only appear in major cities and their scrambling dense suburbs. They have also invaded the remotest towns and villages of South Lebanon, Akkar and the Beqaa Valley. The first thing to attract one's attention as one drives through their desolate hamlets is the proliferation of new shops with enticing displays and catchy logos of global brands and consumer products. The dissonance between the almost abandoned and forsaken villages and the profusion of kitsch ads is much too jarring.

In the mid-1950s when Daniel Lerner (1958) was heralding the advent of modernity in the Arab world, it was the unobtrusive, barely visible, objects

– such as the ballpoint, the wristwatch and eventually the transistor radio and the print media – which were seen as the 'vectors of modernity' and 'mobility multipliers'. In the mid and late 1960s, as television became more accessible, TV antennas on rooftops and balconies became the coveted emblems of modernity. Members of the underclass would even fake such possessions to ward off feelings of exclusion. Today digital cable dishes in all shapes and forms have invaded rooftops, along with the less visible gadgets of electronically mediated cyberlife. In towns and villages, the leafy and lush vines which once graced the rooftops have had to give way to these invasive contraptions of postmodernity.

Lebanon has been characteristically swift in adapting to the new transformations in media networks. In the early days of the internet, the average Lebanese was plugged in to portals like Yahoo and Google to seek information online (more than 80 percent of households have cable access). Today, social networks like Facebook, blogs, RSS Readers and social bookmarking tools are, according to Roland Prince (2009), rapidly gaining notoriety among internet users. Facebook claimed at that point to have around 635,000 Lebanese users that generated 70 millimeters pages per month, with a fascinating daily growing rate. Figures reveal that 53 percent of Lebanese Facebook users are male and 47 percent female. Differentiation by age indicated that the bulk was owned by the 19–25 age group with about a 45 percent share, but a surprisingly 4,600 subscribers were above 55 years of age. These figures are, incidentally, considerably higher than the rest of the Levant and Gulf region (see Prince, 2009, for further details).

This paradigm shift in the internet, abetted by the falling prices of digital technology and the proliferation of broadband access, has opened up a whole range of ways for people to express themselves and communicate with video. For example, recently Facebook started producing what it calls 'engagement ads'. Where conventional online ads are much like billboards advertising a preset message, engagement ads are more like digital bulletin boards, prodding participants to comment, sharing virtual gifts or becoming fans of the ads themselves. Another inventive and civic-minded program introduced by YouTube is the 'Video Republic', intended to support democracy with a witty tagline: 'everyday democracy'.

As in other 'creative industries',[7] Lebanon has always had a headstart over

---

7 'Creative Industries' is adopted from a recent survey conducted by the Olayan School of Business at the American University of Beirut. The label was used to include 'those

other countries in the region in terms of its receptivity to the changing forms of mass media and in being instrumental in exporting them to other parts of the Arab world. As early as the 1950s, Lebanon's exposure to traditional mass media (i.e. movies, print, radio and television) was considerably higher than all adjacent countries. The same is true of the advent of the 'new media', the media content available online. The recent evidence supplied by Roland Prince (2009) appears to confirm that Lebanon enjoys a disproportionate access to the 'Social Media' as well. This means that the Lebanese have more opportunities to express themselves freely. More important, they are no longer duped or passive consumers. They are also in a position to shape and share the media they decide to consume.

During the past few years Beirut has become unrivaled as the marketing, media and graphic design capital of the Arab world. Imposing billboards, employing the latest state-of-the-art technologies, punctuate roadsides and highways, often in violation of aesthetic and safety standards. Mega-brands, with no effort to render them in a more culture-bound vernacular, appear and change instantly. Nothing is spared commoditization: from the portraits of political leaders, assassinated public figures and martyrs of resistance movements, singers and entertainers, to the deepest and most intimate of our personal connections, namely the thriving sex industry, or the commercialization of religion and spirituality.

Even the enabling and patriotic virtues of political struggle and martyrdom are not spared the allure of commodification. In an insightful and graphically illustrated survey of a sample of political posters (150 from an archival collection of 700), Zeina Maasri (2009) shows how the iconography of such visual and aesthetic representations reflected the changing political identities and ideological discourse of the warring factions. Making judicious conceptual use of Stuart Hall and Antonio Gramsci's models of counter-hegemonic struggle, she analyzes the signs, textual discourse, visual and aesthetic representations of posters under study by focusing on four themes: leadership, commemoration, martyrdom and belonging.

---

industries which have their origin in individual creativity, skill and talent and which have a potential for wealth and job creation through the generation and exploitation of intellectual property'. The mapping constructed for the survey allowed the identification of seven creative sectors or industries as follows: (1) Theater, Film, Radio and Television, (2) Music Composition and Production, (3) Heritage, Painting, Photography, Sculpture, Fashion Design and Artisana, (4) Advertising and Graphic Design, (5) Architecture and Design, (6) Writing, Publishing and Print Media, (7) Video Games and New Technologies. For further information see Olayan School of Business.

Schor and Holt asserted that 'little remains sacred and separate from the world of the commodity. As a result people become even more desperate to sacralize the profane consumer worlds around them, worshiping celebrities, collections and brand logos' (Schor and Holt, 2000: p. ix). In the language of Emile Durkheim, the sacred is profaned and the profane is worshiped and sacralized. Durkheim is also relevant in a more compelling sense. He was, after all, among the first classical thinkers who alerted us to some of the unsettling consequences of anomie; where society fails to impose adequate restraints to regulate or tame people's excessive desires. In other words, society translates basic human needs into insatiable desires and hence traps man into a state of constant seeking without fulfillment.

It must be recalled that, to Durkheim, economic progress consisted mainly 'of freeing industrial relations from all regulation. Until very recently it was the function of a whole system of moral forces to exert this discipline, (Durkeim, 1933: 254). These forces included both religion and systems of guilds and corporations, primary traditionalist targets of the liberal bourgeoisie. They have now lost their moral power and can no longer set commanding social aims: 'the amoral character of economic life amounts to a public danger'. Into this moral gap flows the formal utilitarian rationality:

> Nations are supposed to have as their only or principal objective the achievement of industrial prosperity ... industry, instead of continuing to be regarded as a means to end which transcends it, has become the supreme end for individuals and society. But then appetites thus awakened are freed from any limiting authority. By sanctifying these appetites, so to speak, this deification of material well-being has placed them above all human law ... From the top to the bottom of the scale covetous desires are aroused without it being known where they might level out. (Thompson, 1985: 111)

Thus this 'deification of material well-being' becomes embodied in the sphere of consumption. 'One no longer knows what is fair, what are legitimate claims and hopes, and which are excessive. As a result, there is nothing to which one does not aspire ... Appetites no longer accept limits to behavior, since public opinion cannot restrain them' (ibid., p. 110).

Durkheim puts forward one of the grounding themes of the critique of consumer culture: in premodern societies, economic scarcity went hand in hand with social regulation to limit the range of human wants and needs. Modern deregulation and industrial productivity let loose human desires which are in principle insatiable. Indeed, in the acerbic language of Durkheim, 'sensation is a bottomless abyss that nothing can satisfy':

> Human nature in itself cannot set invariable limits to our needs. Consequently, in so far as it is left to the individual alone, these needs are unlimited. Without reference to any external regulating influence our capacity for sensation is a bottomless abyss that nothing can satisfy. But, then, if nothing external manages to restrict this capacity, it can only be a source of torment to itself. Unlimited desires are insatiable by definition, and insatiability is rightly considered a pathological symptom ... Society alone can perform this moderating role ... for it is the only moral power superior to the individual. (Thompson, 1985: 109)

The views of another classical sociologist – George Simmel – are also relevant in helping us understand how modern man, living in a society replete with anxiety, fear and uncertainty, is induced to seek shelter in the delusionary seductions of consumerism. With remarkable intuition and foresight, Simmel advanced the notion that man as resident of the sprawling, immense and crowded modern metropolis, assumes a 'blasé' attitude toward knowledge, work and lifestyle:

> The essence of the blasé attitude consists in the blunting of discrimination. This does not mean that the objects are not perceived, as is the case with the half-wit, but rather that the meaning and differing values of things, and thereby the things themselves, are experienced as insubstantial. They appear to the blasé person in an evenly flat and grey tone; no one object deserves preference over any other ... All things float with equal specific gravity in the constantly moving stream of money. (Simmel, 2004: 15)

To survive, in other words, one is compelled to 'blunt discrimination'. Everything appears in gray, flat tones with no object deserving any special regard over any other. One merely floats in a state of being adrift in a 'constantly moving stream of money'. Hence, the primacy of marketing and commodification. Within the same context Simmel advanced the notion that the 'blasé' person is also riddled with symptoms of 'melancholy': the generic affliction of the consumer. In Simmel's vocabulary:

> It stands for the built-in transitoriness and the contrived insubstantiality of objects that drift over, sink in and re-emerge from the rising tide of stimulation. It stands for the insubstantiality that rebounds in the behavioral code of consumers as indiscriminate omnivorous gluttony. (Ibid., p. 15)

This is also linked, as will be elaborated later, to some of the dismaying features of the 'society of the spectacle'. As rendered by Rolland Munro, the concept of melancholy in its current use represents not so much a state of indecision or uncertainty between choices. Rather, it represents a backing off. It stands for a 'disentanglement from being attached to anything specific ... Because of the infinity of connections, the melancholic is hooked up to nothing. In short, melancholy refers to a *form without content*' (Munro, 2005: 282). This, as we shall see, is one of the defining features of being in a society of the spectacle where appearance, image-making and fetishized and alienated consumerism become salient. To paraphrase Bauman, the consumer is simply drifting with the flow as he sinks into and re-emerges from the rising tide of stimulation. It is then that consumers are deformed into 'indiscriminate, omnivorous gluttony' (Bauman, 2007b: 42).

Some intellectuals and political activists (e.g. Antonio Gramsci, Raymond Williams and Richard Hoggart) acknowledged the parallel existence of popular cultures which constituted an informal 'plebian public sphere', organized through the medium of more restricted oral and visual communications. There is no evidence of such restrictive plebian public spheres in Lebanon. If anything it is the underclass, given the fairly affordable and universal access to television and pirated videos and DVDs, which appears to be addicted to such popular forms of entertainment. As a result, the role of the mass media in attending to the basic needs and issues associated with citizenship, and civic rights and obligations, has grown considerably in recent years. I take my hint here from the persuasive work of Néstor García Canclini (2001) who advances a similar conclusion when he explores the critical effects of urban sprawl, global media and commodity markets on citizens in Latin America. He argues that men and women increasingly feel that many of questions proper to citizenship – 'where do I belong, what rights accrue to me, how can I get information, who represents my interests – are being answered in the private realm of commodity consumption and the mass media more than in the abstract rules of democracy or collective participation in public spaces' (Canclini, 2001: 15).

MERCHANDIZING STRATEGIES

Most of the sociological and anthropological literature on consumerism has attempted to shed light on the meaning and status of consumption in modern society. At the risk of oversimplification, the basic thrust of the extensive volume of writing has been largely concerned with two overriding questions.

First, we are essentially what we consume, in the sense that consumption is a critical aspect of giving meaning, status and identity. More concretely, *what we own, how we use and display what we own, speaks to others of our status and tastes.* Furthermore, access to new and affordable advertising technologies has elevated crass material acquisition to the status of a dominant social paradigm. In such instances, as Princen, Maniates and Conca (2002) argue, commoditization becomes a strategy of substituting marketable goods and services for personal relationships, culture, artistic expressions and other sources of well-being.

Second, like most social phenomena, consumption is socially constructed. It is manufactured and programmed into an irresistible 'consumption trap' beyond the control of individual or community. Hence whether the consumer is simply duped or deceived by the charisma or aura of the hyped product, or whether he can rearrange and manipulate the marketing forces to comply with his interest and desires, becomes a contested issue. So sacrosanct has merchandizing become in everyday life, one can readily understand why it has also become a source of anxiety and apprehension. It is inherent in the fear of being caught, as it were, offguard.

It was Erving Goffman, in much of his intuitive exploration of the rituals of personal interaction and encounters in everyday life, who drew our attention to the importance of appearance and marketing oneself and, hence, to the constant threat of embarrassment. This ubiquitous fear hangs perennially over us: 'To be awkward, or unkempt, to talk or move wrongly, is a dangerous giant, a destroyer of worlds' (Goffman, 1961: 81). In the fluid, transient and episodic encounters of modern society, where consumption is becoming more relevant than productive activity in forging one's status and identity, people become more obsessed with managing their appearance and marketing their selves. It is in this existential sense, Goffman reminds us, that people are not trying to *do* something, but they are trying to *be* something. Clearly, it is the shift from doing to being that leads to the concern with packaging, marketing, taking shortcuts, manipulating circumstances to gain an edge over one's competitors.

In such a setting, as was suggested earlier, a person's worth, esteem and self-regard do not depend on his utility or functions. Rather it is more likely to be a reflection of his skillful ability to mobilize persuasive ploys, props, fronts, face (*wajh* and, hence, *wajaha*) and demeanors to realize his objectives. In such a world, it is not the moral code or respect which are the arbiters of conduct. Instead, it is tact, prudence and sociability which become prized. In the sardonic language of the Lebanese it is the *harbouq,* the chameleon-like character, the ever-changing and adaptable person, the one most adept at taking shortcuts and mastering the art of *shatarah,* that is, being quick-witted, under-handed, even ruthless and clandestine.

Since being adrift has become a ubiquitous condition, people become more adept at living situationally. Everyday life is riddled with uncertainties, unanticipated twists and turns. Nothing can be taken for granted anymore. Hence, agility, being impetuous, watchful and irascible often slips into trick-ery, deception and foul play. This is yet another catch-22 for the Lebanese. The very circumstances which enable the *harbouq* and the *shatir* – the prized national characters – to survive also render them sources of deception and misconduct.

The poor and the underclass are naturally more prone, as Bauman (2007b: 139) reminds us, to be victims of such pervasive fears. In a small country like Lebanon, characterized by fairly intimate, communal and familiar relation-ships, the poor face painful choices. They are forced into situations in which they either spend what little money or resources they have on senseless con-sumer items in order to deflect social humiliation or embarrassment, or face the dishonorable prospects of being teased and ridiculed.

Etel Adnan expressed the same predicament when she argued that this acquisitive impulse is so irresistible that people are willing, as she poignantly put it, 'to sell their honor before anything else, to buy any gadget, and this because material wealth has become the sole image of one's value so that the greatest humiliation seems the one of being poor, or poorer than one's neigh-bors' (Adnan, 1998).

The influence and stature of Lebanon's aggressive and fairly autonomous media, particularly its press and, more recently, its transnational satellite broadcasting and the bourgeoning sector of its creative industries – as noted by a score of scholars – have always been disproportionate to its size. It is also asymmetrical with its real power as one of the smallest and most vulnerable nation-states in the region. It is related that President Nasser of Egypt had the habit of reading the Lebanese press the first thing in the morning. During the three decades of Syria's hegemony over Lebanon, there was a strict embargo on the entry of Lebanon's newspapers into Syria. Yet the Ba'ath party and the ruling regime made a point of securing enough copies of the leading papers to circulate among the political elite and government officials.

The inventiveness and liberal traditions of the Lebanese media, reinforced by its entrepreneurial skills, also enhance its marketing dimensions. The direct impact on consumerism and lifestyle must be immense. About ten years ago both LBC1 and the Future were already employing fairly explicit erotic images and clips to advertise products. Given the restrictive censorship in the Gulf, LBC1 was adept at camouflaging its shows to broadcast erotically charged programs. In one instance they used a benign health and sports program as a prop, while host Haifa, accompanied by a trio of models in tight outfits, went about performing their sexually suggestive erotic sketches.

THE SLOGANS FOR TRANSFORMING CONSUMERS INTO COMMODITIES

What strategies or gimmicks are the Lebanese entrepreneurs employing to market and merchandize their products and to tempt the gullible but eager consumer to purchase new products? In the language of marketing, how are the Lebanese being enticed, nudged, even compelled to transform objects into attractive and desirable commodities? This is not, as Bauman puts it, an idle question:

> In the society of consumers no one can become a subject without first turning into a commodity, and no one can keep his or her subjectness secure without perpetually resuscitating, resurrecting and replenishing the capacities expected and required of a sellable commodity. The 'subjectivity' of the 'subject', and most of what that subjectivity enables the subject to achieve, is focused on an unending effort to itself become, and remain, a sellable commodity. The most prominent feature of the society of consumers – however carefully concealed and most thoroughly covered up – is the *transformation of consumers into commodities*. (Bauman, 2007a: 12)

One recent theme which underlies all marketing campaigns – whether for a car, a home, a facelift, a shopping mall, new fashions, even the maligned cigarette – is the promise of a 'good life', 'the pursuit of beauty, good-looks and happiness', 'a new life' or being 'born again'. The more fanciful, whimsical or spectacular the bait, the more willing consumers become to part with their money (earned money or, more often, borrowed money) to appropriate the hyped products. As was argued earlier, such acquisitiveness is predicated on the premise that the exuberant promises are deceptive and short lived. In a modern society characterized by swift and dissonant change, most valuables rapidly lose their luster and appeal. They are rendered wasteful, discarded and hence need to be disposed of to make room for the new.

The curious habits of the inhabitants of Leonia, as depicted in Italo Calvino's *Invisible Cities*, come to mind. They carry an ironical but telling message with regard to the nature of opulence and its implications for the relationship between excess and waste.

> It is not so much by the things that each day are manufactured, sold, bought that you can measure Leonia's opulence, but rather by the things that each day are thrown out to make room for the new. So you begin to wonder if Leonia's true passion is really, as they say, the enjoyment of new and different things, and not, instead, the joy of expelling, discarding, cleansing itself of recurrent impurity. (Calvino, 1997: 114)

Again, the image of Janus-like and baffling Beirut, with jarring symptoms of private opulence amid public squalor, makes it a facsimile of Calvino's Leonia. Being *adrift* has led the Lebanese to become more indulgent, impetuous, narcissistic but also more unrestrained and wasteful. The insatiable Lebanese consumer is yet to realize that today's crazed and coveted objects are destined to become tomorrow's forgotten fads. What is 'in' and fashionable today is 'out' and 'démodé' tomorrow, in the common parlance of the Lebanese.

The state of being *adrift* acquires a new existential and poignant predicament: in the words of Alberto Melucci, 'Being torn between desire and fear, between anticipation and uncertainty' (Melucci, 1996: 43). This comes close to what Ulrich Beck calls society at *risk*. These are today the misbegotten hallmarks of Lebanon's *adrift* state. It is a culture of fear, uncertainty and broken promises. In such a culture, it is foolhardy if not impossible, to validate one's worth and identity through rational, purposive learning and the accumulation of skills and refined cultural products. Much like the culture of the spectacle, it is appearance, impression management, conspicuous consumption, leisure and style which are more relevant to the existential needs of people adrift. Much of the seminal work of Zygmunt Bauman on our fluid modern world is essentially an elaboration of such reality. 'When destinations move or lose their charms faster than legs can walk, cars drive or planes fly, keeping on the move matters more than the destination' (Bauman, 2004: 116).

Caught in such a persisting state of limbo, an intermediate interlude of being unanchored yet uncertain of reaching one's expected destination need not be so unsettling. Most societies amid rapid social change are gripped by such fluidity and ambivalence. They disengage, become more introspective, more sober in the hope of reaching more agreeable and attainable destinations. More of the Lebanese, however, particularly in the current postwar setting, have not sought such felicitous options. They have become more extravagant in their expectations and more showy and spectacular in their outward behavior.

It is meaningful in this context to document textually the advertising slogans and images employed to commodify six basic amenities and needs: buying a home, beautifying oneself – through fashions and plastic surgery – entertainment and nightlife, and seeking spiritual solace and comfort through religion. I have deliberately employed the term 'touting' to suggest that the marketing strategies of the Lebanese in soliciting their customers are not ordinary advertising ploys. Instead, as touting implies, they resort to aggressive, persistent and often brazen and 'annoying forms of besieging and soliciting importunately' (*Webster's Third New International Dictionary*). The promoted product is always 'boastfully advertized and praised extravagantly' (*Random House Unabridged Dictionary*).

BUYING A HOME: A GATEWAY TO A TIMELESS ADDRESS OR A 'PIECE OF HEAVEN'

Lebanon, Beirut in particular, is today in the throes of an unprecedented construction boon. The magnitude of this sustained increase, as confirmed by a variety of sources, is truly unusual, particularly since it comes at a time of political uncertainly and regional and global economic crises. Most recent estimates indicate that there are currently about 400 major real estate projects in the country, of which 350 are about to be completed. Between 80 and 85 percent of these projects have already been sold. In more explicit terms this translates into about 2,600.000 square meters of built-up surface area which generated between $4 and $5 billion in real estate transactions (for further details, see *an-Nahar*, 30 Nov. 2009: 1–10).

Horrendous real-estate prices (estimated at $7,000 per square meter in Beirut) and increases in mortgage loans do not seem to deter the impulse to invest speculatively in land or in purchasing vacation homes. For example, the

Global Property Guide's annual report on real estate investment trends around the world reveals that Beirut ranks in fifty-seconnd place among ninety-one markets globally and in third place in the MENA region. The assessment is based on the price of a 120-square-meter apartment. The *Guide* is keen to indicate that this spectacular boom in property values, sustained over the past five years, comes in the wake of a global financial crisis. The *Guide* reports that apartments of that size were valued at $60,000 in 2004. They are now estimated at more than $400,000 (*Daily Star*, 22 Dec. 2009: 4).

Lebanon's commercial banks issued an average of 6,000 housing loans in 2006. The number of mortgages leapt to about 12,000 in 2008 (Nash, *Now Lebanon*). The real estate market is largely driven by expatriates and Gulf Arabs. Both groups are considerably wealthier than resident Lebanese. Much like proverbial 'Tulip Mania' in seventeenth-century Holland; the circumstances propelling the surge in land values are fictitious and irrational, based more on perception than reality. (Tulip mania peaked around the 1640s and had ruinous implications for the Dutch economy.)

Given the recent surge in construction, particularly upscale fashionable and exclusive residential compounds or towering skyscrapers, the once pristine and lush urbanscape of Beirut – dotted with suburban red-tiled roof villas – is quickly disappearing. At this same intensity of construction, Beirut will soon begin to look like any of the sprawling city-states in the Arabian Peninsula. Solidere alone has at the moment seventy-eight massive projects under construction in downtown Beirut. They are all marked by eye-catching panels with stylistic designs of the prospective project. What is striking is the swiftness with which the panels are changed; all with bold, high-resolution and often three-dimensional images. Beirut under construction seems like an open and ever-changing art show. The picturesque panels, of course, serve another hidden purpose. They enclose and hide from view the precious archeological relics being devoured in the process.

This ransacking of Beirut's urban legacy is made more deplorable by the way it is ruthlessly but stylistically merchandized. Glistening images and designs camouflage what is being plundered and mystify what is to be built. Here, art and deception are similarly aligned. Joanne Finkelstein tells us that 'the ubiquity of deception in popular culture is an invitation to consider the possibility that behind the surface of appearances there are other realities' (Finkelstein, 2007: 2).

In such a free-for-all context, any concern for the aesthetic, human or cultural dimensions of living space is bound to be dismissed as superfluous or guileless. As a result, it is of little concern whether our public spaces are ugly, whether they debase their inhabitants, whether they are aesthetically, spiritually or physically tolerable, or whether they provide people with opportunities for authentic individuality, privacy and edifying human encounters. If unrestrained, this surge for urban construction and real estate speculation could begin to assume some of the grotesque grandiosity of a Dubai-like skyline; a bonanza of everywhere-and-nowhere culture, spiced with gaudy theme-park attractions, gigantic shopping malls and a bland but monumental architecture.

These unpleasant realities are disguised by the ingenuity, beguiling and artful character of how new buildings and urban complexes under construction are merchandized. Purchasing an apartment or a house becomes a 'signature project', a 'gateway to a timeless address'. One is not only promised the 'good life ... The experience of serenity and natural charm.' Above all, it is an 'experience in the rebirth of luxury living'. One is also promised 'a piece of heaven'. A house, in other words is no longer just a comely roof over one's head but a signature project or a gateway to a timeless address or to 'own a piece of heaven'.

One residential project in an Achrafieh neighborhood is so exultant that its promotional panel identified no less than a dozen vignettes arranged graphically like a labyrinthine tapestry. The tempting myriad included the following: 'Comfort, Lux, Famille, Caractère, Tradition, Art, Anthenticite, Residence Levantine, Racine, Harmonie, Vie de Quartier, Environment.'

The City within the City, dubbed as one of the most monumental urban projects in the region (both in terms of built-up area and height), is designed by Jean Nouvel, a renowned global architect. Upon its completion, it will dwarf everything in sight. In its stylized image, the towering structure – which envelops much of the surface area of Riad El-Solh square, west of the Bourj – is made to appear pockmarked by bombshells and bullet holes, a fitting war memorial, since none exists thus far. Delayed because of the unsettling events of 2005, in the wake of Rafik Hariri's assassination, the project has been recently revived. Jean Nouvel has composed the following which appears on the advertising panel:

> There is a cultural heritage to reinterpret.
> Inside, outside, terraces, loggias, atriums.
> There is light, brilliant sunlight, and its consequences.
> Shade. These are the colors of the city:

Real golden stone and symbolic purple.
There is vegetation
These are our points of departure, our architectural material.
The whole thing is like a city within a city.
Unique, it will have its place along side
The markers and the moments of past centuries on the visitors' map of Beirut.

Another massive upscale residential compound which has been under construction for the past three years, and will most probably take as much before it is completed, is the *Wadi Grand Residence*, part of the 'WadiHill' project. Wadi Abou Jamil, the original Jewish quarter, was totally destroyed during the war. The luxurious project is built on the western and hilly end of the 'Wadi'. Hence its catchy identity. Its advertising panels include the following vignettes:

Tailored space for fine living.
A dream you call home
A unique blend of cultural history and exciting modernity
Revitalize mind, body and soul
Exclusive luxury, shopping and retail
A perfect environment

Bourj Kronful:
In the clutter of Beirut, Bourj Kronful stands tall in front of a lavishly open space. Directly overlooking the vast field of the Beirut Hippodrome ... Gives its spacious apartments even more breathing space and an unobstructed open view.

TITANIUM – Ain El-Tineh:
Adding its signature to a Beirut neighborhood synonymous with
exceptional exclusivity. Amid an absolute epicenter of sheer refinement
in the capital's fashionable quarter of Ain El-Tineh, this luxurious
residential development stands as the pinnacle of luxury and refinement.

L'Armonial:
Transmitting know-how to safeguard identity: Transmitting and safeguarding, two words that join to form a future built upon the idea of protecting and perpetuating Lebanese architectural heritage. L'Armonial is a pioneering residential project aiming to reserve a traditional building at Abdel Wahab El Inglisi Street,

while integrating it into a first-rate real estate undertaking. This method of real estate promotion initiated by Greenstone is an original solution to the erosion of Lebanese heritage, a solution that brings the old into the fold of the new. A legacy, a memory, a future.

The New Beginning: A and H Construction and Development:
We believe in homes that shape lives
We build walls that actually bring people closer together
And we redefine space to surround you and your family with the luxury of better living.

Beit Misk:
All villages have a history. This one's got a future: Beit Misk is that unique blend of the traditional and contemporary: you get all the pleasures of living in a charming village, with all the amenities you need to lead a modern life. That's why in Beit Misk, more than ever, we're answering all your future needs today.

In most of the other large-scale projects under construction – *Bay Towers, Eden Gardens, Park Palace, The Dana Plus Towers, Noor Gardens*, to mention a few – the recurrent motifs converge on: 'new expressions of luxurious living', 'select address', 'the good life', 'rebirth and new beginnings', the 'house of your dreams' with promises of 'authenticity', 'tranquility' and a 'nest of peace'.

Within the context of anomie, and again I cannot refrain from invoking Durkheim, the captivating panels are very telling. Both their defining identity or logos and what they promise to deliver are equally exuberant and hence delusional. One is not only beckoned to live in a 'Majestic Tower', 'Dream House', 'Signature Project', but one is also promised luxury, prestige, authenticity, harmony natural charm and elegance. The Arabic panels repeatedly refer to *al-Rafahiyya* (i.e. luxury, opulence). Quite often, they are dramatically inconsistent in what they promise to deliver. A house in a dense city quarter promises serenity, peace, tranquility and harmony but also the 'rebirth of luxury living'. A town-house or chalet in *Tilal Fakra* becomes an invitation to have not only a 'luxurious and prestigious villa', but also a 'nest of peace in the echo of tranquility'.

All these dissonant expectations are delusional precisely because they embody an inevitable disjunction. Hence one is doomed to a condition of constant seeking without fulfillment. This is after all, as Bauman reminds us, one of the defining features of a consumer society since it manages to render non-satisfaction a permanent condition in society.

PASSION FOR FASHIONS: HAUTE COUTURE CAPITAL

Of all the popular labels conferred on Lebanon, seedy or otherwise, being the 'daring fashion capital' in the Middle East has more than a ring of truth to it. This is evident in the impressive crop of fairly young designers whose outfits are showcased at celebrity events such as the Oscars and the Golden Globe Awards.

Though it had a headstart over other countries in the region, its haute couture and ready-to-wear fashion industry is largely the outcome of the last decade or so. Indeed, with the exception of Elie Saab who held his first show at the Casion du Liban in 1982, all the country's top designers (George Hobeika, Robert Abi-Nader, Zuhair Murad, George Chakra, Naji Hojeily, Pierre Katra, Reem Acra) began to design their lines during the 1990s. Initially, much of their business was directed toward local needs and the princely elites of the Gulf States. Lately though, more than a handful have acquired a stellar international acclaim.

Their designs are frequently seen on the catwalks of New York, Paris and Milan. Elie Saab and Reem Acra, in particular, are sought by movie stars, princesses, queens and the private jetset. Both have opened their own fashion houses in New York and Paris and are beginning to serve as role models to a growing crop of gifted young designers. Acra specializes in wedding dresses and glamorous evening gowns. It is the international reputation of this group of local designers which has enhanced Beirut's standing as the gateway to the burgeoning Middle East fashion and textile industry, estimated at $12 billion. The much anticipated catwalk of Beirut Fashion 2009 hosted some of the world's most prominent models displaying latest trends in the industry.

The 'success story' of Lebanese haute couture is largely a by-product, as in other venues of the creative industries, of the inventiveness and engaging marketing and public relations strategies they have employed in competing internationally with exclusive brand names. Specially alluring are their efforts to 'orientalize' their designs by incorporating local artisanal features – such as embroidery, needlework, the *abayas* and lounging robes women wear at home – into fashionable evening dresses. Yes, of course, the risk of kitsching-up the designs in the vernacular Lebanese wardrobe is inevitable, as seen in the surge of fashion shows featuring night gowns and fetishized lingerie and underwear. Somehow, the industry has resisted such demeaning incursions as it sustained its inventive expansion into ready-to-wear, men's casual clothing and lines for children. Incidentally, many such ventures, though initiated as small-scale family operations, are now franchised throughout the region (for further details, see *Creative Industries in Lebanon*, 2008: 29–44).

Zeina Karam, prefaced her recent Associated Press piece (29 July 2009) by the following:

> the gowns are cut low in the front, slashing down to the navel, or low in the back, swooping below the waist, inset with delicate see-through fabric. They couldn't be further from the modest dresses generally worn by women in the Muslim Arab world ... Yet these fashions came from Lebanon, a tiny Arab country known for military conflicts than the arts has produced.

Elie Saab is emblematic of a generation of gifted young Lebanese, not only in the fashion industry but in other sectors of the global economy, of the so-called 'creative industries'. To varying degrees, they are adept at converting local and vernacular traditions (both the fashion-conscious proclivities of the Lebanese for wearing plunging necklines and suggestive clothes and the rich fabrics and vivid colors) into vectors for inventive artistic creations which appeal to the beautiful people of Hollywood and the international jetset. Saab grew up in a modest home and recalls how he discovered his hobby as a kid sewing dresses for his sisters using his mother's tablecloths and curtains. Lebanon still at war, he established his own atelier in 1982, studied fashion in Paris and quickly climbed his way up.

Given the image and fashion-consciousness of the Lebanese, with the penchant for being glamorous, trendy and debonair, it is not difficult to account for the 'success story' of the fashion industry. By any measure, it is a fairly successful story. Like other creative industries, its products spilled beyond the limited confines of the local market. For example, the 80 percent increase in sales it witnessed in 2000 was largely due to clients in the Arab world. Despite its moderate size, it has swiftly emerged into a multi-million-dollar industry. Today there are at least forty haute couture houses in Lebanon. Each atelier produces an average of 200 dresses per year at prices ranging from $3,000 to $8,000 and reaching five-digit figures for top houses (*Creative Industries in Lebanon*, 2008: 36). It is also a labor-intensive industry. Small houses employ about thrity to sixty tailors and skilled embroiderers, and the figure can leap to about seventy full-timers and 200 part-timers. The volume of activity peaks in preparation of an international show; normally twice a year in either Paris or Milan (for the summer and winter collection) at the cost of $250,000 or $400,000 (ibid., p. 37).

In trying to understand the prominent role that fashion plays in the daily life of the average Lebanese, regardless of socio-economic standing, it should borne in mind that in the classical European humanistic tradition, fashion was always thought to be antithetical to good taste. A person compulsively following the whims of fashion was considered without style. A man of style, however – or a gentleman – was using his own power of judgment and discretion. Immanuel Kant (1734–1808) and Georg Simmel (1858–1918) some years apart and in different socio-historical settings held similar views on fashions. Kant and many of his contemporaries took the high road and were opposed to fashion because it departed from the pure aesthetics of the beautiful and the sublime. Simmel's renowned essay on fashion can be taken as a somewhat ironic commentary on Kant's idea of a *sensus communis*. Bourdieu too thought that Kant had elevated the sense of aesthetics to a purified and universal ideology, almost a second power (Gronow, 1997: 13).

To Simmel, fashion as a social formation always combined two opposite forces. First, the charm of novelty offered by fashion is a purely aesthetic pleasure. Second, and despite its seemingly frivolous, transitory and short-dived elements, the community of fashion reflected the real community of universal taste. It is the 'fun' and 'playful' ethics, along with the 'sensuous impulse and fellow-feeling', precisely because of their 'useless etiquette and irrational habits and customs', that become functional. No social formation, Simmel insisted, can survive without them (2004: 17).

Veblen's interest in pecuniary culture is also relevant for understanding the obsession of the Lebanese with clothing and fashion. Clothing provides an accessible and fairly persuasive way of showing off how wealthy we are. Apparel is naturally more suited to this style of display than any other object. Since dress is ubiquitous, even complete strangers can at a glance infer one's social standing from the quality of their clothes. As Veblen bluntly put it: 'A cheap coat makes a cheap man' (Veblen, 1899: 169). Furthermore, prestige was enhanced if one's clothing indicated that one could not possibly be engaged in manual labor of any kind.

Such observations notwithstanding, it is important to recognize how a group of talented Lebanese, driven and sustained by creative and intuitive entrepreneurship, have managed to transform this cultural predisposition for glamour and fashionable appearance into a viable export industry. Here, as in other venues of creative industries, the symbiotic interplay between culture and enterprise becomes a functional and enabling dialectic. To Paul Boulos, in fact, because of Lebanon's tested accomplishments in such creative pursuits, it has become a 'Creative Brand' in the region and beyond (Boulos, 2009).

What is admirable about this group is that, despite the commercial appeals of the market, quite a few have resisted being co-opted by pecuniary promises, lucrative as they are. Many have become spirited role models for social awareness and community service. Some have created or support grass-roots movements in various creative industries. For example, Sarah Beydoun of 'Sarah Bags' has made judicious use of her training in sociology as well as her enterprising and creative energies. Indeed, Beydoun's business is a form of community rehabilitation perhaps unique to Lebanon. Her program enables women at risk – either because of economic deprivation or the stigma of having a prison record – to acquire skills and a stable source of income.

The recent discourse on fashion continues to be riddled with controversy. Some, reminiscent of the classic tradition, are inclined to argue that fashion is a conspiracy to distract us from the real affairs of society. They bemoan the fashion lover as someone absorbed with the frivolities of trendy fads of unproductive consumerism. On the more positive and functional side, fashions, like any other material possession, are seen as sources of identity and status in otherwise destabilizing and unsettling times (Gay, 2008). The broader structural transformations generated by urbanization, technological innovation and secularism are still with us today. They continue to impinge on individual consciousness and thus exacerbate the polemics over the politics of identity.

Just consider, as elucidated earlier, how city life is constantly exposing us to the scrutiny of strangers. In a dense urban setting where different lifestyles and value systems become sources of anxiety, fashion could easily provide a shortcut which allows us to adopt an identity, join a subculture and thereby insulate us from others. In this manner, as Dick Hebdige (1988: 110) has persuasively argued, fashion goods could easily become 'weapons of exclusion'. They function, in other words, as identity markers. Hence, they are not as benign and frivolous as they appear.

More important, perhaps, as Leslie Rabine reminds us, clothes are 'erotically charged'. Fashion photography and advertising encourage women to gaze at other women with desire. In this regard since fashions eroticize aspects of everyday life, they make us obsessively attentive to details. They also compound our anxieties about appearance. So fashions can offer women more physical freedom and choice in self-representation. This can help us to better understand the 'success story' of the Lebanese in haute couture and their seemingly irresistible passion, often at exorbitant prices, for fashionable clothes. Acquiring a wardrobe, deciding what, when and how to be properly clad, become accessible and meaningful venues for expressing individual agency and social aspirations.

When Christian Dior, considered by many to be the father of modern fashion, was interviewed by *Time* magazine in 1957, he pondered the importance of luxury in contemporary society:

> I'm no philosopher, he said, 'but it seems to me that women – and men too – instinctively yearn to exhibit themselves. In this machine age, which esteems convention and uniformity, fashion is the ultimate refuge of the human, the personal and the inimitable. Even the most outrageous innovations should be welcomed, if only because they shield us against the shabby and the humdrum. Of course fashion is a transient, egotistical indulgence, yet in an era as somber as ours, luxury must be defended centimeter by centimeter.' (As quoted by Thomas, 2007: 7–8)

In her most recent work on the role of image and identity in popular culture, Joanne Finkelstein (2007) has this to say about how gender and status become a playful and expressive part of this interplay:

> The pleasures of voyeurism and exhibitionism have become firmly attached to the visible body making the displays of gender and status a playful part of its repertoire. Fashion can ameliorate the tensions between the masculine and feminine as well as those created by status inequalities and social privilege by creating ambiguous styles. The fashion industries endorse a modernist assumption that societies are progressive and self-renewing; they provide sites for expression of human rationality and creativity. (Finkelstein, 2007: 215)

The inference we can make from the above is that women need not be, as often assumed, passive victims of fashions. Nor are they entirely in control of the meanings attached to material goods. The prophetic and intuitive view of Simmel must be recalled here. He reminded us of two dimensions intrinsic to fashion: at one end, fashion incorporates materially utilitarian elements, at the other, aesthetically decorative, fleeting and situational features.

'THE MAKEOVER OF YOUR DREAMS': THE ALLURE OF PLASTIC
SURGERY

As of this writing (mid-September 2009), the most visible ads and billboards are the portraits of political leaders and electoral candidates. Though
the national elections were held almost four months ago, the commanding
portraits of politicians – often in massive screen panels draping over entire
buildings – still prevail. Even those mutilated by foul weather are promptly
renewed. In her introduction to *Creative Lives* (2009), an edited volume on
the lives of thirty-one Lebanese artists, the posters were the first image or
reality which attracted Sierra Prasada's attention as she drove from Damascus
to Beirut: 'The parade of diverse political posters look festive if somewhat
alien, their glossy surfaces throwing back the sun's light like so many gold
coins' (Prasada, 2009: 5).

Strong competition, because of the summer season, comes from the merchandizing of entertainers in sleazy nightclubs and upscale resorts. The
number and variety of singers, crooners and other vocalists (of both sexes) is
truly dazzling. From the empirical evidence, it seems probable that Lebanon
could boast the highest number of popular entertainers per capita. Clearly,
this is suggested by the selection of new faces, always in high-resolution and
larger-than-life images which punctuate the billboards, and tabloid magazines. This, too, has also become a prosperous export industry.

Equally striking is the merchandizing of a wide variety of new goods and
services normally beyond the reach of aggressive advertising outlets. Other
than the omnipresent ads for cigarettes, lingerie and liquor, advertising
campaigns for upscale hospitals and medical centers – simulating five-star
boutique hotels – are the latest rage. The same is true of specialized clinics,
health and beauty spas. Perhaps most popular are those promoting the
irresistible allure of cosmetic surgery.

Cosmetic surgery generally refers to an increasing range of medical
interventions directed at either improving or modifying the appearance of
the body (Haikein, 1997). It is by no means a recent phenomenon – scholars
provide evidence of such practices dating as far back as 600 BC. What is
new, however, is the sheer magnitude of its technological advancement
and widespread accessibility; particularly out-patient laser procedures.
Expressions such as 'nose jobs', 'boob jobs' and 'tummy tucks' have become
commonplace. What this in effect means is that the body can now be molded
and readily rearranged by liposuction; blepharoplasty (eyelid surgery);

chemical peels; bone reconfiguration; radical dentistry; amputation; implants; sub-incision (splitting of the penis); and skin-bleaching (Hall, 2007). The publicity surrounding labiaplasty (hymnoplasty, the so-called 'designer vagina') suggests that there is little which cannot be tucked or trimmed (Navarno, 2004).

The Lebanese appear to indulge in all the above with abandon and no visible ethical or medical scruples, particularly since all these interventions involve considerable risk and can have long-term physical side-effects. Even hymnoplasty, which elsewhere continues to arouse heated debates, is virtually normalized in Lebanon. Advertising of such procedures, once confined to sections of women's magazines, is now there for all to see. In May 2007, the First National Bank of Lebanon embarked on a unique and, perhaps, unprecedented media campaign. A legion of billboards (estimated at 900) in both Arabic and English sprouted up on a major roadway and thoroughfares. The campaign was not promoting one of the consumer products most cherished by the Lebanese, namely tobacco, alcohol or lingerie. Nor was it offering loans to defray the rising costs of school tuition, medication or home mortgages. The billboards instead were promising 'The makeover of your dreams.'

The corresponding magazine advertisement featured a blonde, blue-eyed woman beckoning the onlookers to 'have a life you've always wanted'. The bank was guaranteed a legion of takers. Lebanon has seen a dramatic surge in the demand for cosmetic surgery. In 1970, there were barely ten plastic surgeons. Today the figure has leapt to about a 100 and, possibly more. The sample of doctors interviewed by Doherty (2008) asserted that the demand for image-enhancing procedures among Lebanese nationals has risen substantially. Many of the surgeons claimed that their practice increased by 50 percent over the past decade. A good portion of this demand is due to the inflow of foreign visitors, leading Beirut to be hailed as the 'cosmetic enhancement capital of the Arab World'.

The motivations for facial and bodily makeover do not depart much from those observed among their Euro-American counterparts. The role of the media, particularly glossy periodicals like *Mondalité Noun, Prestige, Snob, Femme, Layalina, Special* (just to mention few of the top monthly magazines), is decisive in inducing women to submit to the knife. Such tabloids are often devoted to blown-up photospreads of social gatherings, receptions and celebrations, in a mélange of images without any accompanying text. Bereft of any story, they deliver an overarching message about media-imposed aesthetic norms and the irresistible pressure to abide by them. The advertising and cosmetic industries are very resourceful and inventive ventures. Ads for facelifts and cosmetic surgery are framed as the 'makeover of your dreams'. The makeover is not to be taken lightly, particularly 'in one of the world's most aggressive cultures of female display' (Zoepf, 2006). Given the skewed demographic realities, since a substantial number of eligible single young men are seeking employment overseas, women have to compete ruthlessly with other cohorts to attract the gaze of this scarce but coveted entity. As local work opportunities shrink, the gender imbalance is bound to worsen. Eroticizing one's body, being fashionable and sexually appealing and being on display in restaurants, bars, shopping malls, banquets and receptions becomes prized social capital.

The ranks of image-conscious Lebanese undergoing cosmetic enhancement has now a growing breed of new recruits: pre-adolescent girls. More than a handful of beauty spas and parlors have recently opened their well-advertised facilities to this younger generation who wish to emulate their mothers, older sisters and glamorized celebrities. Little wonder that bulimia and anorexia are much more widespread than commonly recognized. The few therapists and public health experts I consulted confirm this likelihood. A substantial number of women and increasingly men are prey to this cultural mystique which prods them to eroticize their bodies. Bulimia, in particular, is becoming more widespread. Hence, addictive smoking, another aberrant public affliction, may be related to the need of young women to suppress their appetite.

Despite the peculiarity of the gender imbalance, this longing to enhance one's physical endowments is certainly not unique to Lebanon. Eric Hobsbawn (1999), among others, has recently argued that modern society runs the risk of creating new forms of discrimination, no longer based on income, class, social status but on what he terms the 'cosmetics of affluence'. What is of relevance here for understanding this overwhelming appeal, almost charisma, of plastic surgery in Lebanon, as elsewhere, is that it is not just the *unhealthy* body but the *unattractive* body that stands out as a 'marker of moral failure' (see Raisborough, 2007: 26–7). If a seemingly benign surgical intervention can promise deliverance from this foreboding 'moral failure', little can be done to restrain its appeal, whatever its egregious side-effects.

A HEDONIST HAVEN: BEIRUT'S NIGHTLIFE AND SEXUAL CONSUMERISM

Lebanon's comparatively libertine and permissive popular culture has always had a special appeal to itinerant visitors and tourists, long before the Gulf and other Arabs started to use it as a party haven where they can indulge their licentious and iniquitous appetites with abandon, away from the taboos they must contend with in their prohibitive societies. Interestingly, it was the European travelers, during the first quarter of the nineteenth century, who first become aware of and wrote about the stylish life, of evening quadrille parties, freedom of movement and European shops and bazaars. They also spoke of the quick and stupendous changes in public life.

For example, the British traveler Frederick Neale, like several others, was almost rhapsodic when he described what he saw in Beirut in 1842. He spoke of the stylish lounging bars and Italian locandas 'with the latest European journals and French papers' (Neale, 1852: 235–6). He wrote amusingly of the evening quadrille parties, musical reunions and balls to which 'all the elite of every religion and costume are invited' (ibid., p. 211), and where the latest polkas and waltzes were admirably performed. 'The ordinary reunions break up before midnight; the people are a strictly mercantile set and late hours would interfere with their daily business.' He spoke of European bazaars and shops kept by Greeks, Ionians, Maltese and Italians selling 'a little of everything that comes from the West' (ibid., p. 217). Others were more impressed by the freedom of movement and the new liberties people were beginning to enjoy in their dress and appearance in public places. Lady Stanhope's physician and author of her *Memoirs,* revisiting Beirut in 1837 after an absence of six years, was moved to observe the following changes:

> The city of Beyrout had undergone great changes since the conquest of Syria by Ibrahim Pasha; not in the tortuosity of its street, not in its broken pavement and the filthy entrances to its houses, but in the appearance of its population. Formerly, a few straggling Europeans, or Levantines in European dresses, were seen hanging about the doors of a warehouse or two in the Frank quarter; and occasionally a European woman, the wife of a consul or a merchant, would steal from one house to another, as if afraid, in her way, of insult from a fanatic Turk. Now the bustle of a crowded mart was visible, and Europeans and their ladies walked about with a freedom which showed that a strong arm kept the haughty Mussulman under control. In 1831, the appearance of a French lady in the streets, wearing a green silk gown, was signalized as a feat of great hardihood; such an assumption of the

colour peculiar to the prophet Mahomet's descendants generally entailing vexations on the wearer: and a gentleman would never have dared to give his arm to a lady out of doors: but now, both the one and the other passed on without any loud remark, although, internally, the grave Mussulmans cherished a feeling of vengeance against those who so openly violated their religious and moral institutions. (Stanhope, 1841: 216–17)

As we have seen, the resilience of the Lebanese in putting up with dark times was also compounded by their proclivity to bounce back to a state of normalcy. During the civil war, particularly in successive cease-fire interludes, or during periods when the intensity of fighting had momentarily subsided, the first manifestations to resurface would be outlets which catered to their passions for leisure and frivolous consumer interests, maintaining the appearance that all is well with the world. It is telling that Lady Stanhope's physician, close to two centuries ago, was struck by similar impressions. He was describing Beirut during the decade of its occupation by Ibrahim Pasha of Egypt (1830–40): he spoke of 'Levantine in European dresses', the 'bustle of crowded marts' in the midst of the 'tortuosity of its streets, its broken pavements and the filthy entrances to homes'.

Again such Janus-like dualities have become more pronounced recently. Already half of the population have acquired the stern, severe, ascetic and joyless demeanor, at least outwardly, of a society engulfed in a culture of permanent resistance and militancy reinforced by a resurgent Islamic fundamentalism. The other half, largely a reaction to such foreboding prospects, have made 'I Love Life' their most abiding leitmotif. Within such a contested setting, it is not surprising that the sharp polarization becomes more pronounced and polemical. As one group seeks shelter in more prohibitive and restrictive lifestyles, the other finds redemption in being freed from any constraints on their epicurean and hedonistic impulses.

It is in this setting, along with the longing to make up for lost time, that a thirst develops for novelties, unfamiliar pleasures and nameless sensations; all of which lose their savor as soon as they are gratified. It creates a world of boorish decadence, with groups free from moral or social restraints, demanding instant gratification for their newly aroused impulses. With the ingenuity of an aggressive advertising industry, such delusionary expectations beget a world of graceless hedonists. Nothing seems out of bounds anymore.

No wonder that Beirut, of late, has been dubbed by the global media as a capital of virtually all the aberrant and disreputable labels: from 'Party City', 'Amusement Park', 'Nightlife Capital', 'Sex Life', 'Gay and Lesbian Capital' of the Arab world to 'Sin city'. Beirut lives up to its mischievous image and is not particularly embarrassed by the offensive attributions. Indeed, it wallows in them with much abandon. And it has been doing so for quite some time. Brothels or houses of prostitution were in existence in Beirut as early as 1880. It was not, however, until 1920 that laws were promulgated as a public health measure to control the outbreak of an epidemic among French troops. Not only prostitutes (*al-mumsat*) but dancers, singers and other so-called 'artistes' were required to register with the police. They were issued identification cards, went about their work in designated brothels and were subject to medical inspection twice a week. The presence of French troops must have played a part in increasing the demand for commercial prostitution.

The first decree to recognize and regulate prostitution (*al-da'arah*) as a legal profession was introduced in 1931. The law defined a prostitute as any woman who submitted to sexual intercourse (*irrtikab al-fahsha'*) in return for a monetary reward. It also distinguished between 'public houses' and other 'places of assignation'. Because of these restrictive measures, the number of registered prostitutes was reduced by almost half: from 1,250 to 624. The number of licensed brothels was confined to about sixty. Though limited in number, the prostitutes and the district in which they were located, east of the Bourj, became more visible and notorious. Like much of the traditional city center of Beirut, it was the period when virtually all enterprises and entertainment ventures were becoming commercially minded and receptive to novel modes of marketing and gentrification. The enterprising *patronas* gave the maligned image of their tainted quarter the facelift it needed to transform it into a welcoming place.

Reference must be made here to the epic-like story of Marica Espiredone, the Greek emigrant who managed to cast her mythical shadow over the entire red light district of the Bourj for over half a century. Her rags-to-riches biography is riveting precisely because she epitomizes the circumstances associated with the metamorphosis of commercial prostitution. Quite ahead of her times, she managed to transform herself from being a *sex object* to a *sex worker*: from being a quintessentially passive and resigned victim of male domination and manipulation to being a willful agent who actively constructed her work life.

The fact that the notorious red light district was becoming so compelling and visible in the very heart of the nation's capital did not go unnoticed. I have elsewhere (Khalaf, 1965) identified three distinct reactions or groups. First, traditionalists, particularly heads of religious communities, were inclined to regard prostitution as a necessary evil, a safety valve for the release of the superfluous sexual energies of the young. In their view, the prostitute in this sense protects the virtue of the family and the sanctity of marriage. Second, there were those who were more inclined to condemn prostitution because it involved the commodification of sexual intimacy, the confinement of women and the restriction of their freedom. Finally, there were those who recognized the need for regulated brothels but who wished to relocate them away from the heart of the city. Given the persistent demand for licensed prostitution, and it is not likely to disappear with the liberalization of sexual mores, this group is of the view that outlawing prostitution carries the risk of shutting off an expedient safety valve. The prostitute, with the help of pimps and procurers, will be driven underground and forced to resort to clandestine and more nefarious means.

The results of a rare empirical survey of the state of legal prostitution in the mid-1960s, based on personal interviews with a sample of resident prostitutes in the red light district, confirm the above projections. While the prostitutes remained comparatively busy, they were already beginning to complain about the decline in the quality of their business. They were also astute and prophetic in attributing this inevitable demise to changing lifestyles associated with the advent of stereo-clubs, mass consumerism, international migration and sexual tourism (Khalaf, 1965).

The destruction of the red light district during the early rounds of the civil war for control of the city center in 1975–6 was altogether a propitious windfall. Already, manifestations of clandestine prostitution, part of the bourgeoning global industry, were beginning to permeate society. By then, and perhaps more so than other societies in the region, Beirut had not been spared some of the aberrant consequences of globalization and mass consumerism. International migration carried with it a dramatic change in the sex industry, particularly in the manner in which a growing number of consumers were purchasing their sexual services and products. Taking advantage of a loophole in the country's public-health laws dating back to 1931, which penalizes those who facilitate, encourage or live off acts of prostitution but not the prostitute herself, bevies of shrewd entrepreneurs emerged to exploit the potential inherent in such a laissez-faire setting. The most thriving part of this largely global industry is represented by the 'super nightclubs' that dot the coastline between Jounieh and Maameltein. There are somewhere between eighty and ninety such upscale joints in those tourist neighborhoods. Each club can employ up to sixty hostesses, mostly girls from Eastern

Europe or the former Soviet Union. Others of lesser quality, and not as concentrated, can be spotted around Hamra, Ain Mreysseh, Mansourieh, Sin El File, Hazmieh and mountain resorts like Aley. To qualify as a 'super nightclub', the establishment must offer a cabaret and the hostesses are recruited as 'artistes' for six-month renewable periods.[8] Only a few of the larger clubs provide such artistic performances or entertainment, however the main attraction is the opportunity to spend time with a girl of one's choice; the fee – ranging from $60 to $100 – depends on the quality of the drink and the time spent, not exceeding ninety minutes. The clubs are not bordellos, and the girls are not allowed to provide any sexual favors. Undercover policemen or Sûreté Générale officers are expected to monitor the premises by making unannounced spot checks. In principle, customers are not permitted to leave with girls from the club. For a certain fee, however, a man is entitled to 'ask the girl out' during her 'off' hours, from one o'clock to seven o'clock. It is during these interludes that the girls tend to their trade. Depending on their personal appeal and resourcefulness, the business could be exceedingly lucrative, even though by the terms of their contract they are expected to share a stipulated portion of their earnings with the club proprietor and, often, the hotel manager for paying off security officers.

The 'super nightclubs', generating an estimated $100 million annually, are by far the most lucrative sector of the expanding sex industry in postwar Lebanon. Since the bulk of the workforce providing the services in this stigmatized profession are itinerant transnationals, some of the ethical reservations that traditional moralists continue to hold with regard to prostitution are partly allayed. Lebanon, however, like other countries involved in the illegal trafficking of women for sexual exploitation, has a questionable record on human rights which on occasion prompts the government to be more prohibitive in its restrictive measures.

Although not as visible or lucrative, the tourist sex industry has other outlets that cater to the eroticized needs of customers. Most prominent are massage parlors, often euphemistically labeled as 'anti-stress centers'. Technically, the parlors are legal since licenses are usually sought for a hygienic 'treatment center'. Under such a therapeutic guise, they openly advertise in the local press, and their premises are located in respectable residential or business quarters. They generate over $20 million annually. Given

---

8   By Lebanese laws, the imported 'artists', as they are officially called, are expected to return home after six months.

their accomplished skills in this regard, most employees are Filipino or Asian women who attend to about seven customers per day. The session, lasting thirty to forty minutes, usually costs around $20 – plus all the other additional services, up to $30 – which are kept by the masseuse.

The three other conventional outlets, the closest to those offered by the traditional brothels, are the bar-girls, call-girls and freelancers. Together they generate another $20 million annually. There are about two dozen such bars, recognizable by their traditional red lights, in the Hamra and Ain Mreysseh districts. They are usually managed by mature, enterprising *patronas* and employ about four women, mostly Egyptian and North African. The cost of a drink is no different from other ordinary bars. Unlike 'super nightclubs', the women are available – for about $50 – for sexual encounters in a secluded modest room behind the bar or elsewhere in the premises. Since these establishments are unlicensed, the police have to be kept quiet and at a distance.

More upscale and glamorous are the rings of fearsomely popular Lebanese girls, often aspiring models, singers, dancers or those seeking marriage partners, who ply their trade in hotel lobbies, lounges and other fashionable resorts. The more ambitious advertise their 'escort' and other services in the many glossy magazines in the hope of being picked up by one of the agents who arrange, under a rich variety of proxies, regular weekend party charter flights between Beirut and the Gulf States.

The lowest on the totem pole of commodified sex, and the most accessible and affordable component, are the ordinary streetwalkers. They are generally Lebanese, Syrians and Africans who may be seen on highways, Raouche, Janah and at popular intersections. Others might be domestic help moonlighting on their days off. Recently, many have been frequenting cafes, bars and open meeting spaces of downtown Beirut: their original abode of old!

As in other societies, particularly those where tourism is likewise a viable sector, prostitution became part and parcel of a thriving adult entertainment industry. The accessibility of X-rated videos, adult cable shows, computer pornography, adult magazines, even commercial telephone sex has, like elsewhere, invaded the inner sanctum of the home. In this respect, the globalization of sexuality began paradoxically to contribute to its privatization. Pornography, both in its 'soft' and 'hardcore' varieties, existed in some of the run-down and dilapidated movie houses in Beirut during the war and shortly after. The past decade has seen porn migrate from the movie houses to the privacy of the viewers' own living rooms. Little can be done to avert or control such an aggressive and tenacious invasion.

The commodification of sexual outlets has not only affected the character of prostitution. The emergent and fluid features which characterize homosexuality as a community, or a subculture, within the context of postwar Beirut, are also beginning to reflect some of the broader changes associated with regional and global transformations.

Discussions of homosexuality, judging by the media and, often, sensational attention it has been receiving, are an indication that it has already become part of the public discourse, though technically it remains illegal, since officials deem it 'unnatural'. More compelling, Lebanon now can already boast of being the first country in the Arab world to establish a gay rights voluntary association (Helem, the Arabic word for dream and acronym for Himaya Lubnaniyya lil Mithliyeen). While other states in the region are prosecuting gays (in Iran and Iraq they are executed), Helem has a regular periodical (*Barra*), its own website and a guide which offers inventories of gay-friendly clubs, bars and safe cruising areas. As a result, the number of gays who have recently 'come out' and who are actively engaged in defending their lifestyle and associated freedoms are becoming more audible. Its recently installed website is already being inundated by over 50,000 hits and postings per month (see McCormick, 2006).

Despite the overt liberalization and less inhibitive socio-cultural setting, evidence extracted from a score of recent studies reveals that most Lebanese are still averse to considering a gay way of life as acceptable.[9] In February 2009, a widely publicized beating by police of two gay men prompted Helem to stage perhaps the first major gay rights rally. The protest in downtown Beirut drew a limited crowd of supporters with rainbow flags and banners calling for gay rights. Many practicing gays lead portions of their lives covertly, particularly in relation to their family. Usually, the father is kept in the dark. At least he is the last to know. Hence, the delicate balancing act – being 'in/out' of the closet – is still riddled with tension, ambivalence and personal anguish. It is interesting to point out in this regard that quite a few who have lived abroad are inclined to show less dissonance between their lived and gay identity. In fact, many of those have come out recently and appear to take many of the Western gay archetypes as a guide and role models in validating their own gay identity. They also are the groups who assume leadership roles in the activities of Helem.

The legal restrictions are so permeable that the 'Bear Arabia Mega Party' was hosted in a beach resort in June 2009. (The label 'Bear' is employed

---

9   For a sample of such recent studies, see Mourabet (2006); Moussawi (2009).

globally to refer to heavy-set, hairy gays, usually older than thirty.) The internationally advertised event attracted scores of participants not only globally but regionally where homophobia is still rampant.

Altogether what is striking about the gay scene is that Beirut is the only place in the region where non-heterosexuals and groups who harbor alternative lifestyles and sexual orientations can still feel fairly secure. Yes, of course, groups are still furtive about the public display of affection. Watchful security guards at clubs can intercede if the display of intimacy gets too frisky. On the whole though, tourists who are seeking Beirut for such outlets are not at all disappointed. One may not as yet identify a concrete subculture, but there is a bourgeoning gay social network with a website, international chat sites and a growing but roving member of clubs, hotels and bars – some not exclusively homosexual – where they can meet and interact without the disgrace of being admonished or rebuked. Though they are fairly at ease about their sexuality, they do not feel the need to carry their sexuality on their sleeve. Likewise, they avoid being flamboyant or openly cavalier. Thus the quest to forge a plausible gay identity is promising. It is bound, despite the current uncertainties, to play a transforming role in the advancement of sexuality and gay rights in Lebanon and perhaps elsewhere in the Arab world.

Its legendary after-dark culture and nightlife, the lavish display of all the resplendent outlets which cater to all the hedonistic and licentious desires of pleasure-seekers, are becoming much more risqué, even outlandish. Nothing seems out of bounds any more. Rooftop clubs, some singled out as unrivaled in the world, stay open until dawn. Bikini-clad ladies lounge in exclusive beach clubs decked with colossal state-of-the-art yachts. The proverbial three S's (sun, sand and sex) are all located on a strip of about twenty kilometers north of Beirut, from Junieh to Maameltein. 'Super nightclubs', over a hundred of them, attend to a thriving clandestine sex industry.

With the destruction of the regulated brothels and red light district east of Martyrs' Square in central Beirut during the civil war, the coastal strip quickly emerged as an alternate disreputable, racy but fashionable nightspot. Here pleasure seekers – and given the prohibitive cultures in adjacent regimes, Arab nationals arrive en masse – can indulge their appetites for glitzy shows and lurid entertainment without any restraints. They can watch women, mostly from Belarus, Ukraine, and Romania, perform nude and strip shows. Though sexual encounters are not permitted on the premises, enterprising pimps for as much as $5000 to $10,000 per night can deliver any of the chosen women (*Daily Star*, 28 Aug. 2009: 3). In less attractive areas, Iraqi women who have fled their country are drawn to commercial prostitution as an accessible lucrative source of income. One Ukrainian woman I interviewed, an English teacher back home (earning about $400/month), averaged more than $45,000 in six months.

In 1998, the government passed a law forbidding brothels or other places where women had access to beds and rooms for sex work. To bypass the law and recognizing the lucrative returns of sexual tourism, the official label of these outlets changed to 'super nightclubs'. Though sexual encounters are not permitted on the premises, women could still be solicited and taken up to other locations, thus reinforcing the shadowy and discreet operation of the thriving sex industry. In this regard, though prostitution is officially prohibited, the country can still reap the benefits of the increase in tourist revenues from those seeking sexual adventure.

Ghada Masri made the following comment after conducting ethnographic fieldwork on sexual tourism in Beirut. Her respondents included local residents, tour guides, tourists and those who worked within the industry:

> The myths of modernity and rebirth drape the image and reputation of Beirut as a place of desire where the fantasy of consumption, designer goods, and commoditized bodies are possible. Beirut's cosmopolitan spirit, taken to excess, as many things are in Beirut, encompasses its tourist consumption of sexualized and nationalized female bodies. Beirut's cosmopolitanism is turned into an 'international buffet' where women of the world, whose bodies are nationally marked (that is Ukrainian, Ethiopian, Syrian and Iraq), are presented on a sampling platter to the highest bidder – giving new meaning to 'national cuisine'. (Masri, 2009: 2)

Gemayzeh, one of Beirut's hotspots for party-goers, barely existed a decade ago. It was a quaint, quiet residential neighborhood with artisans, grocers and traditional craftsmen and novelty shops at street level and homes for mostly lower-middle-class families on top. 'Le Chef', a tiny, nondescript restaurant, frequented by foreign journalists and left-leaning local mavericks, was the only outlet in the entire neighborhood. Today it is jam-packed with about eighty bars and clubs and thirty restaurants and cafes. Oddly, only around 5 percent of the bars are legal, as they do not meet requirements concerning adequate parking space and noise pollution. On weekdays and weekends, the vehicular and pedestrian traffic is so dense that one can barely inch through without literally bumping into others.

Despite such discomforts, perhaps because of them, Gemayzeh continues to be a prime nightlife and tourist attraction and a vital artery of the
Lebanese economy. The demand for such after-dark and party outlets is
so inelastic that Mar Mikhael, its adjoining street and neighborhood, is
already beginning to cope with the spill over. Just as Gemayzeh emerged
in the wake of Monot's decline, Mar Mikhael could well be the harbin-
ger of what lies ahead. Incidentally, Monot – the urban enclosure named
after one of the prominent Jesuits associated with the establishment of St
Joseph University (USJ) – was the first neighborhood to attract a score of
bars, night-clubs, side-walk cafés and restaurants. The commercial viability,
along with the congestion and nuisances generated by such outlets, drove
enterprising capitalists to locate their premises in Gemayzeh.

At the moment, Beirut is also undergoing a startling shopping-mall boom.
The most discernible retail trend during the past few years has been the inexorable rise of Western-style shopping malls, catering mainly to a well-heeled
clientele in and around Beirut. Medium-sized, city-center malls such as ABC
in Ashrafieh or the Metropolitan in Sin el-Fil have been doing thriving business since they opened at the turn of this century. Much larger out-of-town
centers have mushroomed in Dora, Chiyah and other suburbs. They are all
buzzing with customers and aggressive advertising strategies. The competition is so intense that a few are resorting to bolder measures to attract the
bulging generations of shopaholics.

Most striking perhaps is that these manifestations have lately begun to
emerge in the south and the southern suburbs of Beirut. The stigmatized
image of 'Hizbullah Land' as a foreboding place, a breeding ground for
resistance cultures of young militants devoted to the joyless creeds of martyrdom and self-sacrifice, no longer reflects the visible changes on the ground.
Certainly, the appearance of amusement parks, ecotourism facilities in towns
in the south and a relentless string of cybercafes and restaurants in the southern suburbs of Beirut speak otherwise. Interestingly, these are not only built
by a corporate investment group but they reflect the new face of Hizbullah.
They represent, as Lara Deeb and Mona Harb (2009) demonstrate in their
ongoing research on the emergent 'Islamic Milieu', Hizbullah being directly
involved in sponsoring activities which aim at reintegrating elements of
Thaqafa (literally culture) into the religious and political fabric of society.
They are, in effect, 'promoting a particular moral lifestyle that naturally is
accompanied by political allegiance, coupled with notions of education and
class mobility ... *Thaqafa* also includes not only resistance politics and moral

behavior, but also consumerism, historical narratives, heritage, the natural and built environment, and religious practice and debate' (Deeb and Harb, 2009: 199–200). In other words, Hizbullah, with all its avowed virtues of piety, moral and ethical edicts of abstinence and asceticism and its rejection of all the desecrating profanities of Western culture, has not been able to resist the marketing demands for Islamic entertainment.

More pioneering, and on a much larger scale, is the Beirut Souks project which has just been launched after considerable delay because of political unrest. Commanding some 100,000 square meters of space and costing over $100 million, the souks were designed by the world-renowned architect Rafael Moneo in place of the traditional largely makeshift, labyrinthine souks destroyed during the civil war. The commanding complex, designed in the style of a traditional open-air Middle Eastern market, accommodates over 200 outlets representing every conceivable trendy franchise or global brand name. Still in a 'soft opening' phase, it is already dense with traffic. The malls, much like the neighborhoods taken over by upscale restaurants, bars and sleazy night-spots, are also haunts for 'proletarian shoppers' and tourists. There are more people window-shopping, sight-seeing, browsing, loitering or simply parading or cruising up and down. They are there to be seen and attract the public gaze. They consume images and space but not commodities.

In summer 2009, because of the relative lull in political unrest, the Tourist Ministry reported record figures. In the month of July alone one million-plus tourists came for short or extended visits. The inflow was expected to be sustained to exceed two millions by the end of 2009. This is roughly equivalent to half the country's population. Interestingly the bulk of the regional tourists are not attracted by Lebanon's historic, archeological or cultural endowments. Instead, they are overwhelmingly drawn by the shopping, entertainment and sleazy nightlife.

RELIGIOUS TOURISM

Even religious vestiges are not spared commodification. Of all novel forms of tourism currently salient in Lebanon – medical, cosmetic, sexual, amusement and nightlife, shopping – religious tourism is lately becoming more ascend-ant. Monasteries, sanctuaries, mausoleums, churches and shrines abound in Lebanon. Given the eighteen recognized confessional communities, the wealth and diversity of such sacred vestiges and their touristic attractions are immense. The Ministry of Tourism is currently undertaking concerted efforts to boost the touristic potential of this unusual legacy. A documentary book – *The Paths of Faith* – will be released shortly. This is supplemented by a film about the Christian and Muslim holy sites. Both provide vivid portraits and narratives to account for both the proverbial religious pluralism of the country and how it has managed to remain a Christian stronghold in a largely Muslim region.

The holy sites, it should be pointed out, are not limited to the conventional touristic attractions of the coastal cities like Byblos, Tripoli, Beirut, Saida and Tyre, along with Baalbek in the Beqaa Valley. Both *The Paths of Faith* and a recent handsome but rigorous archeological and historical survey on the *Roots of Christianity in Lebanon* by Antoine Harb (2008), provide inviting and persuasive evidence to show that this rich religious legacy is present throughout the country, including obscure towns and remote hamlets. For example it is commonly known that Jbeil (Byblos), as a Phoenician holy city where the Greeks adopted the Phoenician alphabet, was already a prosperous city by the end of the sixth millennium BC, some 7,000 years ago. By then, we are told, it was attracting an inflow of visitors and pilgrims coming to participate in the Adonit celebrations held annually in spring to commemorate the death and revival of the young God Adon (Harb, 2008: 116).

Some of the earliest archaeological vestiges in other less recognized places date back to prehistoric Homo Sapiens, some 40,000 years ago. The Batroun region is distinguished since it contains the largest number of old churches dating back to the Byzantine and Crusader periods. More telling, perhaps, is that most of the churches were built on the ruins of 'pagan' temples (Harb, 2008: 130). Incidentally, the names of many of the towns and villages in the coastal, mid and upper regions of Batroun still carry Semitic names, Aramaic, Phoenician and Syriac. In the Kura district, likewise, towns like Bziza, Kusba, Anfeh, Balamand and Amyoun (where a sepulchral tomb was transformed during the Middle Ages into a shrine dedicated to St Marina) have a rich yet largely unknown legacy of sanctuaries, citadels and shrines. The same is true of the remote Akkar region, largely unknown to local and foreign tourists. The Akkar mountains, in particular, along with tel Arqa, the region of Qobayyat and Akroun have considerable touristic potential.

Two touristic sites stand out: the town of Cana of Galilee and the Qadisha Valley. Cana, the southern village where Jesus performed his first miracles and started preaching the Gospel, has seen a new surge of visitors, particularly after the Israeli air attack of 1996. The vicinity of Cana is replete with rock engravings and grottos; all asserting the relationship of Jesus with the village. The neighboring town of Maghdoushe where, according to customary belief, Mary used to accompany her son on his preaching visits to Tyre and Sidon, is also home of the Grotto where she used to wait for him. The sanctuary was turned into a shrine in honor of the Virgin Mary.

The northern Qadisha Valley (also known as Wadi Qannoubeen) is a truly spellbinding landscape. Despite its rugged topography, the valleys of Qadisha and Qozhaya are dotted with monasteries – the oldest and most renowned is the Monastery of Qannoubeen founded by Theodosius the Coenobit) during the fifth century. (Koinobin in Greek means a place where monks gather.) The original church was constructed inside a hallowed cave and from 1440 until the mid-nineteenth century, it was the seat of the Maronite Patriarchate (see Harb, 2008: 142–8). Within the two valleys there are at least a dozen monasteries and sanctuaries. It was within such austere and foreboding settings that the foundations for Maronite ascetic life were nurtured long before the establishment of the Maronite monastic orders. Fleeing the persecutions they suffered in Syria in the fifth century, they were impelled by feelings of dread and insecurity, and carved sanctuaries straight into the jagged rocky cliffs, barely visible from a distance. The Monastery of Qozhayya stands out because it was there that the first printing press was introduced to the Middle East in 1558, in conjunction with the founding of the Maronite School in Rome. Given this composite legacy, it is no wonder that the valley was named a UNESCO world heritage site in 1998.

I dwell on this distinctive religious legacy in order to point out that, with the exception perhaps of Qannoubeen, these sites remain largely unknown to local and foreign visitors. The sites, however, which are drawing an incessant influx of zealous and devoted visitors, are shrines, graveyards, religious icons or portraits of clerics and nuns associated with 'miraculous healing' or other magical-like redemptive or benevolent attributions. The veneration of such myths and sites is deeply embedded in the religious beliefs, rituals and practices of many Lebanese. Examples are legion and relentless. Brief reference to a few will suffice for purposes of our discussion.

Rituals associated with the worship of Adon are still alive today in coastal towns like Sarba, Tabarja and Bouar. The Adonit rituals involve washing in sea water, in a river or in dew to purify oneself or, and more likely, to seek cure or relief from physical deformities or incurable ailments, particularly skin afflictions and infertility (Harb, 2008: 14). More important, the rituals sometimes invite monetary donations as an expression of gratitude or in return for an anticipated blessing. If not direct financial tokens, gestures could well involve offering the first fruits of a season, flowers or some precious item or idol. Most prevalent perhaps is the votive offering that requires no more than lighting a candle, or hanging a colorful ribbon, or a personal souvenir, on a tree next to the sanctified shrine in anticipated fulfillment of a pledge or a vow.

Two of the most renowned spiritual sites in Lebanon are the famed statue of the Notre Dame du Liban on Harissa's mountaintop and the Monastery of St Charbel in Ihmej. The former, largely because of its dazzling panoramic view, manages to attract about 3,000 daily visits. During holidays and weekends, the number leaps to 15,000–20,000. No wonder that Harissa has been declared one of the most popular religious tourist sites in the Middle East. St Charbel has recently began to compete with Harissa. It is associated with the epic hermetic life of Charbel Makhluf who, since he was beatified in 1965 and canonized in 1977, has emerged as one of the most venerable saints in Lebanon. He was born in 1828 to a poor family in Beqaa Kafra, the highest village next to the Cedars. He spent his boyhood in his native village where he was nicknamed 'the Saint' because of his profound piety and absolute devotion to God. Early in his twenties he entered a Maronite religious order at the monastery of Mayfuq where he studied Syriac, Arabic, liturgy, theology and canon law. In 1859 he was ordained priest and remained at the monastery of Mar Maroun, Annaya, until 1875. It was then that he sought a hermitage attached to the monastery and lived in total seclusion until his death the night before Christmas in 1898. He was entombed in Annaya above Byblos. His body, as noted by a score of biographies, remained intact until 1952. It is then that 'miracles' were performed on his intercession; often 'a brilliant light' was reported by witnesses shining from his sepulcher (for these and other details, see Daou, 1980).

The home page of St Maroun-Annaya Monastery provides an inventory of testimonials supplemented by signed certificates and medical reports of the healing of at least twenty subjects in 1950. All the healings, 'miracles', were attributed to the intercession of Father Charbel. The diseased or malignant organs ranged from serious afflictions like cancerous tumors, cardiological disorders, gastric ulcer, kidney failure, epilepsy and damaged retina to broken limbs and snake bites. The intercession almost always involved either a direct solicitation through visits to Charbel's tomb or through vows and the application of blessed water or oil.

The success stories of such miraculous intercessions have enhanced the touristic potential of St Charbel. The commanding monastery is connected to Annaya Park which covers more than 100,000 square meters. Much like a modern theme park, it is equipped to accommodate all the needs of itinerant visitors: picnic grounds, snack bars, restaurants, museum, bread and breakfast, hiking tracks and, of course, souvenir shops selling not only religious mementos (rosaries, icons, paintings), but gaudy trinkets, knick-knacks and ornaments. The enterprising monks have also ventured into producing wines, jams, artisanal woodwork, grains and food products. Most frequented is the renovated St Charbel Cathedral which is sought for special occasions such as baptism, first communion, weddings and birthday celebrations.

One of the latest episodes of so-called 'miraculous healing' which has recently gained public notoriety is the 'Our Lady of Beshwat' in the Eastern Beqaa Valley. Until 2004 the bulk of the tourist traffic in the Beqaa was directed to Baalbek with incidental stops en route to visit Anjar and the Ksara wine cellars. Beshwat was a desolate small village of not more than 500 inhabitants until the shrine became a popular pilgrimage destination after a score of testimonies of healing. As one enters the tiny church one confronts abandoned wheelchairs and crutches propped up against the doorway – proof of how the Lady of Beshwat had permanently rid them of their infirmities when doctors and medications had failed. By healing the infirm, she has also revived the forsaken village. The government stepped in and paved the old dirt road. Street lights have been installed. A score of souvenir shops and restaurants have opened to cope with the all-year-long tourist influx. There is talk of establishing a modest bed and breakfast and possibly a small hotel. The media has also not neglected this solitary village. Beshwat has, almost overnight, become newsworthy.

In the process the ordinary villagers, mostly shepherds and market-gardeners are suddenly caught in the limelight of an invasive media and prying tourists. The private and unassuming villagers are now compelled to become adept at giving interviews to journalists, engage in small talk with tourists and sell tacky souvenirs, trinkets and postcards. Does this not denature the Beshwati villager? He is suddenly made to leap from being an ordinary and commonplace peasant to a 'postmodern' man attuned to mediated and secondary contacts and attending to the illusionary and, often, apparitional whims of people driven by trance-like moods and sentiments. Also, and perhaps more unsettling, religious rituals are deformed into touristic traps.

One sees elements of such touristic merchandizing in some of the latest projects of Hizbullah. The 'Khiam Detention Center' stands out in this regard. It has recently emerged as part of the growing political and religious tourist industry in Lebanon (Deeb and Harb, 2009: 201). The notoriety of the Khiam Center during the Israeli occupation of Lebanon in 1984, where over 5,000 Lebanese fighters and resistance supporters were subjected to the intimidations and brutalities of torture and imprisonment, gave it the potential to be converted into a national shrine. In no time, after the withdrawal of the Israeli troops in May 2000, a mounting traffic of spontaneous and informal tourism emerged. In consultation with Hizbullah, a group of former detainees established a volunteer committee to develop and administer the site as a touristic attraction. Instruments of torture were on display. Rooms where detainees were killed were particularly highlighted and, more instructive, special narration of the detention experience was made available to enhance the legacy of resistance. Inevitably, the nationalistic and awe-inspiring site could not resist the deformations of kitsch and sleaze. In no time, the Khiam Center has attracted not only stores and cafes but Hizbullah memorabilia including postcards, cassettes, key chains and DVD documentaries about the resistance experience.

Such manifestations are certainly not new. Nor are they unique to Lebanon. As Scruton aptly puts it, some of the earliest manifestations of kitsch can be found in many of the holiest sites: from the doe-eyed madonnas in nineteenth-century Italy to the cult of Christmas and baby Jesus. He too reminds us how pop stars and secular icons are sacralized:

> Hence the earliest manifestations of Kitsch are in religion: the plaster saints and doe-eyed madonnas that sprang up during the nineteenth century in every Italian church, the cult of Christmas and the baby Jesus that replaced the noble tragedy of Easter and the narrative of our hard-won redemption. Kitsch now has its pantheon of deities – deities of make-believe like Santa Claus – and its book of saints and martyrs, saints of sentiment like Linda McCartney and martyrs of self-advertisement like Princess Diana. (Scruton, 1999: 6)

SAIFI VILLAGE: FROM RED LIGHT DISTRICT TO 'QUARTIER D'ART'

Saifi Village is largely a restoration of a cluster of closely knit traditional quarters on the south-eastern fringe of the Bourj. Planned as a residential quarter, in less than five years since it was inaugurated in 2004 by Solidere (the company responsible for the reconstruction of Beirut's city center), the 'Village' has quickly emerged as one of the region's most appealing cultural and artistic destinations. Although fairly compact in size, covering an area of not more than 7,400 square meters, it houses 136 residential flats and provides a total of 30,000 square meters of floor space.

In overall design and execution, the Village epitomizes Solidere's perspectives on the rehabilitation of traditional neighborhoods. Meticulous care is taken to preserve the old city's spatial fabric, with an effort to enhance the distinctive identity of these once intimate but animated urban enclaves. Drawing on the scale and rhythm of the existing structures, the intrinsic character of the neighborhood is not only preserved but is made to give the impression of authenticity, as if the houses were built at different times.

The unmistakable character of the neighborhood stands out: Mediterranean pitched red-tiled roofs, arcaded windows, simple decorative ornaments, gracious trimmings and harmonious soft pastel colors form its architectural language. Some of the houses date back to the 1860s, at the time when the massive rural exodus (in the wake of civil unrest in Mount Lebanon) forced the population to spill beyond the city's medieval walls. Others were turn-of-the-century suburban townhouses and Art Nouveau villas or walk-ups. The restoration process has enhanced and enriched these elements. The delicate care for detail and refined execution – the hallmarks of Solidere projects – are truly stunning. The small-scale cobblestone streets are made narrower by broadened and elevated side-walks lined with rustic lampposts and flowerbeds. Discreet landscaping protects the enclaves from through-traffic. Most appealing, perhaps, are the inner courtyards connected by a network of landscaped walkways and quadrangled but open enclosures.

Like other traditional neighborhoods in Beirut, Saifi was characteristically mixed in land use and largely self-sufficient. Residents generally worked and lived in the same quarter and attended to much of their public and civic needs in adjoining areas. Solidere has been keen to preserve these defining features. Hence, if the original units (mostly two-storied suburban villas or walk-ups) had commercial or vocational outlets on the ground floors, these were retained. Strict zoning, however, consistent with the overall residential character of the Village, is rigidly defined and observed. Only nuisance and noise-free ventures are licensed. Virtually all the available space is already leased to art galleries, artisans, bookstores, wine shops, ateliers, studios, pharmacies, doctors' clinics, health clubs and the like. The Village is thus user-friendly: active and vibrant in daytime and quiet at night. The latest promotional brochure of Solidere identifies a total of fifty premises in the following categories: fashion, interior-design and decoration, artisans, art galleries, gastronomy, children and beautification.

Altogether, one is overwhelmed by the gentle and unobtrusive elegance and beauty of the symbiotic blending of traditional and state-of-the-art elements. Recycled basalt cobblestones and well-crafted masonry complement the hi-tech street furniture, hardscaping and traffic signage. The Village, as a result, has a pastiche-like, almost picture-book, image. The 136 units have either been sold, leased with the option to buy or rented. Already the Village resonates with a sense of commitment to the serene comforts and security of an edifying living environment.

The sustained events and activities associated with the *Intifadah* of 2005 spilled over into Saifi. As the Village was declared a *quartier d'art* (artist quarter), its intimate courtyards and streets erupted with cultural energy. Many of the city's active artists, designers and curators have already taken up premises there. Virtually all the ground-floor shops – which are fitted out with special refractive glass doorways – are already occupied by art galleries, antique shops, design boutiques and artisan outlets of arts and crafts. Periodic shows, exhibits, book launches and opening ceremonies have done much to enhance the lived and interactive quality of the village. It no longer seems like a picture-perfect but sterile and lifeless neighborhood. The traditional carpenters' souk has been reinvented into an upscale art district.

This is indeed a paradigm shift in the life and character of the district. Incidentally, the Beirut's once infamous red light district, which had disgraced the center of thes capital from 1912 to 1975, was located only a block away from Saifi Village. The district not only housed all the seventy-five licensed brothels and the 207 resident prostitutes. It became naturally a tempting spot for other seedy bars and hotels and disreputable places of assignation. In the early 1960s the government introduced plans, as part of an urban renewal project, to relocate the brothels to one of the eastern suburbs and, thereby, restore the tarnished and stigmatized image of Beirut's Central Business District. This was prime urban space at a time when real estate became speculative commercial ventures. The problem was complicated further because much of the desecrated property belonged to the Greek Orthodox Diocese (for further details, see Khalaf, 1965).

In 1964, still a novice sociologist, I was commissioned as part of that project to undertake an empirical survey to explore relevant material regarding the life of the confined prostitutes, the volume of traffic they attracted and prospects for their rehabilitation. Like many other such well-meaning ventures, the project never materialized. The ultimate fate of the district had to await the cruelties of the early rounds of the civil war in 1975–6. The whole area was ravaged and ransacked by factional in-fighting over control of the strategic city center.

The district did not only undergo a paradigm shift, as it were, from the profane to the sublime. By serendipity more than deliberate design, Saifi has evolved into one of the most animated and vibrant artistic and cultural quarters in Beirut and perhaps elsewhere in the region.

Three distinctive and unusual features of Saifi stand out. First, the relentless flow of culturally oriented and artistic ventures it continues to attract displays a formidable degree of inventiveness and, often, unabashed experimentation. Second, and perhaps more strikingly, these activities are virtually a female monopoly. Women are now the undisputed cultural brokers, patrons or actual producers of this explosion in creative and artistic energy. They have been resourceful and enterprising in exploiting their extensive personal networks to reinforce the intensity of collective enthusiasm and mobilization. One cannot but note the historical irony involved in this qualitative shift in the role of gender in defining the identity of this central urban neighborhood. It was women, stigmatized and made captive by prostituting their bodies to meet the demands for lewd and commercialized sexuality, who shaped its debased character during much of its early history. It is women today who are emerging as agents of its ultimate salvation by acting as carriers of moral uplift, socio-economic emancipation and aesthetic and cultural enlightenment.

Finally, this surge in cultural and artistic expression is certainly related to the grass-root populist mobilization sparked off by the *Intifadah*. As the Bourj, barely yards away, was acting as host to the boisterous dimensions of public protest, the seemingly exclusive grounds of the Village offered a more soothing and aesthetically pleasing public sphere. This dialectical interplay between popular mobilization and the proliferation of the arts has symbiotic and mutually reinforcing manifestations. Both are rendered richer and more profound in transforming symptoms of personal autonomy and well-being into instances of empowerment and structural change.

Inevitably, and because of the attentive concern of Solidere to safeguard the safety and exclusive character of the Village, its passageways and inner courtyards have a disproportionate number of security guards with earphones and walkie-talkies. All entrances and gateways to private residences are also equipped with remote security devices and twenty-four-hour surveillance systems. There is more than studied nostalgia to the façades and outward look of the rehabilitated residences and luxury apartments. They all include the latest energy efficiency and thermal and sound installations and underground parking. The entire neighborhood is also electronically friendly, with broadband and short-wave access. To attract recently married couples, a multilingual Montessori nursing school huddles in a quiet and unobtrusive courtyard.

Yes, altogether, the Village remains secure, quiet and impeccably clean. It exudes a feeling of prestige, status and being an upscale hideaway for the well-heeled and connected. Two recent additions are injecting some needed plebeianization into the neighborhoods. Through the commendable grass-roots efforts of Kamal Mouzawck, on Saturday morning, a number of organic farms and Souk el-Tayeb (the Delicious Market), the NGO which sponsors the weekly event, install a makeshift market in an adjoining parking lot. Locals, residents of other areas in Beirut and tourists have become regular shoppers. They also spill over into the courtyards of Saifi.

Earlier during the year, Balima, the only dining outlet in the neighborhood, was permitted to open a semi-outdoor cafe in its central courtyard. A fairly chic and French-styled coffee shop, Balima is attracting, in the absence of a truly side-walk cafe culture, a large clientele of artists, journalists, intellectuals and the younger set of the corporate elite. The courtyard, incidentally, is beautifully landscaped with eye-catching pieces of sculpture by prominent Lebanese artists like Izzat Mezher and Hussain Madi. Saleh Barakat, the proprietor of Maqam, one of the newly established art galleries in Saifi, had this to say about this encouraging trend: 'these sorts of areas exist all over the world. London has Bond Street, Paris has the Rue de Seine, New York has Chelsea and Santa Fe has Canyon Road. It only makes sense that any city that is looking to sell its art to non-residents has to think about creating a central location where they can come and wander through the various galleries and make their purchases' (Barakat, 2009: 1-3).

The commercial success of Saifi Village is most visible in the sharp escalation in the value of its real estate. Hardly four years ago the cost per square meter was estimated at $1,500. Today, it has leapt to about $7,000 – i.e. almost a 400 percent increase. Encouraged by the 'success story' of the village, Solidere was prompted to undertake similar projects in the neighborhood. 'Saifi Village II', a premier luxury project, designed by Nabil Gholam, a leading Lebanese architect, comprises seventy-two residential apartments and penthouses. Five years under construction, the massive project has just been handed over. Markus Giebel, the chief executive of Deyaar (the Dubai-based partner of Solidere), had this to say about this strategically located and new residential landmark: 'The project offers residents an inspirational life-style and a chic environment along with state-of-the-art facilities and ameni-ties. We believe Saifi Village II will be a landmark within the Beirut City Center that fully meets the expectations and living standards of our valued customer base in Lebanon' (Nambiar and Nesson, 2009).

Nabil Gholam has been commissioned to design another two residential extensions to Saifi Village: 178 and 146 Saifi Village. This is how Solidere has heralded what promises to be another landmark in the renovated CBD of Beirut:

> The five-or six-floor buildings, inspired by the Beirut architecture of the fifties, use materials and pastel colors similar to those of the neighborhood. They are organized in a traditional way around the garden courtyard, providing private terrace gardens. Taking into account the Mediterranean climate, they draw on the best features of the central hall plan to create a well-balanced, well-oriented, well-lit space, ensuring optimum efficiency and minimum energy costs. The 45 units, ranging from one to three bedrooms, benefit from modern amenities, ample storage and parking space. (Solidere, 2003: 29)

As suggested earlier, the defining character of Saifi Village is its decisive role in reinforcing artistic and cultural venues in the rehabilitation of Beirut's national character. Modest as they seem at the moment I wish to single out five such venues established recently which stand out in realizing such pros-pects: Nada Debs, Bokja, STARCH, Ceramic Lounge and JF Leather.

Upon returning to Beirut in 1999, Nada Debs realized that the Lebanese have an aversion for locally crafted products. Hence she converted her furniture boutique into a venue to produce and export such home-based innovation and craftsmanship. Her success story is testimony to her enterprising and creative energy and passions. Debs recognized very early in her odyssey – from reluctant Arab raised in Japan to a budding artisan schooled in the US to a self-made entrepreneur drawn back to the Arab world – that she must reconcile these dissonant elements in her life if she is to find redemption and meaning in her creativity. She does this admirably and articulates it in ways relevant to one of the major premises of this work. For example, since Nada had spent her formative years in the Far East, she started to realize that:

If you really dig deep down, I think I'm Japanese in a lot of ways, more than Arab. In Japan, everything is low-profile. The negative is as important as the positive. It's a more introverted society, so people keep things to themselves. Lebanese culture is the opposite: extroverted and appearance-conscious, lavish and warm. (Debs in Prasada, 2009: 130)

Her efforts to bring a fusion of these multicultural elements have been an astounding success. Her furniture and accessories reconcile judiciously the minimalism of Japanese artifacts, contemporary design and the full geographical range of traditional Arab patterns. 'A palette of culture at her fingertips, Nada is well-placed to understand that design is at once an act of surrender and rushing forward to meet the unknown' (Prasada, 2009: 133).

Hoda Baroudi and Mria Hibri of Bokja transformed some of their passionate hobbies – embroidery, decoration, frequenting antique shops, auction houses and second-hand market souks – into a thriving global business. Bokja (literally a bundle, or quantity of material gathered or loosely bound together) is an artisanal furnishing design outlet which celebrates textiles, antique furniture, dazzling colors and bold, innovative ideas. They both credit serendipity for their central design concept: they spread an Uzbek tapestry over an American antique chair, so as to better admire the fabric. Both are also inspired by similar taste for the spectacle, sumptuousness and the search for hidden treasures (Prasada, 2009: 106). Their products are not only popular locally. For several years now, Hollywood celebrities and top designers have been ordering their pieces. They have also exhibited in renowned art shows in Basel, Switzerland, and Miami Beach, Florida.

The clothing shops in Saifi are not just selling foreign imported brand names and logos for snob appeal. The Village is quickly becoming an outlet for the promotion of Lebanon's young design talents. Credit goes to Rabih Kayrouz who recently created STARCH, a boutique offering fashion training to students in the country's universities and design schools. A board of accomplished designers is formed to act as jury to a country-wide competition. About four to six portfolios are selected every season to showcase and promote their designs. As a precocious young man of sixteen Kayrouz left his village in Lebanon for Paris in 1990 to study the French language, geography and culture. But he could not stop himself from pursuing his studies in fashion, a passion he had since the age of eleven. He recalls how he was an indifferent student in school; more excited about flipping through *Vogue* magazine, watching fashion shows on Télé Liban and draping his sisters with towels than doing his homework (see Prasada, 2009: 154–5).

Rabih's precocious gifts were well rewarded. The day he finished his formal schooling in fashion, he got the chance to work as an intern and eventually was hired by the houses of Dior and Chanel. Political stability in Lebanon prodded him to return and establish his shop on the ground floor of his parents' house. In no time he became part of the stellar pool of Lebanese fashion designers. Like some of his colleagues in the thriving haute couture industry, he displayed admirable gifts in reconciling the aesthetic disciplines of his training with local expectations. Prasada captured this predicament while she was interviewing him: 'His style is both a continuation of and a reaction against everything he learned while training as a fashion designer. It is the marriage of respect for discipline and a gradually mounting cry for freedom' (Prasada, 2009: 152).

Where Rabih stands out is in the spirit of social consciousness which animates his creative energies. One of his enabling side-projects is the STARCH boutique he established recently. Cognizant of the privileged tutoring he received at Chanel and Dior, the Saifi boutique is made available to a roster of young gifted designers as they begin their career, showcasing their designs.

The concept of the Ceramic Lounge, though common in Euro-American cities, is a novelty in Lebanon. Given the receptivity of Saifi to innovative ideas, it is not surprising that this version of a 'Paint-Your-Own-Ceramic-Cafe' should find a home in the village. It has been well received since opening two years ago. Clients, mostly children and their families, can choose from a wide selection of white ceramic items, pick their own colors and personalize their own pieces. What is particularly appealing is that young children, regardless of their artistic skills, are getting involved in a participative and productive form of consumerism and entertainment. In the process, mundane and ordinary everyday activities, such as eating and outings with family and friends, are transformed into aesthetically pleasing and culturally meaningful experiences. It is also rewarding to note that the venue is frequently sought for hosting birthday parties and other intimate celebrations and cultural events.

Another innovative venture which has found a creative niche in the Village is the Johnny Farah JF Wabi-Sabi line of leather products. Mr Farah skillfully adopts some of the striking features of Japanese style in the hand-made products – handbags, belts, shoes, accessories – which are cut and sewn in his workshops. The concept sees beauty as essentially 'imperfect, impermanent and incomplete'. Consistent with this tradition, JF designs are naturally irregular in form, lacking uniformity or symmetry. To reinforce this quality, forty-year-old vintage leather, in its raw and natural condition, is used in creating their hand-made line of products. Rather than debasing or devaluing traditional craftsmanship, it is enriched and refined. The products have the disarming quality of disheveled elegance. The intimate and unpretentious bags, belts, wallets and other signature accessories are now marketed globally.

Talking with Johnny Farah in his inviting boutique, engulfed by the colorful display of samples of his latest products, exuding the scent of aged leather, one is struck how this new breed of Lebanese craftsmen/entrepreneurs (as in other venues of the creative industries) has been fairly successful in recreating viable outlets for their enterprising skills. During the war years, he had to relocate his modest leather operation to Canada, Italy and Turkey. Upon his return in 1995, he became convinced that no venture in Lebanon could possibly succeed with the stiff competition from mass-produced synthetic leather.

His fortuitous exposure to the Japanese Wabi-Sabi concept allowed him to make judicious and timely use of two indigenous resources available in Lebanon at the time: a fairly large supply of raw and aged leather and a pool of Armenian artisans in Bourj Hammoud and Qarantina. By retraining the Armenian craftsmen, he has been able to meet the change in the styles and habits of the discerning consumers in favor of hand-produced leather. By so doing, he was able to refine and extend the skills of indigenous craftsmen to meet particular global demands. More than 75 percent of the JF products are for the export market. By limiting the size of his operations he is able to safeguard and refine the quality of his products. More important in his case he can attend to his other two passions, both of which also involve outreach and grass-roots movements: organic farming and gastronomy.

Finally, mention must be made of a recent addition to the Village which is destined to enrich the quality and prospects of the current surge in artistic talent the country is witnessing. Credit goes to two of Lebanon's most accomplished art curators and critics: Saleh Barakat and Joseph Tarrab. In 2010 they established Maqam, a novel art gallery dedicated primarily to enhancing and protecting the quality of modern art and giving it access to credible international venues. Few pressing circumstances prompted the venture. The past few years have displayed a global interest in the contemporary arts in the Middle East, as seen in the surge of auctions in leading houses such as Christies, Sothebys and Bonham. There has also been a marked increase in art collectors – some of questionable credibility. Such a setting, particularly since it is accompanied by a spectacular increase in the sale value of art products, can only beget an equal surge in fake and cheap imitations of the cherished legacy of Lebanon's classical pioneers (such as Khalil Saleeby, Habib Srour, Daoud Corm, Saliba Doueihy, Cesar Gemayel, Omar Onsi, Mustafa Farroukh) and a growing pool of gifted contemporary artists.

Saleh Barakat, in his rationale for the creation of Maqam, does not hesitate to talk about the threats that such conditions pose to genuine and authentic products. Fake and copies are circulating, without effective restrictions or warnings. Likewise, stolen items cannot be traced back or reclaimed. Restoration could well mean total and indiscriminate repainting (Barakat, 2009: 1–3). What Maqam is proposing, to contain this threat, is to reach out for an enlightened and initiated clientele, and help them to select rare and original products, authenticated in terms of source and prospective future value. To expedite this process, four to five exhibitions will be hosted every year on particular themes like landscape and music.

Solidere has recently published a promotional brochure – ironically titled *Saifiholic* – to advertise Saifi Village as the 'best shopping therapy in the region'. Shopping, decried as we have seen, by many of the early classical thinkers for its intrinsic pathologies of greed, gluttony and pursuit of false consciousness, is now being celebrated and promoted in Lebanon as a form of national therapy. A cursory content analysis of the contents, often accented in a laconic power-point style, does provide information about how the outlets or venues are perceived, how they are identified, what they offer or what they promise to deliver to the consumer. Overall, a few overriding themes emerge.

First, no matter what they are selling, most promise a 'unique', 'trend-setting' experience which reflects or complements the 'taste and life-style of the contemporary woman'. They are not at all modest, reserved or measured in expressing this objective. Indeed, a few are so exuberant that they extol their setting or products as 'mindblowing', an invitation to 'indulge your passions', or run away to a magical world of sparkly, fascinating designs and inspiring colors. One Connaissance Des Arts introduces his sculpture studio as a whimsical mix of the surreal, mythological and classical (hence the label 'surreomythoclassical' in which 'form and emotion are aligned').

A second theme is the promise of a harmonious balance, a fusion between seemingly contradictory entities: 'between contemporary simplicity and classical elegance'; between 'traditional crafts and Islamic patterns along with a modern visual vocabulary'; between 'the funky of the postmodern and the dignity and grace of the classical'; between 'the modern, international and local'. For example, Nada Debs's philosophy of her furniture design, and she speaks of it as such, is informed by the 'traditional crafts of the Middle East with the pure lines of the Far East'. Assyla, selling ethnic prêt-à-porter and haute couture lines and accessories, declares that it is inspired by nomadic and Eastern thousand-years-old culture which brings 'sunshine to urban dullness ... It gives women a modern allure between Ethnic-Chic and subtle Bohemian.' Likewise, Balima, a fusion of boutique and cafe, offers a 'mix of oriental magic and French touch, twisted with a zest of Beirut's unique spirit'.

Third, and perhaps most intuitive, is the offer of 'a multi-dimensional destination for the discerning shopper'. *Milia m* states that her fashion boutique, designed as a minimalist corridor where items are casually suspended on a rope, 'talks to a woman across borders, a confident woman at ease with herself, her story and her history'; Cream, a high-end fashion boutique, states that it does not rely on any brand. Instead, the shopper is given the opportunity to 'super-select but never redundant'.

Chapter 5

The Allure of the Spectacle and Kitsch

All that once was directly lived has become mere representation.

(Guy Debord, *The Society of the Spectacle,* 1995)

Both seductive and alienating, the spectacle concurrently enchants while prohibiting any truly human participation.

(George Ritzer, *Explorations in the Sociology of Consumption,* 2001)

As an easily digestible substitute for art, kitsch is the ideal food for a lazy audience that wants to have access to beauty and enjoying it without having to make much of an effort.

(Umberto Eco, *The Structure of Bad Taste,* 1989)

Our house in Saifi Village is hardly a hundred yards away from Martyrs' Square in downtown Beirut. I have been fortunate, as a social scientist and humanist, to witness, during the past five years, all the calamitous transformations unfolding there: the triumphal celebrations of the 'Cedars Revolution' in 2005, its desecration by the invidious forces of 'Tent City', its startling resurrection after the Doha Accord in early May 2008 and a string of other massive public gatherings, that transformed, once again, the Bourj into a vibrant public sphere for collective mobilization.

Throughout its checkered history, I argued elsewhere (2006), Beirut's central square has displayed a relentless proclivity to reinvent itself in order to accommodate the transformations generated by local, regional and global events. Indeed, it has undergone close to a dozen striking mutations in its official identity and assumed popular labels. Three such labels, however, stand out: first, as Place des Canons, connoting its colonial legacy; second, as Martyrs' Square, to commemorate martyrdom and to celebrate the country's liberation from Ottoman control; finally, as the Bourj, perhaps its most enduring label, in reference to its medieval ramparts.

Despite these perpetual changes in its collective identity, it managed to retain its basic character as an open, mixed and cosmopolitan space. It was this malleability which rendered it more receptive in fostering high and popular culture, mass politics and the mobilization of advocacy groups, popular entertainment and, as of late, global consumerism. The latter, as will be elaborated shortly, brought with it some of the disheartening manifestations of excessive commodification, kitsch and the debasement of its architectural heritage, its vernacular arts and crafts and the spirited intellectual debate the Bourj once nurtured during its prewar 'golden' or 'gilded' heyday. This receptivity, eclecticism and cross-cultural context helped the Bourj become the porous, tolerant and pluralistic setting it is today. But it also helped it to acquire some of the vivid attributes of what Guy Debord (1995) labels the 'Society of the Spectacle'. It also made it vulnerable to some of the extreme by-products of postmodernism including nihilism, kitsch, bad taste, and a delight in decadence and mediocrity. In such a setting, public and private events are transformed (or deformed) into objects of curiosity and inappropriate display appealing or intended to appeal to traumatized and duped consumers. The ultimate intention is 'to trap the masses into a simulated culture' (Turner, 1990: 84).

To Debord, this obsession with appearance, image-making, alienated consumption of pseudo-needs and other illusionary whims of false consciousness all leads to the 'inversion of life' (Debord, 1995: 12). Despite all the hype and scintillating appeals such events generate, nothing is truly added to the real world. Indeed, the spectacle corresponds to that historical moment when commoditization completes its 'colonization of social life'. Masses become smug by being seduced by all the distractions and the banalization of commodity consumption, ceremonial expenditure and the preponderance of banquets, festivals, burlesque-like spectacles, trite clichés and cheap sentimentality. Objects, scenes, events are repeatedly exposed to the public gaze. They became little more than a sensational marvel or curiosity. More telling for our purposes, consumption based on genuine and legitimate needs is transformed into consumption driven by desire and exuberant expectations. Hence, an invitation of anomie and a life of constant seeking without fulfillment.

This chapter, albeit briefly, attempts to probe the following questions. What are some of the socio-cultural realities which render postwar Lebanon more vulnerable to some of the dismaying deformations associated with the appeals of the spectacle and kitsch? In what way are they forms of false consciousness and delusionary distractions from the disheartening realities of a traumatized society? Though associated with image-making, virtual and artificial commodification, we also need to ask: why do they manage to remain salient and irrevocable?

THE SPECTACLE AS FALSE CONSCIOUSNESS

There is much in Lebanese culture which renders groups, particularly in times of swift change and uncertainty, susceptible to such prodigious, ostentatious and often unreserved behavior. If one is to identify a core of national character traits, certainly this proclivity for playfulness sparked by a mood of carefree and uncommitted activity is bound to be one of them. At times, it assumes an almost sportive fancy with special fondness for jocular and fun-loving encounters.

This pervasive playful mood and the allure of the spectacle is double-edged. It could well be a source of unflagging resourcefulness, sustained by a sense of experimentation and adventure. When unrestrained, however, and this is a basic premise of this work, it can quickly degenerate into restless expenditure of wasteful energy, mischievous activity and anarchy. Much too often, this heedless bent for play and unplanned activity has permeated the fabric of society. As will be amplified later, this excessive laissez-faire ethos, in such a free-for-all milieu, is clearly a relief to an inept government and welcome to those adept at exploiting it.

The most edifying and enabling feature of the spectacle is, doubtlessly, its convivial and gregarious character. In part because of the survival of a large residue of primordial and intimate social networks, the Lebanese have long displayed a proclivity for festive, light-hearted and fun-loving encounters. The preoccupation of society with feasting, spontaneous social gatherings and companionship is clearly most appealing and visible. Time and budget analysis reveals that an inordinate amount of time and resources is devoted to ceremonial activities, social visits and frequent contacts with close circles of family and friends. Such contacts are invaluable sources of social and psychological support, particularly in times of public distress. As the public world becomes more savage, menacing and insecure, people are more inclined to seek and find refuge and identity in the reassuring comforts of family and community.

In the meantime, however, the simplicity, authenticity and intimacy of such gatherings are gradually being eroded. What remains is highly ritualized and virtual. In effect what this means is that some of the enduring ties and loyalties associated with the family are no longer so meaningful and relevant. Yet, in the absence of other suitable alternatives, the largely hollow shell of the family retains its outward structure. This is social hypocrisy at its best. Though the family is becoming increasingly irrelevant to many Lebanese, particularly the young, they continue to pay outward deference to it.

Such a predicament has broader and more grievous implications. The average Lebanese recognizes no deeper obligations and loyalties. Here lie many of the roots of deficient civility and the erosion of the broader concern for public welfare and national consciousness. To express this more concretely, this is a by-product of a dissonance which has plagued Lebanon for so long: what is enabling at one level is disabling at another. At the local and communal level, conviviality is a source of group solidarity and vital socio-psychological and economic support. At the national and public level, however, it can easily degenerate into parochial and oppressive encounters. Compassion for and an almost obsessive preoccupation with and concern for micro interests coexist with (indeed, are a by-product of) disinterest or indifference to others. Nowhere is this 'inversion of life', to borrow Debord's expression, more apparent than in the disregard the Lebanese display for public spaces or their lack of concern for national and broader issues. For example, societal problems, such as child and family welfare, mental health, orphanages, care for the aged, delinquency, poverty, protection of the environment and habitat, and concern for threatened architectural, archeological and cultural heritage and other such public issues are all articulated as parochial and segmented problems. Indeed, the character of voluntary associations, their membership, financial resources and organizational leadership continue to reflect subnational loyalties. Even interest in competitive sport, normally a benign and affectively neutral and transcending human encounter, has lately shattered into bitter and acrimonious sectarian rivalries.

It is in this sense that Debord regards the spectacle, with all its mixed features, as essentially a form of false consciousness, compounded by delusionary distractions and indifference to some of the unresolved public issues which have beset Lebanon for so long. It is appropriate in this regard

to dwell briefly on some of the recent riveting public events to demonstrate how they are deformed into spectacles. Hariri's martyrdom stands
out as a paradigm instance. It was epochal for the spectacular events and
display of collective grief and mobilization. His poignant and somber
funeral procession, the succession of public protests and demonstrations
and his makeshift shrine next to the Martyrs' monument, prompted the
Bourj once again to play host to momentous transformations. The initial
uprising, together with the counter-mobilizations it provoked, displayed
some of the uplifting elements of pure and spontaneous consciousness-raising. Unlike other forms of collective protest, they had more in common
with emotionally charged rallies, not riotous gatherings. For a while they
remained expressive but peaceful and measured. Above all, the makeshift
grave of Hariri turned into a national shrine for the evocation of collective
grief and deliverance from the oppressive designs of the Syrian regime and
its hapless cronies in Lebanon.

By acquiring a life of its own, the uprising was 'Lebanonised' into a
mélange of seemingly dissonant elements: a Woodstock or a Hyde Park gathering, a triumphal post-World Cup rally or a bit of a carnival, a rock concert,
a 'be-in' or other rejectionist manifestation of early-1970s 'counterculture'.
Youngsters, who could never finish a basketball match without the intervention of the army, were now in restrained frenzy. They observed candlelit
vigils, formed human chains, scribbled artistic manifestos, graffiti and posters
beseeching Syria to 'get out'. Little children in white overalls offered flowers
to stunned soldiers. Others, propped on their parents' shoulders, cheered
joyously. Most touching to see were the Christians and Muslims praying
in unison or bearing cross-religious placards as they observed moments of
silence over Hariri's gravesite.

To commemorate the thirtieth day after Hariri's murder, the coalition of
opposition forces called for a public gathering in Martyrs' Square on March
21, 2005 to reinforce their demands and sustain the peaceful mobilization of
public dissent the youth had been staging there. The gathering, both in sheer
numbers and form, was truly stunning: clearly the largest and most compelling display of collective dissent the country has ever witnessed. It dwarfed
the pro-Syrian public demonstration staged by Hizbullah and its allies a
week earlier. Estimates of the numbers attending range between 800,000
and a million: more than twice the size of that of its political adversaries. This
is almost one quarter of the entire population of the country. In the United
States this would have meant close to eighty million protesters; just imagine

what would have happened had the equivalent of twenty million agitated Egyptians hijacked the streets of Cairo!

Riad el-Solh Square, its adjoining courtyards, parking lots and construction sites were dense with enthusiastic crowds. All major arteries and thoroughfares converging on the city's center were clogged with heavy traffic. Those from the northern coast crossed over by boat. Countless numbers were unable to reach their ultimate destination. More striking was the composition, mood and character of the rally. While the Hizbullah demonstration was somber, stern, homogeneous and almost monolithic in its composition and message, the March 14 event was altogether a much more joyous, ebullient and spirited spectacle. It was also a hybrid of all the sectarian and regional communities, most visible in their outward demeanor, slogans and placards and the rich diversity of dress codes: from traditional horsemen in Arab headscarves and clerics in their distinctive robes and turbans to young girls with bare midriffs and pierced navels. But the dominant image was the red, white and green hues of the Lebanese flag. From a distance, the flickering flags along with the white and red scarves of the protesters seemed like a flaming sea of dazzling gladioli. Those who were not carrying flags had them painted on their faces or tattooed and inscribed on visible parts of their bodies. This was one event in the history of the country when such a unifying and patriotic national symbol transcended all other segmental and subnational loyalties.

Lebanese youth, often berated as a quietist, disaffected, self-seeking generation in wild pursuit of the ephemeral pleasures and consumerism of the new world order, were reawakened with a vengeance. To the surprise of their own parents and mentors, they emerged as the most recalcitrant voices against those undermining the sovereignty, resources and well-being of their country. On their own, and without the support of political parties, blocs and mainstream voluntary associations, they formed a variety of advocacy and emancipatory grass-roots movements to shore up national sentiments and sustain modes of resistance. Most refreshing was the new political language of resistance they were offering, which is in stark contrast to the belligerent overtones of car bombs, suicidal insurgency and counterinsurgency that continue to beleaguer the political landscape in the region.

Also, generations too young to have participated in or to recollect earlier episodes of national emancipation were receiving their own overdue tute-lage in national character-building. They were giving notice, to the gaze and conscience of an attentive world, that the future architects of sovereign, free and independent Lebanon had just made their exultant entry into public life. (For a probing analysis of leadership and mobilization of the Cedars Revolution, see Gahre, 2008.)

The national enthusiasm sparked by the 'Cedars Revolution', as the mass spring protest came to be triumphantly called, managed to mobilize ebullient and expectant sentiments which brought together throngs of multi-faith and cross-generational groups. More compelling, the mass protest went a long way in accomplishing its avowed four objectives: Syria's departure from Lebanon, new elections, an international tribunal to investigate Rafik Hariri's assassination and awakening national consciousness. For a while the Cedars Revolution symbolized two hopeful prospects: non-violence and the search for political and judicial accountability.

Beginning on December 1, 2006, the Bourj was yet to undergo another dramatic turnaround in its basic character. It is ironical that the 'Counter Revolution' launched by Hizbullah and its allies sought to occupy Riad el-Solh Square in order to launch and mobilize their public protest. Historically, *Sahat al-Sur*, located on the southwestern flanks of the old city, had become a natural outlet for the working-class neighborhoods of Basta and Bashura. Migrant and daily workers would congregate early in the morning in the hopes of being recruited at one of the construction sites within the city. During the Ottoman interlude this area in particular was highly politicized and became political space for public processions and the mobilization of dissent on behalf of a variety of national issues and causes (for further details see Khalaf, 2006: 188–90).

After it had proclaimed its 'Divine Victory' over Israel's onslaught in the summer of 2006, Hizbullah and its allies took hostage of the historic center of Beirut. Riad el-Solh Square, adjoining Martyrs' Square, was filled with hundreds of thousands of their embittered supporters. Overnight, the 'Tent City' – the demeaning label it acquired – was outfitted with makeshift tents, electrical generators, audiovisual installations, canteens and portable toilet facilities. The declared objective of the protest was the resignation of Prime Minister Fouad Seniora who was incarcerated in his palatial offices in the Ottoman-era Grand Serail just yards away.

Seniora was accused of trying, with American support, to disarm the military wing of Hizbullah. The Serail was cordoned off by a ring of riot police and massive barbed-wire barricades. Of course, the protest had other more latent and invidious intentions. The restored city center is, after all, the centerpiece of Solidere's postwar reconstruction, perceived by the largely disenfranchised Shi'ite community as an exclusive commercial and entertainment district for the pro-Hariri Sunni Muslims and their political and commercial groups.

In the meantime, the misbegotten Tent City – sustained first by belligerent speeches, recorded manifestos of military anthems, rowdy music and fairly handsome daily allowances – started to lose its momentum. The spectacle elements lost their sparkle and verve. 'The campground became a dusty, semi-deserted shanty town with an air of post-apocalyptic permanence: tattered refugee tents, droning electrical generators and bored old men smoking water-pipes. For 18 months, it was a visible symbol of Lebanon's dysfunction' (Lee, 2008).

I used to stroll by there daily. Hence, I had a chance to witness how this mutinous sit-in degenerated into no more than a malicious expression of *schadenfreude*. It made a mockery of collective acts of public protest and civil disobedience. It was all disobedience but little by way of civility. The forces of opposition, so contemptuous and full of hubris, delighted in the pain, havoc and despoiling they were inflicting on others. The once vibrant and edifying city center, a showcase of urban restoration, degraded into a site of dereliction suffused with symptoms of naked vengeance and retribution. For over eighteen months, probably the longest public strike in recent history, idle and disengaged youth were enticed, by handsome daily allowances and other fringe benefits, to while their time away in wasteful indolence.

More recently, Hizbullah's penchant for self-promotion has kept itself, certainly more than any other of the contending groups, in the public eye and gained popularity by aligning itself with the emancipatory cause of resistance to restore the legitimate rights of Palestinians. The theme of Palestinian suffering also fitfully dovetails with one of the central pillars of the Shi'ite creed; that their fate and destiny is a long and morbid history of oppression, neglect and anguish at the hands of foreign powers. Initially, it was Sunni oppression, a lingering offshoot of the fateful battle of Karbala in 680 when Yazid, the Omayyed Caliph, dispatched an army to kill Hussein, Ali's son and the prophet's grandson.

Waddah Sharara, a noted scholar and a son of a prominent Shi'ite cleric, has argued that Shi'ites have a special bent to follow demagogues rather than seeking true and independent sources of information. Hence, those who make the most compelling and riveting impression are those who can transform the art of public speaking into a dazzling spectacle where the form of delivery overwhelms the content of the message. When clerics appear en masse, as they often do with their distinctive garb and stern demeanor, they present an even more severe and dreaded image. Look how Neil Macfarquhar narrated the scene of such an event in the heart of the banking district in Central Beirut:

> As I watched, row after row of these clerics, around twenty across and all linking arms, marched silently out of the tunnel in one unbroken wave. They arrived with so little warning that I felt they had sprung whole from the earth. I just stood there gaping as two distinct worlds – the moneyed quiet of the downtown and the clamor of the impoverished Shiite neighborhoods – suddenly merged. Behind the clerics flowed a sea of chanting Shiites, many waving Lebanese flags. They had left at home that day their infamous Hizbollah flags – a green fist grasping a Kalashnikov rifle against a yellow background. Their waving the national flag was designed to signal that they were just as Lebanese as everyone else and had a right to be on Banks Street. It was as if the old Beirut, the Beirut of banks and the casino du Liban floor show, was fading into the past with one giant whoosh right before my very eyes. It made me distinctly uneasy, in the way that watching an earthquake made my nerves jangle momentarily because it broke the pattern of the way the earth was supposed to act. (Macfarquhar, 2009: 64)

If elements of the spectacle – particularly attributes of image-making, the emotional contagion of crowds and other forms of false consciousness – had deranged the protest movement into a banal and burlesque-like happening, the reactions of March 14 did not fare any better. As soon as bickering Lebanese politicians announced the Doha Accord on May 21, 2008, the first manifest sign of auspicious change in the political climate was not only the long-awaited election of General Michel Suleiman as President. (The post had remained vacant for about eight months because of the political stalemate.) The dismantling of Tent City, which by then had become a despicable eyesore, certainly no credit to those who had conceived it, was greeted with overwhelming relief.

March 14 and their supporters could not contain their exuberance. They, too, went overboard in their reactions. An alleged non-partisan group (March 11 Movement) launched a three-day marathon celebration where sultry pop stars like Haifa Wehbe, Nancy Ajram, along with Ragheb Alameh, Fadl Shaker and Rami Ayash, among others performed to an enthralled crowd. The concert area in Martyrs' Square became so dense with revelers eager to get a close look at the super stars that several people fainted, which compelled the organizers to cancel the remaining show. Eager to make up for lost time and vent repressed sentiments, the untamed celebrations displayed little by way of conviviality or refined cultural expression. Instead, for five nights, and late into the small hours of the morning, enthralled audiences were entertained by the eroticized divas of mass culture.

The readiness of the Lebanese to transform ordinary episodes into spectacles is not unusual. They have always had a penchant for reveling and merrymaking. Such conviviality is deeply rooted in the folklore of village life. They never partake in or celebrate an occasion – even private and intimate celebrations – without converting it into flashy display, observed with considerable aplomb and fanfare. Obscure, idiosyncratic and eccentric events become a cause for a spectacle. On June 21, 2009, a 'Fête de la Musique' was hosted in downtown Beirut to celebrate the Happy Solstice, the longest day of summer. Over a dozen of spectacular world-class performers were brought in for the occasion. They performed mixed genres of music, choral chants, oriental songs and rap. As a bonus, a foam party was held where kids frolicked with much abandon. As the Fête was going on, the main roadway and streets were uncharacteristically traffic-free. The prolonged European Football Championships kept people glued to their television screens. Banners, flags, insignia of particular teams and posters of star players draped from balconies, store windows or adorned cars. In mid-October, with any eye on the *Guinness Book of Records*, the Bourj square played host to yet another bizarre spectacle. Since Israel had recently been making claims that certain national Lebanese dishes (such as *homos, Tabouleh, Falafel*) were in fact theirs, two successive days were declared 'homos' and 'Tabouleh' days and groups competed to put together the longest or largest plate of either. In the process the Bourj square became literally a garbage dump for trampled and discarded food. Such spectacles of mass frenzy, when uncontrolled, can easily beget grotesque and uncouth conduct, manifestations similar to what Rem Koolhass calls the 'technology of the fantastic'.

TRAPPED BY APPEARANCE AND IMAGE-MAKING

In cultures where spectacles begin to colonize much of a society's social conduct, the emotional contagion of crowd psychology takes over. Hence, traumatized and aroused masses become more susceptible to being stimulated by all forms of persuasion and manipulation. At least in the case of *Ashura*, the sensational commemorations, despite staunch clerical disapproval, have recently proven to be remarkably resilient in mobilizing and reinforcing the political identity of the Shia community. Other aspects of the spectacle, as forms of false consciousness, often extend to the most venial and offensive trivialities. The survival of *Ashura* is particularly interesting because, as a form of popular devotional commemoration, it accentuates the Shi'ite–Sunni polarization and arouses the fears and apprehensions of Christian communities. Indeed, as a score of scholars have pointed out, the ostentatious and spectacular features of such pious and highly dramatized rituals were deliberately avoided in earlier decades to avert such sectarian tensions (see Norton, 2007; Gilsenan, 1982; Khuri, 1975). Vali Nasr (2006) in fact goes further to maintain that the commemoration of Imam Hussein's martyrdom, particularly as evoked in the sensational display of bloodletting and self-flagellation, is perhaps the most vivid demarcation of the rift between the two Muslim communities. In the words of Nasr, it is precisely such grotesque features which 'grate on Sunni sensibilities – the love of visual imagery evident in Shia popular devotionalism. Sunnism tends to frown on the visual arts as possible inducements to, if not outright expression of, idol worship. The piety of the Shia, by contrast is steeped in visual representation' (Nasr, 2006: 44).

In their exaggerated expressions, the reactions of both March 14 and March 8 are futile forms of false consciousness. Neither the eroticized images of Haifa Wehbe or Nancy Ajram, nor the frenzy of turbaned clerics are part of Lebanon's cultural heritage. Nor are they the cherished icons or role models which are likely to redress deepening cultural cleavages or inspire our disinherited and marginalized youth to forge meaningful national identities.

Naturally, these diametrically opposed and misbegotten manifestations are not the only options available to Lebanon. At the popular and most visible level, however, they are, alas, what is being played out. Even some of the leading protagonists and commentators are now fond of depicting Lebanon as being caught between two prototypes: Hanoi or Hong Kong. No wonder that the bulk of embittered youth are today groping to fill this gaping void in their lives by experimenting with a litany of unconventional but expressive outlets. Living up to its image as the party and amusement capital of the region, nightlife in Beirut is resurfacing with a vengeance. A dazzling variety of nightclubs, bars, dancing joints and places of assignation can hardly cope with the mounting traffic. They all bespeak of the appeal of the culture of the cool, uninhibited desires and surrender to faddish and kitschy entertainment.

Under Hizbullah this is deranged further by its almost exclusive association with the commemoration of martyrs and fallen comrades. Only the blood of martyrs, as it were, and other morbid events in the life of a nation merit memorialization. The Hizbullah rally has another grotesque feature. Huddled and quiescent masses are transfixed by the defiant gestures and abusive demagoguery of sullen and obstructionist leaders intent on transforming Lebanon into a perennial war zone or resistance site. Those who do not share this foreboding view are dismissed as traitors or subversive agents.

Even the celebrations of private events in one's life-cycle – christenings, birthdays, anniversaries, weddings and funerals – are hosted with much fanfare and showy display. Birthday parties of children, as if they are being socialized into one of the defining normative expectations of their culture, are converted into lavish venues for pronouncing one's unearned status and elite distinctions. Such snob appeal, particularly in small and closely knit communities and neighborhoods, pays off handsomely. Otherwise people would not indulge in such displays so ravenously. Indeed, banks are known to advance interest-free loans to expedite such ceremonial and unproductive outlays.

Wedding ceremonies, in particular, have not only become a thriving industry but they embody all the dazzling features of a spectacle. From mid-May to mid-September, for sixteen weeks, it is wedding season. A growing number of special 'event managers' and entertainment companies have recently sprouted to cope with the increasing demand as droves of expatriates return to either host or attend nuptials. Like other such events, the conspicuous display becomes coveted social capital. Suffused with so much symbolic value, they are implicitly competitive events as families strive, often with borrowed capital or special bank loans, to outdo others in their social circle.

The cost can be horrendous, way beyond the modest means of average middle-income households. Yet this has not deterred them from expending inordinate sums on extravagant items – garments, decorations, limousines, fireworks, live performances and other special effects. Such spectacles, as one reporter observed, are 'worthy of a Roman Emperor or at the least a Las Vegas show. At a recent wedding in Fakra, the pageantry included a lion!' (Khourchid, 2009). The excessive expenditure is compounded by the time wasted. Hotels, venues, ballrooms, caterers need to be booked well in advance, often close to a year. So do florists, photographers, light and sound engineers, DJs and other performers. For an ordinary family, a bit exacting and selective in its expectations, this could well amount to a full year of intermittent planning and meetings. It is telling that altogether the expended time and resources are considered well spent.

Religious holidays and sacred rituals are also commodified and are already displaying some of the dismaying symptoms of a spectacle. Quaint villages, towns and summer resorts are not spared such bonanzas. Religious festivals, special saints' holidays, become occasions for the debasement of rituals into boisterous display. Each community or sect competes to outdo the other. The modest bonfires and makeshift sparklers of old are now displaced by colossal fireworks to match the momentous national celebrations of 4 July in the US or 14 July in France. As spectacular fireworks subside, overjoyed countrymen punctuate the glittering skies with the sharp rattle of gunfire. Such extravaganzas of sound and light are sustained way beyond midnight with little regard for the offensive noise pollution they generate.

Clearly one of the most uplifting and edifying celebrations was that held on Sunday June 22, 2008 to mark the beatification of Yaaqoub Haddad, the late Capuchin priest, a maverick of a village cleric who gained iconic status because of the outreach welfare and benevolent associations he founded throughout the country and beyond. Way ahead of his times and at a critical interlude in Lebanon's history (between World War I and Independence), he established orders of nuns, mental hospitals, orphanages and expanded the Capuchin schools networks almost single-handedly. Once again, Martyrs' Square played host to this unusual event: the first beatification ever to take place outside the Vatican. Cognizant of how momentous the occasion was, people flocked to the Square in droves. The service was presided over by a representative of Pope Benedict XVI and the head of the Vatican's office of sainthood. Patriarch Sfeir and a litany of Eastern Christian prelates, international envoys and local political leaders attended. On that hot summer day Lebanese girl scouts handed out caps and bottled water to ease the discomfort in the treeless and unshaded Martyrs' Square. Nothing could have dampened the spirits of the exultant audience as the Patriarch ended his sermon by saying that Yaaqoub's work of mercy was an expression of his love of mankind.

The holy month of Ramadan is another sustained thirty-day spectacle, or so it has become lately. Not unlike the commercialization of Christmas or Hanukkah, it too has flouted the strictures of Islam. As the ninth month of the Muslim lunar calendar, Ramadan is considered the holiest month of the year. It is during this month, Muslims believe, that the Prophet Muhammad received his first revelation of the Koran from the Archangel

Gabriel. Believers are called upon to forgo food, water and other worldly pleasures during the day as a pillar of their faith, a sacrifice to demonstrate that they have not forgotten God and the less fortunate. The sacred rituals of fasting – along with asking for forgiveness and taking comfort in community and good deeds – are supposed to be quietly and discreetly observed in the private sanctuaries of homes. But these, as admitted by Muslim religious officials and observant subjects, like other precepts, particularly the call for self-control and restraint, are being betrayed.

The gargantuan *iftars*, with massive spreads of special food and dessert, along with a dazzling coterie of performers, singers and belly-dancers, transform the righteous and ascetic month into an over-indulgent spectacle. With no trace of the modest, ascetic restraint called for by scripture, the glittering events are hosted in grand ballrooms packed to the gills with starlets and celebrities. The intent, as in all spectacles, is to be seen in the company of the most glamorous guests and to advertise one's new look and trendy fashions. Because in 2011 Ramadan coincided with the country's protracted deadlock over the formation of a new cabinet, the nightly fast-breaking *iftars* have been transformed into lavish banquets – not unlike patriotic gatherings of major political conventions – where prominent political leaders deliver keynote speeches to their captive constituencies. The lavish banquets are aired by the media and hence become coveted social events imbued with symbolic status. Being a guest is akin to a badge of honor one bears with an air of elevated self-regard.

Thanks to satellite broadcasts, soap operas and special Ramadan entertainment – mostly lowbrow and sleazy programs – do little to safeguard the desired qualities of righteousness and reflective family gatherings. In 2011 in particular two circumstances have marred the festive spirits of the holy month. Ramadan coincided with the heat of August. Hence nutritionists were duly concerned over the likelihood of weight gain and dehydration. More distressing, the feast was also after a year of mounting sectarian rivalry. As a resident of Saida complained: 'the spirit of Ramadan has changed ... it is no longer the month of forgiveness, sharing and tolerance. Love has turned into hatred and animosities' (Zaatari, 2009).

Largely because of the call for restraint and modesty by religious officials, the special Ramadan tents for *iftar* and *souhour* were not installed. Some residents, in fact, complained that 'Ramadan came shy this year' (Zaatari, 2009). Major hotels and restaurants, however, went out of their way – given the peak in tourism – to advertise special Ramadan banquets.

Another virtuous feature of Ramadan has been violated: the call for charitable and benevolent deeds, the giving of alms discreetly without any
outward display of praise or self-regard. Moutaa al-Majzoub, Director of
the Islamic Welfare Association in Sidon, lamented that 'while charitable
actions were kept secret in the past, they have now found a way to be advertised and publicized ... alms should be given in the spirit of Muslim teach-
ings which means you should help the poor without caring for praise or
gratitude' (Zaatari, 2009).

With daylight fasting and night-time celebrations, people are not only
inclined to over-indulge in eating. Watching television becomes another
all-consuming addictive pastime. In normal times, the quality of television
leaves much to be desired. During Ramadan, stations compete via sleazy
soap operas, sexually explicit video clips and long-winded talk shows, and
programs degenerate into forms of cheap 'infotainment'. The intent is to
dazzle and entertain. One noted exception is the Syrian-produced *musalsal*
(soap opera) *Bab al-Hara* (The Neighborhood Gate), which since its debut
in 2006 continues to attract the largest and most enthusiastic number of
viewers, especially during Ramadan. The show, aired in Lebanon on MBC
and Al-Manar television (the Hizbullah channel), attracts tens of millions of
viewers every day throughout the region. A single episode attracted a staggering 85 million viewers (Galey and Baraki, 2009). Set in Damascus during
the inter-war period of French colonial occupation, the program depicts the
national mood of longing for independence. It is largely a nostalgic recasting
of a world with the cherished but threatened values of dignity, honor, gal-
lantry and the revolutionary spirit.

The *musalsalat* are so appealing that to legions of viewers they have
become an integral part of Ramadan's ritual, particularly since they serve
to bring the family together. It is estimated that there are today 157 original series, amounting to three-quarters of the Arab world's annual televisual
output. Naturally not everybody is enamored by the *musalsal* genre. Critics,
particularly hard-line religious figures, find the permissive themes morally
offensive. Others decry the excessive commercialization and bemoan
that Ramadan has simply taken on some of the commodified trappings of
Christmas and Hanukkah. Streets and major roadways are festooned with
lights, special ornaments and imposing installations. The theme in 2011 is a
colorful mélange of the crescent in varied colors and sizes. All this, of course,
translates into big business for advertisers.

THE ALLURE OF KITSCH IN POSTWAR LEBANON

It is understandable, as suggested earlier, why escapism is a meaningful and legitimate reaction of traumatized and threatened groups. In Lebanon, it is also understandable that such groups should seek shelter in communal solidarities and cloistered spaces. Confessional and territorial attachments, given the country's tenuous pluralism, have always been resilient sources of psychic support, social mobilization and political participation. Though omnipresent, these identities were largely nuanced and subtle. Today, they are becoming sharper and more assertive.

More and more Lebanese are brandishing their confessionalism, if we may invoke a dual metaphor, as both *emblem* and *armor.* It is an *emblem,* because confessional identity has become the most viable medium for asserting presence and securing vital needs and benefits. Without it groups are literally rootless, nameless and voiceless. One is not heard or recognized unless confessional allegiance is first disclosed. It is only when an individual is placed within a confessional context that ideas and assertions are rendered meaningful or worthwhile. Confessionalism is also being used as *armor,* because it has become a shield against real or imagined threats. The more vulnerable the *emblem,* the thicker the *armor.* Conversely, the thicker the *armor,* the more vulnerable and paranoid other communities become. It is precisely this dialectic between threatened communities and the urge to seek shelter in cloistered worlds that has plagued Lebanon for so long.

In addition to such communal reassertions, the Lebanese are also seeking refuge in nostalgic longing and the proliferation of kitsch. Other than the hackneyed and trite images of Lebanon as a protracted battlefield for other people's wars or a breeding ground for Islamic militants, it has recently (Beirut in particular) acquired a set of nefarious and reprehensible labels: a 'hedonistic haven', a 'Sin City', 'Sex Capital' for Gulf Arabs. I am proposing yet another catchy label: Beirut as the capital of Kitsch.

Given the ugly memories of an unfinished war and the persisting anxieties and uncertainties of the postwar era, kitsch which is surfacing in the country with a vengeance has became another mode of retreat from a traumatized society. In many respects, kitsch is a by-product of the spectacle and goes further to embellish some of its scintillating and colorful features. The two feed on each other. After all, kitsch is an expression of the appeal of the popular arts, entertainment and the creative industries whose object is to 'astonish, scintillate, arouse and stir the passions' (Calinescu, 1987: 238).

Normally, it is not perceived as a mode of escape or retreat, at least not in the way Robert Merton (1968) conceptualizes retreatism as a mode of adaptation to anomie.

The rampant allure of kitsch in Lebanon is symptomatic of the need to forget and, hence, it feeds on collective amnesia and the pervasive urge for popular distractions. It is clearly not as benign or frivolous as it may appear. At the least it should not be dismissed lightly, for it has implications for the readiness of the public to be drawn in and become actively and creatively engaged in processes of reconstruction and safeguarding the edifying beauty of their natural habitat and built environment.

The origin of the term 'kitsch' is related to this tension between the refined taste of highly cherished artistic and cultural expressions and their debasement by the undeveloped taste and expectations of mass society. To Norbert Elias, the term probably originated in a particular setting of artists and art dealers in Munich in the early twentieth century. At the time, we are told, artists used to produce 'sketches' which appealed to American tourists. Hence the word 'Kitsch' was thus derived from 'sketch'; more specifically, anything intended to be sold and, interestingly, products not highly regarded by the artists but which they were obliged to produce for economic considerations (Elias, 1988: 31–3). Elias goes further to argue that there was more to the emergence of the kitsch style than the dissonance between high and low culture. It was also linked to the changing tastes of a 'multi-layered mass society cemented together by common experiences and situation, the great destiny which swept all factions along together; a destiny symbolized by wars and social conflict' (Elias, 1988: 32).

Kitsch in other words, and Lebanon here comes to mind, endows a fragmented society with a certain measure of uniformity since it appeals to larger segments of the emerging society. Its fundamental allure is in its ability to offer effortless and easy access to the distractions of global entertainment. It is compatible with the public mood for lethargy, disengagement and disinterest. It is also in this sense that kitsch becomes a form of 'false consciousness' and ideological diversion, a novel opiate for aroused and unanchored masses. To the rest, particularly the large segments who have been uprooted from their familiar moorings, kitsch feeds on their hunger for nostalgia. Much like the spectacle, it is a form of collective deception since it is sustained by the demand for spurious replicas or the reproduction of objects and art forms whose original aesthetic meanings have been compromised. As Calinescu put it, kitsch becomes 'the aesthetics of deception; for it centers around such questions as imitation, forgery, counterfeit. It is basically a form of lying. Beauty turns out to be easy to fabricate' (Calinescu, 1987: 228). Along the same lines, to Meštrovic, who treats kitsch as an extreme by-product of postmodernism, anything and everything, including intellectual products, is kitsched-up.

> These extreme products of postmodernism include nihilism, kitsch, bad taste, and a delight in decadence. In postmodern kitsch, anything and everything is cheaply imitated, endlessly repeated, and made banal – to the delight of audiences and consumers. Not just the media, but intellectuals also produce and cater to kitsch. (Meštrovic, 1991: 27)

This view is shared by Walter Benjamin and Umberto Eco. Although Benjamin expressed his belief in the redemptive and emancipatory features, often evolutional potential, of the mass production of art (Benjamin, 1973), he also maintained that in certain instances art becomes kitsch:

> Kitsch ... is nothing more than art with a 100 percent, absolute and instantaneous availability for consumption. Precisely within the consecrated forms of expression, therefore, kitsch and art stand inconsolably opposed. (Benjamin, 1999: 395)

For Eco, kitsch is a 'substitute for art; *a supplement* and an easily digestible substitute for art' (Eco, 1989: 189). In reviewing these and other dismaying attributes of kitsch, Styhre and Engberg (2003) conclude that kitsch represents 'a certain worldview and a *modus Vivendi*: a form of hedonism. In addition, kitsch shares some important characteristics with the hyper-real. They both go beyond the immediately observable, the really real, and they are distinguishing marks of the modern age.'

Finally, in his analysis of museums and art galleries in a postmodern setting, Mike Featherstone (1991) distinguishes between *discursive* culture and the *spectacular* and *sensual* culture. The former demands a long and relatively difficult apprenticeship reinforced by the Kantian aesthetics of refined and sublime high culture. The latter is more immediate, popular and accessible to untutored masses.

In Lebanon the pathologies of kitsch display more ominous by-products. They not only debase the aesthetic quality of high culture. Folk arts and vernacular architecture are also vulgarized. National symbols, historic and other cherished monuments become expendable trophies or vacuous media images. This frenzy for the prostitution of cherished cultural artifacts and the consumption of pseudo art cannot be attributed merely to the impulse for status-seeking and conspicuous consumption, potent as these predispositions are in Lebanon today. What constitutes the essence of kitsch, as Adorno among others remind us (Adorno, 1973), is its promise for 'easy catharsis'. The object of kitsch, after all, is not to please, charm or refine our tastes and sensibilities. Rather, it promises easy and effortless access to cheap entertainment and scintillating distractions.

Like most traumatized subjects, the attention span of the Lebanese is much too short and episodic. He is not predisposed to wait for more promising future prospects. Postponed gratification is not cherished or valorized. Instead it is the frenzy of fulfilling one's immediate impulses and impetuous desires which is the source of his restless energy. It is in this sense that many of the dismaying features of the spectacle reinforce the appeals of kitsch: the mindless hedonism and narcissism associated with an urge to make up for lost time; the dullness and trivialization of everyday life; the cultural predispositions of the Lebanese for gregariousness, conviviality and fun-loving amusement. All of these have contributed to its appeal. So has the ready access to the vectors of high technology and 'infotainment'. Lebanon is not spared the scintillations of postmodern and global spectacles. Indeed, bourgeois decadence, mediocrity and conspicuous consumption have compounded the public seductions of kitsch.

A score of writers have amplified on how kitsch came to epitomize all the contrived and pseudo elements inherent in forms of false consciousness. To Roger Scruton, for example, it is the 'attempt to appear sublime without the efforts of being so ... the epitome of all that is spurious in the life of our times' (Scruton, 1999: 2). He goes further to maintain that when genuine and authentic cultural and artistic products are not protected from the corrupting influence of the modern media, they can readily pass, as he crudely puts it, 'from junk to crap without an intervening spell of nourishment' (Scruton, 1999: 4). To Ewen (1988) and Richards (1990), the emergence of kitsch cannot be divorced from the needs and anxieties of the middle class. To Ewen, cultural objects that were imitations of elite style aimed at the middle class and produced by mass production became kitsch. In other words, what makes an object kitsch is that 'it is a cheap, mass-produced copy of some original object or copy which was considered elegant' (Ewen, 1988: 64).

In short, kitsch is pretense. The Lebanese are plagued with so many missed opportunities, unrealized national aspirations and unrequited personal

ambitions that pretense, make-believe and social hypocrisy have become legitimate ploys, to borrow Goffman's expression, for the 'management of spoiled
identities'. In much the same way, Richards defines kitsch as 'elaborately aes-
theticized commodities produced in the name of large institution (church,
state, empire, monarchy) for middle-class home-use' (Richards, 1990: 88).
Richards adds another meaningful feature of kitsch: what he calls 'short-order
charisma'. In other words, objects are all designed to satisfy a momentary, suddenly arisen need. Jukka Gronow also employs this notion of momentary
short-term euphoria or charisma to pronounce on the allure of kitsch:

> In their more limited sense, kitsch objects have been designed to satisfy a momen-
> tary, suddenly arisen need. They are commemorative and ornamental objects
> which are useless in themselves; placed on the mantelpiece or shelf, they keep
> the memory of a ceremonial moment or institution, yet at the same time make it
> trivial by turning it into an article of daily use (a provincial coat-of-arms repro-
> duced on the handle of a spoon, for example). Ordinary, mass-produced articles
> of daily use (such as dinner set or furniture) which imitate the earlier elegant
> models and styles also borrow from the 'charisma' attached to the way of life of
> the nobility, for example, at the same time making it more trivial by making them
> accessible to anyone who can afford to buy them. This is why they feel like kitsch
> – somehow artificial and superficial. The impression of kitsch is, however, often
> simply created by the fact that the models in question have been removed from
> their original context. (Gronow, 1997: 42–3)

So eager is the Lebanese to embrace and embellish himself with images and
objects which enhance his traumatized and damaged self, virtually everything in one's habitus – not only works of high art but ceremonies, rituals
and public display of emotion – becomes readily kitsched-up. Employing
Goffman, it is the persisting fear of being debased and embarrassed which
renders kitsch so amenable and seductive. Roger Scruton offers another
insightful hint when he reminds us that the work of the imagination is not
possible for everyone. Hence, 'in an age of mass communication, people learn
to dispense with it. And that is how kitsch arises – when people who are
avoiding the cost of higher life are nevertheless pressured by the surrounding
culture into pretending that they possess it. Kitsch is an attempt to have the
life of the spirit on the cheap' (Scruton, 1999: 5).

All such grotesque manifestations display the paralysis of meanings and
the obsession with drawing public attention. As such, the cultures of shame

and the fear of being disgraced and embarrassed have lost much of their control. Nothing is sheltered from public view anymore. All the emergent fads and foibles have become much too visible and transient. The quicker they surface, the quicker they become obsolete and dispensable. The status- and fashion-conscious Lebanese glory in notoriety and public display. In a prosaic sense, many in fact have become shameless.

JANUS-LIKE LEBANON

How are the Lebanese reacting to city life which denies them intimacy and authenticity? Generally, their reactions fall into two diametrically opposed responses: They either seek shelter in barricaded enclaves or go on a rampage of unrestrained indulgence. This is, after all, what the state of being adrift involves. This also reinforces Lebanon's Janus-like image of seemingly dissonant entities. Throughout its history, and at many levels, Lebanon has always displayed such discordant, often capricious, dualism. As early as the 1820s when American missionaries started to make their appearance in Mount Lebanon, they were invariably impressed by the inconsistent character of the country. William Goodell's graphic description of disembarkation (on 16 November 1823) captured the bizarre features of the local culture. He was stunned by both the 'verdant and lovely beauty' of the habitat, as captivating as the 'hills, dales, fruits and flowers of our own happy country', but also by the 'half naked and barbarous Arabs' (*Missionary Herald*, 1824: Vol. XX, 215).

By the late 1960s, at the height presumably of Beirut's splendor and golden age, the seasoned world traveler John Gunther was so dismayed by what he saw that he prefaced his chapter on the 'Pearl of the Middle East' this way:

> Beirut commits treason against itself. This ancient city, the capital of Lebanon, blessed with a sublime physical location and endowed with a beauty of surroundings unmatched in the world, is a dog-eared shamble – dirtier, just plain dirtier, than any other city of consequence I have ever seen ... In the best quarter of the town, directly adjacent to a brand-new hotel gleaming with lacy marble, there exists a network of grisly small alleys which, so far as I could tell, are never swept at all. Day after day I would see – and learned to know – the same debris: bent chunks of corrugated iron, broken boulders or cement, rags, rotten vegetables, and paper cartons bursting with decayed merchandise. Much of the detritus seems to be of a kind that goes with a rich community, not a poor one. The

cool and sparkling Mediterranean across the boulevard looks enticing for a swim, until you see that the water is full of orange peel, oil slick, blobs of toilet paper, and assorted slimy objects. (Gunther, 1969: 281)

Today, the colliding contradictions are visible almost everywhere; not just between the fairly opulent, cosmopolitan and fashionable neighborhoods of east Beirut and the derelict and embittered southern suburbs. At the most general level, this overriding duality is reflected in the image of Lebanon as a proxy battlefield for unresolved regional rivalries and breeding ground for Islamic militants and resistance groups, but also as a permissive play-ground and tourist destination for pleasure-seekers and itinerant tycoons. The rehabilitated center of Beirut and adjoining eastern neighborhoods are dense with five-star hotels and boutiques, shopping malls, nightclubs, bars, side-walk cafes, art galleries and dealerships of global franchises and consumer icons. Areas under Hizbullah's hegemony, which stretch from South Lebanon to the Northern Beqaa Valley, are by striking contrast dense with thousands of fighters, long-range rockets, underground cells, fortified tunnels and training camps. It is not an exaggerated claim when Hizbullah boasts of being the world's most formidable resistance or guerrilla army. The two political cultures, at least in their latest popular, everyday expressions – let alone ideological perspectives and visions for Lebanon's future – are poles apart. The dissonance, despite avowed expressions to the contrary, is also getting sharper and more starkly visible.

Perhaps because this summer season (August–September 2009) coincided with the holy month of Ramadan, the anomalies became more curious and bizarre. Sparsely clad girls strutted past heavily shrouded women in pitch-black head-to-toe garments. Young men with baggy tracksuits and bling jewelry chatted loudly on mobiles next to bearded sullen Arab men with their white turbans and traditional headgear as they puffed on their sweet-scented hookahs. Run-down and bedraggled 'service' cars competed for space in the dense city traffic with the latest flashy sports cars, limousines and Hummers with tinted windows and Gulf license plates. Beirut's streets and the country's roadways are jam-packed with vehicles. As already noted, Lebanon may well boast among the highest number of cars per capita in the world. The sustained exponential increase in car imports is wedded to the notorious flare of the Lebanese for being reckless and boisterous at the wheel. Hasty and impetuous driving is a national sport, with little regard to the threats to life, havoc and the nuisance generated. No wonder that our inner roads and highways are clogged with gas-guzzling Range Rovers, Hummers and cavalcades of sirened black SUVs. The ordinary pedestrian is a threatened and debased creature; not entitled to any respect, let alone the basic human right of walking on safe streets.

Despite recent commendable efforts to regulate traffic hazards, the magnitude of casualties remains inordinately high. The Youth Association for Social Awareness (YASA) estimate yearly casualties at 940 and about 12,000 injuries per year in comparison to only 200 homicides (*Daily Star,* 31 Dec. 2009). In other words, four times as many are victims of car accidents as of human violence. The magnitude of the problem is exacerbated by the gamut of direct causes. They range from infrastructural defects, such as the absence of road signs, scarcity of traffic lights, erratic public lighting and road construction, to inept and disrespected traffic officers. The system of licensing is so corrupt that virtually no one fails a driving test, not to mention those who secure licenses without a test. This is aggravated by reckless driving and insolence concerning ordinary traffic ordinances, particularly drunk driving and talking on the phone while driving. In only one week in 2009, the International Security Forces (ISF) issued 30,000 tickets for traffic violations in Beirut municipality. Given the deficient system of traffic control, this is extremely high. It amounts to 4,300 violations per day and about 400 every hour.

The spectacle and kitsch have become the locus of illusion and false consciousness. Debord, much like Goffman, argues that the spectacle proclaims the predominance of appearance and, hence, representation and image-making. The first passage in his luminous book begins cogently by asserting 'that all that once was directly lived has become mere representation' (Debord, 1995: 12). It is in this fundamental sense that all social relations between people become mediated by images. When the real world is transformed into images, the human sense of *sight* begins to displace *touch*. To Debord, this transformation has profound implications.

> For one to whom the real world becomes real images, mere images are transformed into real beings – tangible figments which are the efficient motor of trancelike behavior. Since the spectacle's job is to cause a world that is no longer directly perceptible to be *seen* via different specialized mediations, it is inevitable that it should elevate the human sense of sight to the special place once occupied by touch; the most abstract of the senses, and the most easily deceived, sight is naturally the most readily adaptable to present-day society's generalized abstraction. This is not to say, however, that the spectacle itself is perceptible to

the naked eye – even if that eye is assisted by the ear. The spectacle is by definition immune from human activity, inaccessible to any projected review or correction. It is the opposite of dialogue. (Debord, 1995: 17)

The spectacle is not only 'immune from human activity' and averse to human dialogue. To Debord it is also an 'uninterrupted monologue of self-praise' (Debord, 1995: 19). It is precisely this self-indulgent monologue which is emblematic of the needs and state of mind of many Lebanese. Self-exposure, self-love and self-indulgence all become ways to win the ruthless competition for attention. Hence, there is little room for self-effacement and humility. The unassuming and understated Lebanese is a rare, very rare, specimen. Solemn, reclusive and quiet occasions are also scarce. The penchant for overstatement and pomposity, and these are also some of the attributes of kitsch, pervades virtually all aspects of society, from the sublime to the mundane. A recent billboard for C & F (Cosmetics and Fragrance) depicts a luscious woman munching a watermelon with the following unabashed caption: 'Live Out Loud, Love Yourself' – a brazen direct message of overstatement and narcissism.

As noted earlier, all rites of passage in one's life-cycle are celebrated with conspicuous fanfare. Birthday parties, in particular, held in upscale bars and exclusive nightclubs, are always thrown with much self-conscious and lavish expenditure. Even ordinary accomplishments are celebrated with exaggerated aplomb and an eye on social promotion. This aggrandizing process has lately filtered into academia. Mindful of the intense competition from the burgeoning colleges and universities, even established institutions are investing in image building and branding to advertise their products. Commonplace events in the life of a university are held with uncharacteristic flamboyance. It took almost a full year of preparation – the work of two special steering committees of over thirty members – to launch a three-day event in May 2009 to celebrate the inauguration of Peter Dorman as the fifteenth President of the American University of Beirut. The entire month of May was declared as 'Inaugural Month' with relentless reminders -- on the university's website and through colorful leaflets, posters, flags and banners – of the commemorative events. Other than a conference on the prospects for liberal arts, there was nothing cerebral or academic about the celebration. The highlights included a jam session, student concert, folk-dance festival, sports parade (without any competitive events) and a campus-wide picnic where the entire university community was treated to sumptuously catered food. The food was so abundant that students complained, the day after, about the massive amount of leftovers. They were critical of the indiscretion of those responsible for hosting this spectacle when the country was in the midst of a political crisis.

To commemorate the event, a special team was commissioned to redesign the original mace the university used during commencements and opening ceremonies. The justifications the team (mostly from the faculty of Architecture and Design) submitted to account for the mace they created reveal the elaborate and intricate symbolism they employed to arrive at the design. A wooden shaft crafted from a 7,000-year-old cedar log was used. The engraved inscriptions were in Latin and Arabic script from the Kufic mold. The head of the mace is fashioned of modern curvilinear shapes to reflect light and hope. The base, serving as a link to the university's heraldic tradition, is adorned with a replica of a Roman coin bearing the word 'Berytus' and a trident enclosing two stars, with a dolphin entwined about its shaft – the symbol which inspired the original mace. (For further details see *AUB Bulletin Today*, 10/7 (May 2009), 13.)

Incidentally, Dorman is not an ordinary president. Being the great-great-grandson of Daniel Bliss, the founder of the university in 1866, he is a veritable scion of the founding fathers and their puritan heritage of asceticism, modesty and the catchy epigram of 'Doing Big Things with Little Noise'. With an eye on publicity and safeguarding the image of the university as the most distinguished institution of higher learning in the region, the inauguration inevitably assumed the thrills and frills of a spectacle. It also betrayed the sober precepts of its founding fathers.

If established universities are seduced by features of the spectacle and kitsch, it is not surprising that such allure should trickle down to more ordinary ventures. Hence, book-signing events, the inauguration of art shows, new shops, the launching of new products or the elaborate rituals of gift exchange, all become part and parcel of the process of self-advertisement and social climbing. It is in here that the spectacle and kitsch begin to feed on each other. As Jukka Gronow poignantly puts it, 'misplaced social pride corrupts taste' (1997: 46). In a more fundamental sense, this is why spectacles do not produce change. Indeed, the two are incompatible. People are so distracted by the hoopla of being part of the spotlight that they lose focus and discretion and, hence, social control. It is also here that form begins to take precedence over substance. The average Lebanese – and in all walks of life – is so engrossed with outer display that the inner content and subtleties of the message or qualities of the object are routinely forgotten.

The Lebanese have much to learn in this regard from the lessons of history. There is usually an inverse relationship between humility and achievement. For example, the public mood in America after World War II, as in Europe, was most humble when their actual achievements were at their most extraordinary. This is the antithesis of what is so often conspicuous in Lebanon. It is groups with questionable and spurious skills, or those anxious about their social standing, who are inclined to display grandiosity in their outward conduct. Just skim through any of the sleazy, tabloid periodicals that are legion in Lebanon. They are awash, page after page, with images of groups trying to advertise or give an edge to their social climbing. Consorting with the rich and famous is bound to add some luster to one's image. In Lebanon political figures, tycoons, diplomats, media icons, celebrities, even starlets are all high on the totem pole of enviable status.

This penchant for boosting one's image is not strictly a class phenomenon. It is readily seen in how modest and tiny shops and undertakings, even street vendors and makeshift stalls, acquire titanic names and identities. Hence, one is not just vending watermelon, potatoes or falafel. A recent billboard for a home-delivery chicken service is pronounced as chicken *Mahrajan* or festival. One becomes the 'King' of watermelon, the 'Emperor' of potatoes or 'Sultan' of falafel. Likewise, a traditional and unassuming tailor's shop becomes a boutique; a shoe-repairman becomes an establishment; a barber-shop becomes a 'salon'. Hospitals, medical centers and clinics are not spared such glamorizing face-lifts. Instead, they are converted into facsimiles of five-star boutique hotels, customized spas and franchises of exclusive resorts.

The proliferation of restaurants, eating stalls, cafes, pubs, nightclubs, rooftop and underground dancing halls and other entertainment haunts, means that new outlets, which mushroom virtually every day, are compelled to be aggressive in designing and branding their new ventures. None is a facsimile. The intent is to be novel, different and appealing. Hence the debasement of authentic cultural artifacts and the preponderance of kitsch and the spectacle.

As we have seen earlier, the pervasive – often bewitching and captivating – impact of merchandizing technologies in Lebanon has become very compelling. Consequently, it becomes difficult to discern when the Lebanese is consuming an actual product and when he is seduced by the meaning of the commodified goods as constructed by artful advertising and display.

The front page of the *Daily Star* (13 August 2009) carried the following advert for dining at the Habtour Grand Hotel Convention Center and Spa;

a meal is not only treated as a 'destination for luxury or a night of culinary passions', but as a rendezvous with the stars:

Luxury, your only destination

Dining acquires new definition in Le Ciel at Habtour Grand Hotel Convention Center and Spa on the 31st floor. Bask in a panoramic view of Beirut with acclaimed Michelin Star Chef Dominique Blais for a night of culinary passion. With Le Ciel's supreme blend of motivation and passion, float among the stars and experience luxury at its best.

In 2003, a limited edition series of BMW luxury cars was designed especially for the Lebanese market. It was advertised as a source of *muta'a*; literally an experience of unbridled sensuality. The agents, we are told, could not cope with the mounting demand. The price of $80,000 did not act as a restraint on the impulse to purchase the eroticized car. Recently when Porsche launched its 2010 model in a special gala event, over thirty cars at $270,000 each were signed off before the event was over. Virtually all those who purchased the cars, so I was told by the agent, were Lebanese nationals. As we have seen, even purchasing a house is not perceived as a basic human need to seek shelter or to have a roof over one's head. It is elevated by the scintillating promotion campaigns into a 'gateway to a timeless address' or an experience in 'serenity and charm'.

Elements of the spectacle and kitsch are more pronounced because they are emblematic of curious contrasts and anomalies. Beirut is an epicurean, hedonistic city but also a barricaded and militant one. This odd duality, mindful of Durkheim's 'sacred and profane', is in some fundamental respects the *sine qua non* of Lebanon. Many Lebanese, in fact, manage to embrace both without any outward discomfort or unease. Private birthdays, weddings, family celebrations and ordinary parties, as we have seen, are thrown with much pomp, fanfare and an intent to outdo others. They also end up with the rattle of shotguns from rooftops and balconies. The same is true of religious holidays. In multi-sectarian villages and towns, they are an invitation to suffer the boisterous alternation of recorded choral hymns and gunfire.

As alluded to earlier, just as religious rituals are profaned and debased by excessive commodification, we also witness growing manifestations of the profane being sacralized. While some of the righteous and spiritual precepts of Islam – that is, fasting, alms-giving and benevolence – are being commercialized, celebrities, pop singers and brand logos are idolized and worshiped.

Even entertainers with questionable talent (such as Haifa Wehbe and Nancy Ajram), once they are elevated into media-anointed icons, are celebrated as cultural heroes and, hence, endowed with symbolic meaning which transcends their recognized gifts as artists.

A bit more idiosyncratic, a noted nightclub (BO18) designed by Bernard Khoury, one of Lebanon's gifted avant-garde architects, stretches such dissonant elements to a more bizarre degree. The nightclub's tables are constructed out of the coffins of civil war martyrs. The country's hedonists and narcissists dance and frolic on these tables; a symbolic gesture, if ever there was one.

The imposing Al-Amin Mosque dwarfs the historic St George's Maronite Cathedral right next to it. The imposing minarets of the mosque, like others in central Beirut, is barely yards away from the spire of the cathedral. Often the amplified calls for prayer coincide with the pealing of the cathedral bells. Hence, both become inaudible. How the so-called 'Hariri Mosque', a $30 million venture, bestowed on Beirut such a monumental religious landmark, certainly Lebanon's and perhaps the Near East's largest sacred edifice, is a complex and intriguing story, which has been admirably told elsewhere (see Vloeberghs, 2008; Becherer, 2005). Its characteristic blue dome with four imposing minarets overwhelms everything in sight. Resentful of how its own historic icon, which has graced the city center since 1767, is now rendered diminutive, the Maronite diocese is now adding an over-towering steeple topped by a bell and clock spire to exceed the height of the competing minaret.

Meanwhile the 'Hariri Mosque' has metamorphosed into a living shrine to the felled national hero. Ironically, a national tragedy has been converted into a kitschy artistic installation. An iconic, larger-than-life portrait of Hariri is mounted atop a monument of flowers in the shape of an automobile, a reference, one supposes, to the car bomb which took his life along with twenty-one of his close companions. The makeshift shrine, nestled beneath the leviathan mosque, has become a fitting memorial for a secular saint. Since his assassination a steady stream of mourners, heads of state and diplomats, trickles in solemnly to pay their respects.

Yahia Lababidi, an intuitive Lebanese poet, described what he saw when he revisited his birthplace after a decade's absence.

> Across from the extravaganza was another monument of sorts, a five-story Virgin Megastore. Aside from offering a dizzying selection of music and film, the monster music store showcases an impressively liberated book section stocked with contemporary erotic literature,

in addition to the classics. Outside, on the sidewalk, a curious skateboard community congregates. Lebanese teens with long, kinky hair, luxuriant afros, and pierced lips, issue skater-speak in immaculate American accents that abruptly veer into unexpected Lebanese slang: 'yeah, dude, just keep popping ... *yalla, ya zallama*.' Behind this wondrous – strange triptych, bristling with contradictions – mosque-shrine, music store-temple, and inscrutable skateboarders – stood the amoral sea, reconciling all differences. (Lababidi, 2008)

But differences are far from reconciled. The war is almost two decades old, yet buildings pockmarked with craters still stand out as poignant emblems of Lebanon's belligerent past. Residences and quarters of prominent politicians are cordoned off with tanks and military checkpoints. Insecure ordinary citizens resort to their own stopgap measures to blockade their homes. Traumatized Lebanese, willy-nilly, have transformed their residences and neighborhoods into barricaded and dreaded urban spaces. Hence, many ordinary citizens are unable to experience the thrills of urbanity and city life, particularly streets and alleyways as spaces of sociality, aesthetic and sensual sensibilities and encounters. As Steve Seidman (2009) has recently reminded us, streets promise more than steady traffic flows. When cities are colonized by the economies of scale and accelerated circulation of bodies, goods and machines, they undermine the intimacy and conviviality which once were the defining features of Beirut.

As elaborated earlier, the ravages of war and the geography of fear have transformed the once porous, convivial and amiable streets and neighbor-hoods into exclusive enclaves, characterized by distrust, guarded contact and civil indifference. Steve Seidman again:

> Streets that become social enclaves or security risk areas turn into combat zones if they are militarized, for example, regulated by checkpoints and military patrols, cordoned off by fences or walls, subject to surveillance camera networks, or zoned to deny ordinary citizen's access. As a combat zone, the street is framed as a battle-ground, a territory populated by enemies and allies, and a space to be conquered and controlled. (Seidman, 2009: 5)

Seidman goes on to elucidate how this restless desire, so salient in the spaces of postwar Beirut, produces a 'phantasmatic collage of sounds and sights and bodies and machines colliding, exchanging, and always, moving on ... Hamra's streets may be a space of desire and longing but in a street bent to flows and speed it does not encourage intimate sharing' (Seidman, 2009: 6).

I still vividly recall, without any delusionary nostalgia, the inviting streets and labyrinthine alleyways of the residential quarters of Ras Beirut, even downtown Beirut. One felt secure, at home, but also animated by the prospect of socializing. One was induced to slow down, to be more casual and leisurely.

Walking home during the 1960s and 1970s from Bliss to Hamra, through Jeanne d'Arc street, less than a mile apart, was such an inviting and unhurried experience. One invariably encountered familiar and friendly faces. Even shopkeepers inquired about you and noticed your absence if you had been on a short trip. Balconies overlooking the street were always alive with neighbors exchanging news. Shops without any logos or defining identities (other than their kinship affiliation) and without changing their façades remained inveterate icons of the neighborhood. Little of such reassuring encounters survive today. Instead, one is overwhelmed with merciless colonization by fleeting sites, people in haste and without any destination, ruthless commercial competition and marketing ploys – let alone barricaded quarters.

The understandable longing to escape into a re-enchanted past has obviously a nostalgic tinge to it. This, however, need not be seen as a pathological retreat into a delusionary past. It could well serve, as Bryan Turner (1987: 149) has argued, as a redemptive form of heightened sensitivity, a sympathetic awareness of human problems and, hence, it could be 'ethically uplifting'. In this sense it is less of a 'flight' and more a catharsis for human suffering.

Alas, many such retreats have been neither ethically uplifting nor cathartic for the trauma and uncertainty Lebanese have been beset with lately. Perhaps most damaging is the tendency of such retreats, as we have seen, to become jealously guarded enclaves and 'combat zones'. Equally disparaging is the vulgarization of traditional forms of cultural expressions and the commodification of consumerism so rampant in postwar Lebanon. This nostalgic longing, among a growing segment of disenchanted intellectuals, is at least a form of resistance and refusal to partake in the debasement of aesthetic standards or the erosion of *bona fide* and veritable items of cultural heritage. Impotent as such efforts may seem, they express a profound disgust with at least three salient pathologies. First, they are apparent in the trivialization of culture so visible in the emptiness of consumerism. Second, they are visible in the nihilism of the popular cultural industry. Finally, they are also an outcry against the loss of personal autonomy and authenticity. Even commonplace things and daily routines – street smells and sounds and other familiar icons and landmarks of place – let alone historic sites and architectural edifices, are allowed to be defaced or kitsched-up.

Chapter 6

Prospects for Transforming Consumers Into Citizens

Men and women increasingly feel that many of the questions proper to citizenship – where do I belong, what rights accrue to me, how can I get information, who represents my interests? – are being answered in the private realm of commodity consumption and the mass media more than in the abstract rules of democracy or collective participation in public spaces.

(Néstor García Canclini, *Consumers and Citizens*, 2001)

One of the defining premises informing this work is that postwar interludes – particularly those marked by diffuse and protracted civil strife, anarchy and disorder – normally generate moods of restraint, sobriety and moderation. In such settings, people are more inclined to curb their conventional impulses. They become more self-controlled in the interest of reappraising and redirecting their future options. The war in Lebanon – despite or because of its savagery – has paradoxically induced the opposite reaction. As we have seen, rather than freeing them from their prewar excesses, it has unleashed appetites and inflamed people with insatiable desires for acquisitiveness, unearned privileges and transgressions of lawful ordinances.

These have naturally made the Lebanese more vulnerable to some of the dismaying symptoms of mass consumerism, excessive and conspicuous commodification. More ominous is the debasement of aesthetic standards and authentic cultural expressions. These, too, are visible in the preponderance of mindless hedonism and narcissism, bent upon the satisfaction of material and short-lived desires and wants.

With the absence of government authority, such excesses are becoming more rampant. What was not ravaged by war is being eaten up by greedy developers and impetuous consumers. Hardly anything is spared. The once pristine coastline is now littered with tawdry tourist attractions, kitschy resorts, and private marinas as much as by the proliferation of slums and other unlawful makeshift shoddy tenements. The same ravenous defoliation blights the already shrinking greenbelt, public parks and terraced orchards. Even side-walks and private backyards were stripped and defiled. As a result, Beirut today suffers, perhaps, from one of the lowest proportions of open space per capita in the world. The entire metropolitan area of the city claims no more than 600,000 square meters of open space. A UN report stipulates that for an environment to qualify as a healthy one, each person requires approximately 40 square meters of space. Beirut's is as low as 0.8 per person (for these and other estimates see Safe, 2000).

Rampant commercialism, greed and enfeebled state authority could not, on their own, have produced as much damage, and are exacerbated by the ravenous postwar mentality. In the face of an ugly and unfinished war, it is understandable how those moral and aesthetic restraints which normally control public behavior become dispensable virtues.

This is bound to exacerbate some of the aberrant attributes of the perennial state of being *adrift*. Groups have not only lost their moorings and sense of direction. They have also become more impetuous, erratic, often crass and raunchy in their outward behavior. Such excessive display is deliberately exaggerated to demonstrate their rejection of mainstream duplicity, lethargy and indifference.

In such a setting, expectations calling for aesthetic and moral restraints are bound to be too remote. They will certainly be unheeded when pitted against the postwar profligate mood that is overwhelming large portions of society. Victims of collective suffering normally have other, more basic, things on their mind. They rage with bitterness and long to make up for lost time and opportunity. It is then that they become susceptible to gaudy dreams and sleazy consumerism.

It is also then that the environment becomes, as we have seen, an accessible surrogate target on which to vent their wrath. The abandon with which ordinary citizens litter and defile the environment and the total disregard they evince for safeguarding its ecological well-being is alarming. In addition there is a notoriously high incidence of excessive quarrying, deforestation, traffic congestion, reckless driving, air and noise pollution and hazardous motorways which violate minimum safety requirements, let alone the conventional etiquettes and proprieties of public driving.

This cultural disposition to violate or depart from normative expectations is apparent in the preponderance of non-traffic-related violations. These, too, have been persistently increasing. The Bureau of Internal Security normally categorizes as 'ordinary violations' such infractions as the infringement of protective regulations safeguarding forests, public gardens, sand dunes, archeological and tourist sites, as well as building and zoning ordinances. Also included are the transgressions of the rules governing hunting, fishing, quarrying and municipal and public health requirements. These, like all other contraventions of regulations on the use of public utilities, particularly water, electricity, and telephones, are proxy victims of deflected rage and hostility. Recently the press has begun to devote some attention to such violations, particularly flagrant instances of environmental abuse. Many of the other 'ordinary' violations, however, remain unpublicized, and the fines are too low to dissuade violators, even if they are apprehended.

The chapter is in three parts. An attempt is made first to review Lebanon's current experience with consumerism to ascertain the extent to which it complies or departs from patterns observed elsewhere. Second, by way of considering alternatives to excessive commodification, a few promising examples are singled out. Particular focus is placed on those which question the prevailing perceptions regarding the so-called omnipresent and manipulative media and their pliant and submissive clients. Finally, I employ the metaphor of a *playground* as an analytical tool to elucidate and account for Lebanon's double-faced character: both as a 'success story' and as a victim of internal and external exigencies.

PARADIGM SHIFT IN CONSUMERISM

Lebanon is not only caught in an unusual postwar setting and a turbulent region with a residue of unresolved rivalries. More recently, it has become embroiled in all the unsettling forces of globalism and intensification of consumerism and commodification. Though the defining character of postmodernism remains contested, there is a modicum of consensus among observers that we are today in a postmodern interlude with pervasive influence across the globe. This is most visible in the changing character and consequences of consumerism. Indeed, there has been something akin to a paradigm shift in the way material goods, public leisure and mass entertainment are symbolically used. As we have seen, under modernism, there was a relatively fixed relationship between social status and class belonging and consumerism. What one consumed was used to reflect and reinforce one's identity and class allegiance. Today, this reassuring fixity has become loosened. Manifestations of class and social status are being displaced by more individualistic attributes of lifestyle, taste and social distinction. In this regards and to some extent:

> Goods have been freed from their *symbolic moorings* and have begun to *drift* about the world of signs, ready to be used by various groups in various ways. Instead of the coherent collection of cultural practices that characterized modernism, we get a more eclectic grouping – goods and practices become things to be *played* with for a while, then ditched as we move to something else. They are no longer reliable badges of our social status. The old modernist distinction between high and low culture, which certainly served to keep classes in their places is frittered away. (Emphasis added: Corrigan, 1997: 179)

Note the reference that Corrigan makes to being freed from symbolic moorings, being adrift and playful. Likewise Mike Featherstone (1991), another astute observer of such postmodern transformations, alerts us to the vital role that culture, broadly speaking, is assuming today. He tells us that:

> Instead of consuming the goods themselves, we consume the meanings of goods as constructed through advertizing and display (although I think we have been doing that ever since the department store). Instead of going to the museum to receive instruction in high culture, we go to touch, to see, and to experience. (Featherstone, 1991: 97)

This is precisely the manifestation of the public indulgence of the Lebanese. Much of his outward behavior – from the mundane to the sublime – is an effort to make a statement and draw the attention of the public gaze. He is there, whether buying or doing things, to be seen, touched or recognized. It is in this sense that form, style or taste begin to overwhelm and debase substance and genuine content.

The experience of Lebanon with consumerism has not always been consistent with patterns observed in Euro-American societies. For example, Veblen's classical premise which anticipated conspicuous consumption would displace leisure has not as yet become visible in Lebanon. The country, instead, suffers the consequences of both. As a 'Merchant Republic', it had an early exposure to the appeals of shopping, marketing and advertising. This proclivity to be a haven for shoppers and pleasure-seekers is not of recent origin. Nor is it primarily the outcome, as often assumed, of the infusion of petro-dollars or global consumerism and postmodern commodification.

The relentless debate on cultural globalization has often been polarized into whether the recent surge of cultural flows and global consciousness has increased or undermined cultural homogenization. The prevailing view is that the so-called irresistible proliferation of global consumer culture has been realized at the expense of eroding local and vernacular expression. The experience of Lebanon challenges such instances of cultural homogenization or imperialism, American or otherwise. Yes, of course, the Lebanese enjoy relatively free and uncensored access to such cultural inflows: sport spectacles, a rich variety of TV programs, network news and popular entertainment from every possible corner of the globe. Yet, in no way does this mean that the Lebanese consumer displays a totalizing uniformity in his choices and reactions to such exposure. Goods, ideas, symbols and images may be diffused globally. They are, though, consumed locally within distinct socio-cultural and political settings. Eating a Big Mac, a KFC or Dunkin Donuts does not make the Lebanese consumer an apologist for US foreign policy. Likewise, public smoking in large parts of the US is now considered an uncivil, even criminal act. In Lebanon it is still celebrated with much abandon and sense of bravado. The smoker puffing toxic fumes in clear view feels 'cool', 'hip', 'with it'. In these and other such instances there is more evidence of eclecticism, differential adaptation, that is, *glocalization,* where global consumer items are rearranged to render them more accessible to local needs.

Yet in other respects, the recent experiences of Lebanon are beginning to parallel the Euro-American models. This is apparent, for example, in how one's status and self-perception are intimately related to pecuniary emulation and conspicuous consumption. This is particularly relevant to the emergence of the new bourgeoisie which is normally keen on validating its social identity through expressive and liberated lifestyles. The distinction of Featherstone between the *discursive* elements of high culture and the populist and proletarian demands for the *spectacular* and *sensual* is also relevant to understanding the shift in the nature of consumerism, leisure and popular entertainment in Lebanon. This is why, incidentally, the 'virtual mall' is also quickly emerging not only as an ordinary and exclusive site for shopping, but also as a meaningful and accessible site for social interaction and a meeting place for the thrills of play and popular leisure. One could easily spend hours in a mall without actually purchasing anything at all. One French study reported that 'one-third of people exiting from suburban shopping malls had made no purchase' (Shields, 1992: 10). If anything this is an indication of a shift from an actually-existing to virtually-existing space. Hence, leisure services, cultural outlets and other forms of association may become more central than the purchasing of goods.

We are also beginning to see manifestations of discerning and socially conscious citizen groups who participate in advocacy and grass-roots movements to resist some of the abusive consequences of excessive commodification. How one can protect the *discursive* elements of culture from being appropriated and debased by the *spectacular* and *sensual* is of profound importance today. Or, in the language of Habermas, how can one prevent a citizen from being reduced to a client?

Such efforts, however, are still rare, futile and unusual in Lebanon. Participating in such spirited and well-meaning associations might well enhance a person's sense of self-worth and autonomy. Dispossessed and excluded groups begin to feel better about themselves but they remain largely powerless to modify or control the abusive structural impediments. If they cannot rearrange the alienating forces of marginalization and injustice in society, they are gripped by the more trying prospects of rearranging themselves and scaling down their expectations.

ALTERNATIVES TO COMMODIFICATION

Three overriding inferences can be extracted from the bulk of our discussion, particularly in the last three chapters. First, there has been a shift from consumerism to commodification, where symptoms of colonization of society by mass consumption are becoming more salient. Second, such commodification is becoming the preeminent site through which individuals continue to experience and express their identities and social worlds. Who we are, in other words, is largely shaped by *what* and *how* we consume. As we have seen, to some recent scholars this acquisitiveness assumes the pathology of a sickness. To Bauman, it is so irresistible that it becomes a 'sinister demon' suffused with ambient and unanchored fears. To Bourdieu, much of one's status and well-being is gained, lost and reproduced largely through everyday acts of consumption. Third, though such symptoms are becoming increasingly unassailable, one can still find venues through which they can be mitigated and rearranged.

The enduring wisdom of the Frankfurt School, particularly Adorno and Horkheimer, can be once again invoked here, as we consider alternatives to the tyranny of excessive commodification. Though they were appalled by the disheartening symptoms of *mass* production and consumerism they were among the first to alert us that mass production is no longer so mass ... and that the new more flexible technologies allow a proliferation of customized products and niche markets, which grant the consumer far more choice and creativity (Schor and Holt, 2000). In other words, it is possible to escape a world of such ubiquitous commodification. The so-called duped consumer need not be a complacent, unreflective and willing victim of an impetuous and greedy market.

Another intuitive inference comes to mind. As we are reminded by McCracken (1988), goods and commodities are double agents. They can be sources of continuity as well as vehicles of change. Look at what happens when a novelty becomes fashionable. It acquires a conservative authority which persuades others to comply, almost impulsively and uncritically. As long as it remains 'à la mode', it holds things in place. But fashions, particularly in an open, plural and cosmopolitan country like Lebanon – which is also restless and traumatized – have very short life spans. Also, look what happens when the authenticity or aesthetic credibility of a cultural product (art, literature, fashion or architectural style) begins to be questioned. Quite often the sources of open dissent and resistance are embraced and incorporated into the local and vernacular traditions. This, too, accounts for Lebanon's 'success story' as a hybrid and liminal socio-cultural setting; though it appears to be meandering more or less aimlessly, such generative and hybrid manifestations are promising.

As long as the excesses are contained, this state of surrender and wandering may well prove to be recuperative and rejuvenating. Once again being adrift carries the prospect of at least averting the bleak destination ahead. As McCracken (1988) tells us, such a state is especially needed in the early stages of group definition, when one knows that distinctive goods are needed but is not certain as to which goods are the most appropriate. Once some sort of consensus emerges, the goods act as billboard to proclaim group identity. In the language of McCracken this becomes the 'object-code' which reinforces group identity:

It serves as a means by which a society both encourages and endures change. It helps social groups establish alternative ways of seeing themselves that are outside of and contrary to existing cultural definitions. But it also serves to help a society incorporate these changes into the existing cultural framework and to diffuse their destabilizing potential. (McCracken, 1988: 137)

Such a view is a far cry from the critical voices which continue to lambast consumerism. It also has some sobering implications for the experience of Lebanon. Yes, of course, we need to be wary about the dreaded prospects of homogenizing taste. Since the surge in global consumerism is ubiquitous and omnipresent, there is always the likelihood that consumerism will infiltrate and condition every crook and cranny of society. In such instances, the 'market', as Benjamin Barber has cautioned us in his latest book, will 'take over our lives' (Barber, 2007: 222). If uncontained, market forces often narrow rather than expand our choices. But they are not the totalizing 'demons' depicted by Barber, among others. Nor should they be held solely responsible for 'corrupting children, infantilizing adults and swallowing citizens whole', as his subtitle laments.

A few recent promising instances of experimenting with alternative venues for challenging symptoms of excessive or totalizing consumer culture in Euro-American settings and elsewhere are beginning to gain some enthusiastic adherents and advocates. By way of conclusion, passing reference is made to a few, particularly those which parallel or reinforce similar bourgeoning manifestations in Lebanon. Duane Elgin's classic on *Voluntary Simplicity* (1981), reminiscent of earlier such tomes which celebrated the virtues of asceticism, going back to nature, spirituality and self-denial, has been favorably received. Her appeal for voluntary simplicity has not been heeded on the ground, yet 'downsizing', 'living with less', 'just say no' were some of the popular trends in the 1990s. The recent global economic setback has aroused renewed interest in such movements. But these movements are far from new. They had some compelling precursors: the Beats in the 1950s, the hippies of the 1960s, the 'Small is Beautiful' and the pro-environmentalist 'Greens' of the 1970s, and some spokesmen of the religious right of the 1980s. In one way or another they all developed identities based on the rejection of a mainstream culture based on mass consumption.

The plea of Thomas Princen et al. (2000) for 'cautious consuming' is in similar vein. In their efforts to confront overconsumption, they revisited some of the seemingly outmoded norms of thrift, frugality, self-reliance, stewardship and simplicity. To them 'cautious consuming' is an antidote to 'exuberant producing'. To consume cautiously is to defy and resist the imperatives of the market and to question the 'ethical moorings of a political economy that knows no bounds, that acts as if widespread irreversible degradation and growing inequality can be addressed with yet more economic goods' (Princen et al, 2002: 327). In essence, cautious consuming does mean being thoughtful, simplifying one's life to achieve a more equitable balance between private and personal desires and lifestyles and the public good.

Kalle Lasn (2000) advances a more oppositional and radical perspective. Building on the politics of the French Situationists, who believed in staging dramatic social movements that would expose the alienating nature of the 'society of the spectacle', Lasn went as far as to support the movement of 'culture jammers'. Culture jammers employ subversive techniques such as 'sub-vertising', 'de-marketing' and the 'un-cooling' of everything from fashions, fast food and cars to delegitimize the ethos of the consumer culture: 'I consume, therefore I am' (see Lasn, 2000, for further details).

In his 'national bestseller', *Everything Bad is Good for you* (2006) Steven Johnson makes a fairly persuasive plea about the so-called 'infantilized popular culture'. Maligned and decried for so long as a debased form of mass entertainment associated with the dumbing down of high aesthetic culture and its stupefying effects on tomorrow's generation, it can well be seen in a more edifying and enabling perspective. Far from being a dumbed-down version of instant gratification and mass diversion, Johnson claims that popular and mass culture have been growing more sophisticated, more intellectually challenging and cognitively demanding. Drawing on the discipline of narrative theory, social network analysis and neuroscience, he argues that some of the new forms of popular entertainment, particularly video games, involve multiple sources of stimulation. Hence, they are inclined to sharpen intellectual agility of the brain's 'ability to shift from an idle state of inactivity to a focused, task-driven state, and to separate out signal from noise in a complex situation' (Johnson, 2006: 208).

Finally, two probing and seminal works (Cohen, 2004; Canclini, 2001) shift the analysis to how changes in the modes of consumption have direct implications for the nature of citizenship. Cohen prefaces her work – *A Consumer's Republic* – by arguing that our identities as citizens and consumers should not be treated as opposing polarities. For example, after World War II consumption in the US became a prerequisite for the reconstruction of the nation's economy and hence the emergence of a 'Consumer's Republic' became inevitable. It promised to deliver not only economic prosperity but also the loftier social and political ambitions for a more equal, free and democratic nation (Cohen, 2004: 13). If in the final analysis, we are all citizens and we are all consumers, Cohen's message is that how we choose to mix the two reveals a great deal about who we are as individuals as well as about the virtues of the society we live in. Given this tenuous reality, we must be always on guard against elevating consumer wants over civic needs and virtues.

Néstor García Canclini (2001), one of Latin America's most reputable sociologists, is also concerned with the interplay between consumerism and citizenship. Since contemporary society has propelled the masses into public spheres, it is responsible for channeling citizen activity towards consumerism. Hence people today increasingly feel that

> many of the questions proper to citizenship – where do I belong, what rights accrue to me, how can I get information, who represents my interests? – are being answered in the private realm of commodity consumption and the mass media more than in the abstract rules of democracy or collective participation in public places. (Canclini, 2001: 15)

One can extract from Canclini another pertinent inference. He questions the prevailing image of a simple and binary relation between the so-called seductive and manipulative media and docile audiences. Neither the media is that manipulative or suggestive in Lebanon, nor are the consumers duped and undiscerning. I wish to identify a few promising recent examples which provide support, modest as they may seem, to such a claim.

Consumers Lebanon

This is a truly formidable example of what a spirited non-profitable advocacy NGO can accomplish in the short span of ten years, sparked by the inspiring leadership of an executive committee of only six activists. Founded in 2000, just as 'mad cow disease' was arousing global attention, Consumers Lebanon (CL) launched an extensive awareness campaign. In collaboration with the Scientific Committee of the European Union, it lobbied the government to prohibit the addition of crushed bones and meat to cattle feed and to prevent the purchase of non-scientific test procedures for the analysis of new blood. Shortly after, and with the assistance of the Food and Agriculture Organization, it undertook a study of red meat which led to a general 50 percent reduction in meat consumption.

Soon after (September 2001), based on its own survey, it revealed that the costs of cellphone calls in Lebanon are among the highest in the world. The Lebanese, much like their addiction to cigarettes, are compulsive users of cellphones and other digital contraptions. In a joint effort with twenty-three syndicates and economic associations and a campaign for a monthly day boycott, CL managed to negotiate a more favorable deal with the two duopolies which dominated the telecommunication sector. This was followed (February 2002) by an 'Anti-Exclusivity Agency Campaign'. Lebanon is notorious for the excessive number of monopolies in the public and private sector. CL launched a campaign for the abolition of exclusive agencies, the reduction of monopoly power and the promulgation of a Competition Law. A project-law was drafted for the abolition of exclusivity. Its application was postponed until January 2008 (info@consumersLebanon.org). The organization went on to launch a succession of grounded campaigns addressing issues of direct concern to the public: bottled water, air pollution, food safety, sanitary and hygiene, anti-exclusive agency, anti-tobacco, pesticides, household liquid gas security ...

What account for its success are the concerted efforts to establish firm relations with government ministries and parliamentary commissions. More important, it sought assistance and cooperation from a string of international organizations such as the EU, UNIDO, FAO, the World Bank, Amideast and USAID. It also employed many of the successful strategies associated with renowned international foundations and advocacy groups, such as establishing consumer 'hotlines' and circulating periodic newsletters and monthly reports.

Green Party of Lebanon
Another promising, through belated, example is the Green Party of Lebanon (GPL), established in 2004 under the compelling slogan 'the earth knows no religion', by a handful of spirited activists, who were alarmed by the appalling state of the country's environmental deterioration. In his justification for launching GPL its president Philippe Skaff (also CEO of Grey advertising and an intuitive film-maker) exposed the magnitude of the problem and the failure of NGOs and individual initiative to have any direct impact on containing the erosion of the country's most cherished natural resources.

He began, most graphically, by outlining some lamentable realities: '5,000 years ago a squirrel would travel the whole country by merely hopping from tree to tree' (Mahdawi, 2008: 3). By the end of the 1960s, forests covered only 35 percent of the country. By 1972, in about a decade, this had decreased further to about 22 percent. Today, it stands at a mere 13 percent and is threatened to be eaten up further. Skaff invoked Ernest Renan who once described Beirut as the 'Florence of the Orient'. Yet *Paris Match*, one the most reputable French magazines, recently voted Beirut as one of the ugliest cities on the Mediterranean.

Lebanon's abysmal environmental record, if only measured by the incidence of toxic waste, microbiological pollution, deforestation and quarrying, is becoming more deplorable. Such neglect and abuse is not due, as often assumed, to lack of awareness or public consciousness. Repeatedly, special commissions and the platforms of a growing number of NGOs have been providing persuasive evidence of the magnitude and consequences of such neglect. Alas, they remain voices in the wilderness. They only add *insight* to *injury*. The more knowledgeable and insightful we are, the problems become more deplorable. Yet, we are still impotent to provide any concrete future prospects for controlling the abuses.

Some problems are embedded in structural fault lines which seem unassailable. For example, half of the country's 22,000 industrial establishments are concentrated in Beirut and its suburbs. More than 90 percent of these outlets, Skaff tells us, dispose of their toxic and non-toxic waste in the sea. Even the quality of drinking water has lately come into question. While Lebanon boasts of having up to 800 companies selling bottled water, not more than 10 percent are approved by the Ministry of Health (for these and other details, see Mahdawi, 2008).

Lebanese Transparency Association (LTA)
Established in May 1999 as a Lebanese chapter of Transparency International, it is the first NGO to focus on curbing the endemic abuses of corruption and promoting the principles of good governance through civil society. Having become increasing aware of how widespread and abusive such corruption was, a group of devoted public-minded citizens took the initiative to establish the LTA, in an effort to arouse awareness and act forcefully in support of transparency and accountability. The jurisdiction of LTA does not cover individual cases of corruption. Instead, by building coalitions with other stakeholders – particularly state agencies, the media, private sector and international civil society associations – it advocates measures to curb the pervasive pitfalls of the treacherous trilogy of government incompetence, venality and corruption.

Realizing the prospects for mobilizing disaffected and lethargic youth, they established in January 2008 Youth Civil Society Leaders (YCSL). The central objective of the project is to train and promote active youth leaders to address problems of corruption and good governance. The program consists of four mutually reinforcing objectives (taken from the 2009 Lebanese Youth Coalition Against Corruption, LYCAC, Facebook entry):

> Build the capacity of youth civil society leaders in advocacy and anti-corruption techniques;
> Identify issue-based projects that bridge sectarian divides;
> Implement community-driven youth projects that improve government transparency and accountability; and
> Form a nation-wide youth coalition called Lebanese Youth against Corruption.

About 500 youth leaders, selected from close to twenty different regions, received focused instruction (close to ninety hours) on problematic issues (such as citizenship, leadership, conflict resolution, project management). Throughout the training sessions, youth leaders learned to identify the issues related to corrupt governance, to mobilize stakeholders to increase transparency and accountability of local governmental institutions and to unify and consolidate efforts across ethnic and religious boundaries.

In addition to training, the project provided small grants (not exceeding $5,000) amounting to $120,000 to support youth leaders in implementing projects at the community level that encourages transparency and bridge sectarian divides. In total 136 proposals were received, and based on objective selection criteria, 28 anti-corruption small projects have been selected and are currently being implemented in eight different regions. The grantees are 28 young Lebanese, among them 18 females. (Ibid.)

YASA (Youth Association for Social Awareness)

Founded in 1994 as an NGO to raise public awareness and to improve legislation about road safety and injury prevention, it has quickly emerged as a unique initiative in road safety advocacy. YASA considers road safety as a basic human right and collaborates with other partners (both private and public sectors) to lobby and assist the government in addressing the compelling problems which generate formidable adverse effects on the quality of life and public safety. First, to seeks to assist the Lebanese Parliament in legislating a new modern traffic law, since its notoriously defunct system dates back to the 1960s. Second, it aims to improve the quality of law enforcement, to ameliorate road maintenance and, finally, to reform the corrupt system of driving licenses.

Due to the appalling and sustained increase in car accident casualties, YASA has lately been more assertive in its outreach advocacy programs. The released figures in 2009 (94 fatalities and 12,000 injuries, together amounting to about 400 daily victims) had dramatic reverberations throughout society which reinforced YASA's campaigns. For example, in July 2009, it launched a multi-media program to draw the public attention to the pervasive 'culture of bribery' whereby virtually anyone can pass both the theory and practical driving tests. The NGO often resorts, particularly after a calamitous episode, to dramatic gestures to arouse public concern. For example, in November 2009, YASA hosted a widely publicized mass, at the renowned 'Our Lady of Harissa' basilica, to commemorate the victims of car accidents. Perhaps more important is YASA's regional and international outreach activities in persuading policy-makers and decision-makers to treat car accidents as a major public health issue in various Arab countries.

Non-Corporate Architecture

As noted earlier, Lebanon is infamous for the lamentable degradation of its architecture and living space. Fortunately, we have in the making a promising generation of young gifted architects who are beginning to resist massive corporate architecture with its overbearing towers and skyscrapers. These vast, colossal structures have already defaced much of Lebanon's architectural legacy, pristine shoreline and lush landscape. Judging by the impact they have already had, modest as it may seem at the moment, this spirited core of architects is destined to make an indelible mark in resisting mainstream corporate models and/or in offering a minimalist, low-profile, grounded and unobtrusive architecture. Their projects, by virtue of their provisional and temporary character, are not that numerous or visible. They do though stand out precisely because they are in stark contrast to their faceless and imposing surroundings. Those in non-urban settings are more striking because they blend with the cultural and human habitat in which they are grafted.

The group all completed their professional education and training at prominent schools and apprenticeship with noted (often world-class) architects by the mid- or late 1980s and even the early 1990s. They also share, in one way or another, a social and humanistic perspective which predisposes them to favor projects with avowed social welfare, participatory and sustainable dimensions. I wish to single out a handful, identified here in the order in which they commenced their professional practice: the ERGA group of Elie and Randa Gebrayel, Nabil Gholam, Bernard Khoury, Bawader Architects, Hashim Sarkis, George Arbid, Rana Samara Jubayli, Youssef Tohme, Maha Nasrallah, Hani Asfour and Mona Hallak. Of course, one always runs the risk of crimes of omission or commission in making such judgments. The selection is nonetheless made after reviewing their published profiles and portfolios, interviews and discussions with a score of active professionals and my own impressions extracted from direct site visits.

The ERGA group is a project study firm, co-founded in 1982 by the husband/wife team of Elie and Randa Gebrayel. Both are graduates of the Institut National des Beaux Arts, INBA, in 1980 and are among the few local architects not to enjoy the privilege of foreign education or training. Three admirable examples of their work deserve recognition. The refined and meas-ured use of hi-tech elements is made evident in their design of the Order of Doctors, the Badaro Trade Center and the Faubourg St Jean Commercial Center in Hazmieh. The design of the Mövenpick Hotel, stretching across the western slopes of Beirut's seafront, like the Order of Doctors next to Martyrs' Square, evinces a minimalist, simplistic style while seeking monu-mentality in its volume.

The Gebrayel duo have also been involved in restoration work. Most exem-plary in this regard is their rehabilitation and expansion of the Trad Hospital on Clemenceau Street (1993). The construction of a new wing in modern style while preserving the red brick of the old 1930s building is elegant and harmonious. Doubtless their most successful and pacesetting venture is their participation in the reconstruction of the Saifi Village, the traditional urban quarter and carpenters' souk adjoining the eastern flank of Martyrs' Square. The overall project, designed by Francois Spoery, a leading French architect, is a judicious blend of contemporary features while preserving more than outward, cosmetic hints of nostalgia.

Nabil Gholam, a graduate of the Architecture School of Paris-Villemin (1986) and Columbia University (1988), is emerging as arguably one of the most productive of his generation. Soon after his graduation, he joined the workshop of Ricardo Bofill, a leading Catalan architect, which exposed him to global and international trends. Indeed, between 1987 and the establish-ment of his NG architectural and design office in Beirut in 1994, he had a resourceful and enriching career collaborating on major projects in Europe, China and the US. A few of those have won distinguished prizes and awards.

With his young and spirited team of associates, he built a score of hotels and residential compounds in Dubai and Saudi Arabia. In Lebanon, before he undertook some prominent and visible projects, all the outcome of international competitions, he displayed a genuine interest in restoration. He also devoted considerable attention to reclaiming and landscaping coastal and beach areas. To his credit is a score of marinas, yachting clubs, leisure and sports facilities. In the past few years his firm has been associated with many spectacular projects, often in association with world-class architects. Many are currently under construction: the Platinum Towers on Park Avenue overlooking the marina, Foschvill, Block 94 and Saifi II adjoining Martyrs' Square.

Bernard Khoury, a graduate of the Rhodes Island School of Design (1991) and Harvard (1993), has shown considerable inventiveness and originality in his work. Before he completed his Masters at Harvard's Graduate School of Design, he was privileged to work with Jean Nouvel in France. Thus far, most of his projects, although diminutive and unpretentious, are ingenious, often cunning. His BO-18 nightclub, a notorious popular haunt for the young, has become something of an eccentric architectural icon. So too is the Yabani restaurant. Another restaurant in Jemeyze, Central, is a restored building in which the makeshift scaffolding gives the appearance of provisional and temporary structure in the throes of reconstruction. This same temporality, although more dramatic, characterizes the City Center Dome project currently under consideration. The disheveled remains of a once fashionable movie theater, the 'Dome' stands today at the southwest end of Martyrs' Square, an eyesore from the city's belligerent past. Once restored, the 'Red Square', as it is currently labeled, will serve as a short-term cultural and entertainment center (see Arbid, 2004 for further details). Recently it has already served as the premises for a number of exhibitions, performances and artistic installations.

Another promising group is Bawader Architects, established in 1992 by three AUB graduates: Muhammad Adra, Akram Zaatari and Marwan Ghandour. The bulk of their joint efforts thus far has focused on the design and construction of nursery and primary school complexes in various neighborhoods within the city and its suburbs. They have also rehabilitated a score of government hospitals in Saida and Baalbeck. Since the premises are mostly situated in fairly depressed areas, their elegant, rational and airy designs enhance both their own architectural appeal and the quality of their surrounding habitat.

More recently, Hashim Sarkis and George Arbid, both with PhDs from Harvard's Graduate School of Design, have opted to pursue more academic careers. Sarkis is currently the Agha Khan Professor of Islamic Architecture at Harvard while Arbid is at AUB. Of the two, Sarkis has had a decidedly more active and versatile practice. With hardly a decade in the field, and despite his demanding teaching and academic duties, he has already supervised the realization of a score of unusual pacesetting projects, often in remote regions of Lebanon. Most noted are the following: the Fishermen Residential Complex in Tyr, the School of Agronomy in Mejdlaya, the Market and Center for Young People in Zahle and Bab-el-Tabbaneh School in Tripoli. He has also participated in establishing the plan for the development of the University of Balamand in the Kurah district and reconstruction of the public space of the Gefinor Shopping Center. Most recently, his scheme for the International Ideas Competition for the Grand Axis and Martyrs' Square of Beirut was awarded third prize. Through his teaching and studies at Harvard's Graduate School of Design, he has been instrumental in exposing successive generations of students to direct fieldwork on the ground in various cities in the region. One of his students, in fact, has just won first place in the category for Beirut's Martyrs' Square competition.

Not only architects but a core of civic-minded graphic designers are also beginning to break away from the conventional marketing orientation of their programs to address controversial socio-cultural issues. Hence, in addition to creating packaging concepts (such as corporate logos, exhibition posters, comics, digital games and interactive animation), a few have become designers-cum-activists, in that they are adventurous enough to design aggressive anti-abortion posters, on child abuse, smoke-free zones and climate and environmental issues. Much like the other creative industries, Lebanese graphic designers are exporting their skill. In recent years they have managed, despite formidable international competition, to build up an impressive credibility and commercially viable ventures in the region.

FROM BATTLEGROUND TO PLAYGROUND

Throughout its eventful history Lebanon, as we have seen, has always displayed discordant, often binary and diametrically opposed, images. Always Janus-like, it is either adulated or maligned. When marveled at, it is seen as a privileged creation, endowed with a resourceful and resilient pluralism and a captivating natural habitat. When admonished, it is decried as a fractious and precarious polity bent on self-destruction. The two dissonant images are rarely seen as lived dialectical realities which feed on and reinforce each other. For example, during the protracted interlude of civil unrest (1975–92), Lebanon acquired all the atrocious labels associated with random and reckless killing. Lately, it is being celebrated, particularly by the global media, by a slew of catchy and sensational clichés such as a 'sin' or 'licentious' city and permissive resort for loose and uncensored pleasures. So the public image of Lebanon continues to oscillate between arousing all the symptoms of fear – a foreboding place to be avoided – or it is being celebrated as a dazzling and inviting place to visit. Recently Beirut's notorious nightlife, cosmopolitan cuisine and sleazy and nefarious attractions, continue to attract the attention of the global media. Indeed, it is often voted or singled out as among the best ten places in the world to visit.

Both these are extreme and exaggerated images which do not reflect how the two dialectically coexist. This is why, in my view, a *playground* is a more realistic and judicious metaphor. First, and more relevant for the liminal, protean and liquid state of being adrift, a *playground* conjures up images of an open, gregarious, accommodating space, conducive to invention and experimentation but also vulnerable to all the vicissitudes of excessive passion, careless narcissism, complacency and indulgent egoism. In this sense it is a fairly neutral metaphor. It neither adulates nor abnegates. It allows us, instead, to allude to and illuminate certain realities that cannot be wished away, whitewashed or mystified. It is also a more inclusive metaphor, incorporating everyday discursive and sensuous manifestations, which pervade virtually all dimensions of society.

Also a *playground*, incidentally, is more than just a heuristic and analytical tool. It has cathartic and redemptive features. By eliciting latent and hidden longings for play, conviviality and adventure, a 'playground' may serve as an expressive and transcending outlet. It brings out all the 'Homo Ludens' virtues of fair play, the exuberance of self-fulfilling and competitive sports and differential rewards for accomplished feats of excellence (for further elaboration, the interested reader may consult the following: Huizinga, 1949; Illich, 1980; Peattie, 1998). Thus a *playground* becomes an ideal site for cultivating the virtues of civility and commitment to the courtesies of the rules of the game. The very survival of a playground, particularly since it is associated with spaces where children can indulge in play, is predicated on the premise of monitoring and controlling the hazards of reckless, rash and foolhardy impulse. When uncontained, a 'playground' could easily slip into a free-for-all, raucous, rough-and-tumble public ground. At that point the lines demarcating civil and uncivil, vulgar and refined behavior, foul and fair play are blurred.

Second, the curative and healing aspects of a *playground* are naturally more pertinent in times of collective unrest and postwar stress and uncertainties. A boisterous political culture suffused with factional and contentious rivalries can find more than just momentary release in such outlets. Some of the enabling features of a playground – that is, those of fair play, teamwork, equal recognition and the sheer exuberance of doing one's thing without encroaching on the rights and spaces of others – can all become vectors for the restoration of civility. At the very least, they need not be dismissed and trivialized.

Finally, inordinate effort and resources have been squandered on strategies of political and administrative reform and the broader issues of regional conflict and infrastructural reconstruction. Important as these are, they overlook some of the more human and socio-cultural issues of coping with pervasive fear and damaged national identities. It is also these areas that are amenable to individual intervention. Ordinary, otherwise passive and lethargic, citizens are given opportunities to participate and become actively and meaningfully engaged in processes of reconstruction and rehabilitation.

With such considerations in mind, I wish to identify five features of a *playground* which epitomize Lebanon's seemingly lopsided character. In all those features we find many of the enabling and disabling attributes of a *playground* as a metaphor or 'ideal type' analytical tool: that is, those that account for Lebanon's 'success story' and those which render it more vulnerable to all the internal and external contradictions which keep it adrift.

1. By virtue of its location, composition and its historical role as a place of refuge for dissidents or a gateway for itinerant groups, Lebanon has always been a fairly open and free space. Exit from and entry into society has been relatively easy. Indeed, some argue that Lebanon became much too open, too hospitable and, hence, too vulnerable to the vicissitudes of internal and regional disturbances. It laid itself open to abuse by the very forces which sought it as a haven from repression or homelessness. A free press, uncensored media, absence of exchange controls, a 'free zone' in Beirut's port, secret bank accounts, liberal migration laws, receptivity to novelties and fads, progressive and permissive lifestyles, all reinforce the

discordant dualism inherent in its character as a free and open society. Hence its generative and positive attributes were often undermined by subversive elements. Lebanon became all too often no more than an expedient conduit, a transit point, for the trafficking and recycling of displaced groups, goods, capital and ideas.

Naturally, such trafficking was not always of a desirable and lawful character. Inevitably, the country became notorious for smuggling, arms-running, trading in drugs, black-marketing of illicit contraband products and other nefarious activities. The recent unprecedented surge in building construction and real-estate speculation, particularly upscale residential projects beyond the reach of ordinary citizens with modest financial resources, is one such glaring example of this dissonance. Perhaps more damaging is the abandon with which dissident groups exploited this freedom to launch vilifying press campaigns and plots against repressive regimes in the region. This only served to arouse suspicion and retributive acts by the targeted states or groups against Lebanon. On both counts Lebanon became unjustly victimized.

2. As in a *playground*, the Lebanese displayed a proclivity for carefree and uncommitted, almost sportive attitude, with special fondness for jocular and humorous experiences. But this playfulness is double-edged. It is a source of unflagging resourcefulness, sustained by a sense of experimentation and adventure. When unrestrained, however, it could quickly degenerate into restlessness, mischievousness or even anarchy. A thread of careless play and spontaneous activity runs through society. The laissez-faire ethos, in such a free-for-all milieu, is clearly a relief to an inept government and welcome to those adept at exploiting it. Even the corrupt civil servant 'became increasingly appreciated by the national and international business communities, since bribes now served to circumvent red tape and to effect short-cuts; which made conduct of business, in many ways, more "efficient" in Lebanon than in even the most advanced countries' (Tabbarah, 1977: 22).

As we have seen, there are other more grievous manifestations of this predisposition for unrestrained play. It is evident in the wasteful discrepancy between audacious and playful planning on the one hand and executive ineffectiveness on the other. This has plagued government bureaucracy for a long time and has been a blatant source of administrative inefficiency and misuse of resources. Some of the schemes for development are often so adventurous in their vision that they must necessarily remain unrealized blueprints, victims of reckless planning or short-sighted expediency. Examples are legion.

The Litani River Authority of 1954 was supposed to irrigate, once completed, 32,000 hectares in the southwestern regions of the Beqaa Valley. Over fifty years after the establishment of the project and despite the expenditure of hundreds of millions of pounds, the precious waters of the Litani are still draining into the Mediterranean. The Green Plan of 1964, successive urban planning schemes and comprehensive master plans, rent and zoning laws, educational and civil services reforms, to mention a few, are all regrettable by-products of this dissonance between exuberant planning and flawed implementation.

The whole character of the political process, particularly electoral campaigns and contests for public office, is suffused with elements of the spectacle. The style of daily politics is typified by political maneuverings and animated exchanges bordering on public entertainment. Indeed, as one of the smallest nation-states in the world, Lebanon has always suffered from the inordinate number of people who expend their energies and derive their sense of self-worth and esteem from 'playing' politics. This, in itself, is another reflection of the difficult, even ungovernable character of the Lebanese polity. To many of these political actors, prominent and not-so-prominent figures who meddle in the political affairs of their society, the art of politics is often reduced to a self-indulgent game, a morbid form of public amusement and exhibitionism. So alluring is the game that successive generations of politicians have found it extremely difficult to redirect their energies into less self-flattering but more demanding and creative pastimes. Much like others engaged in any addictive or habit-forming activity, some of inveterate Lebanese politicians appear to suffer withdrawal symptoms if they are compelled to retire from politics.

Some of the pathological attributes of both the spectacle and kitsch are alive and thriving in the country's beleaguered political culture. Such dismaying features have become much too obvious lately. To cite one most recent example, for almost five months since the general elections of June 2009, the parliamentary majority was not able to form a national unity government. Yet despite the deadlock, perhaps because of it, politicians continued to engage in a spectacle-like rhetoric. The political discourse has been so trivialized that at times it is no more than a banal and acrimonious exchange of invective banter and indignant and irate attributions.

The more debased and futile the political discourse, the more arrogant and pompous the magisterial presentations. The political game, and it has became such a trite and tedious joke, is not far from an 'opera bouffe'. The cast and major protagonists, though, rarely change. The Lebanese are stuck with the same set of futile and unaccountable politicians who somehow manage to perpetuate their political careers. Even the more astute and smart among them cannot resist the temptation to play politics. They have also mastered the art of representation and image-making. All the *zu'ama* and heads of political factions or parties have a retinue of media experts, consultants and event managers. Many run their own TV stations, own or patronize newspapers and provide sources of livelihoods to legions of henchmen, attendants and bodyguards. Thanks to the electronic, digital state-of-the art information technologies at their disposal, they indulge in such spectacles with the virtuosity of gifted performers. Their public appearances, even impromptu meetings, are always staged. They all have their insignia, logos, coats of arms and, most imposing, an assortment of vehicles, monitoring artifacts and security devices. Their residences and headquarters, just like their peripatetic circulation, are notorious for the nuisance they generate for ordinary citizens. The rerouting of traffic, excessive surveillance, frisking of pedestrians, all render the pleasures of urbanity disagreeable.

The tone and quality of the country's political culture, even its contentious political discourse, are not spared. It is pertinent in this regard to recall, as Jennifer Dueck ably demonstrates in her recent exploration of mass political mobilization in its pre- and post-independence interlude, how much the nascent political leadership and the parties and associations they created were largely a by-product of the orchestrated spectacles of mass rallies reminiscent of the archetypes refined by the fascists and Nazis into accomplished political art forms (Dueck, 2010). Dueck demonstrates how youthful scout movements during the French Mandate, an otherwise idealistic consciousness-raising movement, were deformed by the factional and regional political struggles of the period. For example, in all foreign schools and educational missions (French, German and Italian) the formation of scouts and quasi-scout associations became their conspicuous hallmarks of success. As early as 1937 groups of Lebanese young men were already travelling to Europe to participate in the international jamborees of scouts in Hungary, Italy and of course Hitler's Germany.

We are told by Dueck that the Italian consulate at the time used Italian Catholic schools, community centers, clubs and leisure outlets to recruit subjects. Much like the fascist youth groups in Italy, most local groups also incorporated distinct uniforms, participation in parades, marches with salutes, slogans and athletic drills. These and other spectacles served as powerful symbols in preparation for military training. Such paramilitary features, apparent in many of the youth associations of the late 1930s, cannot be overlooked in accounting for their general appeal. Examples of such associations and political groupings were particularly preponderant in Lebanon given its fragmented political culture.

A few striking examples will suffice. Antoun Sa'adeh's Syrian Socialist Nationalist Party (PPS), the Armenian Tachnaq, the Phalanges, the Nejjada and the 'White Shirts' were all instrumental in shaping the contested political discourse of the period. Pierre Gemayel, founder of the Phalanges, and Husayn Sij'an, president of the Jajjada, both attended the 1936 Berlin Olympics, and were impressed by the collective discipline of the German and Italian youth factions. Dueck appropriately points out that the Germans were interested in wooing Arab youth and many Arab nationalists saw Germany as an ally in their struggle against British and French imperialism (Dueck, 2010).

More dismaying, when political discourse becomes a spectacle where the dazzle of surface and appearance is so seductive, veteran politicians can easily disguise their misconduct. It is then that the disparaging symptoms of 'graftocracy' – that is, embezzling public funds, nepotism, clientelistic politics – so pervasive in failed states, are overlooked. Many of Lebanon's inveterate political leaders are acting like a 'kleptocratic' elite for whom deal-making, favor-swapping have become almost second nature; a way of life where infractions and breaches become guilt-free occurrences divorced from any moral apprehensions. They indulge in notorious quid-pro-quo deals and still manage to sleep well at night. The misuse of public funds, deal-making, nepotism have become so pervasive that the gossip columns of newspapers and tabloids are replete with such sordid accounts. Indeed, gossiping about the failings and foibles of the political class has become something akin to a national sport.

Such symptoms, as we have seen, do not remain a preserve of the elite. They trickle down to other layers of ordinary citizens. Since the political class, with all their unsavory shortcomings, remain coveted role models, their misconduct is not only overlooked. It is also emulated. More grievous, they became sources for validating misconduct. Since they have mastered the cultural skills of being *harbouk* (chameleon-like, adept at cutting corners), *shatarah* (smart, savvy, quick-witted), *qad halou* (confrontational and daring), *bedal wakif* (always upright and on his feet), they are accomplished cultural brokers. These desirable normative traits were after all nurtured during early socialization and have remained resilient and coveted modes of social conduct.

3. A *playground* is, above all, a place that thrives on gamesmanship. In an open, free and competitive milieu, one sustained by the maximization of private initiative and free enterprise, there is a correspondingly high premium placed on individual success and socio-economic mobility. Ruthless competition may propel the Lebanese into new heights, stretch their abilities to new thresholds. As we have seen, the global surge in mass consumerism and digital technologies has reawakened their interests and sharpened their skills to readily employ, often mindlessly, such new technologies. Yet such circumstances also generate forms of 'social Darwinism' and heedless individualism impervious to any controls or ethical restraints. It is then that symptoms of anomie become rampant. Everything and anything become accessible or feasible. Benign play could then readily degenerate into malevolent and foul play.

Within such a context, it is understandable why some of the cherished virtues of reverence along with the sense of awe and respect for the conventional graces of civility which kept people together and made life in society pleasant and bearable have begun to disappear. Instead, what one observes are symptoms of irreverence, hubris, false conceit and immodesty. In a small and tightly knit society like Lebanon, the dividends of such unearned privileged and pretensions are quite inviting.

At the height of Lebanon's golden age (mid- to late 1960s), there was already a growing chorus of dissenting voices decrying the abuses and the desecration of the country's potential. To René Habachi, there was nothing new about the crisis.

The present crisis is a quarter of a century old. It is as old as independence, that is one generation. It is a chronic, latent, disease which has suddenly burst out from under the embers of people's souls. The old style Lebanese, those who wore Ottoman boots, took over a country which had entered the modern age, but they ruled it with the mentality of the Sultan. The level of development of the country, its openness to civilization and its geographic, economic and human resources fitted it to live within the democracy of science and knowledge. Instead they ruled it like someone exploiting a farm he had inherited from his father, with the right to bequeath it in turn to his son. In Lebanon, today, there are two Lebanons ... (Quoted by Awad, 1976: 137)

Gamesmanship after all involves, as we have seen, the internalization of the necessary social skills – those of tact, deftness, acumen, quick-wittedness for *shatarah* and being *harbouq* – for handling and rearranging situations to one's own advantage. It conjures up images of Byzantine maneuvering, manipulation, deals and quid-pro-quos. Everything, including the most cherished values and resources, becomes negotiable. Lebanese entrepreneurship, particularly in its reckless form of speculation and risk-taking, seems guided more by Adam Smith's 'invisible hand' than by rational long-term planning.

4. Another double-edged feature of being a *playground* in a state of being adrift is its implication for debasing some of the convivial and gregarious character of society. In part because of the survival of many primordial and intimate social networks, the Lebanese have long displayed a proclivity for festive, light-hearted and fun-loving experiences. If one were to single out a national pastime, it would be feasting, with its associated carefree social gatherings and companionship. Time and budget analysis reveals that an inordinate amount of time and resources is devoted to ceremonial activities, social visiting and frequent contacts with close circles of family and friends. Such contacts are invaluable sources of social and psychological support, particularly in times of public distress. As the public world becomes more savage, menacing and insecure, people are more inclined to seek and find refuge and identity in the reassuring comforts of family and community. So intense and encompassing are these attachments that the average Lebanese recognizes hardly any obligations and loyalties beyond them. Here lie many of the roots of deficient civility and the erosion of the broader loyalties to public welfare and national consciousness.

Once again, in other words, what enables at one level, disables at another. At the local and communal level, conviviality (even some elements of the spectacle) is a source of group solidarity and a venue for vital socio-psychological and economic support. At the national and public level, it can lead to parochialism and oppression. Compassion for and almost obsessive preoccupation with micro-interests coexist with (are indeed a by-product of) disinterest or indifference for others. Nowhere is this more apparent than in the character or functioning of voluntary associations. The concern for public welfare continues to be inspired and mobilized on sectarian, communal or factional grounds. Hence national and broader societal problems such as child and family welfare, mental health, orphanages, the aged, delinquency, poverty, protection of the environment and habitat, and concern for the threatened architectural, archeological and cultural heritage, and other such public issues are all articulated as parochial and segmented problems. Indeed, the character of voluntary associations, their membership, financial resources and organizational leadership continue to reflect subnational loyalties.

5. Finally, elements of the spectacle and the predisposition of the Lebanese to display their material possessions and conspicuous leisure also reflect a growing multitude who perceive and seek the country as a popular resort, an amusement park or a place of abandon. The country's captivating topography, scenic beauty, temperate climate, historic sites, colorful folklore, reinforced by an aggressive infrastructure of commercial, financial, medical and cultural facilities, have made it an all-year-round tourist attraction, a popular amusement center with all its double implications.

As a national industry, tourism and related services have long invigorated the Lebanese economy. Early in the 1950s it had already comprised the most important invisible export, earning more than half of the value of all exported merchandise (see Gates, 1998: 117–80). Revenue from tourism grew fourfold in the period 1968–74, to provide 10 percent of the gross domestic product (Owen, 1988: 37). By the outbreak of hostilities in 1975 it was contributing significantly (at least $40 million annually) to GNP and thus offsetting the unfavorable trade balance. It opened up society further and enhanced the receptivity of isolated communities to diverse cultural contacts.

There is, however, a darker side to tourism and Lebanon's image as a resort. It exacerbates further the lopsidedness of the Lebanese economy by rechanneling vital resources into largely unproductive sectors of the economy. The country is increasingly becoming a nation of services, middlemen, agents, idle rentiers and hotel-keepers. Popular resorts, invariably, become tempting spots for venial and not-so-venial attractions. Lebanon, as we have seen, is hardly a paragon of virtue in this regard. It has its full share of houses of ill-repute, casinos, gambling parlors, nightclubs, discos, bars, escort bureaux and other abodes of wickedness.

Such aberrant features blemish the country's national character. As a 'merchant republic' Lebanon became a country obsessed with and too eager to please and serve others, with all the cruel ironies that such ingratiation and servility often do to society's self-esteem. Artisans, villagers and farmers abandoned some of their venerated crafts, vocations and sources of traditional status to capitalize on the transient rewards of tourist-affiliated activities. Many became idle much of the year, awaiting the quick and sizeable windfall generated by the influx of 'resorters' during the brief summer months. Others wallowed in aimless indolence.

It is easy to see how tourism, underpinned by the ethics of a mercantile culture, could deepen further the inauspicious consequences of rampant commercialism and the vulgarization of some of the cherished values and institutions. As a result, society at times displays the most lurid features of a bazaar, an amusement park and a dazzling spectacle, where the impulse for fun and profit is there for all to see. Practically everything and anything can be commodified, put up for sale or converted into a sleazy tourist attraction. Every entity and human capacity is conceived as a resource for the acquisition of profit or as a commodity to be sold to the highest bidder. This is most visible in the ruthless plunder of Lebanon's scenic natural habitat and dehumanization of much of its living space. Hardly anything is spared: shorelines, green belt, public parks and private backyards, suburban villas, historic sites and monuments ... they are all giving way to more intensive forms of exploitation to enhance the fashionable attributes of the resorts.

Epilogue

Parting Thoughts

That we do not know our next step does not mean that we are lost. It only means that we have yet to find ourselves.

(Thomas Dumm, *Loneliness*, 2008)

Most conceptions of civility and the virtues of the public sphere assume that all acts of public witness, defiance and mobilization to bring about desired change are meaningful venues for consciousness-raising. At the least, they provide tutelage in movements of cultural resistance and civil disobedience. Even when such movements fail to realize their avowed objectives, this does not detract from their significance. In this sense, Lebanon might well be an instance of double failure. The movements neither meet their desired expectations, nor do they instill within the public any genuine enthusiasm in support of their role in cultivating social awareness to transcend their private or parochial interest.

Alas, what seems salient today in Lebanon does not depart much from the unsavory images propagated by the global media: a society of the spectacle, sustained by unrestrained hedonism, sensuality and symptoms of vulgarity bordering at times on the grotesque and obscene. More disheartening, such aberrant manifestations do not seem to invite any public rebuke. Hence, the indulgent do not need to tame their exuberant desires and impetuous impulses nor to conceal their misconduct. On the contrary one is inclined to elevate one's social standing and self-regard by flouting excessive display, mischief and unearned privileges.

Within such contexts it becomes more meaningful – rather than continuing to lambast some of the dismaying features of the spectacle, excessive commodification or those of entropy and disengagement – to consider strategies of how they can be transformed into participatory agencies for promoting well-being and citizenship. One already sees promising signs of the proliferation of grass-roots movements and other forms of voluntarism launching programs to resist forces of excessive commodification, government dysfunction and drains on public resources and corruption. We should consider strategies and programs developed elsewhere to ascertain how such efforts can encourage the Lebanese to experiment with new institutional arrangements which, in the language of Habermas, can 'resist the transformation of citizens into clients' (Habermas, 1992).

Recent research evidence regarding the role of the new media is beginning to provide encouraging evidence which is redefining the relationship between consumerism and citizenship. For example, prevailing stereotypes regarding the simple and binary interplay between the so-called seductive and manipulative media and docile audiences and gullible consumers is being questioned. Even in totally modern settings, where the media is omnipotent, consumption is not something 'private, atomized and passive' (Appadurai, 1986). Mary Douglas and Baron Isherwood go further to maintain that consumerism, 'in as far as it acts to distinguish us from others and help us communicate with them ... then commodities are good for thinking' (Douglas and Isherwood, 1979: 62).

The Lebanese, particularly young adults, have not been shy in experimenting with the latest gadgetry of the electronic media – from Facebook, YouTube, chat rooms to social media. Disillusioned with the state, disaffiliated from their families and other traditional voices and moral entrepreneurs, they turn to the media to receive what citizen institutions could not deliver: services, justice, enhanced autonomy, entertainment and consumer products which merit their attention.

By far the most promising signs in this regard, as we have seen, are the strategies to which various communities have recently resorted in order to resist threats to their local heritage and identity. Here responses to fear and uncertainty – whether generated by internal displacement, global capital or mass culture and consumerism – have reawakened and mobilized local groups to reclaim their contested spaces and eroded cultural identities. The emergent spaces reveal more than just residues or pockets of resistance. There are encouraging signs of so-called 'third spaces' or in-between cultures of hybridity, mixture and tolerance. Being adrift could well become a precursor to such hopeful realities.

This is, after all, what Bennett implied by 'cultures of resistance', that is, how a 'local spatial system retains many of its traditional institutions and utilizes these to manipulate and control the extreme forces' (Bennett, 1996: 80). Hence, many of the public spaces, more the work of spontaneity than design, are in fact spaces of bargaining and negotiation for national memory and indigenous re-emergence. More so than in other such instances of 'glocalization', what we are witnessing in Lebanon today are manifestations of local groups becoming increasingly globalized and, conversely, global incursions being increasingly localized. In other words, we see symptoms of 'inward shifts', where loyalties are redirected toward renewed localism and subnational groups and institutions. We also see 'outward shifts', where loyalties and interests are being extended to transnational entities (DiMuccio and Rosenau, 1992: 62).

This is, incidentally, a far cry from the portraits one can extract from recent writings on the spatial and cultural implications of this global/local dialectics. For example, in his polemical but engaging work on the interplay between 'jihad' and 'McWorld', Benjamin Barber pits McWorld, as the universe of manufactured needs, mass consumption and mass infotainment against Jihad, the Arabic word meaning holy war, as a shorthand for the belligerent politics of religious, tribal and other forms of bigotry (Barber, 1996). The former is driven by the cash nexus of greedy capitalists and the bland preferences of mass consumers. The latter is propelled by fierce tribal loyalties, rooted in exclusionary and parochial hatreds. Barber goes on to assert that McWorld, with all its promises of a world homogenized by global consumerism, is rapidly dissolving local cultural identities. On the other hand, by recreating parochial loyalties, Jihad is fragmenting the world into tighter and smaller enclosures. Both, in other words, are a threat to civil liberties, tolerance and genuine coexistence. 'Jihad pursues a bloody politics of identity, McWorld a bloodless economics of profit. Belonging by default to McWorld, everyone is a consumer; seeking a repository for identity, everyone belongs to some tribe. But no one is a citizen' (Barber, 1996: 8).

We see little of such sharp dichotomies and diametrical representations in postwar Lebanon. While many of the emergent spatial enclaves are cognizant and jealous of their indigenous identities, they are not averse to experimenting with more global and ephemeral encounters and cultural products. Likewise, global expectations are being reshaped and rearranged to accommodate local needs and preferences. Expressed in the language of globalization and postmodernity, the so-called 'world without borders' is not a prerequisite for global encounters. At least this is not what has been transpiring in Lebanon. Indeed, as Martin Albrow argues, one of the key effects globalization on locality is that people 'can reside in one place and have their meaningful social relations almost entirely outside it and across the globe'. This, Albrow goes on to say, 'means that people use the locality as site and resource for social activities in widely different ways according to the extension of their sociosphere' (1996: 53).

Here as well, the active engagement in the burgeoning voluntary sector can be effective in resisting the forces of excessive commodification, government dysfunction, drains on public resources and corruption. Concerted efforts must be made in this regard to shift or redirect the obsessive interest of the Lebanese in the hedonistic and ephemeral pleasures of consumerism to more productive and resourceful outlets. Consumption, as has been implied all along, is essentially a passive preoccupation when compared to the more productive and creative pursuits of doing things for oneself in association with others. This distinction is not a benign or self-evident as it may seem. Nor should it be belittled as a source of collective healing and rejuvenation. All productive activities are inherently cooperative. Hence any active engagement in a medley of activities – be it in sports, music, neighborhood improvement, social welfare, human rights, programs for continuing special education or participation in advocacy groups on behalf of the excluded and marginalized and above all cultural and artistic outlets – is destined to become a transformative transcending experience.

By transforming the private concerns of *autonomy* into sites of political *empowerment*, where issues of public concern are debated and addressed, such venues will also become the ultimate and most redemptive settings for the cultivation of civil virtues. It is in such hybrid and open spaces that this cultivation in civility will allow groups to appreciate their *differences* without being *indifferent* to others. Is this not, after all, what the virtues of tolerance and cosmopolitanism are all about?

Lebanon's recent experience in this regard offers some promising prospects. At the popular cultural level, this resistance to the threat of disappearance is seen in the revival of folk arts, popular music, flea markets, artisan shops and other such exhibits and galleries. Personal memoirs, autobiographies, nostalgic recollections of early childhood and life in gregarious and convivial quarters and neighborhoods of old Beirut are now popular narrative genres. So are glossy illustrated anthologies of Beirut's urban history, old postcards, maps and other such collectibles. They are all a thriving business. Even the media and advertising industry are exploiting such imagery and nostalgic longing to market their products.

At the more substantive and concrete level such manifestations are more encouraging; particularly for urbanists, architects and other cultural producers and those involved in the creative industries. Modest as they may seem at the moment, they can restrain some of the dismaying features of kitsch and the spectacle and redirect them into more redemptive and creative avenues. This is not an easy task. Above all, it involves the incorporation or reconciliation of two seemingly opposing options: to tame and restrain the excessive features of commodification while acting as sentinels to arouse the disengaged and disinterested by infusing their world with some rejuvenated concern for well-being and the public good.

The distinctive views of Emile Durkheim and Max Weber with regard to the role of moral values in coping with this basic anomaly in contemporary society come to mind. To Durkheim, as we have seen, the problem is one of anomie and excessive desires. Society, in a sense, fails to provide meaningful controls on people's aroused impulses. Hence, he emphasized the role of moral values (religion, myth, even non-rational rituals) as inhibiting and restraining functions. To Weber, however, the compelling problems of modern society are inherent in its over-rationalized, impersonal and alienating character. Everyday life, as a result, was bound to become lifeless and spiritless. This calls for the need to ignite and arouse passions and 're-enchant' life with some élan, ardor and zest. In Lebanon today we need to heed the sagacious messages of both Weber and Durkheim. Weber would have urged us to infuse some excitement into an otherwise dull and dreary world. Durkheim would have counseled us to be moderate, sober and reasonable. Otherwise we will be perennial victims of that anguishing condition of constant seeking without fulfillment.

Reconciling both is perplexing but not formidable. It requires that we cultivate and sustain the cultural predispositions of the Lebanese for playfulness, *joie de vivre*, ingenuity, love of adventure. More problematic though, they must be sheltered from the excesses of material acquisition and immoderate lifestyles. The former is a highly cherished cultural expectation. It is also more inviting since both the popular media and the ostentatious lifestyles of the newly rich and political elite are so seductive. It is far more difficult to propagate and celebrate the virtues of simplicity and authenticity. They are though no longer just hopeful prospects. Foreboding threats of global warming and climate change are having a profound impact – reinforced by early resocialization, schooling and green activism – to endorse such pragmatic strategies and programs.

Care must be taken to avoid both extremes. Neither the self-denying ascetic nor the opulence of the ornate and flamboyant are judicious and plausible in Lebanon today. We must seek a third way which makes the best of both. How, in explicit terms, can the ordinary Lebanese sustain his love for adventure and public display but also how he can be made more reasonable in his desires and expectations?

While clearing my old book shelves the other day, I came across Roy Heath's *The Reasonable Adventurer* (1967), a slim book with a ringing message reminiscent of the time. The poignant message is still pertinent today. Among other things, being a 'reasonable adventurer' implies that one's expectations are redirected to seemingly more ordinary things. One becomes more receptive to cultivating uncommon interests in the commonplace. At the personal and existential level such prospects are much more fulfilling. As Heath tells us, his protagonist will certainly face many problems, but by being a reasonable adventurer, his least likely problem is boredom, lethargy or disinterest. 'Somehow, in the ordinary more is seen, more is felt ... Can you imagine, for example, a Pascal, an Emerson, or a Churchill being bored?' (Heath, 1967: 34).

At the concrete and pragmatic level, providing outlets for the release of such seemingly common and moderate creative energies should not be belittled or trivialized. Nietzsche here also comes to mind. He was keen on reminding us that an aesthetic solution through artistic creation can well serve as a powerful expression for releasing individuals from the constraints of nihilism and resentment. 'It is in art that we appear to realize fully our abilities and potential to break through the limitations of our own circumstances' (Stauth and Turner, 1988: 517).

My parting thought is inspired by the sobering aphorism with which Thomas Dumm concludes his own impassionate book on *Loneliness* (2008): 'that we do not know our next step does not mean that we are lost. It only means that we have yet to find ourselves' (Dumm, 2008: 179). It is my hope that this book will inspire this kind of self-reflection on how ordinary Lebanese citizens can shelter themselves from being colonized by global markets or reduced to clients. More concretely the book is also an invitation to start cultivating alternative venues for enhancing prospects for civility and the 'good life'. Lebanon's experience in this regard, perplexing and treacherous as it has been, is not unique. In considering the preferred setting, the most supportive environment for what Michael Walzer calls the 'good life', he arrives (after reviewing predominant socialist and capitalist ideologies in the nineteenth and twentieth centuries) at a similar conclusion. To 'live well', he tells us, 'is to participate with other men and women in remembering, cultivating and passing on a national heritage', and such a 'good life' can only be realized in a civil society. 'The realm of fragmentation and struggle but also of concrete and authentic solidarities where we fulfill E. M. Foster's injunction of only connect, become social or communal men and women' (Walzer, 1991: 298).

Walzer goes on to assert:

> The picture here is of people freely associating and communicating with one another, forming and reforming groups of all sorts, not for the sake of any particular formation – family, tribe, nation, religion, commune, brotherhood or sisterhood, interest group or ideological movement – but for the sake of sociability itself. For we are by nature social, before we are political or economic beings, ... What is true is that the quality of our political and economic activity and of our national culture is intimately connected to the strength and vitality of our associations. Ideally, civil society is a setting of settings: all are included, none is preferred. (Walzer, 1991: 298)

This is not another elusive pipe dream. Just as commodification, image-making and the allure of the spectacle and kitsch have been socially constructed and culturally sanctioned, they can also be unlearned. Under the spur of visionary and enlightened leadership ordinary Lebanese can be resocialized to consider alternative sources for validating their social identities without undermining the sense of collective well-being and the public good. As we have seen, over the past few years, and largely the outcome of a growing core of young activists, advocacy groups and NGOs – environmentalists, anti-consumerists, human rights and urban design – are all beginning to articulate visions of programs in support of a quality of life more conducive for cultivating the ethics of voluntary simplicity, living with less, expressive and authentic lifestyles, decency and the joys of small delights.

Bibliography

Adnan, E. 1998. 'Letter from Beirut: Lebanon Loses What War Did Not Destroy', *Al-Jadid*, 4/24.

Adorno, Theodor. 1973. *Philosophy of Modern Music* (New York: Seabury Press).

Albrow, M. 1996. 'Travelling beyond Local Cultures', in J. Eade (ed), *Living the Global City* (London and New York: Routledge), 37–55.

Almond, G. and J. S. Coleman (eds). 1960. *Politics and Developing Areas* (Princeton: Princeton University Press).

Almond, G. and G. B. Powell (eds). 1966. *Comparative Politics: A Development Approach* (Boston: Little Brown).

Appadurai, A. 1986. *The Social Life of Things: Commodities in Cultural Perspective* (New York: Cambridge University Press).

— 1996. *Modernity at Large: Cultural Dimensions of Modernity* (Minneapolis: University of Minnesota Press).

Apter, David. 1965. *The Politics of Modernization* (Chicago: University of Chicago Press).

Arabi, Afif. 1996. 'The History of Lebanese Cinema 1929–1979: An Analytical Study of The Evolution and Development of Lebanese Cinema' (Ph.D. dissertation, Ohio State University).

Arbid, George. 2004. 'Habile détournement, restaurant and bar La Central à Beyrouth', *Faces* ([architectural periodical], Geneva, Autumn), 38–41.

Arendt, Hannah. 1958. *The Human Condition* (New York: Doubleday Archon Books).

Arkali, Engin. 1993. *The Long Peace, 1861–1920* (Berkeley, CA: University of California Press).

AUB Bulletin Today, 10/7 (May 2009), 13.

Baer, G. 1982. *Fellah and Townsmen in the Middle East* (London: Frank Cass).

De Balzac, H. 1833. *The Girl with the Golden Eyes*, tr. Ellen Marriage, in Lewis Coser (ed), *Sociology through Literature* (Englewood, NJ: Prentice Hall), 240–9.

Barakat, Saleh. 2009. 'A Word about *Maqam*', *Landscapes Cityscapes 1* (Saifi Village: *Maqam*), 1–3.

Barber, Benjamin. 1996. *Jihad vs. McWorld* (New York: Ballantine Books).

— 2007. *Consumed: How Markets Corrupt Children, Infantilize Adults and Swallow Citizens Whole* (London: W. W. Norton & Co.).

Bauman, Zygmunt. 1990. *Thinking Sociologically* (Oxford: Blackwell).

— 2000. *Liquid Modernity* (Malden, MA: Blackwell).

— 2004. *Wasted Lives* (Cambridge: Polity Press).

— 2005. *Liquid Life* (Cambridge: Polity Press).

— 2006. *Liquid Fear* (Malden, MA: Polity).

— 2007a, *Consuming Life* (Cambridge: Polity).

— 2007b. *Liquid Times: Living in an Age of Uncertainty* (Cambridge: Polity).

Becherer, Richard. 2005. 'A Matter of Life and Debt: The Untold Costs of Rafiq Hariri's New Beirut', *Journal of Architecture*, Vol. 10. No.1: 1-42

Benjamin, Walter. 1973. 'The Work of Art in the Age of Mechanical Reproduction', in *Illuminations* (London: Fontana).

— 1999. *The Arcades Project* (Cambridge, MA: Belknap).

Bennett, Clinton. 1996. *In Search of the Sacred: Anthropology and Study of Religions* (London: Cassell).

Bhabha, H. 1994. *The Location of Culture* (London and New York: Routledge).

Bienen, H. 1984. 'Urbanization and Third World Stability', *World Development*, 12/7: 661–91.

Black, Perry. 1966. *The Dynamics of Modernization: A Study in Comparative History* (New York: Harper & Row).

Bouheiry, Marwan. 1987. *Beirut's Role in the Political Economy of the French Mandate: 1919–39* (Center for Lebanese Studies, Oxford).

Boulos, Paul. 2009. 'Lebanon as a Creative Brand', *Zawiya*, 17 Aug.

Bourdieu, Pierre. 1984. *Distinction: A Social Critique of the Judgment of Taste* (London: Routledge & Kegan Paul).

Bouyer-Bell, J. 1987. *The Gun in Politics: An Analysis of Irish Political Conflict, 1916–1986* (New Brunswick, NJ: Transaction).

Bustani, Emile. 1961. *March Arabesque* (London: Robert Hale Ld.).

Calinescu, M. 1987. *Five Faces of Modernity* (Durham, NC: Duke University Press).

Calvino, Italo. 1997. *Invisible Cities* (New York: William Weaver (Vintage)).

Campbell, Colin. 1987. *The Romantic Ethics and the Spirit of Modern Consumerism* (London: Blackwell).

— 1995. 'The Sociology of Consumption', in D. Miller (ed), *Acknowledging Consumption* (London: Routledge), 96–126.

Campbell, Joseph. 1949. *The Hero with a Thousand Faces* (New York: Pantheon).

Canclini, Néstor García. 2001. *Consumers and Citizens: Globalization and Multicultural Conflicts* (Minneapolis: University of Minnesota Press).

Carroll, Bernice A. 1980. 'Victory and Defeat: The Mystique of Dominance', in S. Albert and E. Luck (eds), *On the Endings of War* (Port Washington, NY: Kennikat Press).

Chevallier, Dominique. 1971. *La Société du Mont Liban à l'époque de la Révolution Industrielle en Europe* (Paris: Librarie Orientaliste Paul Geuther).

Clinard, Marshall. 1964. *Anomie and Deviant Behavior* (London: Free Press).

Cohen, Lizabeth. 2004. *A Consumers' Republic: The Politics of Mass Consumption in Postwar America* (New York: Vintage).

Collins, R. 1974. 'The Three Faces of Cruelty: Towards a Comparative Study of Violence', *Theory and Society*, 1: 415–40.

Connerton, P. 1989. *How Societies Remember* (Cambridge: Cambridge University Press).

Corrigan, Peter. 1997. *The Sociology of Consumption* (London: Sage Publications).

Coser, Lewis. 1963. 'The Anatomy of Paris: Honoré de Balzac', in *Sociology through Literature* (Englewood Cliffs, NJ: Prentice Hall), 240–9.

Creative Industries in Lebanon. 2008. (American University of Beirut: Suleiman Olayan School of Business)

Daghestani, Kazem. 1931. *La famille musulmane contemporaine en Syrie* (Paris: Librairie Ernest Le Roux)

Daily Star. 2009. 'Beirut: Sex Capital for Arab Tourists' (28 Aug.): 3.

Daou, Revd Butors. 1980. *Tarikh al-Mawarinah* (History of the Maronites) (Saidon: Saidon Press).

Davis, Fred. 1992. *Fashion, Culture and Identity* (Chicago: University of Chicago Press).

Debbas, Fouad. 1986. *Beirut, our Memory* (Beirut: Naufal Group).

Debord, G. 1995. *The Society of the Spectacle* (Brooklyn, NY: Zone Books).

De Certeau, Michel. 1984. *The Practice of Everyday Life* (Berkeley, CA: University of California Press).

Deeb, Lara, and Mona Harb. 2009. 'Politics, Culture, Religion: How Hizbullah is Constructing an Islamic Milieu in Lebanon', *Review of Middle East Studies*, 43/2 (Winter): 198–206.

Deutsch, Karl. 1961. 'Social Mobilization and Political Development', *American Political Science Review*, 55 (Sept.): 493–514.

DiMuccio, R. B. A., and J. Rosenau. 1992. 'Turbulence and Sovereignty in World Politics: Explaining the Relocation of Legitimacy in the 1990s and beyond', in Z. Milnar (ed), *Globalization and Territorial Identities* (Aldershot, England: Avebury).

Dittmar, Helga. 1992. *The Social Psychology of Material Possessions* (Hemel Hempstead: Harvester Wheatsheaf).

Doherty, Sandra Beth. 2008. 'Cosmetic Surgery and the Beauty Regime in Lebanon', *MERIP*, 249 (Winter): 28–31.

Douglas, Mary, and Baron Isherwood. 1979. *The World of Goods* (New York: Basic Books).

Dueck, Jennifer. 2010. *The Claims of Culture at Empire's End* (Oxford: Oxford University Press).

Dumm, Thomas. 2008. *Loneliness as a Way of Life* (Cambridge, MA: Harvard University Press).

Durkheim, Emile. 1933. *The Division of Labor in Society* (N.Y.: Free Press).

Eco, Umberto. 1989. 'The Structure of Bad Taste', in the *Open Works* (London: Hutchinson Radius).

Eckstein, Harry. 1965. 'On the Etiology of Internal Wars', *History and Theory*, 4/2: 133–63.

Eisenstadt, S. N. 1966. *Modernization: Protest and Change* (Englewood Cliffs, NJ: Prentice Hall).

Elgin, Duane, 1981. *Voluntary Simplicity* (New York: Harper Collins Publishers, Inc.).

Elias, Norbert. 1988. 'Violence and Civilization: The State Monopoly of Physical Violence and its Infringement', in John Keane (ed), *Civil Society and the State* (London and New York: Verso).

Erikson, K. 1976. *Everything in its Path: Destruction of the Community in the Buffalo Creek Flood* (New York: Simon & Schuster).

Esman, M.J. & I Rabinovich. 1988. *Ethnicity, Pluralism and the State in the Middle East* (Ithaca: Cornell University Press).

Ewen, S. 1988. *All Consuming Images* (New York: Basic Books).

Fawaz, Leila Tarazi. 1983. *Merchants and Migrants in Nineteenth-Century Beirut* (Cambridge, MA: Harvard University Press).

Featherstone, Mike. 1990. 'Perspectives on Consumer Culture', *Sociology*, 24/1: 5–22.

— 1991. *Consumer Culture and Postmodernism* (London: Sage).

Feierabend, I. K., and Feierabend, R. L. 1966. 'Aggressive Behaviors within Polities, 1948–1962: A Cross-National Study', *Journal of Conflict Resolution*, 10/3 (Sept.): 249–71.

Festinger, L. 1957. *A Theory of Cognitive Dissonance* (Evanston, IL: Row, Peterson).

Finkelstein, Joanne. 2007. *Art and Self Invention* (London: I. B. Tauris).

Fiske, John. 2000. 'Shopping for Pleasure: Malls, Power, and Resistance', In Juliet B. Schor and Douglas B. Holt (eds), *The Consumer Society Reader* (New York: New York Press), 306–59.

Forty, Adrian. 2001. Introduction', in A. Forty and S. Küchler (eds), *The Art of Forgetting* (Oxford: Berg).

Freud, S. 1969. *Civilization and its Discontents* (London: Hogarth Press).

Fromm, Erich. 1941. *Escape from Freedom* (New York: Farrar & Reinhart).

Gahre, C. 2008. 'Staging the Lebanese Nation: Urban Public Space and Political Mobilization in the Aftermath of Hariri's Assassination' (Unpublished MA thesis, American University of Beirut).

Galey, P., and Baraki, Nayla. 2009. 'Soaps Take Center Stage during Holy Month', *Daily Star*, 11 Sept.: 3.

Gates, Carolyn. 1998. *The Merchant Republic of Lebanon: Rise of an Open Economy* (London: I. B. Tauris).

Gay, Peter. 1993. *The Cultivation of Hatred* (New York: W. W. Norton).

— 2008. *Modernism: The Lure of Heresy* (N.Y.: Norton & Co.).

Geertz, Clifford. 1968. *Agricultural Involution: The Process of Ecological Change in Indonesia* (Berkeley, CA: University of California Press).

Gellner, Ernest. 1987. *Culture, Identity and Politics* (Cambridge: Cambridge University Press).

Gerges, Fawaz. 1997. 'Lebanon', in Yezid Sayigh and Avi Shlaim (eds), *The Cold War and the Middle East* (Oxford: Clarendon Press), 77–101.

Geyer, Georgie Anne. 1985. 'Our Disintegrating World: The Menace of Global Anarchy', in *Encyclopedia Britannica, Book of the Year, 1985.* (Chicago: University of Chicago Press), 11–25.

Giddens, Anthony. 1991. *Modernity and Self-Identity* (Cambridge: Polity).

Gillian, James. 1996. *Violence* (N.Y.: Vintage Books).

Gilsenan, Michael. 1982. *Recognizing Islam: Religion and Society in the Modern Arab World* (New York: Pantheon Books).

Girard, R. 1977. *Violence and the Sacred* (Baltimore: Johns Hopkins University Press).

Girouard, M. 1985. *Cities and Societies* (New Haven: Yale University Press).

Giroux, H. 1994. *Disturbing Pleasures: Learning Popular Culture* (New York: Routledge).

Goffman, E., 1961. *Encounters: Two Essays on the Sociology of Interaction* (Indianopolis: Bobbs-Merrill).

— 1963. *Stigma: Notes on the Management of Spoiled Identity* (Eaglewood Cliffs, NJ: Prentice-Hall).

Gronow, Jukka. 1997. *The Sociology of Taste* (London: Routledge).

Gunther, John. 1969. *Twelve Cities* (New York: Harper & Row).

Gurr, T. R. 1980. *Handbook of Political Conflict* (New York: Free Press).

Habermas, Jürgen. 1992. 'L'espace publique, 30 ans après', *Quaderni*, 18 (Paris, autumn).

Hage, Ghassan. 2003. *Against Paranoid Nationalism: Searching for Hope in a Shrinking Society* (London: Pluto Press).

— 2009. 'Introduction', in Ghassan Hage (ed), *Waiting Out* (Melbourne: Melbourne University Press), 1–12.

Haikein, E. 1997. *Venus Envy: A History of Cosmetic Surgery* (Baltimore: Johns Hopkins University Press).

Halbwachs, M. 1991. *On Collective Memory*, ed. and tr. Lewis Coser (Chicago: University of Chicago Press).

Hall, S. 2007. 'Doctors Warning of Liposuction Op Rise by 90%', *Guardian Unlimited* (http://www.guardian.co.uk/uk/2007/jan/29/health.healthandwellbeing, 29 Jan.).

Hanf, Theodor. 1993. *Coexistence in Wartime Lebanon: Decline of a State and Rise of a Nation* (London: I. B. Tauris).
— 1995. 'Ethnergy: On the Analytical Use and Normative Abuse of the Concept of 'Ethnic Identity' in Keebet Von Berda-Bechman and Utrecht Verknyten (eds), *Nationalism, Ethnicity and Cultural Identity* (Utrecht: Utrecht University).
Hannerz, U. 1996. *Transnational Connections* (London and New York: Routledge).
Hanssen, Jens. 2005. *Fin de Siècle Beirut* (Oxford: Oxford Historical Monographs).
— and Genberg, D. 2002. 'Beirut in Memoriam: A Kaleidoscopic Space out of Focus', in A. Pflitsch and A. Neuwirth (eds), *Crisis and Memory: Dimensions of their Relationship in Islam and Adjacent Cultures* (Berlin and Beirut: Orient Institute), 231–62.
Harb, Antoine Khoury. 2008. *The Roots of Christianity in Lebanon* (Beirut: Lebanese Heritage Foundation).
Harik, Iliya. 1968. *Politics and Change in a Traditional Society: Lebanon 1711–1845* (Princeton: Princeton University Press).
Harris, William. 1997. *Faces of Lebanon: Sects, Wars and Global Extensions* (Princeton, NJ: Markus Wiener Publishers).
Hebdige, D. 1988. 'Object as Image: The Italian Scooter Cycle', in Juliet B. Schor and Douglas B. Holt (eds), *The Consumer Society Reader* (New York: New York Press), 117–54.
Hirschman, Albert. 1970. *Exit, Voice and Loyalty* (Cambridge, MA: Harvard University Press).
Hitti, Philip. 1957. *Lebanon in History* (London: Macmillan & Co.).
Hobsbawn, Eric. 1999. *On the Edge of the New Century* (New York: New Press).
Horowitz, Donald. 1985. *Ethnic Groups in Conflict* (Berkeley, CA: University of California Press).
— 1993. *The Morality of Spending: Attitudes towards the Consumer Society in America* (Chicago: I. R. Dee).
Hottinger, Arnold. 1961. 'Zu'ama and Parties in the Lebanese Crisis of 1958', *Middle East Journal*, 15/2 (spring): 127–40.
Hourani, Albert. 1962. *Arabic Thought in a Liberal Age, 1798–1939* (London: Oxford University Press).
Hudson, Micheal. 1968. *The Precarious Republic* (New York: Random House).
Huizinga, Johan. 1949. *Homo Ludens* (London: Routledge, Kegan Paul).
Huntington, Samuel. 1993. 'The Clash of Civilizations?', *Foreign Affairs*, 72 (summer): 22–49.

Ignatieff, Michael. 1994. *Blood and Belonging: Journeys into the New Nationalism* (New York: Farrar, Strauss and Giroux).
Ikle, Fred Charles. 1971. *Every War Must End* (New York: Columbia University Press).
Illich, Ivan. 1980. *Tools for Conviviality* (New York: Harper & Row).
Issawi, Charles. 1964. 'Economic Development and Political Liberalism in Lebanon', in Leonard Binder (ed), *Politics in Lebanon* (New York: John Wiley & Sons).
— 1966. 'Economic Development and Political Liberalism in Lebanon', in L. Binder (ed), *Politics in Lebanon* (New York: Wiley).
— 1977. 'British Trade and the Rise of Beirut, 1830–1860', *International Journal of Middle Eastern Studies*, 8: 92–3.

Jarman, Neil. 2001. 'Commemorating 1916, Celebrating Difference: Parading and Painting in Befast', in A. Forty and S. Küchler (eds), *The Art of Forgetting* (Oxford: Berg), 171–210.
Jedlowski, P. 1990. 'Simmel on Memory', in M. Kaern, B. S. Phillips and R. S. Cohen (eds). *George Simmel and Contemporary Sociology* (Dordrecht: Kluwer).
Johnson, Steven. 2006. *Everything Bad is Good for you* (New York: Riverhead Books).

Jumblat, Kamal. 1959. *Haqiqat al-Thawrah al-Lubnaniyah* (The Truth about the Lebanese Revolution) (Beirut: Dar al-Nashr al-'Arabiyah).

Kakar, Sudhir. 1996. *The Colors of Violence* (Chicago and London: University of Chicago Press).

Kaplan, Jay. 1980. 'Victors and Vanquished: The Postwar Relations', in S. Albert and E. Luch (eds), *On the Endings of Wars* (New York: Kennikat Press), 72–117.

Karam, Zeina. 2009. 'Lebanon is Middle East's Daring Fashion Capital', *Daily Star* (29 July).

Keane, John. 1996. *Reflections on Violence* (New York: Verso).

— 2001. *Civil Society: Old Images, New Visions* (Oxford and Stanford, CA: Stanford University Press).

Keen, Sam. 1986. *Faces of the Enemy: Reflections of the Hostile Imagination* (New York: Harper & Row).

Kelly, Kevin. 1994. *Out of Control: The Rise of Neo-Biological Civilization* (Reading Mass: Addison-Wesley).

Kelman, H. 1987. 'On the Sources of Attachment to the Nation', paper presented at the meeting of the International Society of Political Psychology (San Francisco, 6 July).

Khalaf, Samir. 1965. *Prostitution in a Changing Society* (Beirut: Khayat Publishers).

— 1979. *Persistence and Change in Nineteenth Century Lebanon* (Beirut: American University of Beirut and Syracuse University Press).

— 1991. 'Ties that Bind', *Beirut Review*, 1/1 (spring): 32–61.

— 1992. 'Urban Design and the Recovery of Beirut', in S. Khalaf and P. Khoury (eds) *Recovering Beirut* (Leiden: E. J. Brill).

— 1998. 'Contested Space and the Forging of New Cultural Identities', in P. Rowe and H. Sarkis (eds), *Projecting Beirut: Urban Design and Post-War Reconstruction* (Munich: Prestel Verlag), 140–64.

— 2001. *Cultural Resistance: Global and Local Encounters in the Middle East* (London: Saqi Books).

— 2002. *Civil and Uncivil Violence: The Internationalization of Communal Conflict* (New York: Columbia University Press).

— 2006. 'Reclaiming the Bourj: As a Cultural and Cosmopolitan Sphere', in H. Sarkis and M. Dwyer (eds), *Two Squares* (Cambridge, MA: Harvard Graduate School of Design), 24–49.

— 2010. 'The Inside/Outside Dialectics and Protracted Civil Unrest in Lebanon', in Amy Freedman (ed), *Sites of Opportunity: The Nexus between Internal and External Security Threats* (Toronto: University of Toronto Press).

Khalaf, S., and Denoeux, G. 1988. 'Urban Networks and Political Conflict in Lebanon', in N. Shehadi and D. Haffar Mills (eds), *Lebanon: A History of Conflict and Consensus* (London: I. B. Tauris), 181–209.

Khourchid, Maya. 2009. 'The Tourist Boom', *Now* (www.nowLebanon.com, 31 Aug.), 1–3.

Khuri, Fuad I. 1975. *From Village to Suburbs: Order and Change in Greater Beirut* (Chicago: University of Chicago Press).

King, A. D. 2003. 'Writing Transnational Planning Histories', in J. Nasr, J. and M. Volait (eds), *Urbanism: Imported or Exported* (Chichester: John Wiley & Sons), 1–14.

Korbani, Agnes. 1991. *U.S. Intervention in Lebanon, 1958 and 1982* (New York: Praeger).

Küchler, Susanne. 2001. 'The Place of Memory', in A. Forty and S. Küchler (eds), *The Art of Forgetting* (Oxford and New York: Berg): 21–52.

Lababidi, Yahia. 2008. 'Dancing on the Graves: Beirut before the Last War'. *Levnatine Cultural Center.* Retrieved 19 July 2010, from http://www.levantinecenter.org.

Lasn, Kalle. 2000. 'Culture Jamming', in Juliet Schor and Douglas Holt (eds), *The Consumer Society Reader* (New York: New Press), 414–32.

Lee, Andrew. 2008. 'Beirut Reopens for Business', *Time Inc.* (23 May).

Lerner, D. 1958. *The Passing of Traditional Society* (Glencoe, IL: Free Press).

Lowenthal, David. 2001. 'Preface', in A. Forty and Susanne Küchler (eds), *The Art of Forgetting* (New York: Berg).

Lury, C. 1996. *Consumer Culture* (Cambridge: Polity Press).

Maasri, Zena. 2009. *Off the Wall: Political Posters of the Lebanese Civil War* (London: I. B. Tauris)

MacCannell, D. 1989. *The Tourist: A New Theory of the Leisure Class* (New York: Schocken).

McCormick, J. 2006. 'Transition Beirut: Gay Identities, Lived Realities', in S. Khalaf and J. Gagnon (eds), *Sexuality in the Arab World* (London: Saqi Books), 243–60.

McCracken, Grant. 1988. *Culture and Consumption: New Approaches to the Symbolic Character of Consumer Goods and Activities* (Bloomington, IN: Indiana University Press).

Macfarquhar, Neil. 2009. *The Media Relations Department of Hizbollah Wishes you a Happy Birthday* (New York: Public Affairs Books).

Mack, J. E. 1979. Foreword to: V. D. Volkan (ed), *Cyprus: War and Adaptation. A Psychoanalytic History of Two Ethnic Groups in Conflict* (Charlottesville, VA: University of Virginia).

— 1988. 'The Enemy System', *The Lancet* (13 August), vol. 332, issue 8607: 385–7.

Mahdawi, Dalila. 2008. 'Green Party Aims to Enforce Laws that Protect Environment', *Daily Star* (22 Aug.): 3

Makdisi, J. S. 1990. *Beirut Fragments* (New York: Persea Books).

Masri, Ghada. 2009. 'Tourism, Sex and Beirut', *Global Studies Journal* (26 June): 1–4.

Mathur, M. 1999. 'Neither Wilderness Nor Home: The Indian Maiden', in J. Corner (ed,). *Recovering Landscape* (Princeton, NJ: Princeton Architectural Press), 205–19.

Melikian, L., and L. Diab. 1974. 'Stability and Change in Group Affiliation of University Students in the Arab Middle East', *Journal of Social Psychology*, 93: 13–21.

Melucci, Alberto. 1996. *The Playing Self: Person and Meaning in Planetary Society* (Cambridge: Cambridge University Press).

Merton, Robert. 1968. *Social Theory and Social Structure* (New York: The Free Press).

Meštrovic, Stjepan. 1991. *The Coming Fin de Siecle* (London: Routledge).

Milnar, Z. 1996. *Globalization and Territorial Identities* (Aldershot, England: Avebury)

Moore, Barrington. 1966. *Social Origins of Dictatorship and Democracy* (Boston, MA: Beacon Press).

Moussawi, Ghassan. 2009. 'Compulsory Heterosexuality and the Construction of Non-Heterosexual Masculinities in Beirut' M.A. Dissertation (Sociology Department, American University of Beirut).

Moynihan, Daniel Patrick. 1993. *Pandaemonium: Ethnicity in International Politics* (New York: Oxford University Press).

Munro, Rolland. 2005. 'Outside Paradise: Melancholy and the Follies of Modernization', *Culture and Organization*, 4: 275–89.

Nambiar, N., and N. V. Nesson. 2009. 'Deyaar to Hand over Saifi Village II in July', in (ASDA'A Burson-Marsteller) Press Release.

Nan, E. 1997. *Architecture of Fear* (Princeton, NJ: Princeton Architectural Press).

Nasr, J., and M. Volait (eds) 2003. *Urbanism Imported or Exported* (Chichester: Wiley & Sons).

Nasr, S. 1993. 'New Social Realities and Postwar Lebanon', in S. Khalaf and P. Khoury (eds), *Recovering Beirut: Urban Design and Post-War Reconstruction* (Leiden: E. J. Brill), 63–80.

Nasr, Vali. 2006. *The Shia Revival: How Conflicts within Islam Will Shape the Future* (N.Y. W.W. Norton & Company).

Navarno, M. 2004. 'The Most Private Makeovers', *New York Times* (http://www.nytimes.com/2004/11/28/fashion/28PLAS.html, 1 Dec.).

Neale, I. A. 1852. *Eight Years in Syria, Palestine and Asia Minor,* vol. 1, 2nd edn (London: Colburn & Co.).

Norton, Augustus Richard. 2007. *Hezbollah* (Princeton, N.J.: Princeton University Press).

Nussbaum, M. C. 1997. 'Kant and Cosmopolitanism', in J. Bohman and M. Lutz-Bachman (eds), *Perpetual Peace* (Cambridge, MA: MIT Press), 25–57.

al-Nusuli, Muhi al-Din. 1936. *al-Zawaj min al-ajnabiyyat* (Marriage to foreign women). (Beirut: Dar al-Nashr)

Owen, Roger. 1981. *The Middle East in the World Economy, 1800–1914* (London: Methuen).

— 1988. 'The Economic History of Lebanon, 1943–1974: The Salient Features', in Halim Barakat (ed), *Toward a Viable Lebanon* (London: Croom Helm), 27–41.

Oxford Business Group. 2006. 'Shop till you Drop: Demanding Consumers have Made Beirut a Retail Paradise', *The Report: Emerging Lebanon 2006* (Beirut: Arab Printing Press): 133–8.

Peattie, Lisa. 1998. 'Convivial Cities', in Mike Douglass and John Friedmann (eds), *Cities for Citizens* (New York: John Wiley & Sons), 245–53.

Picard, Elizabeth. 1996. *Lebanon: A Shattered Country* (New York: Holmes and Meier).

Pinderhughes, C. A., 1979. 'Differential Bonding: Toward a Psychophysiological Theory of Stereotyping', *American Journal of Psychiatry,* 136/1 (Jan.): 33–7.

Prasada, Sierra. 2009. *Creative Lives in Lebanon.* (Beirut: Turning Point).

Prince, Roland. 2009. 'The Case of Social Media', *Arab Ad,* 19/7 (Aug.): 30–4.

Princen, Thomas, Maniates, Michael, and Conca, Ken. 2002. *Confronting Consumption* (Cambridge, MA: MIT Press).

— et al. 2000. *Cautious Consuming* (Cambridge, MA: MIT Press).

Prothro, E. T., and L. N. Diab. 1974. *Changing Family Patterns in the Arab World* (Beirut: American University of Beirut).

Pye, Lucian W. 1966. *Aspects of Political Development: An Analytical Study* (Boston, MA: Little, Brown).

Qubain, Fahim. 1961. *Crisis in Lebanon* (Washington, DC: Middle East Institute).

Raisborough, Jayne. 2007. 'Context of Choice: The Risky Business of Elective Cosmetic Surgery', in J. Scott Jones and J. Raisborough (eds), *Risk, Identities and the Everyday* (London: Ashgate), 19–35.

Randal, Jonathan. 1984. *Going All the Way* (New York: Vintage).

Richards, T. 1990. *The Community Culture of Victorian England: Advertising and Spectacle 1851–1914* (Stanford, CA: Stanford University Press).

Ritzer, George. 2001. *Explorations in the Sociology of Consumption* (London: Sage Publication).

Robertson, Roland. 1992. *Globalization: Social Theory and Global Culture* (London: Sage Publication).

Rorty, Richard. 1989. *Contingency, Irony and Solidarity* (Cambridge: Cambridge University Press).

Rugh, William. 1979. *The Arab Press: News Media and Political Process in the Arab World* (New York: Syracuse University Press).

Rule, James. 1988. *Theories of Civil Violence* (Berkeley, CA: University of California Press).

Rupesinghe, Kumar. 1992. 'The Disappearing Boundaries Between Internal and External Conflicts.' In K. Rupesinghe (ed). *Internal Conflict and Governance*. (New York: St. Martin's Press).

Rutgers University 1990. 'Conference on How Civil Wars End', *Proceedings* (2–4 March).

Safe, Joe. 2000. *The State of Human Rights in Lebanon, 1999* (Beirut: Foundation for Human and Humanitarian Rights).

Said, Edward. 2000. 'Identity, Authority and Freedom: The Potentate and the Traveler', in *Reflections on Exile* (Cambridge, MA: Harvard University Press), 386–404.

Salecl, R. 2008. 'Subjectivity in Times of Abundance and Choice', in David Held and Henrietta Moore (eds). *Cultural Politics in a Global Age* (Oxford: One World Publications), 360–8.

Salibi, Kamal. 1965. *The Modern History of Lebanon* (London: Weidenfeld & Nicolson).

— 1988. *A House of Many Mansions* (London: I. B. Tauris).

Sarkis, Hashim. 1993. 'Territorial Claims: Post-War Attitudes Towards the Built Environment', in S. Khalaf and P. Khoury (eds), *Recovering Beirut: Prospects of Urban Reconstruction* (Leiden: E. J. Brill).

Scarry, Elaine. 1985. *The Body in Pain: The Making and Unmaking of the World* (New York: Oxford University Press).

Schor, J., and Holt, D. B. 2000. *The Consumer Reader* (New York: New Press).

Scruton, Roger. 1999. 'Kitsch and the Modern Predicament', *City Journal*, 9/1 (winter): 82-95.

Seidman, Steve. 2009. 'Streets in Beirut: Self and the Encounter with the Other': Arabic version appeared in *Idafat*, 5: 41–69.

al-Shidiaq, Tannus. 1954. *Akhbar al-A'yan fi Jabal Lubnan* (Beirut: Lebanese University).

Shields, Rob. 1992. *Lifestyle Shopping: The Subject of Consumption* (London: Routledge).

Shils, E. 1965. *Political Development in the New States* (The Hague: Mouton).

Short, J. 2001. *Global Dimensions: Space, Place and the Contemporary World* (London: Reaktion Books).

Simmel, George. 2004. 'The Metropolis and Mental Life', in M. Miles and Tim Hall (eds), *The City Culture Reader* (London: Routledge), 12–19.

Slater, Don. 1998. *Consumer Culture and Modernity* (Cambridge: Polity)

Smilianskaya, I. M. 1972. *Al-Harakat Al-Fullahiyyah Fi Lubnan.* (Peasant uprising in Lebanon). (Beirut: Dar al-Farabi Press).

Solidere, 2003. *Annual Report* (Beirut: Solidere), 28–9.

Stanhope, Lady Hester. 1846. Charles Lewis Meryon (ed). *Memoirs of the Lady Hester Stanhope*, 2nd vol.(London: Henry Colburn).

Stauth, G., and B. S. Turner. 1988. 'Nostalgia, Postmodernism and the Critique of Mass Culture', *Theory, Culture and Society*, vol. 5, no. 2: 509–26.

Stearns, Peter. 2001. *Consumerism in World History* (London: Routledge).

Stewart, Desmond. 1959. *Turmoil in Beirut* (London: Allan Wingate).

Storr, A. 1968. *Human Aggression* (New York: Bantam).

Styhre, A., and Engberg, T. 2003. 'Spaces of Consumption: From Margin to Centre', *Ephemera*, 3(2): 115–25.

Szmigin, Isabelle. 2003. *Understanding the Consumer* (London: Sage Publications).

Tabbarah, Riad. 1977. 'Rural Development and Urbanization in Lebanon', *Population Bulletin of the United Nations*, 4 (Beirut: ECWA): 3–25.

Tarazi, Vicomte Phillipe de. 1914. *Tarik as-Sahafa al-Arabiyah* (in Arabic, History of the Arab press), vol. 2 (Beirut, al-Matba'a al Adabiyah).

Tarcici, Adnan. 1941. *L'education actuelle de la jeune fille Musulmane au Liban* (Vitry-sur-Seine: Librairie Mariale).

Tawney, R. H. 1920. *The Acquisitive Society* (New York: Harcourt, Brace & Co.).

Thomas, Dana. 2007. *Delux: How Luxury Lost its Luster* (New York: Penguin Press).

Thompson, E. 2000. *Colonial Citizen* (New York: Columbia University Press).

Thompson, Kenneth (ed) 1985. *Readings from Emile Durkheim* (London: Routledge).

Thomson, W. M. 1886. *The Land of the Book: Lebanon, Damascus and beyond Jordan* (London: T. Nelson & Sons).

Tilly, Charles. 1978. *From Mobilization to Revolution* (New York: Random House).

Traboulsi, Fawwaz. 2007. *A History of Modern Lebanon* (London: Pluto Press).

Tueni, Ghassan. 1971. *Freedom of the Press in a Developing Society* (Beirut: Dar an-Nahar).

— 1985. *Une guerre pour les autres* (Paris: J. C. Lattes).

— 1995. *Sir al Mehnah wa Asrar Oukhra* (Professional secrets and others) (Beirut: Dar an-nahar).

— and F. Sassine (eds) 2000. *El-Bourj: Place de La Liberté et Port du Levant* (Beirut: Dar an-nahar).

Turner, B. 1987. 'A Note on Nostalgia', *Theory, Culture and Society,* 4/1: 147–156.

— 1990. *Theories of Modernity and Postmodernity* (London: Sage Publications).

UNESCO statistical yearbook 1965.

UNESCO statistical yearbook 1985.

Veblen, T. 1899. *The Theory of the Leisure Class* (New York: Macmillan).

Vloeberghs, Ward. 2008. 'The Genesis of a Mosque: Negotiating Sacred Space in Downtown Beirut'. EUI Working Papers RSCAS. Retrieved July 19,2010, from http://cadmus.eui.eu.

Volkan, V. D. 1979. *Cyprus: War and Adaptation: A Psychoanalytic History of Two Ethnic Groups in Conflict* (Charlottesville, VA: University Press of Virginia).

— 1985. 'The Need to have Enemies and Allies: A Developmental Approach', *Political Psychology,* 6/2: 219–47.

Walzer, Michael. 1991. 'The Idea of a Civil Society', *Dissent* (spring): 293–304.

Warde, Allen. 1991. 'Notes on the Relationship between Production and Consumption', in R. Burrows and C. March (eds), *Consumption of Class: Divisions and Change* (London: Macmillan), 15–31.

— 1994. 'Consumption, Identity-Formation and Uncertainty', *Sociology,* 28/4: 877–98.

— 1996. 'Afterwards: The Future of the Sociology of Consumption', in S. Edgell, K. Hetherington and A. Warde (eds), *Consumption Matters* (Cambridge, MA: Blackwell), 302–12.

— 2006. 'Consumer Society and Consumption', in Bryan S. Turner (ed), *The Cambridge Dictionary of Sociology* (Cambridge: Cambridge University Press), 88–90.

Weber, Marx. 1947. *The Theory of Social and Economic Organization,* tr. A. R. Henderson and Talcott Parsons (New York: Oxford University Press).

Williams, Robin. 1981. 'Legitimate and Illegitimate Uses of Violence', in Gaylin, W., Macklin, R., and Powledge, T. M. (eds), *Violence and the Politics of Research* (New York: Plenum), 23-45.

Williams, Raymond. 1985. 'Consumer', *Keywords: A Vocabulary of Culture and Society* (New York: Oxford University Press).

Wills, Garry. 1990. 'The Politics of Grievance', *New York Review of Books* (19 July).

Wilson-Goldie, Kaelen. 2009. 'Guerilla Marketing' *The National* (July 19) Retrieved from http://www.thenational.ae/arts-culture.

Winslow, Charles. 1996. *Lebanon: War and Politics in a Fragmented Society* (London and New York: Routledge).

Wolf, K. W. 1995. *Transformation in the Writing: A Case of Surrender and Catch* (Dordrecht: Kluwer Academic).

Wolin, S. S. 1989. *The Presence of the Past* (Baltimore: Johns Hopkins University Press).

Yacoub, Gebran. 2003. *Architectures au Liban* (Beirut: Dar Qabis).

Yahya, Maha. 1993. 'Reconstituting Space: The Aberration of the Urban in Beirut', in S. Khalaf and P. S. Khoury (eds), *Recovering Beirut* (Leiden: E. J. Brill).

Yates, Frances. 1966. *The Art of Memory* (Harmondsworth: Penguin).

Yazbek, Natacha. 2007. 'Culture of the Catch: A Glimpse into Sexual Scripts of the Eligible Beiruti Bachelor' (MA dissertation SBS Department, American University of Beirut).

Young, I. M. 1990. *Justice and the Politics of Difference* (Princeton, NJ: Princeton University Press).

Young, J. 1993. *The Texture of Memory* (New Haven and London: Yale University Press).

Zaatari, M. 2009. 'Sidon's Khan al-Franj Hosts Events during Ramadan', *Daily Star* (1 Dec.).

Zoepf, Katherine. 2006. 'Where the Boys are, at Least for Now, the Girls Pounce', *New York Times* (2 Nov.).

Zola, Emile. 2010. *Au bonheur des dames* (*Shop Girls of Paris*), tr. Mary Sherwood (Biblio Bazaar). Original work published 1833.

Zur, O. 1987. 'The Psychohistory of Warfare: The Co-Evolution of Culture-Psyche and Enemy', *Journal of Peace Research*, 24/2: 125–34.

Acknowledgments

This is a book I had not planned to write. It just happened. As I started to consider the prospect, it somehow acquired a life of its own unrelated to the circumstances that might have incited it. Credit goes to my good friend and colleague Ghassan Hage. He was instrumental in inviting me to give three lectures at the universities of Melbourne and Sydney in April 2009. It was he who suggested that I elaborated on the topics and issues I covered – the pathologies of protracted and displaced civil violence in Lebanon, collective memory and identity, and rampant consumerism in a traumatized society.

As I started working on the book, it gradually became clear to me that the experience of the pathos of being adrift is not too germane to understanding by only the conventional tools of dispassionate description, critique and analysis. Being adrift is an ambient state; nowhere in particular but everywhere at once. Hence, one must be adept at supplementing the formalistic and essentialist research methodologies by other unobtrusive and mundane tools of inquiry. These allow one to capture the discursive, hidden and unrecognized features of being adrift. Personal intuitions, subjective impressions and viewpoints need not be suspended or mystified. Indeed, since some of the dismaying symptoms of being adrift are violations of cherished personal and public values, the substance and tone of the book became inevitably personal. Given some of the grotesque symptoms I am decrying, the personal indignation and outrage are, in my view, pardonable and welcome.

Judging by the sources I consulted – scholarly treatments, narrative accounts and journalistic expositions – I found that I was just one among a legion of other critical voices. The extensive bibliography is a testimony of how liberally I borrowed from others. I am also privileged – and I am not employing the term loosely

– to enjoy a small circle of friends and colleagues who never shy away, despite the taxing demands of their own commitments, from reacting generously to earlier drafts or queries I solicit from them. Foremost, I need to acknowledge the preface of Ghassan Hage, which graces the book. It is vintage Ghassan: intuitive, engaging and relevant to central issues explored in the book. 'Eefneh, incidentally, is a collo- quial expression which, literally, connotes 'leave me alone' or 'let me be'. It captures many of the symptoms associated with being 'adrift'. I also wish to single out, at the risk of the sins of omission, the following: Myrna Bustani, Micheal el Khoury, Sari Hanafi, John Keane, Salim El Meouchi, Ibrahim Rizk, Randa Serhan, Riad Tabbarah, Walter Wallace and Micheal Young. I also benefited from the critical evaluations of two anonymous reviewers. I owe my students, in a score of classes and seminars, a special debt for being such a willing captive and engaging audience. It is refreshing to recognize, and applaud, the predisposition of young students today to challenge the conventional expectations of deference to professorial and presumed sacrosanct authority. Bereft of such reverence, one is kept on his toes. I also wish to acknowledge the generous funds advanced by Talal Shair, CEO of Dar Al-Handasah, which supported my research assistants. Talal, much like his departed father, sustains a benevolent penchant for academic philanthropy.

Mrs Leila Jbara, my genial and accommodating assistance, has had, as usual, to put up with all the tedious chores of preparing various versions of the manu- script. Youssef el-Khoury and Angie Nassar provided invaluable help in scouting for and validating sources.

My wife Roseanne continues to invest an inordinate portion of her time and writing skills, beyond the call of filial piety or personal affection, on uplifting the quality of my prose. With time, I hope I am inching closer to meeting her judi- cious urgings to write leaner, shorter and crisper sentences.

As I was putting the final touches on the manuscript, I was blessed by the birth of Gavin, my first grandchild. Earlier works of mine, particularly those published during Lebanon's interludes of civil strife, were dedicated to Gavin's father (George) and his uncle (Ramzi). Both were coming-of-age during that dark period of Lebanon's beleaguered history. The joys of parenting two lovable children were a soothing antidote to a cruel world. I am now discovering that welcoming a grandchild into that world is equally thrilling.

Though less belligerent, the country, alas, remains 'adrift' between the dismay- ing futilities of an ugly and unfinished war, and the uncertainties of an ambiva- lent future. By dedicating the book to Gavin, I harbor the hope that he will come to live in more auspicious times. Better still, he might partake in his country's cross-over into a more tolerant, civil and cosmopolitan society.

Index

Abdul Hamid, Sultan 94, 158
Abi-Nader, Robert 176
Abu Musa 64
Acra, Reem 176
Adam and Eve (film) 153
Adam, Henry 54
Adnan, Etel 168
Adorno, Theodor 126, 129, 228, 246
Adra, Muhammad (architect) 255
adrift
    consequences of 168, 170, 264–5
    definitions of 17
    symptoms of 17–18, 241
Ajram, Nancy 218, 220, 237
Alameh, Ragheb 218
Albrow, Martin 89–90, 270
Al-Amin mosque 102, 237
Al-Khoury, President Bishara 138
an-Nahar 49, 159, 171
anomie 140–1, 175, 211, 261
Aoun, General 57, 65
Appadurai, A 103, 268
Apter, David 32
Arabi, Afif 152
Arab–Israeli
    conflict 49
    peace talks 60
Arafat, Yasser 64
Arbid, George (architect) 254, 255, 256
architecture, non-Corporate 253–6
Arendt, Hannah 34
arghileh smoking 7–9

Arida, Antoine, Maronite Patriarch 153
Aristotle 106
Arkali, Engin 49
Asfour, Hani (architect) 254
Ashura 219–20
AUB (American University of Beirut) 75
AUB Bulletin Today 234
Awad 264
Ayash, Rami 218

Baer, G 51
Baghdad Pact (1955) 47
Balzac, Honoré de 120–1
Barakat, Saleh 203, 207–8
Barber, Benjamin 89, 104, 247, 269
Baroudi, Hoda 205
al-Bashir (Jesuit newspaper) 152
Bauman, Zygmunt 22–3, 28, 75, 88, 115,
    122, 132, 134, 135, 136, 166, 167, 169, 170,
    175–6, 245
Bawader Architects 254, 255
Bayrut (daily newspaper) 153
Becherer, Richard 237
Beck, Ulrich 134, 170
Begin, Prime Minister Menachem 63
Beirut
    billboards of the dead 74
    capital of Kitsch 225
    changes in the Bourj 93–4
    communal identities 83, 88, 264, 268
    competition for spatial identity 85–6
    destruction of common spaces 57, 82, 238

destruction of urban legacy 172–5, 239
economic growth 137–8, 148–9
epochal history 28, 91
fashion capital 176–8
financial centre 98, 137, 148
formation of exclusive enclaves 83, 239,
    269
low proportion of open space 241
marketing and media capital 28, 91,
    115–16, 137–8, 163
Martyrs' Square 95, 107
memory of unfinished war 77
nightlife 185–9, 191–3
production of social space 100
reconstruction 75–6, 99–100, 105
shopping malls 193–4, 245
vulnerable openness 112–13, 258–9
Benedict XVI, Pope 221
Benjamin, Walter 105, 126, 227
Bennett, Clinton 88, 269
Beshwat, Lady of 198
Beydoun, Sarah 179
Bhabha, H 103
Bienen, H 33
billboards
    advertising 161, 163, 182
    of the dead 74
    politicians 181
Black, Perry 32
Bliss, Daniel 234
Bofill, Ricardo (architect) 254
Bouheiry, Marwan 144, 147, 148, 149
Boulos, Paul 179
Bourdieu, Pierre 28, 122, 133, 136, 154, 178,
    245–6
    Distinction: A Social Critique of the
        Judgement of Taste 130–1
Bourj 27, 77, 82, 90–5, 98, 111–13, 149–50,
    154, 155, 156–7, 210–11
Bouyer-Bell, J 37, 69
Bustani, Emile 53

Cairo Accord (1969) 71
Calinescu, M 225, 226–7
Calvino, Italo, Invisible Cities 170
Campbell, Colin 124, 130
Campbell, Joseph, The Hero with a
    Thousand Faces 127
Cana of Galilee 195–6

Canclini, Néstor García 115, 166, 240, 248,
    249
Carroll, Bernice A 70
Cedars Revolution (2005) 44, 55, 57, 210,
    216
Chakra, George 176
Chamoun, Dany 64
Chamoun, Dory (shop-keeper) 53
Chamoun, President Camille 47, 51, 54, 138
Charbel, Saint 197–8
Christmas 222, 224
cinemas 28, 96–7, 149–52, 155
civil unrest, deflection to violence 24, 35, 38,
    45–6, 59
civil war 37, 69
    1958 50–4
    1975–6 71
    2006 57, 80
Clinard, Marshall 141
Cohen, Lizabeth, A Consumer's Republic
    248–9
Cold War, superpower rivalry 47
'collective action' (1958) 33, 39, 51–2
collective amnesia 78, 103–5, 109, 226
collective memory 27, 78, 103–4, 108
Collins, Randall 86
commodification 28–9, 30, 117–18, 211, 235,
    245–6, 266
communalism 67, 73
    brutality of 86
    solidarities of 87, 264
confessionalism 42, 68, 225
Connerton, Paul 104, 105
conspicuous consumption 122–3, 131–2,
    134, 156, 167, 211, 244
conspicuous leisure 123, 124, 125–6, 265
construction boom 171–5
consumerism 18, 27–8, 95–6, 102, 117,
    119–25, 130, 164–5, 239, 270
    changing 243
    luxurious constructs 235–6
Consumers Lebanon (CL) 249–50
Corm, Daoud 208
Corrigan, Peter 243
corruption 251–2
Coser, Lewis 121
cosmetic surgery 181–2
Creative Industries in Lebanon 177
cultural revival 270

al-Dabbur 154
Daghestani, Kazem 154
Daily Star 142, 172, 192, 232, 235–6
Damour (Maronite town) 62
Danton, Arthur 111
Daou, Revd Butors 197
Davis, Fred 123
Dāwūd Pasha 93
de Certau, Michel 105, 106, 130
Debbas, Fouad 145
Debord, Guy, *The Society of the Spectacle* 15, 23, 210, 211, 213, 232–3
Debs, Nada 204–5, 209
Deeb, Lara and Harb, Mona 193–4, 199
Deutsch, Karl 32
DiMuccio, R B A and Rosenau, J 89, 269
Dior, Christian 180
Dittmar, Helga 133
Doha Accord (2008) 210, 218
Doherty, Sandra Beth 182
Dorman, Peter, University President 233–4
Doueihy, Saliba 208
Douglas, Mary 268
Dueck, Jennifer 261–2
Dulles, Foster, US Secretary of State 47
Dumm, Thomas, *Loneliness as a Way of Life* 132, 267, 272
Durkheim, Emile 19, 28, 102, 140, 164–5, 175, 236, 271

Eco, Umberto 210, 227
Eisenhower Doctrine 47, 49
Eisenstadt, S N 32
elections, May 2009 58
Elgin, Duane, *Voluntary Simplicity* 247
Elias, Norbert 226
'Elisar' project 90
enmity 54–5, 56
environment
    disregard for 230–1, 241–2, 250–1
    violation of the habitat 16
Erikson, K 81
Espiredone, Marica 186
ethnic identity 66
Ewen, S 228

Fakhrī Bek 94
Farah, Johnny 206–7
Farroukh, Mustafa 208

Fatah 52, 64
Fawaz, Leila Tarazi 144, 147
Faysal Ibn al-Husayn, Prince 94
Featherstone, Mike 122, 124, 133, 154, 161, 227, 243, 244
Feierabend, I K and Feierabend, R L 33
Festinger, L 33
film censorship 152–3
Finkelstein, Joanne 124, 135–6, 172, 180
Fiske, John 122, 130
Food and Agriculture Organization (FAO) 249
foreign intervention 25, 46–7, 59
foreign labour 126
Forster, E M 273
Forty, Adrian 105, 106, 108
fragmentation 32
Franjieh, Tony 64
Frankfurt School 122, 126, 127, 129, 246
French
    relief and reconstruction programme 148–9
    suspend publications 159
Freud, Sigmund 105, 106
Fromm, Erich, *Escape from Freedom* 127

Gahre, C 216
Galey, P and Baraki, Nayla 224
Gates, Carolyn 136, 265
Gay, Peter, *The Cultivation of Hatred* 31, 71, 179
Gebrayel, Elie and Randa (architects) 254
Geertz, Clifford 32
Gellner, Ernest 40–1, 41, 103
Gemayel, Bashir 62, 64
Gemayel, Cesar 208
Gemayel, Pierre (Kata'ib Party) 61, 74, 262
Genberg, Daniel 109
geography of fear 88, 101–2, 238
Gerges, Fawaz 48
Ghandour, Marwan (architect) 255
Gholam, Nabil (architect) 203, 204, 254–5
Giddens, Anthony 28, 117–18, 134
Giebel, Marcus 204
Gillian, James 21
Gilsenan, Michael 220
Girard, René, *Violence and the Sacred* 25–6, 31, 59, 65–6, 139
Girouard, M 148

292LEBANON ADRIFT

Giroux, Henry 161
Glass, Charles 61
Global Property Guide 172
globalization 100–1, 244, 269–70
'glocalization' 29, 89–90, 244, 269
Goffman, Erving 28, 124, 157, 167, 229, 232
Golan Heights 63
Goodell, William 230
Graham, Sylvester 120
Gramsci, Antonio 130, 163, 166
'Green Lines' 84, 107
Green Party of Lebanon (GPL) 250–1
Gronow, Jukka 178, 229, 234
Gunther, John 230–1
Gurr, T R 33

Habachi, René 263–4
Habermas, Jürgen 245, 268
Haddad, Father Yaaqoub 222
Haddad, Major 62
Hadiqat al-Akhbar (newspaper) 147, 157–8
Hage, Ghassan 76, 136, 143
Haiken, E 181
Halbwachs, M 104
Hall, Stuart 163, 181–2
Hallak, Mona (architect) 254
Hanf, Theodor 26, 40, 48, 54, 66, 69
Hannerz, Ulf 103
Hanssen, Jens 109, 147
Hanukkah 222, 224
Harb, Antoine, *Roots of Christianity in Lebanon* 195–6
Hariri, Prime Minister Rafik 44, 55, 74, 80, 98, 214, 237
Hariri, Prime Minister Saad 58
Harris, William 22
Heath, Roy, *The Reasonable Adventurer* 271
Hebdige, Dick 179
Heidegger, Martin 105
Hibri, Mria 205
Hirschman, Albert 33
Hitti, Philip 49
Hizbullah 22, 55, 56, 57, 58, 60
    attacks on Israel 60–1
    controlled areas 231
    Counter Revolution (2006) 216–17, 221
    in-fighting 64
    Islamic entertainment 193–4
    Khiam Detention Center 198–9

pro-Syrian demonstration 214, 215
Hobbes, Thomas 104, 107
Hobeika, Elie 64–5
Hobeika, George 176
Hobsbawn, Eric 183
Hoggart, Richard 166
Hojeily, Naji 176
homelessness 81–2
homosexuality 190–1
Horkheimer, Max 126, 129, 246
Horowitz, Donald 66, 120
Hottinger, Arnold 53
Hourani, Albert 144, 147
Hudson, Micheal 138
Huizinga, Johan 257
Huntington, Samuel 32
Hussein Ibn Ali, Imam 217, 220
Hussein, Saddam 65

Ibrahim Pasha 185
'ideal types' 22–3
Ikle, Fred 70
Illich, Ivan 92, 257
image boosting 235
import of consumer goods 95–6
Independence uprising (2005) 98–9, 214–16
infantile regression 9
'inside–outside' polemics 32, 45, 58
International Urban Design competition 110
Intifadah (2005) 201, 202
Iran, supports Hizbullah 60
Isherwood, Baron 268
Islamic fundamentalism 19
Israeli
    dispr
    invasio
Israeli Defe
Issawi, Char

Ja'ja, Samir 64
Jamal Pasha 94
Jarman, Neil 108
Jedlowski, P 103
Jesus 196
Jihad 89, 269
Johnson, Steven, *Everything Bad is Good for You* 248

journalism 97
Jubayli, Rana Samara (architect) 254
Jumblat, Kamal 54, 62

Kakar, Sudhir 67
Kant, Immanuel 178, 227
Kaplan, Jay, 'Victors and Vanquished' 31, 70
Karam, Zeina 177
Kata'ib militia 61–2, 71
Katra, Pierre 176
Kayrouz, Rabih 205–6
Keane, John 73, 113
Keen, Sam 68
Kelman, H 68
Khalaf, S and Denoeux, G 33, 42
Khalaf, Samir
    Civil and Uncivil Violence 21, 26, 55, 59, 147
    'Contested Space and the Formation of
        New Cultural Identities' 90
    Cultural Resistance 79
    *Persistence and Change in Nineteenth
        Century Lebanon* 144
    Prostitution in a Changing Society 186,
        187, 201
    'Reclaiming the Bourj' 216
    'Ties that Bind' 42, 67
    'Urban Design and the Recovery of
        Beirut' 96
Khourchid, Maya 221
Khoury, Bernard (architect) 237, 254, 255
Khuri, Fuad I 220
King, A D 100, 101
Kisrwan 46
Kissinger, Henry 25, 48
kitsch 29, 212, 220, 225–30, 234, 237
Klein, Naomi 129
Koolhass, Rem 219
Korbani, Agnes 49
Küchler, Susanne 110

Lababidi, Yahia 237–8
labelling 19–20
Larousse dictionary 21
Lasn, Kalle 248
Lebanese Army, neutrality 53
Lebanese Transparency Association (LTA)
    251–2
Lebanese Youth Coalition Against
    Corruption (LYCAC) 252

'Lebanization' 20–2
Lebanon
    contrasting entities 230–1, 236, 257
    corruption of values 141, 262–3
    damage sustained 80
    decline of social order 139–40
    designated Ottoman province 47
    open but vulnerable 258–9
    playfulness 259–60
    political culture 260–3
    political history 41
    postmodern globalism 14, 78
    postwar uncertainties 13–14, 139–40
    reconstruction problematic 77
    ruthless competitiveness 263–4
    socio-cultural realities 14–15
    strategies for healing 78
    surrender of national security 48
    unresolved rivalries 14
L'Ecran (Catholic movie magazine) 153
Lee, Andrew 217
Lerner, Daniel 32, 161
liminality 19
Litani River Project 260
Lowenthal, David, *The Art of Forgetting*
    104–5, 107
Lury, Celia 115, 122, 132, 133

Maasri, Zeina 163
MacCannell, D 103
Macfarquhar, Neil 218
Mack, John 73
McCormick, J 190
McCracken, Grant 124, 246–7
McWorld 89, 269
Madi, Hussain 203
Mahdawi, Dalila 250, 251
al-Majzoub, Moutaa 224
Makdisi, J S 84
Makhluf, Father Charbel 197
Malik, Charles, Foreign Minister 47
March 8 (political faction) 44, 56, 57, 220
March 11 Movement 218
March 14 Alliance (political faction) 44,
    55, 56, 214–15, 218, 220
Marcuse, Hebert 126
marketing strategies 169–71, 181
Maronite
    clerics 46

militias 64
turf wars 65
martyrs 94–5, 107, 158–9
Martyrs Square 107, 159, 211, 214, 218, 222
Mary, Virgin 106
Masri, Ghada 192
mass protest (2005) 214–16
Mathur, M 92
Maydān 91–3
media 162–3, 168–9, 182, 268
Melikian, L and Diab, L 43
Melucci, Alberto 170
memorial *versus* monument 110–11
mercantilism 16, 98, 136–8
Merton, Robert 226
Meštrovic, Stjepan 227
metaphors 23
Mezher, Izzat 203
Milnar, Z 88
Missionary Herald 230
Moneo, Rafael (architect) 194
Moore, Barrington 33
Mount Lebanon
    region 46, 49
    uprisings 24, 25, 32, 45, 59, 200
Mouzawck, Kamal 203
movie attendance 28, 96–7, 150–4, 155
    women 153–4
Mughniyeh, Imad 55, 55–6
Muhammad, Prophet 222–3
Munro, Rolland 23, 166
al-Murabitun (Nasserist movement) 52
Murad, Zuhair 176

Nambiar, N and Nesson, M V 204
Nan, E 86
Nash, *Now Lebanon* 172
Nasr, J and Volait, M 100
Nasr, Salim 83
Nasr, Vali 220
Nasrallah, Maha (architect) 254
Nasrallah, Sayyed Hassan 56
Nasser, President Gamal Abdel 47, 168
Navarno, M 182
Nazism 121–2
Neale, Frederick 184
Neale, I A 137
newspapers 157–60
Nietzsche, Friedrich 57, 139, 272

Nimr, Faris 158
Norton, Augustus Richard 220
Notre Dame du Liban 197
Nouvel, Jean (architect) 173, 254
Nussbaum, M C 113
al-Nusuli, Muhi al-Din 153

Onsi, Omar 208
Orosdi-Back (department store) 28, 146–7,
    147–8
Orwell, George 115
Ottoman Turks 41, 46, 47, 94, 146, 158
Owen, Roger 144, 147, 265
Oxford Business Group 116, 125

Palestine Liberation Organization (PLO)
    49, 60, 64, 71
Palestinian
    in-fighting 64
    militants from Jordan 60, 71
    refugees 52, 62
    self-rule negotiations 63
paramilitary youth movements 261–2
Paris Match magazine 251
Peattie, Lisa 257
Persky and Weiwel 90
Phalange 64, 71, 262
Pinderhughes, C A 73
pirated products 125
'playground' 29–30, 83, 95, 156, 231, 257–66
political misconduct 262–3
postwar
    psychic toll 80
    spiritual consequences 80–1
Prasada, Sierra, *Creative Lives* 181, 204–6
primordial ties 38, 40–1
Prince, Roland 162, 163
Princen, Thomas, Maniates, Michael and
    Conca, Ken 117, 167, 247–8
prostitution 186–9, 192, 201
Prothro, E T and Diab, L N 154
proxy battlefield 48, 52, 109–10
proxy victimization 60, 61–2
Pye, Lucian W 32

Qarantina ('liberation' of) 62
Qubain, Fahim 53
Qulailat, Ibrahim 52

Rabine, Leslie 179–80
radicalization of communal identity 24, 54
Radio-Orient 149
Raisborough, Jayne 183
Randal, Jonathan 66
Random House Unabridged Dictionary 171
Reagan, President Ronald 48, 49, 63
reconstruction processes 99–100, 105
Réglement Organique 47
relative deprivation 33, 50–1
religiosity 18, 67
Renan, Ernest 105, 106, 108–9, 251
'retribalization' 41–2, 43, 77–8
Richards, T 228, 229
Ritzer, George 123, 210
'road rage' 9–10
Robertson, Roland 100
Rorty, Richard 87
Rugh, William 158
Rule, James 25, 50
Rupesinghe, Kumar 21
Rutgers University 70

Saab, Elie 176, 177
Sa'adeh, Antoun, Syrian Socialist Party 262
Sabra and Shatila camps 62
Sadat, President Anwar 48
Safe, Joe 241
Said, Edward 20
Saifi village 199–204, 205–9, 254
Salecl, Renata 128–9
Saleeby, Khalil 208
Salibi, Kamal 144, 147, 148
Sarkis, Hashim (architect) 83, 254, 256
Sarruf, Yaqub 158
Scarry, Elaine 87
schadenfreude 57, 217
Schor, J and Holt, D B 129, 130, 164, 246
Scruton, Roger 199, 228, 229
sectarian and confessional rivalry 26, 54,
    69, 72
Seidman, Steve 238
Seniora, Prime Minister Fouad 57, 216
sexual consumerism 184–92
Sfeir, Patriarch Nusrallah 65, 222
Shaker, Fadl 218
Sharara, Waddah 217
al-Shidiaq, Tannus 46
Shields, Rob 245

Shi'ites 64, 217–18, 220
Shils, E 32
Short, John 103
Sij'an, Husayn (Jajjada) 262
Simmel, George 23, 28, 165, 178, 180
Sinai Observers Agreement 63
Skaff, Philippe 250, 251
Slater, Don 123
SLT (UN Special Lebanese Tribunal) 44
Smilianskaya, I M 46
Smith, Adam 264
smoking 141–3, 244
soap operas (*musalsalat*) 224
social hypocrisy 213
social order, decline of 139–40
'social strife' 36–7
Society of the Spectacle, The, Guy Debord
    15, 23
socio-economic disputes 26, 39, 54, 68
Solidere 105, 109, 110, 172, 199–200, 202,
    203, 208, 216
South Lebanese Army (SLA) 62
South Lebanon
    pre-invasion 63
    war zone 60
spatial
    changes caused by war 84
    identities 81, 101
    sensibility 79
spectacles 29, 212, 213–14, 232–3
    academic 233–4
    Ashura 219–20
    private celebrations 221–2, 233, 236
    Ramadan 222–4
    religious festivals 222–3
    sacralization of the profane 236–7
    soap operas 224
    unconnected events 219
Spoery, François (architect) 254
Srour, Habib 208
St George's Maronite Cathedral 102, 237
Stanhope, Lady Hester 184–5
Stauth, G and Turner, B S 272
Stearns, Peter 119, 122
Stevenson, Robert Louis 19
Stewart, Desmond 53
Storr, Anthony 72
Styhre, A and Engberg, T 227
Suez Crisis (1956) 47

Suleiman, General Michel, President 128, 218

Syria, arms conduit 60

Szmigin, Isabelle 123

Tabbarah, Riad 259

Taif 43

Taqla, Salim and Bishara 158

Tarazi, Vicomte Phillipe de 158

Tarcici, Adnan 153

Tarrab, Joseph 207

Tawney, Richard H 119

Tel al-Zaatar 62

'Tent City' 216–17, 218

Thompson, E 95, 96, 152, 153, 154, 164–5

Thomson, William 144–5

Tilly, Charles 33*bis*

Time magazine 180

Tohme, Youssef (architect) 254

tourism 265–6

    religious 194–8

Tourism, Ministry of, *The Paths of Faith* 195

Traboulsi, Fawwaz 136

traffic casualties 232, 253

Tueni, Ghassan 49, 97, 160

Tueni, Ghassan and Sassine, F 94

Turner, Bryan 107, 211, 239

UN Resolutions

    1559: withdrawal of Syrian troops 99

    1595: international inquiry into Hariri assassination 99

UNESCO

    statistical yearbook 96, 97, 155

    world heritage site 196

United Arab Republic (formation) 47

urbanization 33, 144–6, 156

US, deployment of marines 47, 49, 53

Veblen, Thorstein 28, 122–3, 124, 130, 154, 178, 243

    The Theory of the Leisure Class 122

violence

    consumatory and instrumental 25, 50–1

    displaced 25–6, 34, 58–9, 60

    domestication 53–4

    internecine 63–4

    intraconfessional 34, 65, 71

    legitimization of 73

    protracted 35–6, 59, 70

    random and diffuse 35

    self-generative cycle 39

Virgin Megastore 125

Vloeberghs, Ward 237

Volkan, V D 68

voluntary associations for reconciliation 107, 213, 264–5

Walzer, Michael 273

Warde, Alan 119, 122, 124, 131, 133–4

Weber, Max 22, 23, 127, 128, 271

Webster's Third New International Dictionary 171

weddings 221–2

Wehbe, Haifa 218, 220, 237

WHO (World Health Organization) 142

wilayat al-faqih 74

Williams, Raymond 120, 166

Williams, Robin 73

Wills, Gary 54

Wilson, Elizabeth 33, 122

Wilson-Goldie, Kaelen 127–8

Winslow, Charles 65

Wiske, John 132

Wolf, K W 19–20

Wolin, S S 109

Yahya, Maha 84

Yates, Francis 110

Yazbek, Natacha 129

Yazid, Caliph 217

Young, Iris 113

Young, James 111

Youth Association for Social Awareness (YASA) 232, 252–3

Youth Civil Society Leaders (YCSL) 252

youth protest 215–16, 220

Zaatari, Akram (architect 255

Zaatari, M 223–4

Zoepf, Katharine 183

Zola, Emile, *Au Bonheur des Dames* 120

Zur, O 68